The World of Agriculture

This textbook takes a truly international approach towards agricultural economics, uniting many different perspectives on the subject and providing insight into agriculture in general, and into how practical farming works in particular. The book is laced throughout with real world examples and other pedagogical features.

Topics covered are wide-ranging and include:

- world food production and population
- the food chain and food safety
- non-foods derived from farming
- land and soil issues
- arable and animal production and management at farm level.

The World of Agricultural Economics: an introduction is primarily an introductory textbook for students in agricultural economics, agronomy and adjacent fields. However, its accessible approach means that it is also suitable for readers without any previous knowledge in the field, who are seeking an introduction to agriculture.

Carin Martiin is Associate Professor of Agricultural History in the Department of Economics at the Swedish University of Agricultural Sciences, Uppsala, Sweden.

Routledge textbooks in environmental and agricultural economics

The World of Agricultural Economics

An introduction

Carin Martiin

Routledge
Taylor & Francis Group

LONDON AND NEW YORK

First published 2013
by Routledge
2 Park Square, Milton Park, Abingdon, Oxon OX14 4RN

Simultaneously published in the USA and Canada
by Routledge
711 Third Avenue, New York, NY 10017

Routledge is an imprint of the Taylor & Francis Group, an informa business

British Library Cataloguing in Publication Data
A catalogue record for this book is available from the British Library

Library of Congress Cataloging in Publication Data
Martiin, Carin.
The world of agricultural economics: an introduction / Carin Martiin.
    p. cm.
Includes bibliographical references and index.
1. Agriculture–Economic aspects. I. Title.
HD1415.M337 2013
338.1–dc23   2012034243

ISBN: 978-0-415-59359-5 (hbk)
ISBN: 978-0-415-59360-1 (pbk)
ISBN: 978-0-203-58843-7 (ebk)

Typeset in Times New Roman
by Cenveo Publisher Services

Printed and bound in Great Britain by
TJ International Ltd, Padstow, Cornwall

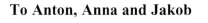

To Anton, Anna and Jakob

Contents

Figures

Tables

Boxes

Acknowledgements

It has been a great opportunity for me to be able to write this book, which may never have come true had not Robert Langham, Senior Publisher at Routledge, suggested that I write it. The challenge to write a wide-ranging basic textbook gave me a reason to sit down and systematize and structure the multifaceted world of agriculture, to turn fragments into a whole, and to combine together my threefold background in agronomy, economic and agricultural history, and practical farm work and farm management.

Along the way the book has benefitted from support by colleagues and many others. The heaviest work has probably been done by two students, by that time at masters level, at the Swedish University of Agricultural Sciences, William Redekop from Canada and Shanshan Zhang from China. Will and Shanshan have read, discussed and commented with never ending enthusiasm without which the writing process would have been much more difficult. I am deeply grateful for this! I am also particularly grateful to Anna Martiin who managed to combine her studies with frequent reading and discussion of the early stages of mum's book. Further, I owe much to the colleagues whom I have bothered with my chapters: Associate Professor James Watson, Massey University, New Zealand; Assistant Lecturer Alice Turinawe-Ainembabazi, Makerere University, Uganda; and, at the Swedish University of Agricultural Sciences, PhD Magnus Simonsson, Department of Soil and Environment; Professor Lars Andersson, Department of Crop Production Ecology; Professor Lotta Rydhmer, Department of Animal Breeding and Genetics; Professor Hans Andersson, Department of Economics; Professor Ivar Vågsholm, Department of Biomedical Sciences and Veterinary Public Health; and Associate Professor Anders Wästfelt, Agricultural History, also at the Department of Human Geography at Stockholm University. Additional information has, among others, also been provided by Anamaria Iuga, Bucharest, Romania and Rodolfo Magne at the Swedish Society for Nature Conservation. In spite of the experts' reading it is almost unavoidable that a wide-reaching book like this may include some mistakes, and these are all my responsibility.

I would also like to thank my colleagues at the Department of Economics at the Swedish University of Agricultural Sciences, especially Professor Janken Myrdal and my other research and teaching workmates in the Agricultural History section. Many thanks also to my colleagues at the Department of Urban and Rural Development and in the interdisciplinary research programme Future Agriculture.

Special thanks are due to the anonymous referees who contributed with constructive suggestions, remarks and ideas on the basis of very early drafts of what would later be developed into this book. At Routledge I would like to thank Senior Publisher Robert Langham for encouraging support; Louisa Earls and Natalie Tomlinson for their support during the writing process and manuscript delivery; Emily Davies, Production Editor, for keeping it all together during the process of production; Lisa Williams for copyediting and polishing the language; and Eliza Wright for the proofreading.

Directly and indirectly the book has also benefitted from my students at the Swedish University of Agricultural Sciences and at the Department of Economic History at Stockholm University. It would in fact hardly have been possible to write this textbook without being influenced by questions and perspectives from the students. Another key asset for textbook writing is libraries. The SLU library in Uppsala has been most generous in letting me borrow (and keep for so long) hundreds of books. Many thanks also to the generous staff at the Royal Swedish Academy of Agriculture and Forestry library in Stockholm.

I am happy to have been able to illustrate the text with photos from different parts of the world. Many thanks to Viktoria Olausson who has let me use some of her beautiful South African photos. The other photos are somewhat of a family business to which Anna, Jakob and Anton have all contributed and deserve many thanks.

Writing a book takes time and requires many breaks. Among the friends who have supported this I especially appreciate Agneta Liljestam, for our night-time talks about our first stumbling steps as agronomy students, about life and about the state of the world. Finally, my family Gunnar, Anton, Anna, Jakob and other dear family members have supported both writing and breaks, through reading and questioning, and by taking the author out into the farmed landscape.

Abbreviations

AI	artificial insemination
AU	African Union
CAC	Codex Alimentarius Commission
CAP	Common Agricultural Policy
CGIAR	Consultative Group on International Agricultural Research
CIS	Commonwealth of Independent States
Defra	Department for Environment, Food and Rural Affairs, UK
EU	European Union
FAO	Food and Agriculture Organization of the United Nations
FAOSTAT	the FAO statistical database
FMD	foot and mouth disease
HYV	high yielding varieties
ICG	International Grains Council
IFPRI	International Food Policy Research Institute
IMF	International Monetary Fund
NGO	non-governmental organization
OECD	Organization for Economic Co-operation and Development
OIE	World Organization for Animal Health
SPS	Agreement on the Application of Sanitary and Phytosanitary Measures
TAD	transboundary animal diseases
UN	United Nations
USDA	United States Department of Agriculture
WFP	World Food Programme
WHO	World Health Organization
WRB	World Reference Base for Soil Resources
WTO	World Trade Organization

Introduction

The cover photo shows a blue sky and newly harrowed soil. This is where agriculture takes place, as a tension between the sky and the land. Sometimes the land suffers from too much sun and heat, sometimes from the contrary. World agriculture is also characterized by contrasts in the material and social conditions under which farm production is operated, such as differences in scale, access to resources, methods of production, yields and sales opportunities.

This book includes the diverse world of farming, as well as the agricultural sector at large. It touches on many topics, of which some are frequently debated, but aims at maintaining the character of a basic textbook, still without ignoring that the world of agriculture includes both challenging farm work and aspects such as: world food supply, food trade conditions, resource use, environmental impact, rural–urban issues and degrees of political involvement. The following chapters include questions and subjects that engage thousands of researchers and representatives of different kinds of organizations. As a farmer you may face many of these issues every day. Farming is no easy task; it is both physically and intellectually challenging, whether you have thousands of hectares or just half a hectare to cultivate under the open sky.

What this book is about

In brief this book outlines what world agriculture is about and how it works. The book thus tells about agricultural economics in its widest meaning, and does not replace introductory books in economics. The twenty-one chapters combine macro and micro perspectives that range from nature dependency, food security and international trade to practical matters such as crop cultivation, animal feeding and the managing of a farm. All kinds of farming are included, irrespective of methods of production, geographical position, and political, socioeconomic and demographic circumstances. The book covers large-scale commercial agriculture as well as subsistence oriented farming under poor conditions. If some key words and perspectives should be highlighted as characterizing the book as a whole, these would be: farmers, farm production, food security, and access to and economizing with resources.

Suggested readers

The book is of interest to a wide audience in need of an introduction to the agricultural sector and practical farming, although it addresses students in the first place. The primary intended readers are first year agronomy students. The book is also beneficial for undergraduate students in topics such as demography, human geography, international relations, natural resources, environmental studies, landscaping, biodiversity, rural development, rural sociology, animal ethics and veterinary medicine. Moreover, the content may be useful for postgraduate students who are engaged in essays or other projects that require insights into agriculture.

What is more, the book may be of interest to professionals who come into contact with agriculture in one way or another, for example in financing, trade, marketing, retailing, or in various kinds of administration. Further, the book may be of value to journalists, debaters, teachers and politicians in search of a broad introduction to world agriculture. If you belong to categories other than students you must have patience with the learning objectives and the issues for discussion at the beginning and end of each chapter.

You can study the content without any previous agricultural knowledge or experience of practical farming, but the wide range of topics and inclusion of all kinds of farming around the world also make the book interesting for people who are already involved in food and farming in one way or another.

How the book is structured

Writing a book about all kinds of agriculture is a challenge, in terms of content as well as structure. In order to handle this, the book is organized as a kind of hourglass that begins with a broad picture about food security and global agriculture, followed by more detailed reasoning about practical farming, after which the perspective is successively widened to matters of international trade and food safety.

In addition to this hourglass structure, the book is based on three connecting thoughts. First, that agriculture as characterized by a number of fundamentals that all kinds of farming have in common, such as nature dependency and everybody's need for food. A second thought is that degrees of market versus subsistence orientation are highly decisive for farmers' decisions and abilities to produce. Third, you will find that the food chain is referred to as a concept to understand resource flows and the actors involved.

All chapters open with an introductory text, learning objectives and key words; and conclude with a chapter summary and study questions. The learning objectives are basic, while some of the study questions encourage more analysis and discussion. In addition to the main chapter texts you will find accompanying boxes with the most varying contents, from practical examples and extracts to additional facts. Lists with black bullets are not further commented upon, while lists with unfilled bullets are. You will also find explanatory figures and photos from various parts of the agricultural sector. There is also a list of abbreviations at the front of the book and a bibliography at the end.

Chapter by chapter

The book is structured in five major parts with four or five chapters in each. Part I presents major perspectives and connecting thoughts, and Part II provides a worldwide survey of world agriculture. Parts III and IV have a more practical approach and deal with soils, cultivation and animal husbandry, whereas farm management and the market are covered in Part V. The content of each chapter is outlined in more detail below.

In Part I, Chapter 1, you will find definitions of basic terms, such as agricultural economics and farming. Chapter 2 outlines fundamental characteristics that all kinds of agriculture have in common, albeit to varying extents and with different consequences. Chapter 3 discusses market and subsistence oriented agriculture and Chapter 4 focuses on the food chain.

The presentation of world agriculture at large, in Part II, is largely based on statistics and begins with population issues and demographic trends, in Chapter 5. Chapter 6 focuses on agricultural areas and presents production of various crops around the world. Attention then turns to world animal production, which is described in Chapter 7, after which Chapter 8 discusses production of a wide range of non-foods such as fibres and bio-energy.

Part III of this book deals with land, soils, plant nutrients and water, which provide the basis for all kinds of cultivation and plant growth, and thus for both crop and animal farming. Chapter 9 deals with farmers' access to land in the form of ownership, lease and other forms. Thereafter we will discuss areas and field structures in Chapter 10. Further, you will get a relatively detailed description of soils and soil functions in Chapter 11, which is followed by an account of water and plant nutrients in Chapter 12.

Part IV takes you closer to practical farming. First you will read about the principal parts of the growing season, in Chapter 13. The crop cultivation theme continues in Chapter 14, which covers seeds, weeds, agro-chemicals and other aspects of practical crop farming. Farm animals are the focus of attention in Chapters 15 and 16, the first of which discusses various strategies in animal farming, from backyard farming to factory-like production. In the latter you will learn about feeding, animal health and animal breeding.

The fifth and final part of the book has a more diverse content. Chapter 17 emphasizes the importance of managing the farm, and Chapter 18 discusses various aspects of time and farm work. In Chapter 19 we will discuss farmers' sale of products, while Chapter 20 focuses on international trade of agricultural products. The concluding chapter, Chapter 21, deviates slightly from the previous ones in that it deals with food hygiene and food safety, which is of the greatest importance in ensuring that the foods produced can be fully utilized.

There are no automatic deliveries of food

In the very last stages of the writing of this book global agriculture has attracted considerable attention around the world. The primary reason is severe draught in the US (July 2012), but also weather problems in other countries, such as drought in India and Russia, flooding in the Philippines and record high precipitation in northern Europe. Not least reduced yields of maize and soybeans in US, the world's leading producer and exporter, are expected to bring far-reaching consequences, on global trade, food prices, feed costs and on the bio-fuel market. A third global food price crisis is thus feared, the third within five years. There may obviously be contemporary failures – there is no natural law saying that poor harvests in one part of the world would automatically be compensated for by abundant yields somewhere else. Global agriculture is no zero-sum game and there are no automatic deliveries of food.

Part I
Ways into agriculture

1 Agricultural economics, a common ground

What is agricultural economics? And what is farming? We will answer the first question later, but give a brief answer to the latter question by saying that farming is an organized way to produce food, fibre, bio-energy and other non-foods by cultivation or grazing.

This short opening chapter deals with definitions of a few central terms that you have to grasp completely to be able to follow the reasoning in the following chapters. We will, among other things, discuss how the basic terms 'agricultural economics', 'farming' and 'farmer' are used in this book. You probably already have an idea about these terms, but as definitions differ with disciplines, authors and individual readers, it is wise to start with a key vocabulary that can serve as a common ground for the following chapters.

After this chapter you are expected to:

○ Know the terms agricultural economics, farming and farmer, as defined in this chapter
○ Be familiar with the meaning of farm work, farm, farm household and farm family, as discussed in this chapter

Key words

Agricultural economics, farming, farm work, farmer, farm, farm household, farm family, agriculture.

Agricultural economics

The term agricultural economics is part of the book title. We will deal with the subject matter in a broad sense, in line with the widening of the field in recent decades. In 2011 the US based Agricultural and Applied Economics Association described its field of interest as being about 'the economics of agriculture, international and rural development, resources and the environment, food and consumer issues, and agribusiness' (http://www.aaea.org, accessed 17 June 2011).

Box 1.1 Topics within the field of agricultural economics, some examples

- Production economics in agriculture
- Methods of production in farming
- Agricultural marketing and trade
- Environment and natural resources in agriculture
- Supply and demand for agricultural products
- Food security and food safety   *(Food technology)*
- Rural development

This understanding of agricultural economics differs from the original view from the early twentieth century, which focused on farm management and production technologies. Likewise the wide and interdisciplinary approach deviates from more specific studies in agricultural economics, such as econometrics. Box 1.1 gives some examples of topics within the wide field of agricultural economics.

You will find the examples in Box 1.1, and many others, in the following chapters. Some deal specifically with a certain topic, for example food safety, which is discussed in Chapter 21, whereas, for instance, environmental issues are interwoven in many chapters.

If we turn from a general understanding of the field of agricultural economics to a specific definition of the term agricultural economics, we find that it is slightly differently defined by various authors but that key terms such as production, resources, decisions and distribution are frequently included. In this book, with its introductory and interdisciplinary approach, the term agricultural economics is defined as follows:

> Agricultural economics deals with how we organize and use resources for farm production of food, fibre, bio-energy and other non-foods; how the products are distributed, handled and consumed; and with the local and global impact this has on living conditions, societies, environment and economies.

Practical farming is an essential and basic part of agricultural economics, and is given substantial space and attention in this book, especially in Part IV, and serves as point of reference for much of the reasoning, albeit in a wide context that includes socioeconomic and environmental concerns. We will thus pay special attention to the terms farming, farmer and related words – speaking about farming is not as easy as just saying that farming takes place on farms that are run by farmers.

Farming

It is no exaggeration to say that farming and farm products constitute the pure essence of the world of agricultural economics. You read a short explanation of the term farming at the beginning of this chapter. An extended version of that definition says that

> Farming can be defined as an organized way to grow crops and rear animals in order to provide food, fibre, bio-energy and other non-foods through cultivation or grazing, stationary or not, with the purpose of selling the products, or using them in kind.

Our definition of farming includes all kinds of arable and animal farming everywhere, in each corner of the world, irrespective of location, aims of production, methods of production, economy and society. It refers to all kinds of outdoor crop cultivation, plus greenhouse cultivation, and to stationary and nomadic forms of animal husbandry. We will not exclude fish farming, which for instance is important for many Asian farmers, but we will not examine fish farming as such.

Farm work

We will also apply a wide definition of farm work. Farming activities include all kinds of farm work that is conducted with or without the help of machinery and equipment, such as tractor driving, control of automatic milking, field inspections, machine and equipment repairs, digging ditches, mending fences, carrying feed and water for farm animals, making budgets and discussion with agricultural advisers.

Farmer

You will frequently come across the term farmer all through this book. A farmer is often thought of as a person who works at and leads the work at a farm holding, while others involved are considered as family members, employees, etc. We will, however, apply a wider definition that includes all categories of people who are engaged in farm work. This simplification makes it possible to discuss farm work without becoming entangled in the impossible undertaking of distinguishing exactly who does what; at a particular farm or in farming in general. The same kind of job, feeding pigs for example, may in one case be done by a landowning farmer, in another case by a farmhand and in a third case by a child. Only the first one, however, probably calls him/herself 'farmer'.

The simplification to one single term, farmer, does not mean that we will overlook the diversity of categories that are engaged in real farming. On the contrary, the inclusion of many categories in one term means that we perceive farm work as conducted by a wide range of people of different age, sex and position. It should be emphasized that the term farmer includes both men and women. Women's work in agriculture is decisive all over the world and they form a majority of the agricultural labour force, especially in South Asia and Sub-Saharan Africa. Bringing together all categories of labour in one term, farmer, does, however, require that you, as a reader, are continuously aware of the wide meaning all through the book (see Box 1.2).

Box 1.2 Some categories that are included in the term farmer as it is used in this book. (It is possible to belong to more than one category)

- Full-time farmers
- Part-time farmers
- Landowners who operate their land actively
- Leaseholders
- Pastoral nomads
- Poor smallholders
- Households with backyard farming, with or without access to land
- Year-round farmhands
- Casual farmhands with farming as a major source of income
- Farming men, women and children

Although the inclusion of categories is generous, some are, however, excluded from being called farmers. Hired-in specialists, such as veterinarians, sheep shearers and economic consultants, are not farmers, and the same is true of staff from machinery stations, and other people who work at a particular farm unit for a very short period of time and then take on other kinds of jobs. Neither is it relevant to include investors, whose primary aim is to invest in agriculture rather than produce. As this book has a utility perspective, it would be relevant to exclude hobby farmers too, but it is not easy to distinguish between farming as livelihood and the plethora of intermediate forms that are found between professional and hobby farming. By now we have reached a definition of the term farmer, as understood in this book:

> Farmers are here defined as men and women of all ages who, for utility purposes, are directly involved in practical farming, as defined above.

Farm

The term farm is perhaps the most complex of the basic terms that are discussed in this introductory chapter. You may have a picture of what a farm looks like, maybe a few fields and some houses that are situated in the countryside. You may consider a farm as a physically and legally defined unit that is delineated from other farms and possible to identify on a map. The reality is, however, more complicated than that. Even when there is a delineated farm unit this may not be the same as the operational unit. The operational farm unit can be bigger or smaller, and organized in various ways, for example because of collaboration, or because a physical unit is split up in one way or another. Farming is also operated on the basis of customary rights, without specified delimitations. You will read more about land rights in Chapter 9 and about organization of farming in Chapters 10, 17 and 18. As our main focus is on production, we will generally consider a farm as an operational unit, which sometimes is the same as the physically delineated farm, sometimes not.

Farm households and farm families

A few words should also be said about the terms farm household and farm family, which are important as points of reference in some agricultural economies. The two are sometimes, but far from always, identical. Farm households and farm families may overlap, for example at so-called family farms in Western Europe and North America. You also find farm households with extended families; and households with both family members and employees. At big farm units many separate households can be found, such as camps for casual farm hands. Another example is when employees live in separate households at some distance from the farm. You will find both farm households and farm families in the following chapters, with the former term used most often.

Agriculture

Finally, it should be said that the word agriculture will be used more generally. Agriculture covers a wider field than farming, but is narrower than agricultural economics. We will use the term agriculture freely, in line with common language, for example in formulations such as agricultural production, agricultural sectors and agricultural politics.

Summary

This chapter introduces some basic terms that are frequently used in the following chapters. Agricultural economics is given a rather wide definition which says that agricultural economics deals with how we organize and use resources for farm production of food, fibre, bio-energy and other non-foods; how the products are distributed, handled and consumed; and the local and global impact this has on living conditions, societies, environment and economies. Farming is defined as an organized way to grow crops and rear animals in order to provide food, fibre, bio-energy and other non-foods through cultivation or grazing, with the purpose of selling the products, or using them in kind. Moreover, farm work is defined as all kinds of farming activities, including manual work as well as farm management. The term farmer is here defined as men and women of all ages who, for utility purposes, are directly involved in practical farming, as defined above. As regards the term farm, this is generally considered as an operational unit, which sometimes is the same as the physically delineated farm, sometimes not. There is also some discussion of the terms farm household and farm family, and the term agriculture, which is used in a general way in this book.

Next

In Chapter 2 you will read about fundamental characteristics that all kinds of farming have in common, such as its dependency on natural forces, and necessity for world food supply.

To discuss

o   Study some photos of 'African farming', 'Australian farming', etc. by using a search engine on the Internet, in order to get a general idea of what farming can look like in different parts of the world.

2   Fundamentals of agriculture

This chapter highlights fundamental characteristics of agriculture, characteristics that all kinds of farming have in common. We will study these fundamentals as nine themes, which argue that agriculture is a meeting between nature and human society; is necessary for human survival; is dependent on land; is ruled by weather, seasons and biological rhythms; is both predictable and unpredictable; is a matter of economizing with resources; is found on almost all continents; is conducted by large numbers of farmers; and may be highly influenced by social and cultural factors. Thinking about agriculture in terms of typical characteristics, as the nine points just listed, is helpful for your understanding of agriculture as a phenomenon and makes it easier to grasp the multiplicity in agriculture that we will deal with in the following chapters, for which the fundamental characteristics serve as general points of reference.

After this chapter you are expected to:

o   Be familiar with fundamental characteristics in terms of nine themes about agriculture's roles for humanity, nature related prerequisites and common realities in all kinds of farming

Key words

Nature, human society, economic activity, necessities, human survival, land, weather, seasons, biological rhythm, unpredictability, economizing, social and cultural impact.

As the point of departure for the challenge of combining and handling the multiplicity in world agriculture, we will use this chapter to search for common features, aspects that unite the many different kinds of farming. As mentioned, you will read about nine characteristics that include agriculture's roles for humanity; prerequisites to be able to farm at all; realities, such as the unpredictable; and other features such as that farming is operated worldwide. The uniting characters point to the fact that agriculture is:

○   A meeting between nature and human society
○   Necessary for human survival
○   Dependent on land
○   Ruled by weather, seasons and biological rhythm
○   Both predictable and unpredictable
○   A matter of economizing with resources
○   Found on almost every continent
○   Conducted by large numbers of farmers
○   Influenced by social and cultural factors

Throughout this chapter we will discuss the listed characteristics one by one. You may argue that that some features are valid for other sectors too, which is true to a greater or lesser extent when it comes to nature-dependent activities such as fishing, forestry, some tourism and road building and other kinds of outdoor jobs.

Agriculture is a meeting between nature and human society

Agriculture is an economic activity that is more or less closely related to nature. Depending on how agriculture is conducted and on the perspective of the individual, agriculture can be seen as a kind of collaboration between nature and humans; as humankind's necessary and more or less sustainable utilization of nature; or as different forms of exploitation of nature and natural resources. According to the perspectives of this book, agriculture is positioned at the intersection between nature, the limits set by nature and the global need for food. In addition, the economy at large and relevant living conditions at farm level are vital parts of this understanding of world agriculture.

The meeting between nature and society, in order to produce food, fibre, bio-energy and other non-food products from the land, is to a great extent delegated from urban consumers to farmers anywhere in the world. We may formulate the situation thus: urban society expects the agricultural sector to produce and deliver desired quantities and quality, at the right point of time, and at affordable prices – irrespective of eventual nature related problems at farm level. To manage this is a challenge for everybody involved, primarily for the world's many farmers but also for many other professionals in the field. Citing Cramer *et al.* in their *Agricultural Economics and Agribusiness*:

> Getting food and fibre to all people in the world in the right form at the right time is an extremely complex process.

> (Cramer *et al.* 2001: 9)

At the same time the world's many poor smallholders are heavily dependent on subsistence production, and the ability to produce as much as possible of the household's needs for survival.

Agriculture is necessary for human survival

> With a child dying every six seconds because of undernourishment-related problems, hunger remains the world's largest tragedy and scandal.
>
> (Jacques Diouf, FAO Director General, 14 September 2010,
> Rome; http://www.un-foodsecurity.org/node/787)

Few necessities are as necessary as food. Each of us is thus inevitably dependent on agriculture, which supplies almost everything we eat, plus the sweaters we wear and numerous other necessities. It would not actually be possible to feed either the present or prospective world population without farming. The general dependency on agriculture makes the sector unique; although it is debated whether agriculture should be considered as special or as like any other kind of business as regards economy and politics. Recent peaks in food prices, in 2007/2008 and 2011, have boosted the international interest in the world food supply and highlighted that we can hardly expect food to be supplied as a matter of course in the future.

Agriculture is dependent on land

Land is a prerequisite for agriculture and a symbol for farming. You may object that some forms of production are conducted without land, for example advanced greenhouse cultivation. This is right, but in wide and long-term perspectives there is no doubt that agriculture depends on land, and that this distinguishes the sector from most other kinds of business. In addition, different types of farming depend on various kinds of land, such as highly fertile land for intensive vegetable cultivation or vast and cheap pasture areas for large-scale sheep farming. As will be discussed in Chapters 10 and 15, factory-like animal production can be based on feed that is purchased from far away, and is then not directly dependent on the surrounding land. However, the purchased feed is grown somewhere.

The connection with land means that farming generally also is characterized by geographical distances, such as distances from neighbours, communications and markets. There are, however, big differences between various corners of the world. Some farmers live in crowded villages, whereas others run farms in remote areas; and while some areas enjoy good communications and smooth contacts with services and markets, many regions suffer from the opposite.

Agriculture is ruled by weather, seasons and biological rhythm

The fourth point in the list of fundamentals refers to the fact that almost all farming is located outdoors, which means that farming has to cope with weather,

Figure 2.1 Agriculture is a meeting between nature and human society. It depends on land, and is ruled by weather, seasons and biological rhythm. Cambodia, 2010.
Photo: Anna Martiin.

seasons and other forces of nature (see Figure 2.1). The impact of nature is an absolute prerequisite; farming would not be possible without sun radiation, precipitation and certain temperatures. On the other hand nature can be cruel. Drought, flooding, hurricanes and severe frost frequently cause devastation and tragedy among farmers in different regions. You have possibly heard this reported, or even experienced it yourself. Some farmers have better chances of modifying weather problems, for example irrigation during periods of drought, but not even the most high-tech outdoor farming is uninfluenced by nature. Farming is thus ruled by nature, for good and bad, and to a greater or lesser extent.

Seasonality influences practical farming, agricultural business and food consumption. If the harvest fails, one generally has to wait for the right season before it is possible to start it all over again. Similarly, some forms of animal husbandry are greatly dependent on the season, for example on grazing seasons. Seasonality thus characterizes much of farm work and the yearly rhythm in farming. What is more, the season impacts supply and demand for agricultural products, and price levels on inputs such as sowing seed, and outputs such as grains and meats.

Each plant and animal species has its specific biological rhythm, which has to harmonize with ordinary seasonal conditions at the farm. Seasonal and biological constraints mean that agricultural production generally has to begin at a certain time of the year, and that the biological processes have to be completed once they have been set in train. If not, the work, land, sowing seed or animal feed will probably get lost.

Agriculture is both predictable and unpredictable

Farming's dependency on nature means that agriculture is both highly predictable and unpredictable. Days and seasons come and go, which gives farming a repetitive and foreseeable character, at least in the eyes of an external observer. This kind of rhythm is, however, a prerequisite for most kinds of farming. Both crop farming and livestock production are vulnerable to disruptions in ordinary weather patterns and seasons. Prolonged rainy seasons can, for example, delay seeding and thereby disturb the entire growing season. Problems like these are often heard in discussions about climate change and fears of extreme consequences for farmers in some parts of the world. In addition to disrupted weather patterns and seasonal rhythms, agriculture is exposed to sudden natural events, such as hailstorms, which can ruin an arable field within a few hours.

The combination of stable rhythm and unpredictabilities means that farmers have to act on the assumption that things will be normal, as if sown seed always will be harvested, even though some more or less severe events may occur.

Agriculture is a matter of economizing with resources

Like other economic activities agriculture has to deal with economizing with resources. It is obvious that the available area of arable land has to be used as efficiently as possible with regard to short- and long-term perspectives. The same is true for labour, and generally also for crop nutrients, animal feed, energy and water, just to mention some of the resources that are frequently used. You will find more about resources all through the book.

Agriculture is found on almost every continent

With a few extreme exceptions, such as the Antarctic and completely barren mountain areas, farming is found in all corners of the world. Animal farming can generally be found in both fertile and harsh regions, whereas the distribution of crop farming is somewhat more restricted. Some products, such as coffee, are grown in some regions only, while others, for example potatoes, are widely grown. Even though farming is found almost all over the world, it is not proportional to the distribution of the world population. We will get back to ongoing tendencies in these matters in Chapter 9, which highlights access to land from different angles.

Agriculture is conducted by large numbers of farmers

In comparison with many other kinds of economic activities agriculture is characterized by an enormous number of farm units that generally are small or very small. You will find more about farm numbers and farm sizes in Chapter 10. Furthermore, agriculture is characterized by geographical spread, and by market conditions with more or less independently acting farmers, although with exceptions. No single farmer is able to influence the global market; the dominance of the food market appears higher up in the food supply chain. This picture presents farming as an almost textbook example of a perfectly competitive market. In order to strengthen their negotiating positions with purchasers farmers in some countries are, to varying degrees, collaborating in producer cooperatives or other types of arrangements, which is touched on in Chapters 18 and 19.

Agriculture is influenced by social and cultural factors

In addition to being an economic activity that is closely related to nature, agriculture is also related to social and cultural factors. A fair understanding of agriculture and farming requires attention to these aspects, which often adds dimensions to farmers' actions and may contribute to decisions beyond economic rationality, beyond economic revenues and returns on investments in terms of capital and labour.

The character and strength of social and cultural features differ greatly between various forms of agriculture, and around the world, including traditional views on relations between humans and nature as well as aims for the entrepreneurial development of farming. Belonging to a certain local society and cultivating the same land as previous generations are other aspects. Similarly, farming is often influenced by close connections between farm economy and household economy, work time and leisure time, and by the fact that the place of work also is the home of most farmers. The world of agriculture includes a plethora of life styles and views; still, being a farmer is often a round-the-clock identity.

From similarities to differences

To sum up, most of the uniting characteristics of agriculture we have discussed are timeless and nature related phenomena that are independent of shifting social and economic conditions. From the first attempts to cultivate the land and to domesticate animals farming has been a meeting between nature and human societies. And with an increased world population, agriculture has become increasingly important for human survival. Without doubt both cultivation and grazing require land areas, and depend on weather, the seasons and biological rhythms, which provide both high degrees of predictability and unpredictability. Resources have often been scarce, such as land or labour, but the proportions have varied over time, which also could be said about the distribution of farming between continents, the number of farmers, the societal and cultural impact, and about the forms in which farming has been conducted.

The differences in farming highlight huge gaps within the world of agriculture. The major differences are to a great extent connected with degree of market orientation, farm size, technologies, methods of production and yield levels.

Moreover, differences between farmers' situations can be explained by circumstances in the surrounding society, such as infrastructure, consumer demand, trade, education, health, confidence, financing, laws and regulations, and threats from armed conflicts. We will not be able to examine all these topics, but will focus on a selection.

Summary

In this second, introductory chapter agriculture has been discussed in view of fundamental characteristics that unite all kinds of farming. Most of these are nature related, due to the fact that agriculture utilizes nature and natural resources and operates on the land, in most cases as an open-air activity. We have briefly discussed agriculture as a geographically, socially and culturally widespread and necessary activity, which is in part an unpredictable meeting between nature and human societies, and ultimately is ruled by nature.

Next

Chapter 3 turns our perspectives the other way around, from characteristics that unite agriculture to those that differ. We will discuss this in terms of market and subsistence orientation. Whether products are sold or not is decisive for how a farm holding can be operated in terms of methods of production, outcome and livelihoods.

To discuss

○ Consider each of the nine themes discussed, one by one, and try to exemplify each of them as concretely as possible, on the basis of your current understanding of agriculture.

3　Market and subsistence oriented agriculture

One of the challenges for comprehensive studies of world agriculture is to deal with its diversity. Despite Chapter 2's focus on shared features, the sector is certainly also characterized by enormous disparities. Just imagine the contrasts between gigantic combines that harvest vast North American maize fields and manual harvest on small Sub-Saharan plots. And compare the supply of ready-to-eat foods on gigantic supermarket shelves with outdoor cooking in a village in Bangladesh. As we said in Chapter 2, the similarities are generally related to nature, whereas the dissimilarities are primarily connected with human actions and socioeconomic differences, such as access to and use of resources and technologies.

This chapter emphasizes differences in world agriculture and introduces you to how parts of the diversity are handled in this book. Instead of the more common approach of considering the world on the basis of nationalities, or as developed and developing countries, we will use degree of market orientation as the point of departure to explain some major dissimilarities in agriculture. Market orientation means production for sale, which generates revenues that, among other things, open up choices about how to produce in terms of resources and aims of production. How production is conducted is highly decisive for yield levels, outcomes and farmers' livelihoods – all greatly contributing to the differences within the world of agriculture. We will combine the term market orientation with its opposite, subsistence orientation, but also consider the wide span in between.

After this chapter you are expected to:

o　Be able to identify main characteristics of typical market oriented agriculture
o　Similarly be able to identify major features of subsistence oriented agriculture
o　Have an idea about how surpluses for sale can influence farm practices and farmers' livelihoods, in comparison with situations without any revenues from farming

Key words

Market orientation, subsistence orientation, sale, resources, cash crops, food crops.

A quick glance at the miscellaneous world of farming

Let us begin with a quick glance at practical farming around the globe. Imagine a late summer afternoon in the middle of the United States where enormous combines are seen roaring across the horizon, rapidly harvesting thousands of tons of maize. The same afternoon, a Ugandan smallholder feeds her poultry with food scraps, and keeps an eye on the children and on the pot with boiling maize which was manually harvested. Turning north, we find a Finnish dairy farmer who studies the latest milk-quality report before it is high time for the afternoon routines, which begin with moving silage to an automatic feeder with the help of a tractor. Far away, in south-east India, a boy takes the family's buffalo to a water pond but stops here and there to let it graze along the roadside. Further eastwards, in the middle of China, a young man is seen repairing the ventilation system at a newly built plant for 10,000 hogs. Down under, an Australian herd of 5,000 sheep is being moved to the farm centre, by which professional shearers are hired and where they soon will arrive. Returning to the Americas, a Uruguayan herd of thousands of beef cattle is heard screaming through a cloud of dust, while being moved to more fertile grasslands. The examples give a hint of the many ways in which farming is operated. How do we handle this miscellaneous world of farming?

Why not simply a geographic point of departure?

The choice to use degree of market orientation as a way to handle some of the differences in world farming is motivated by the fact that neither countries nor continents or geographic regions are homogenous in regard to agriculture. Some kinds of farming are certainly much more frequent in some parts of the world than in others, but there is also a heterogeneity that complicates the view. We can, for example, find both big commercial farms and poor smallholdings in Kenya, India, China and Brazil; sometimes within sight of each other. There may also be homogenous farming on transboundary plains where farmers have more in common with colleagues across the border than with smallholders in other parts of the same country.

We will not ignore differences between varying parts of the world, far from it, but nor will we generalize so that local differences are passed over. By using the terms market and subsistence orientation, rather than country or classification as developed or developing, it is possible to discuss farmers' different situations regarding methods of production and farmers' actions in various situations.

Market versus subsistence orientation

Whether products are sold or not is largely decisive for how a farm holding can be operated, and for living conditions in farm households and rural areas at large. If money is coming in, parts of the money can be used for purchases that support production. If not, the farmer is often more severely exposed to forces of nature and has fewer chances of coping with upcoming problems and otherwise directing his/her production through methods that require access to money.

In brief, market oriented farming can typically be seen as production for sale against payment in cash. With revenues coming into the business it is, as just mentioned, possible for the farmer to decide to buy inputs to continue or even increase production, for example fertilizer and sowing seed, and to make investments, such as in farm machinery and irrigation equipment. The purchased resources can then be expected to result in new products to sell. At the same time the farmer's freedom of action is increased. When he/she has access to more resources and cash, a wider range of choices and decisions becomes relevant. The alternative of buying additional feed in order to compensate for shortages due to drought in the local area is, for example, irrelevant without the possibility of paying for it. The term cash crop is often used for this type of production, and includes not only crops but also fibres, bio-energy and other non-food farm products.

As a counterpart to cash crops we speak about subsistence production of food crops, crops that are intended to be consumed by the producer. The term subsistence originally refers to the bare necessities that are needed to be able to continue to exist, which means minimal levels of food and other essentials. Even this is, however, a challenging equation, among other things because of scarcities of resources, exposure to nature and variations from year to year. Most so-called subsistence farms are in reality based on combinations of different sources of income, where the smallholding provides a basis for the food supply and generates some cash from occasional sales. In many cases purchases of additional food are the rule, especially during the last months before the next harvest, and even more in years that follow bad harvests. Subsistence production can also include products other than food, and the entire production can be part of local exchanges in kind, against other products, work or as various forms of social responsibility.

With some exceptions, such as specialized large-scale crop farming, most agriculture is neither extremely market or subsistence oriented, but rather consists of combinations of production for sale and internal use. This explains why the word orientation has been added to the terms market and subsistence in this book.

Alternatively, crops can, for example, be used as animal feed instead of being sold. In many cases the final use is not decided until after harvest. Cash and food crops can therefore be considered as multipurpose crops, which may be sold or maintained for one's own needs, depending on how things work out each particular year. When the products are perishable, such as milk, fresh vegetables and berries, decisions about whether to sell or not have to be taken quickly, but in other cases the products may be stored and the decisions taken successively.

Resources versus degree of market orientation

The degree of market orientation is strongly related to the use of resources. Thinking in terms of flows of resources provides a useful tool for our understanding of market and subsistence oriented agriculture and the many nuances in between as regards different types of farm production, methods of production, yield levels, and farmers' various choices and decisions.

Generally speaking, the flows of resources, such as fertilizer and animal feed, can be expected to increase with the degree of market orientation. Or the degree of market orientation can be supposed to increase with increased use of resources, which raises the production potential and what can possibly be sold. Matters of resource use and surplus production for sale thus have similarities with the question about the hen and the egg.

Production for use in kind only, without any sale, means no cash income from farming and consequently that it is very difficult for the farmer to pay for inputs, such as sowing seed and fertilizer. This limits production to what it is possible to obtain on the basis of recirculation within the farm, such as animal manure and home-saved seed, plus other resources that might be available for free. Accordingly, it is relevant to assume comparably high resource use and production in market oriented farming, but low inputs and outputs when the degree of market orientation is low or zero. You can follow this reasoning in Figure 3.1,

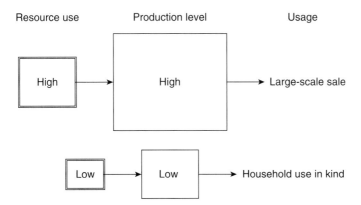

Figure 3.1 Principal links between resource use, potential level of production and whether the products are marketed or used in kind. The sizes of the boxes are not proportional.

which illustrates the principal links between use of resources and market and subsistence oriented agriculture.

Although the boxes in Figure 3.1 are not proportional, they indicate principal differences between market and subsistence oriented farming, and between input and output within the two alternatives. Due to the connections between resource use and degree of market orientation we may alternatively consider this as an output driven form of production, for which the outputs, such as grain or milk yields, serve as point of departure for methods of production.

Similarly, subsistence oriented farming can be understood as input driven, because the available inputs set the upper limits for what it is possible to obtain from production. You will read more about this in Chapter 12, where we will discuss output and input driven production in relation to plant nutrient supply.

High degrees of market orientation are chiefly found in large-scale farming, whereas low degrees dominate smallholder farming. The connections between sale and size are logical; it is hardly possible to consume the entire production from a big farm, and more difficult to create a surplus for sale from a smallholding. Still, many smallholder farmers sell products occasionally, as illustrated by Figure 3.2, which shows smallholder produced eggs for sale at a local market in South-East Asia.

Figure 3.2 Smallholder produced eggs sold at a local market in South-East Asia, 2010.
Photo: Anna Martiin.

Drawbacks and vicious circles

Neither market nor subsistence oriented farming is unproblematic. Not from farmers' perspectives, and not from societal views. There is in fact a variety of pros and cons in each system. Market oriented farming may generate high levels of production but also has drawbacks such as high use of water for irrigation and of non-renewable resources, such as fossil energy. Moreover, the individual market oriented farmer may worry about imbalances between costs and revenues; high levels of indebtedness; and the functioning of infrastructures and markets.

As private consumption is likely to be a minor part of the total turnover of big market oriented farms, the household will probably be able to maintain relatively unchanged their material standard of living even during problematic years. This contrasts with typical subsistence farming, where seasonal variations can directly affect livelihoods, including the daily food supply.

Shortages of resources and cash in subsistence farming mean high vulnerability and cruel exposure to forces of nature. Many poor smallholder farmers are more or less trapped in vicous circles with rather limited possibilities for preventing or dealing with upcoming problems such as diseases of plants and animals and long-lasting periods of drought. These problems highlight one of the current challenges for world agriculture: to break the vicious circle of resource scarcity in poor smallholder farming. As discussed in Box 3.1, the numbers of explicitly market oriented farms are few compared with the large numbers that are more subsistence oriented.

Box 3.1 Proportions of market and subsistence oriented farming

The proportions of market and subsistence oriented farming may at best be roughly approximated. Degrees of market orientation differ over the year and between years, and individually, also between neighbouring farmers. Moreover, access to land and farm sizes are too multifaceted matters to provide an exact figure (Chapters 9 and 10). Nevertheless, the question is worth some consideration. According to Table 10.1, there are more than half a billion farm holdings around the world. Of these only about 0.6 per cent are supposed to have more than 100 hectares, which undoubtedly can be seen as a category where highly market oriented farming is the only relevant alternative. Moreover, 2.7 per cent of all farms are thought to have between 10 and 100 hectares, which, with reservations, can be supposed to be a farm size with high degrees of market orientation, albeit some of these may be operated part time (Chapter 18). Farms with between 2 and 10 hectares of arable land form a third group which is estimated to comprise 11.7 per cent of all farms. Most probably this category includes various degrees of market orientation. Farms like these may be operated on a hobby basis in Western Europe, but can on the contrary be seen as relatively wealthy businesses in smallholder dominated regions, for example in parts of Sub-Saharan Africa. The remaining approximately 85 per cent of the estimated half a billion farm holdings have less than 2 hectares. This makes it relevant to assume that hundreds of millions of smallholdings are chiefly operated in order to fulfil as much as possible of the households' needs, albeit with occasional small-scale sales as well as additional purchases. It is thus, in spite of the approximate figures, obvious that highly market oriented farming is operated on a minority of all farm holdings. The picture would change if we were to study the total production, or farm areas, instead of the number of farmers.

Production and consumption in kind are principally managed without direct contact with the market, without purchases and sales, which ought to make subsistence farming independent of volatile price levels and other pressures from national and international markets. The small-scale sale and the supplementary purchases of food are, however, highly vulnerable to price volatilities. Many smallholders may use 50, 60 or even 70 per cent of their cash income on purchases of food, which means that reduced prices for the products and/or increases in food prices bring a high risk of undernourishment in the farm household.

Real life, a matter of nuances and combinations

As mentioned, the principal categorization in market and subsistence oriented farming is widely modified in real life. There certainly are farms where 100 per cent of production is sold, and there are farms where all products are used at home. But a great deal of all farming is operated as combinations, with larger or smaller shares for sale and internal use, respectively. This is exemplified in Boxes 3.2–3.5, which take you to four different farms, in Canada, New Zealand, Romania and Uganda. Before this, we will study the four cases in terms of relations between resource use and market orientation, as shown in Figure 3.3.

The four letters in Figure 3.3 indicate four different types of farms. In the top right, A shows a 100 per cent market oriented farm with high use of purchased inputs. Likewise, B illustrates 100 per cent market orientation, but on the basis of modest use of purchased inputs. C indicates combined market and subsistence oriented farming with relatively low use of purchased resources and with emphasis on both sale and use in kind. In the bottom left, D represents farming that is primarily aimed at subsistence needs, but with some occasional sale. Smallholding D is operated with very limited possibilities of using purchased input resources. The letters A to D are exemplified in Boxes 3.2–3.5, which are based on fictitious examples from around the world.

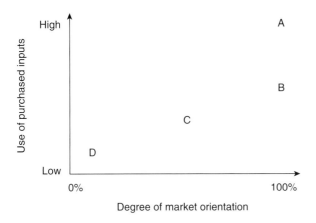

Figure 3.3 The letters A to D indicate different kinds of farming with respect to degree of market orientation (horizontal axis) and use of purchased input resources (vertical axis). The A to D farms are exemplified in Boxes 3.2–3.5.

Box 3.2 A. 100 per cent market oriented farming and high use of purchased inputs

Sue and Jeff Johnson cultivate 1,400 hectares of arable land in the Canadian prairies. About one-quarter of the area is maize (corn), one-quarter is winter wheat and the remaining hectares are made up of canola, soybeans, barley and oats. The Johnsons also operate a farrow-to-finish hog operation, with 1,500 sows that produce approximately 35,000 hogs per year. Despite raising crops, they feed hogs on ready-made feed delivered by the local feed mill. Sue and Jeff operate their farm intensively, with high levels of purchased fertilizers and regular use of chemical pesticides. Moreover, tractors and harvesters consume a couple of hundred cubic metres of fossil fuel, even though the latest purchased tractor runs on bio-fuel. The Johnsons have also invested in thorough drainage of the fields. Approximately half of the crop is sold via futures contracts provided prices are attractive in spring, while the remainder is stored at the farm and then sold when economically favourable. Hogs are sold for slaughter at about six months of age when they have reached a market weight of 115 kg. These are also sold on contract to a large nationwide processor with slaughtering operations in the region. This part of the business also generates animal manure that is used as a fertilizer, even though it is not sufficient for the entire area. Accordingly, the business makes some use of internally produced means of production; however, the primary benefit of the mixed farming operations is the balancing of otherwise seasonal workloads and cash flows. Still, the Johnsons are 100 per cent market oriented and manage the farm on the basis of high use of purchased resources. This example refers to A in Figure 3.3 and to the upper alternative in Figure 3.1.

Box 3.3 B. 100 per cent market orientation but relatively low level of
purchased inputs

The brothers Alex and Stephen McArthur have 1,200 breeding ewes and 800 steers that graze an area of 1,400 acres on the North Island of New Zealand. All animals are primarily pasture fed, supplemented with silage when needed. Costs of inputs are relatively low. Necessary expenses are, among other things, purchase of young calves, costs of silage production, petrol, veterinary, insurance, fences and maintenance of a few buildings, plus various taxes. The production is paid extra since the farm was certified as environmentally friendly a few years ago. Like the example in Box 3.2, Alex and Stephen are 100 per cent market oriented in their farming, even though they base this on relatively low inputs and yields. This kind of farming exemplifies B in Figure 3.3.

Box 3.4 C. both market and subsistence orientation with relatively low
use of purchased inputs

The Petrescu family owns a farm in Transylvania, Romania. Seven hectares of arable land are intensively cultivated with maize, sunflower, roots, vegetables, wine and grains. In addition, hay for the animals is partly grown on arable land, partly on pasture along the hillside, which is also used for grazing. The family has four dairy cows, eight sheep and some poultry. Occasionally a pig is bred for slaughter. Some sowing seed, fertilizer and a little feed concentrate is bought, as well as petrol and lubricant for a tractor, which is shared with a neighbouring family. Some cash money is earned through daily sale of milk to a local dairy. Still, as much as possible of the diverse production is used in kind in the household. Elderly family members especially work conserving and preparing food and refining wool. It is, however, increasingly difficult to manage this old-fashioned subsistence strategy, not least after far-reaching drought problems a few years ago, which strained the family's economy. To maintain the household, the younger parents commute weekly for work at a factory, while the grandparents take care of the children and the farm. Without this external income they would not be able to keep the farm. This kind of farming exemplifies C in Figure 3.3.

Box 3.5 D. chiefly subsistence orientation and low use of purchased inputs

The Byarugaba family in south-western Uganda cultivate about one hectare, which is split up into many small plots along the hillside. The area is rain fed and the family cultivates cassava, sorghum, maize, beans, potatoes, bananas, fresh vegetables and some tobacco. Most of what is grown is consumed by the extended family, but the tobacco is sold. The possibility of selling other products differs from year to year, primarily depending on the weather. Moreover, the family has a few cattle, pigs and poultry, which are important for the household but occasionally also provide surpluses for sale. The sowing seed is usually home saved, and fertilizer is limited to the available manure and other organic matter that can be obtained for free. Each plot is small and manually operated at this intensively farmed smallholding, which generates very little money. Cash expenditures are, however, unavoidable and the needs are currently managed with the help of money sent home by relatives working abroad. This kind of farming exemplifies D in Figure 3.3 and the bottom alternative in Figure 3.1.

Summary

Two major and principally different forms of agriculture are introduced in this chapter: market oriented farming, aiming at sale and subsistence oriented farming, which is primarily intended for consumption in the producer household. As the two strategies are often combined in reality, we may alternatively speak about various degrees of market orientation. The flows of resources into and out of the farm can be expected to increase with the degree of market orientation. With money coming in from sales, it becomes possible to buy more inputs, such as fertilizer and animal feed, and thereby continue or even increase production for sale. Highly market oriented farming is generally found in large-scale farming, and vice versa, which is logical, but smallholder farming is also largely involved in occasional sales. The reasoning about resource use and market and subsistence orientation is exemplified by four farm examples from different parts of the world.

Next

In Chapter 4 you will study the food chain, which you may know of from expressions such as 'from farm to fork'. We will leave the previous focus on matters that unite and distinguish different kinds of farming, and turn our attention to the many stages of the food chain, from farm inputs to final consumption of the products. Much of the reasoning is also valid for other kinds of farm products, such as fibres, bio-energy and other non-food products.

To discuss

○   Make use of the Internet, and look for examples of farming that seem to be characterized by varying degrees of market orientation. Depending on how much time you can spend, study different continents and regions. Discuss the findings with your student colleagues.

○   Discuss the pros and cons of large-scale production for the national or international market, on the one hand, and small-scale farming for the household and local society, on the other. Consider aspects such as the advantages and disadvantages of each with respect to yearly variations, seasonal surpluses and shortages, access to resources for farming, environmental aspects of transport, and long-term perspectives on farming and food supply.

○   Think of a farm holding that you either have long personal experience of, have visited, or have come into contact with through the media. To what extent do you believe this particular holding is/was market oriented? Can you remember what kinds of products were used in the household and what kind were sold?

4   The food chain

You have probably heard expressions like 'from farm to fork', 'from stable to table' or 'from gate to plate'. They are all used as umbrella terms for the food chain and referring to how foods are being produced, transformed and distributed from the farms to the final food consumer. Other kinds of agricultural products can be thought of in similar ways, such as fibre chains and bio-energy chains, although the reasoning in this chapter has the food chain as the point of reference.

You will be introduced to the characteristics of chains for marketed foods and learn about similarities and differences in comparison with situations where the food is consumed in the producer's household. In addition to the use of the food chain model to study production–handling–consumption, the concept can help us identify and analyse resource flows, by-products and emissions. The thinking in terms of chains provides the third of three main points of reference to which much of the reasoning in this book refers, together with the fundamental characteristics and degree of market orientation.

After this chapter you are expected to:

- ○ Understand the food chain as a concept
- ○ Be able to account for the main stages in a commercial food chain
- ○ Be able to describe major differences between food chains in market and subsistence economies
- ○ Be able to consider food chains and other kinds of agricultural product chains as a way to study resources and environmental impact

Key words

Food chain, marketed food, use in kind, inputs, post-harvest processes, storage, transport, distribution, wholesale, food processing, food packaging, retailing, consumption, by-products, resource flows.

The 'from farm to fork' approach

Each time we eat we are engaged in the food chain. For many of us the plate provides a colourful map, with food from almost all over the world. Even a small biscuit can be a globetrotter. It is not just that the final biscuit may have been baked on another continent and then been stored, packaged and repackaged at various places. Each ingredient often has its own story of origin, such as wheat flour from the US, whey powder from Australia, powdered eggs from India, sugar from Brazil, glucose syrup from China, salt from Mexico; plus artificial additives of varying backgrounds. In addition, the fats in our biscuit may be a mixture of palm oil from Indonesia, palm kernel oil from Malaysia, coconut oil from Viet Nam and rapeseed oil from Canada.

In brief, a food chain can be defined as a linear sequential structure that shows various stages along the processes of production, handling and consumption of food. The food chain approach is widely applied, and a way to highlight the actors involved, such as the farmer, the transport sector and the consumer. It is also applicable to fibre, bio-energy and other non-food chains that are being produced in the agricultural sector.

Chains for marketed foods

Market oriented food chains are often long and complex, and include a large number of actors. The intermediate stages between farmers and consumers especially can engage a broad range of interested parties. The food chain actors can be individuals, which generally is the case with farmers and consumers, whereas others may be giants, such as national or international grain trading companies. You will find a general model of the food chain for marketed foods in Figure 4.1.

Depending on the focus of interest, food chains can be lengthened, for example in order to involve health aspects for consumers; or shortened, in order to go deeper into a specific part of the chain. You may, for instance, concentrate on the different stages that are operated at the farm level, or in the many transports that occur throughout the chain. The box 'Intermediate stages' in Figure 4.1 is particularly simplified. In reality this stage may include a wide range of actors, such as truck drivers, traders, workers in processing industries and staff at fast-food restaurants. The following list describes the various stages of the commercial food chain.

- Input supply: the purchased input resources that are put into the food chain. Among the input suppliers to farm production you may find: fertilizer

Figure 4.1 General outline of the chain for marketed foods.

industries, seed companies, animal feed companies, farm machinery companies, agro-chemical industries, petrochemical companies and electricity suppliers. Energy and chemicals are also continuously required during later stages, which also use large amounts of inputs such as packaging materials, transport and storage facilities.

- Farmers: market oriented farm production of crops, animal products, fibres, bio-energy and varying by-products form the basis for food chains and other agricultural chains.
- Intermediate stages: intermediate stages constitute larger or smaller parts of the total handling and final costs for agricultural products. Some of these activities are frequently repeated along the chain, not least transport, repackaging and intermediate storage. The following list includes a more detailed account of the intermediate stages than was relevant to include in Figure 4.1:
  - Post-harvest processes: processes that are carried out at the farm or elsewhere in order to make the products storable and/or able to be handled. Chilling of milk before it is delivered to a dairy plant is one example; drying of grains is another; ensiling of grass for internal use is a third.
  - Storage: storage is repeatedly undertaken along the food chain, in which it serves as a stage in between other activities. The more complex the chain, the more frequently will products probably be stored.
  - Transport: like storage, transport is an intermediate activity that often takes place repeatedly, over longer or shorter distances. Transportation begins in the arable field, and is then frequently repeated along the food chain.
  - Distribution: the term distribution includes more than the actual transportation as it refers to allocation, geographically, between people and over time.
  - Wholesale: wholesalers may be involved in many stages of the food chain, where they act as purchasers or agents in buying and selling agricultural commodities for further sale to other actors, such as other wholesalers, food processing industries or retailers.
  - Processing: food processing refers to mechanical and/or chemical operations in order to change and/or preserve foods. Processing takes a number of varying forms that range from large-scale processing plants to small-scale manual operations, for example in a small-scale bakery.
  - Packaging: packaging and repackaging in order to preserve the food make it moveable, and portion it into saleable consumer packages.
  - Retailing: retailers are in more direct contact with the final consumers, who buy food in order to consume it. Retailer roles can be played by supermarkets, stores, street vendors and others, and retailing is, in contrast with local barter, generally based on cash.
- Consumption: besides eating, the consumption stage can include related consumer activities such as the trip to the supermarket, storing in the

household and cooking, and eventually also some care with packaging and food waste.

- Waste: waste is produced all along the chain, and so are a plethora of by-products. The distinction between waste and by-products may be a grey zone that to a great extent is decided by the ambition to reuse or otherwise recycle. Nonetheless, waste occurs, stored in landfills and/or emitted into air and water.

Food chains can thus include a large number of players and many of these form separate branches that can be gigantic, for example feed concentrate companies, air transportation of fresh fruits around the world and dairy packaging industries. Many of these are potential places of work for agronomists and adjacent professions with different kinds of expertise. Box 4.1 exemplifies a dairy chain in a European context.

Thus far we have emphasized the complexity of chains for marketed foods. As the continuing text turns the attention to subsistence farming you will find that the food chain is shorter and of a somewhat different character, but also that this hardly means that food supply in kind would be an easy task.

Food chains in subsistence farming

Among the most important differences between food chains in commercial and subsistence economies are that you hardly find any external intermediate actors in the latter, where the farmer and the consumer are the same person, or members of the same household. Put in another way, many of the functions along food chains in subsistence systems have to be managed at the farm producing units, which is in contrast to commercial chains, where numerous specialized actors are involved. The wholesaler and retailer functions are excluded from subsistence chains but the other functions remain in one way or another. In addition, the many kinds of undertakings are often carried out under simple conditions: outdoors, manually

---

Box 4.1 The dairy chain, an example

The basic chain structure can be exemplified by the milk chain. The milk is produced at a farm with the help of input supplies such as feed concentrate and electricity. The post-harvest stage is here represented by transportation of the milk through pipes in a milking parlour to a tank, where it is cooled and temporarily stored before it is transported to the dairy plant where the milk is processed, for instance fermented into yoghurt. The yoghurt is then packed in cartons or pots, and temporarily stored before the further transportation to stores and supermarkets, nearby or far away.

The food chain in subsistence farming

The producer = The consumer, and the one who has to guarantee:

✓ Input supply
✓ Post-harvest processes (thresh, dry, conserve, etc.)
✓ Storage
✓ Internal transportation
✓ Distribution within the household and over time
✓ Food processing and cooking
✓ Waste management

Figure 4.2 When the producer and the consumer are the same person, or belong to the same household, many of the sequences of the food chain have to be guaranteed at the farm.

with simple tools, without electricity and with poor storage facilities. Figure 4.2 highlights the many stages of the food chain that have to be guaranteed where farm products are used in kind.

The first stage in Figure 4.2, input supply, is usually limited to the resources that possibly can be obtained in kind, which you will read more about in Parts II and III. Post-harvest processes aimed at making the products storable, or ready to use, can be exemplified be threshing in the farmyard, or drying fish from a fish pond. Perishable products, such as fresh milk and many vegetables and fruits, often have to be consumed directly. The combined producer-consumer also has to take care of storage and shelter, so that the products are not damaged by moisture, mould or vermin. Transportation in this context is often the same as carrying, which may have to be done more than once, for example from fields to farmyards, to a first place for storage, and then for further handling and storing. Moreover, the products have to be distributed between use in kind and eventual sale, between the household and other alternative use in kind, such as exchanges, and payment for labour. Distribution over time, until the next harvest, is another challenge. Storing and packaging are closely intertwined in subsistence farming, where we speak about sacks, baskets, boxes and pots, rather than about the throw-away plastic and paper packaging that dominates commercial food chains. Finally, the subsistence economy also includes frequent cleaning and time-consuming grinding, chopping and boiling of home-produced foods.

Current characteristics and trends

The world of agriculture includes the most varied kinds of food chains. The differences are generally bigger between commercial and subsistence chains, but there are also large dissimilarities between various chains for marketed foods. You can probably find both locally produced foods and commodities from other parts of the world in most food stores and supermarkets. Still, chains for marketed foods can in general be characterized by:

- Relatively few suppliers of commercial inputs, such as inorganic fertilizers and agrochemicals
- Many farmers, in comparison with input suppliers and intermediate actors
- Many intermediate stages, but comparably few actors, especially in some stages such as multinational retailer corporations
- A great many consumers

What is more, the world is currently experiencing rapid changes in food chain structures for marketed foods. First, ongoing urbanization means that the gaps between production and consumption are increasing, in terms of physical distance as well as when it comes to understanding how food is produced, before it reaches the food store or the supermarket. Second, the global food trade is intensive, and distances are often ignored in favour of the opportunity to sell. Transportation of fresh strawberries and roses from one continent to another illustrates this trend. Third, we are facing a situation in which power is increasingly concentrated in the hands of intermediaries, not least retailers, which widens the gaps between producers and consumers.

We are also facing a situation in which many smallholders are becoming increasingly dependent on supplementary purchases of food. This can in part be explained by increased fragmentation of already small farm units, but may also be due to weather events and/or political instability. In addition to tendencies of reduced subsistence production per household in some regions, prices for food have lately been more volatile than during previous decades. The transportation of food by bicycle, pictured in Figure 4.3 may illustrate the diversity, and at the same time one of the transport sequences along the chain.

From the farmer's point of view it is natural to consider the food chain as fundamentally based on the processes of production that takes place at the farm, for example as the wheat chain, while the consumer rather sees this as the bread chain. In Box 4.2 you will find some examples of specific chains, with the farmer's view at the beginning of each row, and suggested consumer perspectives by the end.

Crop versus animal production chains

Whether a product originates from plants or animals influences the chain sequence at farm level. While cash crops are sold, sooner or later after harvest, feed crops are recirculated through the animals. You can see the principle in Figure 4.4, which demonstrates the recirculation of cultivated crops through the animals, from which the manure is recirculated too. The principles outlined in Figure 4.4 are valid for types of farming where farm animals are fed on cultivated crops from the farm. Where the animals are fed solely on grazing the animal production chain is less complicated.

Figure 4.3 Transportation by bicycle of sacks, for instance of rice, illustrating one of the many types of transport that may be included in the food chain.

Photo: Anna Martiin.

Box 4.2 Corresponding producer–consumer perspectives, some examples

- The wheat chain – the pasta chain; or the bread chain; or the pancake chain
- The maize (corn) chain – the breakfast cereal chain; or the maize oil chain
- The cassava chain – the cassava porridge chain; or the cassava cake chain
- The rapeseed chain – the margarine chain; or the rapeseed honey chain
- The milk chain – the yoghurt chain; or the cheese chain
- The hog chain – the ham chain; or the bacon chain
- The fish pond chain – the smoked fish chain; or the fishcake chain
- The cotton chain – the textile chain; or the T-shirt chain

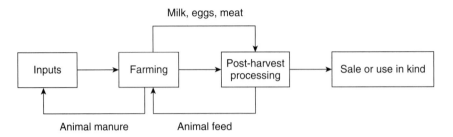

Figure 4.4 Parts of the food chain that take place at the farm. While cash crops may be sold or consumed after harvest, feed crops are recirculated through the animals before the products, animal products, are sold or used in kind.

Summary

The food chain outlines how foods are being produced, transformed and distributed, from farm level to the final food consumer. In addition, the model can also be applied to other agricultural products, such as fibres, bio-energy and other non-foods. The chain model is based on a step-by-step approach which often focuses on the actors involved, but also on the differ-ent functions. With reference to market and subsistence oriented farming it is argued that the world of agriculture includes varying kinds of food chains that differ in length, complexity and the actors involved. In addition, food chains can be used for studies of emissions and on how resources are used along the chain. On the one hand, the text highlights the increased impact of intermediate actors on chains for marketed foods. On the other hand, atten-tion is focused on the work required to manage production and consump-tion of food in kind. The chapter also touches on current trends in matters of food chains and, among other things, touches on current urbanization, a strengthened retailer sector and volatile food prices.

Next

The sum of all agricultural chains results in enormous, although not always sufficient, quantities of food and other farm products. These are focused on in Part II of the book, which highlights world agriculture in large-scale perspectives. First, in Chapter 5, we will explore the population situation with regard to general trends, differences between continents and propor-tions between rural and urban populations.

To discuss

○   Reflect on what you have eaten during the last few days, and try to get an idea of the origin of the different foods. Try to be as detailed as possible as regards place of origin, possible chains for each kind of food and possible actors involved.

Part II
World agriculture

5   World population and food

There are inescapable correlations between farming and the number of mouths that can be fed. World food supply is more complicated than that, but it is undeniable that the initial stages of the food chain impact the final stages and vice versa. We are currently experiencing substantial increases in total world population, in parallel with worries about environmental constraints such as climate change, water supply and use of non-renewable resources. Each of these phenomena has consequences for farming and has contributed to increased concerns about the global food supply.

This chapter highlights the world population, the number of food consumers for which farming actually is conducted. The scale is primarily global, but also continental and national. We will examine the present situation and then consider the projections for 2050 and 2090, and take a glance back to 1950. Attention is also turned to current trends in food consumption patterns, which in fact are deepening the effects of population growth. Changes in proportions of people in rural and urban areas are also discussed, as well as the number of farmers and proportions of male and female farmers.

After this chapter you are expected to:

- Have a fair idea of the size of the world population in 1950 and today, and of forecasts for this century
- Be able to discuss expected changes in world population distribution between the continents
- Be familiar with today's major trends in consumption of vegetable versus animal foods
- Have a fair idea of the proportions of rural and urban populations at a global scale, today and in recent decades
- Account for the approximate number of people who are economically active in farming, in the world, and in so-called developed and developing countries

    o   Be familiar with approximate proportions of male and female farmers in the world, including some differences between the continents

    o   Be able to define the term food security

Key words

World population, demography, population forecasts, trends, food consumption patterns, rural, urban, economically active, male farmers, female farmers, food security.

Inevitable correlations between population and food

The survival of a certain number of people requires a certain and continuous flow of food, which means that there are basic and inevitable links between what is grown and harvested and the number of mouths that can be fed. The attention paid to the fundamental link between world population and world farming has increased in recent years. We have in fact experienced a kind of shift in the international discussion, a shift that highlights both total food production and the ways in which the food is being produced. This contrasts with the major debate during the last decades of the twentieth century, which chiefly focused on global agricultural trade and fair socioeconomic distribution of food. The Nobel Prize laureate Amartya Sen, for example, claimed the importance of fair information about prices and food availability, rather than production as such.

Current discussions in the international arena still emphasize these factors but the perspectives have been extended to include farming methods and total farm production as well. This trend should be seen in the light of emerging general concern about the demographic and environmental challenges that lie ahead. It is interesting to note that the widened focus has brought about a newly awakened interest in farming among international organizations, governments, non-governmental organizations (NGOs) and agri-business corporations. Their basic interests differ but during the last years many organizations and companies have formulated relatively similar declarations about future challenges in agriculture; at conferences, on websites and in other media.

The ongoing increase in world population, which we will study in the major part of this chapter, means growing pressure on the resources for food production, such as arable and pasture land, water, energy and crop nutrients. At the same time as we need more food, production has to take increasing account of problems such as climate change, environmental impact and sustainable use of limited resources.

With reduced margins, the solving of one problem cannot be allowed to cause negative effects somewhere else. This means that understanding of the agricultural sector, not least of practical farming, is necessary not only for the production of food as such, but to manage population growth and the food supply in the long run.

Transforming reality into figures

As the continuous examination of the world population situation, as well as the other chapters in this part of the book, is largely based on statistics, some attention should be paid to statistics as such. The real world is far from easy to transform into homogenous, manageable and comparable tables. This is true for all kinds of statistics but global population and agricultural statistics can be more tricky than the average. Among the problems with worldwide agricultural statistics are the difficulties in formulating questionnaires that are relevant for all countries and easy to understand in spite of differences in terminology, culture and practices. Measurement units of farm land can differ, for example, and so can local categories for farm animals. In addition, the time for collection of data may differ between countries and regions, so that international statistics for practical reasons have to be based on information from several years. These issues are also discussed in Chapter 10 with examples in Box 10.1.

Due to the wide range of different geographical, economic, social and cultural structures under which agriculture is conducted, and that you will learn about throughout this book, it is hardly relevant to expect that global statistics are completely comparable. We thus have to be aware of the risks of various kinds of bias, and consider whether and how this might affect a certain study. The applied statistical methods are advanced and able to handle some weaknesses in the underlying material, but it is still appropriate to regard the figures as good approximates, rather than as exact information.

Studies of numbers of inhabitants and other kinds of population issues belong to demographics, which is the discipline that studies human populations. In terms of agriculture, demographic perspectives are important for our understanding of current and future needs for food, patterns of consumption, demand for non-food products from farming, farm labour and for analyses of migration between rural and urban areas.

The following reasoning about the world's population is largely based on population statistics from the United Nations Population Division, while the agricultural statistics in this and subsequent chapters chiefly derive from the statistical database FAOSTAT at the Food and Agricultural Organization of the United Nations, FAO. These are leading sources of global population and agricultural statistics, respectively, the common points of reference to which many authors and debaters refer. You can also find the two databases on UN websites; see the Bibliography.

Increased world population

The world population continues to rise. The first billion was reached about two hundred years ago, around the year 1800, and by 1950 total world population was 2.5 billion. Just fifty years later, by the turn of the millennium, we were at 6 billion, and a decade later 7 billion! Prospects for the future suggest further increases, to about 8.3 billion by 2030 and 9.3 billion by 2050. Growth is

Table 5.1 World population 1950–2010 and forecasts to 2090. The forecasts refer to the so-called medium alternative of the United Nations Population Division

	1950	*1970*	*1990*	*2010*	*2030*	*2050*	*2070*	*2090*
World population, billions	2.5	3.7	5.3	6.9	8.3	9.3	9.8	10.1

Source: *World Population Prospects, the 2010 Revision* (accessed 26 September 2012).

supposed to slow down during the second half of this century and reach approximately 10 billion around the year 2085. Table 5.1 illustrates the increase in world population from 1950 to 2010, and forecasts to 2090, all in twenty-year intervals.

The figures in Table 5.1 refer to the medium level of current estimates by the United Nations Population Division. The medium variant is often referred to but, as you can see in Table 5.2, there are higher and lower forecasts as well, forecasts that highlight dramatic differences for the future.

As you can see in Table 5.2, the four alternative trends lead to widely different population levels. While the low variant points at a slightly lower level than today, 6.7 billion, the so-called high variant suggests more than a doubling compared with today, 14.6 billion people by 2090. The fourth alternative, the so-called constant-fertility variant, forecasts a three-fold increase, to an astronomical 21.3 billion, by the end of the century. When considering the reliability of prognoses like these it is interesting to find that a UN report in 1973 foresaw 6.4 billion by the turn of the millennium, which was close to the actual figure of 6.1 billion.

A number of factors will, however, influence which of the alternatives turns out to be most relevant. The prognoses include estimates about increased life expectancy and deaths due to diseases such as HIV/AIDS, but fertility (in brief, the average number of children per woman) is seen as the key factor. The medium variant in Table 5.2 assumes that the average fertility in the world will go down from 2.52 children per woman in 2005–2010, to 2.17 in 2045–2050 and to 2.04 in

Table 5.2 World population situation in 2010 and four different levels of forecasts up to 2090

	World population, billions				
	2010	*2030*	*2050*	*2070*	*2090*
Low variant	6.9	7.9	8.1	7.6	6.7
Medium variant	6.9	8.3	9.3	9.8	10.1
High variant	6.9	8.8	10.6	12.5	14.6
Constant-fertility variant	6.9	8.7	10.9	14.5	21.3

Source: *World Population Prospects, the 2010 Revision* (accessed 26 September 2012).

2085–2090. By 2045–2050 the low variant suggests 1.71 children per woman, the high variant 2.64 and the constant-fertility rate variant 3.22 children per woman. Accordingly, relatively small differences at the individual level contribute to enormous long-term differences in global perspective.

As mentioned, the alternative most commonly believed to be likely is the medium variant; however, it is commonly claimed that this requires improvements in education, food security and health care in countries with many poor households with many children.

Differences between continents

As important as the total population expansion is the fact that growth is expected to be unequally distributed between the continents. You can see this in Table 5.3, which demonstrates that the percentage increase is assumed to be especially high in Africa.

The forecasts in Table 5.3 suggest big differences in population increases, from more than a doubling in Africa to a slight reduction in Europe. The percentage growth is more similar in Asia, Latin America and North America, between 23 and 30 per cent. In real numbers, the Asian and African populations are assumed to increase by about one billion each, but the relative change in Asia, 23 per cent, appears less dramatic than the forecasted 114 per cent rise in Africa.

According to these figures Africa seems to face enormous demographic changes that, among other things, highlight African agriculture and food supply. As the present food security situation is already troublesome in many countries, there is no doubt that the future supply is a challenge. Looking just twenty years ahead, to 2030, the UN medium level forecasts that the number of people in Africa and Asia will equal the total world population today. These examples illustrate the rapidity with which the demographic changes are taking place, and the necessity

Table 5.3 Distribution of world population between continents in 2010 and expectations for 2050, according to the medium alternative of the United Nations Population Division

	2010, millions	*2050, millions*	*Increase, millions*	*Increase, %*
Africa	1,022	2,192	1,070	114
Asia	4,164	5,142	978	23
Europe	738	719	−19	−3
North America	345	447	102	30
Latin America and Caribbean	590	751	161	27
Oceania	37	55	18	49
World	6,896	9,306	2,410	35

Source: *World Population Prospects, the 2010 Revision* (accessed 27 September 2012).

Table 5.4 Comparison of the number of inhabitants in Africa and Europe in 1950 and 2090, according to the medium alternative of the United Nations Population Division

	1950		2090	
	Millions of people	*% of world population*	*Millions of people*	*% of world population*
Africa	230	9	3,358	33
Europe	547	22	675	7
World	2,532	100	10,062	100

Source: *World Population Prospects, the 2010 Revision* (accessed 27 September 2010).

of managing world farming, functioning food chains and fair access to foods. The contrasting future prospects for Africa and Europe are further developed in Table 5.4, which compares the populations back in 1950 with the suggested situation by 2090.

If the forecasts in Table 5.4 come true the African continent will have one-third of the world population by the end of this century, compared to one-tenth in the middle of the last century. At the same time Europe is expected to turn from about one-fifth of the world population in 1950 to less than 7 per cent by the close of this century. Accordingly we face both increases in numbers and percentages and altered proportions between the continents. This raises a plethora of questions, not least about agriculture, and even though we do not know how the population forecasts will turn out, we know for certain that agriculture has to be developed in order to feed the world population in the long run – everywhere.

Changes in food consumption patterns

In addition to the increased numbers of mouths to feed, current food consumption trends are exacerbating the effects of the demographic trends. People eat more, waste food and demand more foods of animal origin, which generally require more resources compared with the production of vegetable foods. The latter trend has been tellingly formulated by Joachim von Braun, formerly of the International Food Policy Research Institute (IFPRI), who says that the expected 9 billion people by the middle of the century will be eating like 12.

The exact global consumption of food is hard to determine. A lot of food is home produced or bartered, and thus hardly registered. In contrast, food sales in supermarkets can be registered in the utmost detail, via varying kinds of customer membership cards or in other ways. In between, a variety of stores, restaurants and street vendors are supplying a large number of consumers; daily or more irregularly. And, even if were able to estimate what is produced and bought, there are difficulties in knowing exactly how much of various kinds of foods is actually eaten or wasted.

Table 5.5 Comparison of some marketed food commodities between 1999 and 2009, world. Index 100 = 1999

Marketed food commodities for consumption	Year 2009. Index 100 = 1999
Beef and veal	110
Pig meat	121
Poultry meat	146
Sheep meat	119
Fresh dairy products	112
Cheese	109
Whole milk powder	107
Wheat	107
Rice	113
Vegetable oils	166
Sugar	133

Source: OECD–FAO Agricultural Outlook 2011–2020 database (accessed 30 December 2012).

Due to these difficulties we will study world food consumption in the form of some marketed food commodities, which is shown in Table 5.5. The table compares marketed quantities of some foods in the years 1999 and 2009 and shows the changes in the form of an index, with Index 100 = 1999. If we take pig meat as an example, the index 121 in 2009 says that the total marketed quantity of pig meat increased by 11 per cent from 1999 to 2009.

Comparisons like the one in Table 5.5 are highly dependent on the specific years that are chosen, and neither eventual ups and downs in between the two highlighted years nor diverging levels just before and after the years studied are brought to light. In the case of Table 5.5 some variations appear between 1999 and 2009, and just before and after the period, but they are relatively modest and do not confuse the general impression of the table.

The table demonstrates increases for meats, especially for poultry meat, which rose dramatically from a relatively high level in 1999. Pig meat sales rose too, especially in view of the high total quantities in 1999. As the marketed quantities of sheep meat are relatively low, the higher index for sheep meat in 2009 refers to relatively modest quantities, counted in kilos. Table 5.5 also points at increased sales of dairy products, exemplified by fresh dairy products and cheese. The most dramatic change is, however, the increased sales of vegetable oils, which was 66 per cent higher in 2009 than in 1999. Sales of sugar also increased significantly. Similar tables are also found in Chapters 7 and 20, where 7.3–7.4 and 20.5–20.7 highlight production and export respectively.

The impact of population growth must, however, also be taken into account and, at least as much, how the increases are distributed. Global averages may conceal huge differences and can hide decreases as well. If we extend the perspective further back in time, the FAO publication *Livestock's Long Shadow* (2006b) highlights a three-fold increase in the supply of meat between 1980 and 2002, and comments:

> Driven by population growth and rising income in many developing countries, the global livestock sector has seen a dramatic expansion over the past decades, though with considerable differences between developing and developed countries.
>
> (Steinfeld *et al.* 2006b: 15)

The illustrated changes in patterns of consumption are generally believed to be set to continue, and eventually also to expand. Along with urbanization, we can also expect that larger shares of food sales will take place in supermarkets, which can be expected to strengthen their impact on the food chain, considering kinds of production, farming methods, deliveries from farmers and other actors along the chain, and, in addition, to exert a strong impact on consumer demand.

Rural and urban populations

We also have to consider demographic changes in terms of the ongoing trend of strong urbanization. More people in towns and cities means greater numbers of food customers and thereby increased opportunities for sales of farm products. It is easier to market farm products to urban customers without farmyards of their own than in areas where almost everybody is engaged in some kind of food production.

A general insight into rural–urban issues is necessary to grasp world agriculture. The topic is complex and interdisciplinary and deals, among other things, with the proportions of people who live in the countryside and in cities; and with the ongoing migration from rural to urban areas. The rural population is not the same as the farming population. Many people live in the countryside without being directly involved in farming, and farming can to some degree take place in urban areas. Moreover, rural and urban areas differ in how they are defined in national statistics, which means that global statistics include a wide range of different kinds of rural and urban areas. In spite of this it is possible to get a general picture of the situation and the ongoing changes. In Table 5.6 you can study the shares of rural and urban inhabitants around the world in 1980, 1995 and 2010, in total numbers and percentages.

According to Table 5.6 the rural share of world population exceeded the urban in 1980 and 1995, whereas the urban share exceeded the rural in 2010. The reduced share does not mean, however, that the absolute number of people in the countryside has reduced. On the contrary, both rural and urban populations grew from 1980 to 2010, the rural from 2.7 to 3.4 billion and the urban from 1.7 to 3.5 billion. The urban increase was thus much bigger; it approximately doubled from 1980 to 2010. Behind these figures you will find both population increases as such, and far-reaching migration from rural to urban areas (see Figure 5.1).

The modest population growth in rural areas and the dramatic increase in urban regions is far from equally distributed. Many rural areas suffer from far-reaching

Table 5.6 Comparison of the number of people in rural and urban areas in 1980, 1995 and 2010

	1980	*1995*	*2010*
Total world population, billions	4.5	5.7	6.9
Rural world population, billions	2.7	3.2	3.3
Urban world population, billions	1.8	2.6	3.6
Rural world population, %	61	55	48
Urban world population, %	39	45	52

Source: *World Urbanization Prospects, the 2009 Revision* (accessed 27 September 2012).

Figure 5.1 The number of people living in urban areas recently came to exceed the number of people in the countryside. Hong Kong, 2010.

Photo: Anna Martiin.

decreases in the number of inhabitants, especially in remote, already sparsely populated areas, for example in northern Scandinavia. In contrast, many urban areas suffer from inordinate growth.

Due to population increases and migration we are currently, for the first time in history, facing a situation where about one-half of the global population lives in rural and one-half in urban areas. This can also be formulated as follows: about half of the world is heavily dependent on functioning food chains that allow flows of food from the countryside to reach urban consumers, daily and at prices that are relevant for both consumers and farmers. At the same time more food is needed in rural areas, which may increase pressure on subsistence farming, at the same time as the opportunities for market orientation may increase.

Migration from rural to urban areas is a matter not only of the number of people but also of altered age structures. In general, young people leave, while the remaining rural population consists of increasing shares of elderly people. Where urban migration is thought to be temporary, it is common to leave the children to be taken care of by elderly relatives while the parents are away. Box 5.1 illustrates the reverse phenomenon, people leaving the city, which, however, should be understood as a small-scale movement with marginal effects in comparison with the intensive flows of migrants that are heading towards the cities.

As mentioned, the rural population is not the same as the farming population. In many Western European countries, for example, the countryside has a mixed population, with a few farmers who operate large farms in areas that also are popular among people who work elsewhere but find the countryside a good place to live. On the other hand, we can assume that large shares of all inhabitants in

---

Box 5.1 Unemployed city dwellers may return to the countryside

In some regions increasing unemployment in the cities makes former migrants return to the countryside. For example, some Chinese farmers who left the land in order to work in the cities were instead hit by urban unemployment and have therefore returned to farming, at least for a while. On a small scale, reports from Greece told of a kind of green wave in the summer of 2011, when young people left Athens in search of cheaper ways to make a living in the countryside.

A relevant understanding of these forms of what we may call reverse migration is, however, that they chiefly reflect temporary solutions, while waiting for new opportunities in town. Still, the phenomenon is interesting and in part sheds new light on otherwise relatively unbroken tendencies of worldwide urbanization.

Source: *The Financial Times*, 21 July 2011; *Guardian*, 13 May 2011.

regions with many poor smallholders are farming at home or engaged in neighbouring more or less subsistence oriented farming. The following text deals with the number of farmers, which apparently is lower than the number of countryside residents in the world.

Number of people engaged in farming

According to the publication *The State of Food and Agriculture 2010–11* (FAO 2011), approximately 40 per cent of all economically active people around the world are engaged in farming. You will find the total number of economically active people in the world and the proportion who are engaged in farming in Table 5.7, which, in contrast with much of the reasoning in this book, categorizes the world in so-called developing or developed regions because available statistics are based on this.

The figures in Table 5.7 originate from databases, published by the FAO, that use the term economically active for people who work or are seeking work in agriculture, hunting, fishing or forestry, and are doing this as self-employed, paid or unpaid workers, or as assisting family members. This coincides well with how the term farmer is used in this book. As explained in Chapter 1, we define farmers as men and women of all ages who are directly involved in practical farming for utility purposes. What is more, we include farming irrespective of ownership, stationary or nomadic forms, size of land and herds, and whether the engagement is full or part time. Still, the figure 1.3 billion in Table 5.7 is probably overestimated in comparison with our definition, because the former also includes hunting, fishing and forestry even when these are not operated as part of farming. On the other hand there might be underestimates too, due to the many children and elderly people that are included in our definition of farmer, but not in Table 5.7. We also have to remember that many people who are economically active in farming also can be economically active in other sectors. Still, it is beneficial to have this estimate that says that approximately four out of ten of all economically active people around the world are engaged in farming.

According to Table 5.7 almost half of all economically active persons in so-called developing countries are engaged in farming, 48.2 per cent, or 2,657

Table 5.7 Total number of economically active people in the world and the proportion active in farming in 2010

	Countries in developing regions	*Countries in developed regions*	*World*
Total labour force, millions of people	2,657	625	3,282
Proportion in farming, %	48.2	4.2	39.9
Numbers in farming, millions of people	1,282	26	1,308

Source: FAO 2011: Table A4 (accessed 27 September 2012).

million people. As is further discussed in Chapter 10, a large proportion of these farmers is involved in smallholder farming. In the regions classified as developing, the percentage farmers in agriculture went down from 65.3 per cent in 1980 to 57.2 per cent in 1995 and 48.2 per cent by 2010. The average of 48.2 per cent farming versus other kinds of economic activities does, however, conceal that the percentages vary widely between countries, from about 90 to just a few per cent. Extremely high proportions are found, for example, in Burundi, Rwanda, Burkina Faso and Nepal, but notably lower in South Africa. The average for developing regions contrasts strongly with the average in developed regions, 4.2 per cent and about 26 million farmers. Among interesting variations within this category it could be mentioned that the US, which is the world's largest exporter of many farm products, only has 1.6 per cent of its population in farming. Comparably high proportions are, for instance, found in Poland, with 17 per cent, and New Zealand, 7.9 per cent.

If we extend our perspective to include the many actors who are engaged along the entire food and non-food agricultural chains, the number of people is widely increased. This is not least true for market oriented agriculture, which, as discussed in Chapter 4, often engages a large number of actors at many stages between farmer and consumer. The low proportion of farmers in so-called developed countries may thus, to some degree, be offset by comparably high numbers of intermediaries.

The proportion of people who are engaged in practical farming is diminishing worldwide. As is shown in Table 5.8 the proportion decreased from about 50 to 40 per cent of all economically active people from 1980 to 2010. However, as with the previous discussion about rural and urban inhabitants, the number of people in farming has increased, although not as much as the numbers in other kinds of economic activity.

Most probably the increased number of farmers from 1980 to 2010 is found on very small farm-holdings in developing regions, whereas there is no doubt that the number of people in farming in so-called developed regions generally has decreased. In these regions structural rationalization and mechanization have long since directed farming to larger, more highly mechanized and less labour intensive units. During the last three decades the percentage of farmers in developed

Table 5.8 Number of people in world farming and as a proportion of all economically active people in the world in 1980, 1995 and 2010

	1980	*1995*	*2010*
Economically active persons in the world, millions	1,895	2,575	3,282
Economically active persons in world agriculture, millions	955	1,187	1,308
Economically active persons in world agriculture, %	50.4	46.1	39.9

Source: FAO 2011: Table A4 (accessed 27 September 2012).

regions has been drastically reduced, from on average 13.1 per cent in 1980 to 7.5 per cent in 1995 and 4.2 per cent in 2010, and it is safe to say that the absolute numbers have gone down as well.

Men and women in farming

Depending on your point of reference your inner view of a farmer may show a male or a female person. According to a generalized view the farmer on a highly mechanized and market oriented farm is often a man, whereas primarily subsistence oriented and manually operated farming is often conducted by women. The real world is, however, more nuanced and includes many variations, individually and between regions and countries, which is reflected in the following quotation:

> The roles and status of women in agriculture and rural areas vary widely by region, age, ethnicity and social class and are changing rapidly in some parts of the world.
>
> (FAO 2011d: 4)

In 2011 the FAO publication *The State of Food and Agriculture 2010–11: Women in agriculture* reported that women make up about 43 per cent of the world's agricultural labour. The average proportion in developing countries is assumed to be about the same as the world average. The FAO figures are not based on complete information and should thus be seen as rough estimates. The global average includes wide variations, such as especially high proportions of female farmers in Lesotho and Mozambique. Generally speaking, female farmers are more common in Sub-Saharan Africa than in Southern Asia, including India. In contrast, farming in Latin America and the Caribbean seems to be dominated by men. Furthermore, the report estimated the proportion of women in developed regions at about 33 per cent of the total agricultural workforce.

In real numbers, 43 per cent of the global labour makes roughly 560 million women worldwide, of whom about 550 million are working in developing regions and only 9 million in developed countries. It is worth repeating that the figures refer to a wide definition of agricultural labour, and that this is far from always the same as being the one who controls production. In addition, it is hard to know how much of the practical work is done by women and men, respectively, for example when a male farmer at first sight appears to be the main operator. In recent decades the number of female farmers in many countries seems to have increased, due to armed conflict, HIV/AIDS and the more widespread migration of men than of women from rural to urban areas.

Many international organizations highlight female farmers as a strong potential for rural development. The previously referred to FAO report may symbolize the ambitions to strengthen female farmers in poor smallholder farming. In this context frequently heard expressions such as 'closing the gender gap' refer to the difficulties women face in getting hold of land and other resources. It is believed that by improving access to land for women, production as well as smallholder farmers' living conditions will be improved.

Food for all

The same planet that housed 2.5 billion people around 1950 and 6 billion in 2000 is generally expected to have to manage around 9 billion in 2050. We have to cope both with population increase and with the current situation, with the fact that about one in eight people are hungry today. According to recent figures, about 870 million people are undernourished, or about 12 per cent of the world population, to compare with almost 19 per cent 20 years ago. At the same time rising numbers of people worry about eating too much. Looking forward from the somewhat absurd current situation, a main task will nevertheless be to safeguard and improve food security for all. The term food security, which is a key term in these matters, is defined by the United Nations as follows:

> Food security exists when all people, at all times, have physical, social and economic access to sufficient safe and nutritious food that meets their dietary needs and food preferences for an active and healthy life.
>
> (From the UN definition of food security, published by the Committee on World Food Security, www.fao.org/cfs)

The term food security thus claims everybody's right to fair access to food, and the term should not be confused with the term food safety (accounted for in Chapter 21), which refers to hygiene standards all along the food chain.

The challenge of balancing food production and consumption has followed human history ever since agriculture was introduced more than ten thousand years ago. Population versus farming capacity is a classic dilemma that, among others, troubled the English scholar Thomas Malthus. Simplified, Malthus' famous 'An Essay on the Principle of Population' (first published in 1798) claimed that long-term population increase was almost impossible. Each increase would, Malthus argued, increase the pressure on the society and its resources, which would cause famines and diseases that in turn would reduce the population. Humankind was therefore thought to be doomed to cruel, cyclical ups and downs in population size. These pessimistic thoughts were, however, overcome during the nineteenth and twentieth centuries when fossil fuels and global transportation, among other factors, relieved many human societies from being almost totally bound to the local land and forces of nature. When fossil fuel could replace human labour and otherwise contribute to production, and when local harvest failures could be compensated for by trade, it became possible to manage population growth through maintained increases in food production.

In spite of the last two centuries' success in feeding the world, the ongoing increase in the world's population and its coincidence with climate change and other global concerns shed new light on Malthusian principles. Malthus' eventual relevance for the future is controversial and much debated, but some debaters suggest that his thoughts should be considered as delayed, rather than set aside for ever.

Summary

This chapter claims inescapable links between farming and population issues. World population continues to increase, which requires substantial improvements in the food supply. The most common forecasts suggest that the present 7 billion will become 9 billion by 2050 and 10 billion by the end of this century, but there are both lower and higher alternatives.

Future population changes are expected to differ between continents and increase most dramatically in Africa, which highlights the importance of African farming. In addition to increased numbers of mouths to feed, current food consumption trends are accentuating the consequences, among other things because of increased consumption of meat.

Moreover, this chapter highlights the proportions of rural and urban populations, and current trends of migration from rural to urban areas. We are currently facing reduced proportions of farmers and rural inhabitants, even though the absolute numbers are not reduced. Approximately 40 per cent of all economically active people in the world were thought to be active in farming in 2010, of which about 48 per cent were found in so-called developing regions. Only about 4 per cent are active in farming in developed regions around the world, and the share continues to decrease. Much of the work is conducted by female farmers, especially in developing regions, although lack of influence over farm resources can be problematic. In this chapter you have learned the definition of the term food security, which claims the right to fair access to food.

Next

In Chapter 6 we turn our attention from the number of people to be fed to what is being produced. You will read about areas of arable and pasture land around the world, and the crops that are produced on arable land. We will keep to the chiefly quantitative approach that has been applied in this chapter, which means that much of the reasoning is built up around agricultural statistics from around the world.

To discuss

- Look for the UN publication *World Population Prospects: The 2010 revision* (free electronic resource). Examine the future prospects for some countries that you are especially interested in and discuss how population increases change with different fertility rates and years.
- Discuss current trends in patterns of food consumption with your colleagues. What do you think about possible short- and long-term future trends?
- Combine your analysis in the two questions above, and try to imagine the food and population situation in 2030 and 2050, eventually further into the future.
- Consider rural–urban migration in a region that you are familiar with. What does the current trend look like? Try to imagine the rural–urban situation in this region in 2050 and 2090.
- Try to figure out whether male or female farmers dominate the practical work in some countries of specific interest for you. Does there seem to be any difference between the kind of work that is done by men and women?

6   Areas and crops

The following chapter is the first out of three that outline global farm production. In this chapter you will learn about land areas and crops; and thereafter about animal production and non-food production respectively. The three chapters make up a continuation of the previous discussion about world population, and all three have a quantitative character. Practical production is further explained in Parts III and IV.

The following account of areas for crops begins with a description of total land areas and of the areas that are available for agriculture. We will turn our attention to the arable and pasture lands in some countries around the world, but thereafter focus is put on cultivation only, leaving matters of pasture land to the subsequent animal production chapter (Chapter 7). You will read about different categories of crops, such as cereals, oilseeds and fruits; and about the quantities that are being produced at the global level. Some major crops in world agriculture will be given special attention with regard to main producer countries and the quantities produced. In line with the previous discussion about world food production and food security we will also consider the enormous rise in crop production that took place between 1970 and 2009, and that managed to exceed the parallel population increase.

After this chapter you are expected to:

- ○ Be able to define the main categories of agricultural areas and their principal use
- ○ Be able to exemplify countries with extensive arable and/or pasture land areas
- ○ Know the major categories of farm crops for direct human consumption and provide examples of crops in these categories
- ○ Be able to account for major farm crops in the world
- ○ Be aware of the significant increases in total production of farm crops in recent decades

Key words

Agricultural area, forest area, arable land, permanent crops, meadows and pastures, cereals, oilseed, pulses, roots and tubers, sugar crops, vegetables, fruits, global production.

Reading the farmed landscape

Farming has influenced and shaped the landscape in the course of millennia and centuries. Cultivation, grazing and utilization of forests have successively, at a varying pace, framed the landscape and created arable land, pastures and forest. Each piece of farmed land is in part unique and differs in nuances from place to place, but the main differences are usually found between arable, pasture and forest land respectively.

The experienced farmer's eye is often able to read and interpret the farmed landscape in detail; in terms of current usage, weather problems, underperforming crops, grazing potential and any kind of temporary deviation that calls for attention. The temporary visitor may on the other hand observe the large-scale topography of a farmed landscape; whether it is characterized by plains, mountains and lakes, or by a mosaic of small fields and various kinds of vegetation. Eye-catching elements, such as towers or walls, will then probably also soon be perceived, followed by people and animals, farm buildings, solitary trees, roads, ponds and ditches. Seasonal shades may also be noticed, for example if parts of the area are ploughed up; or if the landscape is decorated by a colourful flowering oilseed rape. Agricultural land can be categorized for specific purposes, for instance in order to categorize soils, methods of cultivation or land rights. When, however, the task is to outline agricultural areas worldwide, one of the major ideas of this chapter, then the perspective has to be in line with commonly used categories and definitions. We will thus keep to the FAOSTAT definitions in the following attempt to make the diverse global agricultural landscape manageable and to relate it to other kinds of statistics, such as population and production figures.

Classification of land areas

This text concentrates on how areas are classified with reference to farm production. The internationally applied categories of agricultural land may deviate from national statistics and, even more, from local terminologies. Differences between authorities' and farmers' ways of defining land may cause problems, for example in terms of taxation and land legislation. The same applies to situations with subsidy systems that are based on land, which, for instance, has long been the case in the European Union's Common Agricultural Policy (CAP).

According to FAOSTAT, the world's total land area can be seen as the sum of three main categories: agricultural land, forest land and other land. The total land

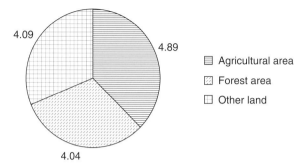

Total land areas in the world (billion hectares)

4.09

4.89

4.04

☰ Agricultural area

▨ Forest area

☐ Other land

Figure 6.1 The world's total land area 2009, categorized as agricultural area, forest area and other land.
Source: FAOSTAT (accessed 2 August 2011).

area excludes major rivers, lakes and water reservoirs. The proportions between agricultural, forest and other land are shown in Figure 6.1, which shows that the world's total land area, about 13 billion hectares, is almost equally divided between the three main categories.

According to Figure 6.1, 4.89 billion hectares are classified as agricultural areas, 4.04 billion hectares as forest and 4.09 billion hectares as other land, which includes urban areas, barren land and all other kinds of land that are neither agricultural nor forest land. The areas are expressed in hectares, with one hectare being 10,000 square metres. We will get back to matters of land areas in Chapter 10.

Before focusing on agricultural areas we will pay some attention to forest areas. In brief the FAOSTAT defines a forest area as a piece of land that fulfils three requirements. First, the area should be more than 0.5 hectares. Second, the area should contain trees that either are or will become higher than 5 metres. Third, the trees' canopy cover should be, or be expected to reach, more than 10 per cent. Areas under reforestation, or land that is expected to regenerate to forest, are included in this generous definition of forest areas. Neither fruit plantations nor agroforestry systems are seen as forest lands, but are instead categorized as permanent crops, which you will read more about further on. As definitions of forests are complicated you will have to go deeper into the details in some other source to get a proper idea of the field. At least parts of the approximately 4.04 billion hectares that are defined as forest land in FAOSTAT may play an important role for some farmers. Market oriented farmers in wooded regions may operate forestry actively and as an integrated part of the farm economy. In subsistence oriented farming access to forest land can offer a valuable source for a variety of necessities such as grazing, firewood, fruits, nuts and berries, hunting and building materials. From the variety of forests we will now move on to a more detailed examination of the world's agricultural areas.

Main kinds of agricultural areas

The global area of agricultural land is categorized as arable land, permanent meadows and pastures, and land with permanent crops. The most extensive category is meadows and pastures, which cover about two and a half times the area of arable land. The dominance of meadows and pastures, in terms of area, does not mean, however, that the category is as economically important as arable land. Figure 6.2 demonstrates the proportions between the three main categories of agricultural areas.

Each of the three main categories of agricultural land is described below, where you can read about alternative ways to use arable land, about permanent crops and about the grazing of meadows and pastures.

Arable land

Arable land covers 1.38 billion hectares, which is about 28 per cent of the world's agricultural area and 11 per cent of the total land area. The arable area includes neither abandoned areas in shifting cultivation systems nor land that potentially may be cultivated. Arable land is the most multifunctional of the categories of agricultural area and can fulfil the functions of the other two, for example its use as grassland. According to the FAOSTAT definition, arable land can be understood as having four subcategories:

○   Arable fields with temporary agricultural crops
○   Horticultural fields and gardens for market or subsistence production
○   Arable fields that are temporarily follow for less than five years
○   Arable fields used for mowing or pasture for periods of less than five years

The first of the subcategories is probably more or less identical to the common understanding of the term arable land. In areas with favourable conditions, some

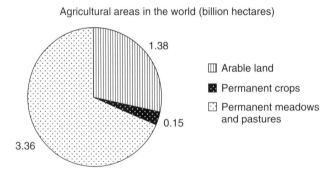

Agricultural areas in the world (billion hectares)

1.38

▦ Arable land
▨ Permanent crops
▨ Permanent meadows and pastures

0.15

3.36

Figure 6.2 Proportions of the three main categories of agricultural areas, 2009: permanent meadows and pastures, arable land and land with permanent crops.

Source: FAOSTAT (accessed 2 August 2011).

crops might even be sown and harvested more than once a year. Typically, arable lands are ploughed or hoed as a part of the yearly rhythm that is characterized by seasonal changes between open land, fresh green sprouts and mature crops (also see Chapter 13). The circumstances differ, however, from seemingly endless plains to small plots surrounded by dense shrubs. This category of arable land produces (1) food for direct human consumption, such as rice and potatoes; (2) animal forage, for example barley; (3) fibres, for instance cotton; (4) other non-foods from arable land, not least bio-energy.

The second subcategory refers to horticulture and includes both areas in large-scale market oriented production and subsistence oriented gardening. The area can alternatively be used for greenhouse cultivation, where glass or plastic covers the land. Although the areas and conditions differ, horticultural arable fields are often comparably small and intensively cultivated.

The third arable subcategory refers to land that is temporarily follow during periods shorter than five years. This kind of arable land is thus temporarily not used for ordinary crop production, although it does not have to be totally abandoned. There are several varying forms of fallow land, as well as a number of reasons for these, which we will get back to in Chapter 14.

The fourth subcategory applies to arable fields that are temporarily used as pasture, with five years as the upper limit. The area is cultivated with grass or herbaceous plants throughout the time period, without being ploughed. The crop is utilized for grazing, or is harvested as hay or silage, a process which can be conducted several times a year. The term temporary pasture land should not be confused with the term permanent meadows and pastures, which, as we have already said, is the largest major category of agricultural area, and which you will read more about further on.

Land used for permanent crops

The category permanent crops makes up the smallest of the three main categories of agricultural area. About 0.15 billion hectares, or 3 per cent of all agricultural land, is used for permanent crops, such as cocoa, tea, coffee, grapes and fruit trees. Permanent crops constitute a specific category because they occupy arable land for many years. The plant growth as such often takes several years, after which the crop is made use of for many years. Apparently permanent crops require long-term planning and investments in comparison with the cultivation of annual crops. The share of the total land area is only about 1 per cent, but permanent crops are more important than that. You find Indonesia, China, India, Brazil, Canada, Malaysia, Spain and Côte d'Ivoire among the countries where the permanent crop area is substantial and of great importance.

Permanent meadows and pastures

As mentioned earlier, permanent meadows and pastures form the main category of the major kinds of agricultural areas. The world's approximately 3.36 billion hectares of permanent meadows and pastures cover nearly 69 per cent of the total agricultural area and 26 per cent of the globe's total land area. The category includes:

- Cultivated permanent meadows and pastures, for periods longer than five years
- Naturally grown permanent meadows and pastures

The distinguishing factor between the two categories is whether the area has been cultivated with grass and herbaceous plants or is naturally grown. In both cases the land is permanently covered with plants that can serve as animal forage, and in both cases the area may be irrigated or fertilized, although this is comparably rare in the latter case. It is the time factor that distinguishes the FAOSTAT category cultivated permanent meadow and pasture from temporary meadow and pasture on arable land. If an arable area is not ploughed up within five years it will be reclassified from arable land to permanent meadow and pasture.

A great deal of the world's permanent meadows and pastures are low-productive land that is not fertilized and which it is not possible to irrigate. The common view of this land category is instead that of vast meagre grazed landscapes that have been used for grazing for decades, centuries or even millennia, and that are highly exposed to drought, winds and other forces of nature. In most cases this kind of land cannot be ploughed up and turned into arable land because the land then soon would be devastated through soil erosion and nutrient leakage. Figure 6.3 illustrates both pasture and arable land through a picture from Central Asia.

Among countries with large areas of permanent meadows and pastures you will find: China, Australia, the US, Brazil, Kazakhstan, Saudi Arabia and Mongolia. As you have now become familiar with the main land categories in general, we will narrow the perspective and consider how the largest, most extensive countries are supplied with varying categories of agricultural land.

Agricultural areas, some country examples

You will find some of the world's largest countries by total land area in Table 6.1, in which, as you can see, all states are well known for their agricultural production. The table presents each country's total land area, and how much of this is used as arable land and permanent meadows and pastures, respectively. Due to the small areas for permanent crops this land category has been included in arable land.

Among other things it is interesting to study the areas of agricultural land in the world's two most populous nations, the Republic of India and the People's Republic of China. As you can see in Table 6.1, the arable area is bigger in India than in China, whereas the pasture areas are enormous in China but comparatively modest in India. It is also interesting to note, that as much as 57 per cent of India's total land area is cultivated, in comparison with 12 per cent of the global area. The Australian figures highlight abundant areas of meadows and pastures but only 6 per cent arable land and permanent crops. In one of the suggested study questions at the end of this chapter you are encouraged to compare the agricultural areas in

Figure 6.3 Permanent pasture land slopes exposed to soil erosion and arable land in the valley. Tibet, 2007.

Photo: Anna Martiin.

Table 6.1 Agricultural areas in some of the world's largest countries by total land area in 2009

Country	Total land area, million hectares	Agricultural area			
		Arable land and permanent crops		Meadows and pastures	
		Million hectares	% of the country's total land area	Million hectares	% of the country's total land area
Russia	1,638	124	8	92	6
China	933	124	13	400	43
US	915	165	18	238	26
Canada	909	52	6	15	2
Brazil	846	69	8	196	23
Australia	768	48	6	362	47
India	297	170	57	10	3
Argentina	274	32	12	109	40
World	13,003	1,533	12	3,356	26

Source: FAOSTAT (accessed 5 August 2011).

Table 6.1 with the populations in the respective countries. This opens up reflections about food security, on the one hand, and export and import of vegetable and animal foods, on the other. In addition it is thought-provoking to consider the available agricultural areas in the light of the forecasted population increases that were discussed in Chapter 5.

Crops for direct human consumption

What is grown in the world's agricultural areas is hardly decided by any master plan for the world food supply, but rather is the result of individual decisions that, with some exceptions, are taken by individual farmers around the world. The agricultural economists Southgate, Graham and Tweeten express this phenomenon as follows:

> no supreme agency exists to strike a desirable balance between food consumption and its availability. At a global level, there is no central bureau that decides on the production of food in various places ... Instead, decision making is highly decentralized.
>
> (Southgate *et al.* 2007: 74)

While the decision making as such is left to Chapter 17, the following pages will focus on the different main categories of crops that may be grown. We will study agricultural and horticultural crops on arable land and areas with permanent crops, but leave meadows and pastures to the later chapters that focus on farm animals. The primary attention is paid to the production of crops that are intended for direct human consumption, although it is sometimes difficult to know whether a crop is consumed directly or finds its way to our tables via animal feed and livestock production.

The number of vegetable species is counted in the many hundreds, in comparison with animal species, which are counted in tens. In Table 6.2 you can see the main categories of crops that are grown by the world's farmers, and the biggest crops by quantity within each category in 2009. Some of the categories include crops that are grown almost only for human consumption, for example rice, tomatoes and bananas. Others, for example maize, can be used either as human food or as animal feed, or as bio-energy or for other non-food purposes.

In some cases the classification can be problematic. Soybeans (soya beans), for example, are both important oilseeds and pulses. Likewise, maize (corn) can be looked at as a cereal, an oilseed, a sugar crop or, when green, as a vegetable. The classification in Table 6.2 coincides with the FAOSTAT one, but you may, as just mentioned, find some of the crops categorized in other ways in other sources or in everyday speech. Many of the crop categories in Table 6.2 are cultivated worldwide, for example potatoes and tomatoes, although the botanic variety may differ. Other crops can only be cultivated in some parts of the world, such as bananas and rice, which are rare in Europe compared with grains such as wheat. In the next section you will find a more detailed account of each of the categories in Table 6.2.

Table 6.2 Main categories of agricultural and horticultural crops, illustrated by some big crops in each category as regards total world production in 2009. The cultivated areas of these crops are also shown

Crop	Production, million tonnes	Harvested area, million hectares
Cereals:		
Maize (corn)	819	159
Wheat	687	225
Rice, paddy	685	159
Oilcrops:		
Soybeans	223	99
Oil palm fruit	218	15
Sugar crops:		
Sugar cane	1,687	24
Pulses:		
Beans, dry	21	25
Roots and tubers:		
Potatoes	332	19
Cassava	235	19
Sweet potatoes	103	8
Vegetables:		
Tomatoes	154	4
Watermelons	99	3
Fruits:		
Bananas	97	5
Apples	71	5
Oranges	68	4
Grapes	69	7
Other:		
Cashew nuts	3	5
Coffee, green	8	10
Cocoa	4	10
Tea	4	3

Source: FAOSTAT (accessed 28 September 2012).

The major crop categories

The following reasoning presents the major crop categories in Table 6.2 one by one. You will read about the most common crops in each category and important producer countries, at the same time as getting a more colourful picture of what is being produced.

Cereals form the leading category of crops; in areas, quantities, values and usage. You find different kinds of cereals in almost every corner of the world. Cereals have a great influence on the agricultural sector at large, and are of great interest for stock markets as well as for world food security. Among the cereals are: maize (corn), wheat, rice, barley, sorghum, millet, oats, rye, triticale and quinoa. The first three of these, maize, wheat and rice, are giants in world agricultural economics and will be further examined later in this chapter. Cereals have the most varying usage, ranging from food and feed to bio-fuels and new technological fields of application. Some cereals are more or less complementary, for example wheat and maize, which among other things means that the price level of wheat has a great influence on the price of maize, and vice versa.

The second category in Table 6.2 is oilcrops, which include a wide range of crops, from groundnuts and rapeseed, which are grown on arable land, to oil palms and other permanent crops. Within the oilseed categories you can, for example, palm fruit find: soybeans, palm fruit, coconuts, rapeseed, cottonseed, groundnuts, sunflower seed and olives. Oilseeds are used in the most varied ways, such as cooking, feed concentrates, industrial fats and bio-fuels. Furthermore, oilseeds are widely traded commodities that, like cereals, have a huge influence on the international economy.

Sugar crops form a third category of crops that, together with cereals and oilseeds, are highly important as farm crops and as players on the international market. Sugar cane dominates widely over sugar beet, both quantitatively and on the global sugar market, where it is involved in food as well as bio-fuel markets. Both crops give high yields per hectare. Moreover, by-products of sugar production are used as animal feed. Large producer countries of sugar cane are Brazil and India; and of sugar beet France, US, Germany and Russia.

Pulses constitute a comparably small category as regards produced quantities, cultivated areas and trade. Among the pulses you find protein rich beans and peas, which are used for direct human consumption or as animal feed. If the botanic classification had been used as the basis for the FAOSTAT categorization to which we are referring, soybeans and groundnuts would be included among pulses, instead of oil crops. Pulses are leguminous plants and are thus able to utilize nitrogen from the air instead of being dependent on nitrogen fertilization. Many pulses are of great importance in subsistence farming and varying species are found in many parts of the world.

Roots and tubers are rich in starch and yield large quantities per hectare. Moreover, roots and tubers can be stored, presuming that the storage facilities are adequate. This is favourable in comparison with many fresh vegetables and fruits, although the storability is not as good as for cereals and beans. Together with cereals and pulses, roots and tubers are major staples in poor smallholder subsistence farming around the world. Among the most important roots and tubers are: potatoes, cassava, sweet potatoes, taro and yams. The production primarily aims at human consumption, although both main products and by-products also can be used as forage. The crops are grown on arable land, not least on small intensively cultivated plots. When traded, roots and tubers are primarily consumed within the region.

Vegetables constitute a diverse category that includes cultivation on big arable fields, small plots in smallholder farming and in greenhouses of various kinds. Many vegetables are intensively traded all over the world, but they are also of great importance in subsistence farming. Producers in leading export countries often specialize in the production of a few vegetables for export, for example tomatoes. Among the many vegetables on the FAOSTAT list are: asparagus, cabbages, carrots, cauliflower, broccoli, cucumbers, eggplants (aubergines), garlic, lettuce, green maize, mushrooms, okra, onions, melons, pumpkins, squash, spinach and tomatoes.

Fruits are generally permanent crops, grown and used for many years, and cover substantial shares of the world's area of permanent crops. Like vegetables, fruits are widely traded, but also of great importance on domestic markets and in subsistence farming. Commercial fruit cultivation is often large-scale and highly specialized, such as oranges, apples and bananas (see Figure 6.4). Among the other important fruits are grapes, mangos, pears, peaches, pineapples, plums, dates, avocados, cherries, kiwis and figs.

Nuts are grown on arable fields, and on bushes and trees. Treenuts form a specific FAOSTAT category, in which you find cashew nuts, walnuts and almonds, which are all widely traded throughout the world, but also important in

Figure 6.4 Bananas, one of the world's most important fruits. India is the biggest producer, followed by the Philippines, China, Ecuador, Brazil, Indonesia, Tanzania, Guatemala and Mexico.

Photo: Anna Martiin.

subsistence farming households. Viet Nam, Nigeria and India are among the most important producers of cashew nuts. The leading producer countries of walnuts are China, US, Turkey and Iran, while the US dominates the production of almonds.

Coffee, cocoa and tea do not belong to any specific statistical category, but are instead registered as specific crops. They are all permanent crops. All three are important internationally traded commodities, and are of great importance for farmers in regions where coffee, cocoa or tea are able to be produced. Among large coffee producing countries are Brazil, Viet Nam, Colombia and Indonesia. Cocoa is largely produced in Côte d'Ivoire, Indonesia, Ghana and Nigeria, and tea in China, India, Kenya and Sri Lanka.

In contrast with the diverse menu above, we will now concentrate on the biggest crops in world agriculture, on the crops that cover the largest areas, provide the largest quantities, generate most value, and that are influential players on agricultural markets and in the world economy at large. At first we will highlight maize, rice and wheat, and thereafter sugar cane, soybeans and palm oil fruit.

A focus on cereals

Without question, the three biggest crops in world agriculture are the cereals maize, wheat and rice. As mentioned earlier, the three crops are widely grown and consumed all over the world, in market as well as in subsistence oriented farming. In terms of produced quantities the production is, however, dominated by a few countries. Table 6.3 highlights this dominance.

As you can see from Table 6.3, the US is the utmost biggest maize producing country, harvesting as much as 41 per cent of the total world production of maize in 2009. During the same year the three leading producers, US, China and Brazil, produced about two-thirds of all maize. As shown earlier, in Table 6.2, the figures

Table 6.3 The world's largest producers of maize, wheat and rice in 2009

Crop	Total world production, million tonnes	Main producing countries	Production, million tonnes	Share of world production, %
Maize	819	US	333	41
		China	164	20
		Brazil	51	6
Wheat	687	China	115	17
		India	81	12
		Russia	62	9
		US	60	9
Rice, paddy	685	China	197	29
		India	134	20
		Indonesia	64	9

Source: FAOSTAT (accessed 28 September 2012).

for total production of wheat and rice were almost equal in 2009, 687 and 685 million tonnes respectively, although the wheat acreage was much larger. According to the FAOSTAT, China was the largest producer of both wheat and rice in 2009 and was in both cases followed by India. In 2009 Russia was the third largest wheat producer, closely followed by the US. As regards rice, China, India and Indonesia accounted for more than half of the global production.

In addition, it is interesting to consider Table 6.3 in terms of exposure and influence. A country that is heavily dependent on a certain farm crop is at the same time greatly exposed to forces of nature, and the risk of low or even failing harvests. Moreover, the national economy is greatly influenced by the market in the dominating agricultural crop. On the other hand, the position as a leading producer means impact and power on the world market. As an example, Indonesia cultivated rice on as much as 55 per cent of the country's arable land in 2009, while the other leading cereal producers in Table 6.3 used between 12 and 28 per cent of their areas for cultivation of maize, wheat or rice, respectively.

Other crops of major importance

Key positions are also held by some other crops, such as sugar cane, soybeans and oil palm fruit, which are of great importance in world agriculture. All three are frequently used in processed foods, and soybeans are also widely used as animal feed. The total world production and the leading producer countries' production of the three crops is presented in Table 6.4.

The most remarkable information in Table 6.4 might be the extremely concentrated production of oil palm fruit in Indonesia and Malaysia, which contributed 81 per cent of global production in 2009. You may remember the biscuit example in Chapter 4, which included fats from the oil palm, in part from Indonesia and in part from Malaysia.

Table 6.4 The largest producers of sugar cane, soybeans and oil palm fruit in 2009. Production (million tonnes) and shares of world production

Crops	Total world production, million tonnes	Main producing countries	Production, million tonnes	Share of world production, %
Sugar cane	1,687	Brazil	692	41
		India	285	17
		China	116	7
Soybeans	223	US	91	41
		Brazil	57	26
		Argentina	31	14
Oil palm fruit	218	Indonesia	90	41
		Malaysia	88	40

Source: FAOSTAT (accessed 28 September 2012).

Global soybean production is also rather concentrated, with 80 per cent produced by three countries: the US, Brazil and Argentina. Sugar cane was slightly less concentrated in 2009, when 65 per cent of the world's sugar cane was produced in Brazil, India and China. As regards cultivated areas, soybeans were grown on about 7 per cent of the world's arable land in 2009, while sugar cane and oil palm fruit covered just a few per cent of the global arable area, which, however, produced high yields per hectare.

Greatly increased global production

In the final part of this chapter we will reflect on the development of cereal production, and combine this with matters of population. The total quantities have increased impressively during the last two centuries, as formulated by the economic historian Giovanni Federico:

> From 1800 to 2000, the world population has risen about six- to sevenfold, from less than one billion to six billion. Yet, world agricultural production has increased substantially faster – at the very least, tenfold in the same period.
>
> (Federico 2005: 1)

Similarly, it is relevant to highlight the high productivity during the last four decades. Table 6.5 demonstrates this through indexed figures, with Index 100 = 1970.

According to Table 6.5 the total production of maize, wheat and rice increased substantially more than the number of mouths to feed. While world population expanded about 84 per cent from 1970 to 2009, the production of maize increased threefold, and the production of wheat and rice more than doubled. What is more, the increases have generally been managed without reductions in other kinds of arable production. On the contrary, the trend has been directed upwards also for other crops and, not least, animal production.

The fact that food supply thus far has managed to exceed the population increase is a wonderful story that few debaters could even imagine in the early 1970s, when, as today, questions about food and population were high on the international agenda. Among the explanations for this success story we can find intensified fertilization and irrigation, and implementation of new breeds. You can read

Table 6.5 Long-term changes in world production of the three main cereal crops, maize, wheat and rice, in comparison with world population increase. Index 100 = 1970

	1970	*1980*	*1990*	*2000*	*2009*
Maize	100	149	182	223	308
Wheat	100	141	191	188	221
Rice, paddy	100	125	164	189	216
World population	100	120	144	166	184

Source: FAOSTAT (accessed 4 October 2012) and *World Population Prospects, the 2010 Revision* (accessed 26 September 2012).

more about these factors in Chapters 12 and 14. In Box 14.2 in Chapter 14 you will find an overview of the so-called Green Revolution, which has contributed to greatly increased yields in many parts of Asia and Latin America but is also widely criticized. There have, however, also been successively increasing yields in, for example, Europe and North America. What is more, attention should be paid to intensive work by farmers, researchers and others people in the agricultural sector, who have all been contributing, albeit not always in the global spotlight.

We may speak about a success story; billions more people are being fed today, although the number of people going hungry is still high. It is, however, hard to believe that yesterday's recipe for success could be used as a blueprint for the future. On the contrary, the future has to economize with resources but still produce more than today.

Summary

About one-third of the total land area is categorized as agricultural area. The total agricultural area is dominated by meadows and pastures, which cover two-thirds, while arable land covers slightly less than one-third. In addition a few per cent of the agricultural area is used for permanent crops. When considering the largest countries, there are interesting differences between the areas available for crops and animal production. This chapter also pays attention to various categories of crops, in terms of cereals, oilseeds, sugar crops, pulses, roots and tubers, vegetables, fruits, etc. Moreover, the most common crops in each category are presented. There is a specific focus on the giants maize, wheat and rice, in terms of total production, major producing countries and their shares of global production. Similar attention is also given to sugar cane, soybeans and palm oil, which are also of greatest interest for world food supply and global agricultural trade. The final part of this chapter connects the total crop production with the ongoing population increase, and discusses the greatly increased crop production of recent decades in terms of current and future challenges.

Next

In Chapter 7, we will continue the quantitative survey of world agriculture and turn to animal production. You will study the stocks of farm animals on a global scale, their geographical distribution and the production of meats, milk and other animal products.

To discuss

○ Study statistics on arable and pasture areas in some countries of special interest. What are the proportions between arable and pasture land?

○ Compare the areas of arable and pasture lands in Table 6.1 and the population size in the respective countries. How much land is available per person in the highlighted countries, today and tomorrow?

○ Chose some crops that you are interested in and find out which are the large producers of these in terms of quantities and areas.

○ Look for some particularly multifunctional crops, for example maize, and describe their different fields of application.

○ Study and analyse the last decade's history of soybean, palm oil, cassava and kiwi production as regards produced quantities and big producer countries. What are your reflections?

○ Study how the production of maize, wheat and rice have changed from 1970 to today in some countries that you are especially interested in. Compare these changes with the changes in population, as has been done at global scale in Table 6.5.

7   World animal production

World animal farming is a rapidly expanding and changing part of agricultural economics. The total output of meat, milk and eggs has boosted in recent years, and at the same time technologies and market structures have contributed to increased scale, altered methods of production and changes in the geographical location of animal production.

This chapter highlights livestock production on global and continental levels, while you can read about more practical aspects of animal husbandry in Chapters 15 and 16. In the following you will study land use for animal production and a variety of products and other benefits from animal farming are highlighted. We will also consider the global stocks of the different kinds of farm animal species and how these are distributed over the world. Moreover, attention is paid to the global production of meat, milk and eggs, in terms of quantities and leading producer countries, and, as in Chapter 6, to a great extent this is based on information from FAOSTAT. By the end of the chapter we will discuss livestock production in terms of environmental impact, negative but also positive, and consider current trends in the production and consumption of animal products.

After this chapter you are expected to:

○   Be able to discuss animal farming in terms of land use aspects
○   Be familiar with the variety of benefits from animal farming around the world
○   Have a fair idea of the numbers of different kinds of farm animal species, and the proportions between the main categories of livestock
○   Have a fair idea of how the global stock of farm animals is distributed between the continents
○   Be familiar with the proportions of various kinds of meat and milk that are produced over the world
○   Have a fair idea of the leading producer countries in meat, milk and eggs

○   Be aware of the main arguments about various negative and positive impacts of animal production
○   Be familiar with recent quantitative changes in world animal production
○   Be familiar with the largest producer countries for milk, eggs and various kinds of meat
○   Have a fair idea of the major environmental problems linked to livestock production

Key words

Land use, pasture land, arable land, cattle, buffaloes, sheep, goats, pigs, camels, camelids, horses, asses, mules, chickens, poultry, global distribution, meats, milk, eggs, negative and positive side-effects, production, consumption, trends.

Livestock and land use

Studies of farm animals around the world take us to the most varied types of landscapes and places, such as windblown moorlands, muddy backyards and enormous pig or chicken plants. Some kinds of animal farming are based on vast land areas, such as nomadism and large-scale rearing of sheep or cattle on low-yielding pastures. In contrast, we find increasing numbers of plants with tens of thousands of hogs or chickens, to which the feed is transported from far away.

As you will remember from Chapter 6, about 26 per cent of the global land area, or 69 per cent of the world's agricultural area, is categorized as pasture land. Parts of these areas are less frequently grazed than others, but it is fascinating to consider the global land use in this perspective. The extensive use of pasture land for animal production does not mean that grazing animals are occupying enormous areas that otherwise would be available for production of crops for direct human consumption. On the contrary, major parts of these areas are situated in sparsely populated regions, such as parts of Central Asia and Australia, for which it is difficult to find alternative relevant use.

Too intensive grazing may cause soil erosion and other damage that threatens the future use of the area. We have numerous current and historical examples of these kinds of problems, for example from the so-called Fertile Crescent area by the Tigris and Euphrates rivers. The area is called 'the cradle of agriculture', due to the early domestication of several crops and farm animals in the area, which, however, came to suffer from too intensive grazing, which has reduced the fertility severely. Sheep and goats are able to graze intensively, sometimes aggressively, which calls for thorough watching of these otherwise quite useful animals that were domesticated at least 9,500 years ago:

Both species are relatively placid and slow-moving foragers. Neither species is territorial, and both sheep and goats form highly social groups having a single dominant leader. In addition, such small groups maintain small home ranges, and thus are predisposed to human constraint.

(Smith 1995: 27)

In addition to permanent pastures substantial areas of arable land are used for the production of animal feed such as maize, barley, wheat and soybeans. According to Steinfeld *et al.* (2006b: 271), about 33 per cent of the total arable area is used for the production of animal feed. Some arable land is also grown with grass, clover and other herbaceous plants in order to be grazed, or harvested as hay or silage. Silage bales are shown in Figure 7.1.

If animals are fed on arable land, the area can alternatively be seen as a potential resource for production of food for direct human consumption. A common example in debates about these matters refers to the feeding of soybeans to beef cattle instead of cooking the beans for direct human consumption. We will get back to this aspect in Chapter 15. It should also be said that many of the world's smallholders have limited or no possibility of feeding the animals on pastures or arable land, but make the best out of more or less marginal land areas and resources, such as roadside grazing, waste and a variety of collected feed stuffs.

Figure 7.1 Silage bales, 2011. Technology for anaerobic fermentation and storing of high-moisture forage crops through tight wrapping in plastic by a specific bale wrapper.
Photo: Carin Martiin.

Accordingly, and as you will read more about in Chapter 15, animal farming can, on the one hand, be seen as a way to make good use of otherwise unutilized areas and other resources, but can, on the other hand, compete for resources that alternatively may be more efficiently used for the production of food for direct human needs. In brief, we can distinguish three main forms of benefits from animal farming: food; large-scale economic and societal impact; and benefits at farm level.

Animal farming for food supply

First and foremost, animal farming is carried out in order to produce nutritious food for human consumption. Food of animal origin is more concentrated and has a more complete content of proteins and some minerals and vitamins, compared with vegetable foods. At the same time as increased portions of animal food can be valuable to improve meagre and insufficient diets, wealthy and even obese individuals might benefit from reduced consumption of animal foods. According to FAOSTAT, the global average per capita consumption of animal protein was close to 30 grams per day in 2007, or 39 per cent of the total average protein consumption of 77 grams per capita per day, obtained from both vegetable and animal foods. The dissimilarities between the different parts of the world were striking, however, with many times higher protein consumption in the US compared with many African countries.

If livestock farming is based on arable land the production generally requires more resources than production of similar nutrients via crop farming, especially production of meat. In addition, water use can be substantially higher, compared with non-irrigated arable farming.

Large-scale impact of animal farming

Second, animal products contribute substantially to domestic and international economies, for example the meat exports from many Latin American countries, and Australia and New Zealand. Furthermore, animal production can contribute to commercial sub-sectors, for sale of feed and other commodities, as well as services. This production is also creating several activities further along the food chain, activities that increase the value of the products and that create a number of jobs.

What is more, animal farming is currently given increased attention as a key to improved livelihoods in smallholder farming. Production of even small quantities of meat, milk and eggs for regular sale is often highlighted as a path out of poverty, a way to support women in farming and to encourage rural development in general (see Figure 7.2). The 'overwhelming social importance' of animal farming for the world's many smallholder farmers is, among others, highlighted by Steinfeld *et al.* (2006b: 281) in their well-read publication *Livestock's Long Shadow*, which is otherwise most known for highlighting environmental problems due to the currently expanding livestock sector. We will get back to the report and other aspects of livestock and environment by the end of this chapter.

Figure 7.2 Small-scale animal farming is of decisive importance for many smallholders
around the world. Cambodia, 2010.

Photo: Anna Martiin.

Benefits at farm level

Third, animal farming fulfils a number of functions for farmers. The character
and outcome of the production differ greatly, depending on degree of market
orientation, methods of production, herd size and animal species, and are also
influenced by factors such as geography, economic and social structures, politics
and culture. A large-scale beef breeding plant in the US is a world away from
nomadic livestock farming in Eastern Africa, even though both are producing
meat. The various kinds of benefits from animal farming are summarized below
and then briefly commented on:

- Meat, milk, eggs
- Cash income
- Savings, capital, serving as social and economic safety nets
- Offspring
- Fibres, hides, feathers, offal and similar by-products
- Animal manure
- Animal draught power
- Possibility of making use of labour and marginal lands

    ○   Spread of economic risk, compared with crop farming only

    ○   Distribution of work over the year, compared with crop farming only

Leaving meat, milk and eggs to separate discussions, it should be said that livestock farming is not only an important source of income in highly market oriented farming but also a common way for subsistence oriented farmers to earn some cash money. The animals as such serve as capital and economic and social safety nets for many smallholders around the world. These functions have deep historical and cultural roots, which are mirrored in the fact that the words for capital derive from the words for cattle in, for example, English and Russian.

    Moreover, production of offspring is important, either for sale or further breeding at the farm. Animal fibres, hides and by-products from slaughter can be part of market oriented livestock production, but may be more appreciated in subsistence oriented agriculture. The production of animal manure is beneficial for both market and subsistence oriented farming, and is a subject that we will get back to in Chapter 12. Animal traction should also be mentioned as an important function for cultivation and transportation, even though ownership of draught animals is out of reach for large sections of the world's poor smallholders.

    Moreover, animals can be a good way to utilize labour, marginal lands and other resources. The last two points on the list remind us of the benefits of combining animal and crop farming, in part as a strategy to spread economic risk, in part as a way to distribute the workload over the year instead of being solely dependent on seasonal peaks in either arable or animal farming.

Farm animals around the world

Varieties of the major farm animal species are found almost all around the world. Cattle, for example, are represented by Holstein breeds in Northern America, Europe and Oceania, and by Zebu varieties in India, Brazil and Africa. And some kinds of pigs are found in factory-like production anywhere in the world, while others are specifically adapted to backyard farming.

    In brief, we have four main categories of food producing farm animals: cattle and buffaloes; sheep and goats; pigs; and poultry. All are large in numbers, widely located around the globe, and main suppliers of animal products. Figure 7.3 illustrates the proportions between cattle and buffaloes; sheep and goats; and pigs, omitting the stock of chickens and other poultry, which is about twenty times larger.

    As you can see from Figure 7.3, the sum of cattle and buffaloes is exceeded by the sum of sheep and goats. If the larger body size of cattle and buffaloes is taken into account, however, there is no doubt that cattle and buffaloes form the largest group. A more comprehensive list of farm animals is shown in Table 7.1, where you can see the total number of farm animals worldwide in 2009.

    In addition to the figures in Table 7.1 you will find the animals described in Boxes 7.1–7.6, which, among other things, show in which countries large numbers of each kind of animal are found, globally and within the continents.

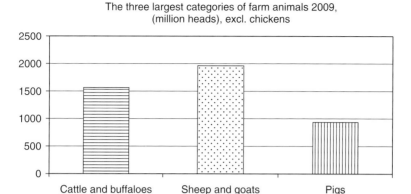

Figure 7.3 The three largest farm animal categories, omitting chicken, at approximately 19,000 million heads.

Source: FAOSTAT (accessed 29 September 2012).

The global distribution of livestock

The large numbers of farm animals in some countries, as shown in Boxes 7.1–7.6, can in part be explained by the simple fact that the countries are big, in size and population. There are also additional reasons, such as export opportunities, access to grasslands, climate, farming structures, culture, social structures in the country-side, and in some cases also specific factors such as the tsetse fly, which hampers cattle farming in many Sub-Saharan countries. In order to get an overview that is

Table 7.1 Numbers of farm animals in 2009

Animal species	*Number of animals*
	Million heads
Cattle	1,419
Buffaloes	190
Camels	24
Other camelids	8
Sheep	1,080
Goats	898
Pigs	955
Horses	60
Asses and mules	53
	1,000 million heads
Chickens	19
Other poultry	2

Source: FAOSTAT 2009 (accessed 29 September 2012).

Box 7.1 Cattle and buffaloes

Cattle are spread almost all over the world and form the largest single category of farm animals. As cattle and buffaloes are ruminants they are able to digest grass and roughage and can thus be fed on roughage and pasture lands. Many cattle are, however, also, to greater or lesser extent, fed on grains, maize, soybeans and other crops, especially in high yielding dairy production and intensive beef cattle production. Among the world's more than 1.6 billion cattle and buffaloes you can find specialized dairy breeds and beef cattle as well as multifunctional cattle and buffaloes, which yield less milk, meat and manure but fulfil many of the previously discussed beneficial functions of animal farming.

According to FAOSTAT, which does not distinguish between dairy and beef cattle, the largest number of cattle is found in India, with about 206 million in 2009. Brazil is also at the top of the global ranking list, with over 205 million cattle. This means that India and Brazil had almost 15 per cent each of the global stock of 1.4 billion cattle. Large numbers of cattle were also found in the US and China, but also in Argentina, Ethiopia and Sudan. Among the African countries, Ethiopia and Sudan were followed by Tanzania, Kenya, Nigeria and South Africa. In Asia, Pakistan, Bangladesh, Burma and Indonesia should be mentioned. The US and Canada are known for large herds of specialized dairy and beef cattle, and down south substantial numbers of cattle are found in Mexico. In South America the world-leading Brazil is accompanied by Argentina, Colombia, Venezuela, Uruguay and Paraguay. Europe was the leading milk producing continent in 2009, and cattle for intensive milk and meat production are important in many countries. Russia had the largest numbers of cattle, followed by France, Germany and the UK. Even more important, on a country level, is the large-scale milk and meat production in Australia and New Zealand.

Of the world's buffalo stock of 190 million heads in 2009, 97 per cent were found in Asia. Undoubtedly the largest national herd of buffaloes is found in India. Buffaloes are also important in, for example, China, Pakistan, Egypt, Brazil and in Italy, where buffaloes are kept for mozzarella cheese.

Box 7.2 Sheep and goats

Sheep and, even more so, goats are able to survive on meagre meadows and pastures, and hardy varieties can additionally withstand harsh climates and high as well as low temperatures. Goats in particular may, however, graze too intensively, which can damage bushes and trees and increase the risk of soil erosion. Sheep and goats are found in the most different contexts, such as densely populated Sub-Saharan villages, vast Australian grasslands and remote islands in distant corners of the world. Both species are used in market oriented farming, but it is fair to say that goats in particular are chiefly found in poor smallholder farming.

Many of world's 1,080 million sheep (in 2009) are found in China, India, Australia, Iran and Sudan. In Africa the largest numbers of sheep were reported in Sudan, Nigeria, Ethiopia, South Africa and Algeria. Continuing to Asia, we find the largest numbers of sheep in China, India, Iran, Pakistan, Turkey and also in Mongolia. The numbers of sheep in the US and Canada are strikingly low. Among the countries in South America, Brazil, Argentina and Peru in particular have large stocks of sheep, and in Europe most sheep are found in the UK, Spain and Russia, followed by Greece, Romania and Italy. Australia and New Zealand have long been known for the large-scale export of wool and mutton, and in 2009 about 10 per cent of the global stock of sheep was found in these countries.

Of the world's almost 900 million goats in 2009 about 60 per cent were found in Asia and about 34 per cent in Africa, where goats and sheep supply milk and meat and fulfil many other functions. As regards stocks, China and India were the world's leading countries in Asia, followed by Pakistan, Bangladesh, Iran, Mongolia and Indonesia. Among the African countries, large numbers of goats were found in Nigeria, former Sudan, Ethiopia, Mali, Kenya, Niger, Somalia, Tanzania and Burkina Faso. Haiti and Cuba hold relatively large herds of goats, but stocks are larger in Brazil, Mexico, Argentina, Bolivia and Peru. European goat farming is primarily found in Greece, Spain and Russia, followed by France, and among the countries in Oceania Australia has a relatively large stock of goats that produce meat, milk, and mohair and cashmere fibres.

According to FAOSTAT the global number of goats increased by as much as 33 per cent from 1995 to 2009, which is the second largest percentage increase of livestock, after chickens, which rose 44 per cent. As a comparison, the number of cattle and pigs rose about 7 and 6 per cent respectively during the same period. The increase in the number of goats occurred chiefly in Asia and Africa, and Western Africa has experienced an enormous increase, as much as 83 per cent within the period 1995–2009. The larger African and Asian stocks of goats can be viewed in the light of the so-called livestock revolution, which is discussed later in this chapter.

Box 7.3 Pigs

Similarly, pigs are found almost all over the world and in the most contrasting environments, from high-tech factory-like plants to backyards. As pigs are non-ruminants, they are not able to survive on roughage and are in principle competing with human beings, for example in cereals. Pigs can, however, also make use of waste, which gives pigs valuable functions in terms of economizing with resources. This kind of recirculation may take place in large-scale pig breeding, but can be seen as most important in subsistence oriented smallholdings. Irrespective of scale, feeding with waste includes risks for the spread of contagious diseases which is mentioned several times in this book. Especially leftovers of animal origin are risky and can, for example, cause large-scale spread of foot and mouth disease. Therefore feeding with waste of animal origin is illegal in many countries, and, even if it is not illegal, it is necessary to boil the material before it is fed to the animals. You will read more about these matters in Chapter 21, which deals specifically with food safety.

The world's largest stocks of pigs are found in China, US, Brazil, Viet Nam, Germany and Spain, followed by Russia, Mexico, France, Poland, the Philippines, Denmark, Canada and the Netherlands. Among Sub-Saharan countries Nigeria stands out, but also Uganda, Burkina Faso, Malawi, South Africa, Madagascar and Mozambique have large numbers of pigs. Among the Caribbean countries Cuba, Haiti and the Dominican Republic could be mentioned. Brazil and Mexico stand out as pig producers among the South American countries. A great deal of the world's pig meat exporters are however, found in Europe, where the largest numbers of pigs are found in Germany, Spain, Russia, France, Poland, Denmark and the Netherlands.

Box 7.4 Poultry

Like pigs, we find poultry in crowded large-scale industrial plants, as well as strolling around in backyards. Chickens are the largest category, but a number of other birds are also found in world farming, such as ducks, turkeys, geese and guinea fowl. Ostriches should also be mentioned. Chicken meat production is a hugely expanding sector in world animal production. This growth is more visible in national and international trade, and in urban eating habits around the world, than the ongoing expansion of goat farming, which to a great extent occurs in subsistence oriented farming.

The largest stocks of chickens in 2009 were found in China, the US, Indonesia and Brazil. Other Asian countries with large numbers of chickens are India and Iran, followed by Pakistan, Japan, Turkey, Thailand and Bangladesh. Chickens and other kinds of poultry are common in almost all African countries, with the largest numbers in Nigeria, Morocco, South Africa and Algeria. Across the Atlantic Ocean the world-leading US and Brazil stand out, but Mexico should be mentioned too. About one-tenth of the global stock of chickens are found in Europe, especially in Russia, the UK, Ukraine, Spain, Poland, France, Italy and Germany.

Box 7.5 Camels and other camelids

The global stock of camels, dromedaries and two-humped camels was in 2009 primarily found in African faming, especially in Somalia, Sudan, Niger, Chad, Mauritania and Mali, but also in some Asian countries, primarily in Pakistan, India, Mongolia and China. The camelids, llamas and alpacas are chiefly found in Bolivia and Peru, where llamas are used for transport and fibre production, while the alpaca primarily known for its valuable fibres for high quality fabrics.

Box 7.6 Horses, asses and mules

In farming, horses, asses and mules are used for the transportation of commodities and people, for cultivation and, depending on culture, for meat and in some cases for milk. Draught and riding animals can be functional solutions in large-scale cattle husbandry in South America, or in the absence of roads in mountainous areas. In smallholder farming asses and mules may be functional, even though the slower moving cattle and buffaloes may serve more multifunctional purposes. The largest number of horses is found in the US, followed by China, Mexico, Brazil, Argentina, Colombia, Mongolia, Ethiopia, Kazakhstan and Russia; all with vast landscapes and horses as traditional means for transporting people and goods. As regards asses, FAOSTAT reports the largest numbers in China, Ethiopia, Pakistan, Egypt, Mexico, Iran, Niger, Afghanistan and Nigeria, while the largest numbers of mules, crossbreeds between horses and asses, are found in Mexico, China and Brazil.

Table 7.2 The distribution of farm animals between the continents in 2009

	Cattle, %	Sheep, %	Goats, %	Pigs, %	Chickens, %
Africa	19	27	33	3	8
Asia	33	42	59	60	53
Europe	9	12	2	20	10
North America	8	1	1	8	12
Latin America and Caribbean	28	8	4	8	16
Oceania	3	10	1	1	1
World	100	100	100	100	100

Source: FAOSTAT 2009 (accessed 30 September 2012).

more detailed than the global scale, but still possible to handle, Table 7.2 shows how the global stock of various farm animals is distributed between the continents. For further details on the country level, or even more specific details, you are encouraged to search FAOSTAT yourself, in line with one of the 'To discuss' questions at the end of this chapter.

As you can see from Table 7.2, Africa has a relatively big share of the global stock of cattle, sheep and goats, but comparatively few pigs and poultry, which, however, may be distributed throughout a large number of smallholdings. Asia, with its large human population and extensive land areas, has the largest share of all the farm animal categories in the table, but the high shares of pigs and chickens are noteworthy. When it comes to Europe, with its relatively small human population and agricultural area, the many pigs should be noted. In North America the global shares of chickens, pigs and cattle are high, while sheep and goat numbers are few, indicating that the wide grasslands in North America are primarily used for beef production. Furthermore, the table highlights the importance of cattle in Latin America and the Caribbean, and of cattle and sheep in Oceania, primarily in Australia and New Zealand.

Table 7.2 can also be seen in the light of the many different functions that are obtained from the many various forms of animal farming conducted around the globe. Each cell in the table can be seen as representing the production of meat, milk and eggs and many other kinds of benefits that are achieved on each continent, such as the many different utilities that are obtained from sheep farming in Africa, and the functions of chickens in Latin America and the Caribbean. In the following we will concentrate on the production of meat, milk and eggs, while leaving the other functions that were touched on earlier in this chapter, such as the value of livestock as capital assets and the production of by-products from the animals.

Global production of meat

The major quantities of meat originate from pigs, followed by chicken and cattle meat, while sheep, goat and other kinds of meat provide a minor share. The different sizes of various animal species certainly are important for the quantities of meat, but the low shares from sheep and goats also reflect the fact that many sheep and goats are found in poor smallholder farming, where they are sparsely fed and kept for multifunctional purposes rather than specialized meat production. The main categories of meat produced in the world in 2009 are demonstrated in Figure 7.4.

As mentioned, pigs provided for the largest share, 37 per cent, of world meat production in 2009, which is clearly visible in Figure 7.4. China dominated production, followed some way behind by the US. Large quantities were also produced in Germany, Spain, Brazil, Viet Nam, France, Russia, Canada and Poland. The second largest kind of meat produced was chicken, with 28 per cent of total world production in 2009. Global chicken meat production was led by the US, after which China and Brazil produced almost equal quantities. Substantial volumes also came from Mexico, Russia, Iran, Argentina, Indonesia, Japan, South Africa, Turkey, the UK, Spain, Thailand, France, Poland, Canada, Colombia and Malaysia.

Although cattle are the most common animal around the world, and in spite of their body size, meat from cattle was only the third largest category in 2009, when 22 per cent of global meat production originated from cattle. Among the main cattle meat producers are the US, followed by Brazil and China, after which Argentina, Australia, Russia, Mexico, France and Canada should be mentioned.

There is a big difference between numbers of sheep and their contribution to the global meat supply, which only was about 3 per cent in 2009, in spite of their dominance in Figure 7.2. The largest quantities of meat from sheep were produced in China, followed by Australia, New Zealand, Iran, former Sudan, the UK, Turkey, India, Syrian Arab Republic, Algeria, Russia, Pakistan, Nigeria and South Africa. Many of these countries have extensive pasture areas, such as China and Australia, in which, according to Table 6.1 in Chapter 6, more than 40 per cent of the agricultural area is categorized as meadows and pastures. Close connections between mutton and pastures are in part also the case in

Global production of various kinds of meat in 2009

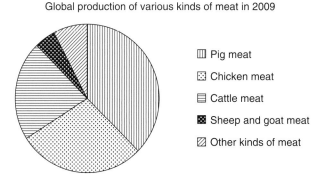

Figure 7.4 Global production of various kinds of meat in 2009.
Source: FAOSTAT (accessed 29 September 2012).

the production of goat meat, which, according to FAOSTAT, provided about 2 per cent of total meat production in 2009. As many of the world's goats are managed by smallholder farmers with limited access to land for grazing, we can, however, assume that the connection between goats and pasture areas is weaker than in the case of sheep.

According to FAOSTAT, China was the largest producer of goat meat in 2009, long after followed by India, Nigeria, Pakistan, Australia, Bangladesh, former Sudan and Iran. The remaining 8 per cent of the pie chart in Figure 7.4 consists of meats of diverse origin, primarily turkey, duck and buffalo, and, more limited, of meat from camels, horses and a variety of birds, rabbits, etc.

You may have noticed some discrepancies between countries with large numbers of animals and the leading producer countries of meat. The differences can generally be explained by the fact that numerous stocks do not automatically mean high production of meat. Neither do leading export countries by necessity have the largest numbers of animals or produce the largest total quantities. Denmark is, for example, a leading exporter of pig meat, but is found neither among the countries with the largest number of pigs nor among those with the largest quantities of product. Another additional aspect of the output of meat is that occasional increases in supply may wrongly be seen as increased production, when the true reason actually is that unusual numbers of animals have had to be slaughtered because of a crisis, such as lack of feed and water, or due to armed conflicts. We can see this back in history, for example in Europe during the twentieth century's two world wars, and quite recently in the Horn of Africa.

World milk production

Global milk production is dominated by milk from dairy cows. Substantial volumes are also achieved from buffaloes, goats, sheep and camels; quantities that can be of decisive importance regionally, locally and in individual households, although this is not mirrored in global ranking lists. Figure 7.5 illustrates the proportions of the various kinds of milk that were produced globally in 2009.

According to Figure 7.5, the 84 per cent of global milk production in 2009 was made up of cow's milk. The same year the US was the largest cow's milk producer, followed by India, China, Russia, Brazil, Germany, France, New Zealand, the UK, Poland, Pakistan, Turkey, the Netherlands, Ukraine, Italy, Mexico, Argentina, Australia, Canada and Japan. As you can see from the long list, large quantities of cow's milk are being produced in countries that are spread almost all over the world, with the exception of Africa.

In contrast, and as a logical consequence of the global distribution of buffaloes shown earlier in the chapter, buffalo milk is chiefly being produced in India and Pakistan. If all milk from cattle and buffaloes is summarized, India was the world's largest milk producer in 2009, followed by the US. More than half of total Indian milk production came from the many buffaloes on the Indian subcontinent, compared with the global average of 13 per cent.

World production of different kinds of milk in 2009

☐ Cow's milk

☐ Buffalo's milk

☒ Sheep's milk

☒ Goat's milk

☒ Camel's milk

Figure 7.5 Proportions of milk of varying origin. Total world production in 2009.
Source: FAOSTAT (accessed 29 September 2012).

According to FAOSTAT only about 1 per cent of all milk comes from sheep, primarily from China, Greece, Turkey, Syrian Arab Republic, Romania, Iran, former Sudan, Spain, Somalia and Italy. The volumes of goat's milk are slightly higher, about 2 per cent of the global milk yield. The main goat's milk producing countries are India, Bangladesh, former Sudan, Pakistan and France. In addition, the figures for 2009 report that 0.3 per cent of world milk production originated from camels, with Somalia, Mali and Ethiopia as the largest producers.

Main egg producing countries

Egg production is important globally, occurs all over the world and is increasing. About 92 per cent of all eggs come from hens, and 8 per cent from other birds. China was the largest producer of hens' eggs in 2009, followed by the US, India, Japan, Mexico, Russia, Brazil, Indonesia, France, Ukraine, Turkey, Spain, Italy, Iran, Germany, the Netherlands, Nigeria, Poland, the UK and Colombia. China is also leading in eggs from other birds, followed by Thailand and Indonesia.

So far our attention has chiefly been given to foods and other benefits of animal farming, although some negative environmental aspects were mentioned earlier in this chapter. We focus on these in the following section, although it concludes with some positive side-effects.

Livestock production and the environment

The report mentioned earlier, *Livestock's Long Shadow*, argues strongly against the combination of expanded beef production and exploitation of natural habitats that has taken place, for instance, in the Amazon rainforest. The report is in part written by the same authors who coined the expression 'the livestock revolution' in 1999, for the predicted dramatic increase in global demand for animal foods.

The livestock revolution has both positive and negative connotations. On the one hand, small-scale animal production is looked at as a path for the development of smallholder farming and rural economies. Small-scale sale of milk and eggs, for instance, may serve as a first step towards market orientation and a regular cash income. On the other hand, large-scale animal production in particular generally requires much more resources and is also criticized as a source of greenhouse gas emissions, such as methane from ruminants. The importance of a balanced view to manage the environmental problems was clearly expressed in a third publication, *The State of Food and Agriculture 2009: Livestock in the balance*, that was published in 2009, in part by the same authors, who modified the earlier criticism by saying that

> The livestock sector, like much of agriculture, plays a complex economic, social and environmental role. Society expects the sector to continue to meet rising world demand for animal products cheaply, quickly and safely. It must do so in an environmentally sustainable way, while managing the incidence and consequences of animal diseases and providing opportunities for rural development, poverty reduction and food security.
>
> (FAO 2009a: 6)

One of the environmental problems with ruminating animals is that the process of ruminating generates greenhouse gases. These processes have been going on for thousands of years but are now seen in another light because of the current combination of increased numbers of ruminants and enlarged emissions from other sources, for instance from fossil fuel. Parts of the emissions from ruminants may be compensated for if the production is based on extensive grazing on meadows and pastures, which, as well as other green vegetation, are able to capture carbon via the photosynthesis process (see Chapter 13, Box 13.5). You will find this and other environmental problems that are associated with livestock production listed in Box 7.7.

The extent to which farming is responsible for the many environmental problems that are listed in Box 7.7 can be debated. In some cases individuals are clearly responsible, for example companies that exploit rainforests for breeding beef cattle, or for cultivation of soybeans intended for feeding purposes. But poor smallholders with a few cattle that are fed on roadside grazing can hardly be blamed. In between we may find farmers who are personally concerned about the problems, but also the opposite.

At the same time as farming contributes to environmental problems, farmers and animals may be victims of these processes. In many cases it is the people who live close to nature who suffer most from environmental changes, and they may also be the first to observe what is going on. If monsoon rains are delayed, or are longer than usual, it is the farmers, first and foremost, who have to deal with this.

Box 7.7 Environmental problems with various kinds of livestock production

Directly connected with the animals

- Emissions of greenhouse gases, such as carbon dioxide and methane from ruminants
- Emissions of nitrous oxide from animal manure
- Overgrazing, causing soil erosion and reduced biodiversity
- Leakage of nutrients from animal manure into watercourses
- High consumption of water, especially by high-producing dairy cattle

Connected with feed production

- Emissions of greenhouse gases due to methods of cultivation
- Land degradation due to eventual exploitation of forests and permanent pastures
- Problems due to use, or overuse, of fertilizer and pesticides
- Water problems due to irrigation of feed crops

Connected with other parts of the food chain

- Emissions from transportation, cooling, processing and packaging along the animal food chain

---

And if the water in the well is contaminated, this troubles, first and foremost, the farm household, farm animals and neighbours in the surrounding area. Similarly, reduced biodiversity in a rural landscape is experienced, first and foremost, by people working and living there.

A number of positive side-effects, apart from the previously highlighted primary aims, also accompany animal farming. The function of grazing areas as carbon sinks has already been mentioned. As a second advantage modest grazing and use of manure can improve ecosystems and biodiversity, in the form of herbs, trees, wildlife and beneficial insects. Third, grazed landscapes are often appreciated for their beauty by people who live and work in the landscape, as well as by visitors from near and far.

Current trends in global livestock production

As previously discussed, the world has experienced large-scale increases in demand for food of animal origin. This trend was shown in Chapter 5, where

Table 7.3 Total global production of meat, milk and eggs in 2000 and 2009

Production, million tonnes	2000	2009
Meats, all kinds, incl. chicken	234	288
Milk, all kinds	579	708
Eggs, all kinds	55	68

Source: FAOSTAT 2009 (accessed 29 September 2012).

Table 5.5, among other things, highlighted the increasingly marketed quantities of poultry meat. In Table 7.3 you can study the increased global production of meats, milk and eggs in the years 2000 and 2009.

Table 7.3 shows all kinds of meat as one figure, which conceals the fact that the production of chicken meat was about 40 per cent higher in 2009 than in the year 2000, while the corresponding figure for pig meat was 19 per cent, cattle meat 14 per cent, sheep meat 10 per cent and goat meat 36 per cent.

According to the report *Livestock in the balance* (FAO 2009a: Table A1), the annual rise in world meat production was on average 2.7 per cent between 1995 and 2007. In more detail, East and South-East Asia experienced as much as a 5.1 per cent annual increase in production of meat, while production rose 3.2 per cent in Latin America and the Caribbean as well as in the Near East and Northern Africa too. The increase was lower in Sub-Saharan Africa, where the annual increase was 2.2 per cent. At the same time many European countries experienced reduced production, which indicates a trend of geographic shift in production. In the same way the global production of milk has risen, albeit less strongly than the production of meat and eggs. From 1995 to 2007 the average annual global increase in milk production was 1.8 per cent, but as much as 12.6 per cent in Viet Nam and 12.3 per cent in China. In contrast many European countries saw low increases or even a negative trend in milk production. Among traditional export-ers of dairy products New Zealand stands out, with 4.6 per cent annual increase in milk production between 1995 and 2007. The strongest global increase between 1995 and 2007 was, however, seen in the production of eggs (3.1 per cent per year), which generally has been paid less attention than the expansion of meat and milk. Increased egg production was relatively equally distributed between the continents, but higher in South, East and South-East Asia.

Increases in production of animal products also went on before 1995, as demonstrated in Table 7.4, which presents relative increases in the production of meat, milk and eggs from 1970 to 2009, and relates these to the parallel increase in world population. According to Table 7.4 the relative changes in production of milk were of the same magnitude as world population growth from 1970 to 2009, whereas the relative increases in the production of meat and eggs were notably higher. The driving force behind the expanding world animal

Table 7.4 Relative changes in production of meat, milk and eggs from 1970 to 2009, and in world population during the same time period. Index 100 = 1970

Category	1970	1980	1990	2000	2009
Meats, all kinds, incl. chicken	100	136	179	232	282
Milk, all kinds	100	119	138	148	179
Eggs, all kinds	100	134	184	270	333
World population, index	100	121	144	166	185

Source: FAOSTAT (accessed 29 September 2012) and *World Population Prospects, the 2010 Revision* (accessed 26 September 2012).

production is often considered in terms of the aforementioned so-called livestock revolution:

> Put simply, the Livestock Revolution is a fundamental change in the way people eat. As their incomes rise, people diversify their diets, giving up traditional staple cereals in favour of more milk, meat, fish and eggs. The change is accentuated in cities, where incomes are higher [...]
>
> (ILRI 2000: 3)

In addition to the emphasis on higher income and urbanization in the quotation, we have to add effects of increased world population. More, but not all, people eat more meat, dairy products and eggs. We can see that animal products have become more easily available, due to relative reductions in price and the expansion of supermarkets on all continents. In conclusion, several trends can be distinguished, of which some amplify each other:

- Increased world population
- Increased per capita consumption of animal foods
- Increased livestock production, partly on the basis of highly resource intensive methods of production
- Increased attention to the livestock sector's negative impact on climate change
- Increased attention to the livestock sector's negative impact on other environmental problems
- Increased attention to the value of animal production for reducing poverty and generating cash income and developing smallholder farming

If we consider Chapters 5, 6 and 7 together, there is a clear trend of increased pressure on natural resources and agriculture at large. Chapter 5 highlights the increased world population, Chapter 6 the relatively stable but limited access to land and Chapter 7 the contemporary increase in resources requiring animal production.

Summary

Substantial parts of all land around the globe are used for animal farming, for grazing or for production of animal feed. While well-balanced grazing can be a good way to make use of otherwise unutilized resources, animal feed from arable land can be seen as a way to compete for resources that might have been available for direct human consumption. Food of animal origin is, however, more concentrated in nutrients, compared with vegetable food. Apart from the production of meat, milk and eggs, animal farming is beneficial from many other points of views, not least in subsistence oriented farming, where livestock often serve multifunctional purposes, such as meat, milk, fibres, manure, and as social and economic assets.

If poultry is excluded, cattle form the largest single category of farm animals but, taken together, sheep and goats dominate in numbers. The third largest category is pigs. We find varieties of all these kinds of farm animals all over the world; and in both market and subsistence oriented agriculture, but the distribution varies between the continents and different countries. In addition, other farm animals such as camelids and horses are briefly mentioned. Due to differences in animal size and productivity the quantitative production of meat, milk and eggs is not always proportional to the number of animals. Pig and chicken meat dominate over cattle meat and other kinds of meat; and in milk, cattle largely dominate, even though milk from buffaloes, goats, sheep and camels can be of great importance.

Livestock production is often debated in terms of environmental impact. A number of negative environmental side-effects of livestock production are touched on in this chapter, which, however, also points out several positive effects besides the production as such. Finally, current trends in world animal production and consumption are put into a wider perspective that connects the ongoing world population growth, the limited global land area, and the increased numbers of farm animals and livestock production in many parts of the world.

Next

Chapter 8 deals with farm production of non-foods. You will primarily read about vegetable and animal fibres and bio-energy production, which are important parts of world agriculture. Some of these products are by-products of other kinds of crop or animal farming; others are produced explicitly in order to be used as fibres, such as cotton; or as bio-energy, such as parts of the world's sugar cane production. Moreover, the chapter is also about as diverse subjects as floriculture. recycling and farmers' engagement in different kinds of services.

To discuss

○   Select your favourite farm animal, and study in which countries the animal is most and least common, and the produced quantities.
○   Study how different kinds of farm animals are distributed between the continents and relate this to the number of people on each continent, today and by 2050.
○   Compare the production of meat, milk and eggs per person in 2000 and today, in the world and in some specific countries.

8 Agricultural production of non-foods

This chapter introduces you to a wide variety of farming activities for which the only common feature is that they result in other products than food. You will read about cotton and other natural fibres from plants, and about wool, hides and other materials of animal origin. Moreover, we will pay some attention to large-scale production of cut flowers, which is an expanding sector. According to the wide definition of non-foods that is applied in this chapter, we will also study recycling, for example of animal manure, which can be seen as a kind of production of inputs for continued production.

Furthermore, farmers' engagement in various kinds of services are discussed, in terms of transports, so-called ecosystem services and agro-tourism. This can be interesting for both market and subsistence oriented farmers, presuming that they have access to unutilized resources and that this kind of engagement does not hamper the crop or animal farming. To have access to land is to have access to large-scale exposure to solar radiation, which gives agriculture unique roles in the conversion of solar energy into various forms of renewable energy.

After this chapter you are expected to:

- ○ Know the major functions of agriculture in other kinds of production than food
- ○ Be able to discuss production of non-foods in terms of main products and by-products
- ○ Be familiar with the global production of plant and animal fibres
- ○ Be aware of the production of hides and other by-products, which takes place in parallel with the production of meat, milk and eggs.
- ○ Be familiar with the term ecosystem services and be able to mention some examples that may be conducted in parallel with food production
- ○ Be able to give an account of the transformation of energy in the bio-energy chain, beginning with the sun and the farmer
- ○ Be able to give some practical examples of bio-energy chains

Key words

Non-foods, main product, by-product, plant fibres, animal fibres, animal by-products, recycling, ecosystem service, agro-tourism, solar energy, biomass, bio-fuel, bio-energy.

Farming generates a multiplicity of non-foods

Put simply, agricultural non-food production includes all kinds of products that are obtained through farming for other purposes than to be eaten. Dealing with agricultural non-food production includes a plethora of different activities, such as: production of commodities; utilization of by-products; recycling of organic matter; various service undertakings; and extraction of bio-energy. Bearing in mind that one-third of the global land area is agricultural land (plus another one-third of forest land), farming is involved in gigantic flows of energy and in continuous growth of enormous quantities of organic substances in the form of vegetable and animal matter. This gives the agricultural sector a unique position in the borderland between agriculture, energy and other natural resources. In this perspective we may perceive the farmed landscape as an arena for the production of foods, fibres and energy, together with more or less ambitious utilization of by-products and recycling of resources, plus numerous other activities.

We may categorize the many different kinds of non-foods on the basis of their character as main or by-products, which draws attention to aspects of economizing with resources. Alternatively, the main focus can be put on four major kinds of functions. First, agriculture generates a wide range of non-food materials, for example cotton and hides. Second, recycling, for example of manure and straw, serves important functions for nutrient supply and continued general production. Third, agriculture can be involved in a number of service functions; in transportation, so-called ecosystem services and agro-tourism. Fourth, the large-scale capturing of energy in all green plants gives farming key functions for the supply of bio-energy. You will find an overview, with examples, of different non-food products in Table 8.1, categorized with regard to functions (vertical) and character as main products or as different kinds of by-products (horizontal).

Among the examples in Table 8.1 you find cotton as a main product intended to be used as a material, not as food. The last cell in the same row points to gelatine as a by-product of a by-product, as it is extracted from hides that in turn are by-products of the production of meat. As you can see, some by-products are mentioned more than once because they can be obtained from food, such as food grains, or from cotton or other non-food crops. The categorization in main and by-products of services should be understood as whether this kind of work is considered as a main or subordinate part of farming. The biogas examples that

Table 8.1 Examples of non-food agricultural production categorized as one of four major kinds of functions (vertical) and with regard to source of origin in terms of main products or different kinds of by-products (horizontal)

Function	*The function is obtained as a:*			
	Main product	*By-product from food production*	*By-product from non-food production*	*By-product of by-products*
Materials, goods	Cotton	Straw, hides, feathers	Fibrous matter	Crop residuals, gelatine
Recycling	So-called green manure	Straw, manure	Straw, manure	Crop residuals
Services	Transportation, agro-tourism	Transportation, agro-tourism	Transportation, agro-tourism	
Bio-fuels	Ethanol from maize	Biogas from composted biomass	Biogas from composted biomass	Biogas from manure

refer to composted biomass can, for instance, derive from leaves from the cultivation of vegetables. You will find more about the included examples later in this chapter.

Non-foods in view of economizing with resources

Agricultural production of non-foods is closely associated with use of resources, positively and negatively. As the products are renewable – wool, for example – we may assume that the production can reduce the use of non-renewable resources, such as nylon. On the other hand the production of non-foods may conflict with food production. Sugar cane for ethanol, for example, competes with bread wheat: for land, and for other resources such as crop nutrients, energy, water and labour.

Bio-energy from arable land is thus controversial, not least in view of the challenge of managing population increase, food security, climate change, limited land areas and the necessity of economizing with natural resources. Universal generalizations for or against are, however, hardly relevant. Production of wool and other animal fibres on the basis of permanent pastures can, for example, often be conducted without competing with other resources. In addition, we may also find mutual advantages between food and non-food production, for example when biogas can be obtained from farm residues of little alternative use. We will get back to these and other questions further on in this chapter, which is structured in line with the following headings:

○ Natural fibres from crops and other plants
○ Natural fibres of animal origin
○ Hides and other by-products of animal production

- ○ Cut flowers and other non-food farm commodities
- ○ Recycling for continued production
- ○ Farmers' engagement in different kinds of services
- ○ Conversion of solar energy to bio-energy

Natural fibres from crops and other plants

Natural fibres from crops and other plants contribute to substantial parts of the entire agricultural non-food production. In cotton farming cotton lint is usually the main purpose, with cotton seed as by-product, although both are highly valuable. Other plant fibres are of more typical by-product character. Coir fibres from coconuts, for example, are quite useful for mats and brushes, but hardly the primary motive for coconut production. In addition, fibre crops generate straw and husks at early stages of the fibre chains, and further along the chains other fibrous residues may be achieved. Some of these may be used in animal husbandry, as building material or composted to be recycled back into the land. At the same time as some of the traditional use of fibres is replaced by plastics, new fields of application are being developed, such as mixtures between natural and synthetic fibres for industrial purposes.

Plant fibre production takes place on all continents and in widely varying contexts. We find endless cotton fields in the so-called Cotton Belt in the Southeastern US, in contrast to small-scale cotton farming in Burkina Faso and smallholder production of jute in Bangladesh. In highly subsistence oriented economies crop fibres are used for a variety of purposes, such as packaging, baskets, ropes and building material, in addition to the worldwide general use of fibres for textiles. Moreover, baskets and various other commodities made of fibres are sold at local markets and to traders for further distribution nationally and internationally. Figure 8.1 shows an example of the small-scale plant fibre sector.

The dominant kind of crop fibre is cotton. In 2009 cotton was followed by jute, flax and sisal. These and a number of other important plant fibres are listed in Table 8.2, which makes no attempt to specify the exact production or ranking. According to the cited source, the global production of cotton is about ten times higher than of jute, and in the order of 1,000 times higher than kapok and henequen.

Cotton is globally traded and an important commodity in the world economy with regard to both the fibres and its valuable oil and protein rich cotton seed. In addition, cotton is also important at regional and local levels, like many other plant fibres. According to FAOSTAT, the largest amount of cotton lint was in 2009 produced by China, with India in second place, US in third and Pakistan as number four. Taken together, the four leading cotton producing countries accounted for as much as 72 per cent of the total quantity. Substantial quantities were also produced by Brazil, Uzbekistan, Turkey, Australia, Greece, Turkmenistan, Syrian Arab Republic, Burkina Faso, Nigeria, Argentina, Tajikistan, Kazakhstan and Egypt. You will read more about cotton in Box 8.1. Jute, the second largest crop fibre, is largely dominated by India and Bangladesh,

Figure 8.1 Small-scale transportation of natural fibres by water in South-East Asia in
2010.
Photo: Anna Martiin.

which, at comparably lower levels, were followed by: China, Uzbekistan, Nepal,
Viet Nam, Burma, Zimbabwe, former Sudan, Thailand and Egypt.

Natural fibres of animal origin

Animal fibres are produced wherever animal farming takes place, although some
animals are more important producers than others. Like crop fibres, animal fibres
can be understood as main or by-products, depending on the main purpose of

Table 8.2 Major fibres of plant origin

Important fibres of plant origin	
Cotton	Ramie
Jute	Hemp
Flax	Manila fibre (abaca)
Kenaf	Kapok
Coir	Henequen
Sisal	

Source: Van Dam 2009: 4.

Box 8.1 Cotton yields, doubled in forty years

On a global scale the produced cotton quantities have doubled since 1969/71; at the same time world population almost doubled too; although it actually seems as if the number of cotton T-shirts per person have increased as well. The increased production of cotton is a result of an, almost doubled yield per hectare, while the global cotton area has been notably stable during the last four decades; around 34 million hectares according to FAOSTAT. The share of the global area on which cotton is grown is thus modest, only a few per cent, but when cotton is grown with large amounts of fertilizer and water for irrigation, the share of resources can be substantial, not least in regions with far-reaching and intensive cotton cultivation.

---

production, which can differ from farm to farm. Wool can be the main purpose of sheep production for some farmers, but is in other cases seen as a by-product, secondary to meat or milk. In contrast, it is safe to say that animal fibre is never the main aim of cattle husbandry, while it often is for the owners of alpacas. In no particular order, Table 8.3 gives you an idea of the variety of animal fibres that are being produced.

Many of the fibres in Table 8.3, silk, alpaca, cashmere, mohair and some other qualities of wool are attractive on the world market, while, with some exceptions, the different kinds of hair primarily are utilized in subsistence economies. Box 8.2 exemplifies the different kinds of wool in the form of alpaca production in the Peruvian Andes.

As in many other forms of agricultural production, the number of animals in a region may but does not have to coincide with the production of fibres. India, for example, was the second leading country in number of sheep in 2009, but was ranked much lower in terms of produced quantities of wool.

China, Australia and New Zealand were the globally leading wool producers in 2010, together producing almost half of global production. Before that Australia

Table 8.3 Examples of main fibres of animal origin

Important fibres of animal origin	
Wool, merino	Goat hair
Wool, mohair	Camel hair
Wool, cashmere	Hair from cattle, yak, horses, etc.
Wool, alpaca	Silk
Wool, camel	Feathers

Box 8.2 Alpaca wool production in the Peruvian Andes

A large proportion of the world's alpacas are found at high altitudes in the southern parts of Peru, where the alpaca is closely connected with the Peruvian identity. More than 100,000 families are estimated to have their main source of living from the alpacas, which commonly are kept in herds of fewer than fifty heads each. Approximately between 1.5 and 2.8 kg of fibres are produced annually per animal or, alternatively expressed, each alpaca may deliver warm and hygroscopic wool for three or four sweaters. Most of the Peruvian alpaca wool is white, but as many as twenty-three different colours have been distinguished.

Source: Cardellino and Mueller 2009.

---

was for a long time the leading producer, but has recently experienced drastic decreases in the number of sheep, about one-third from 2005 to 2010. Besides, changes like these are taking place in some countries at the same time as the total numbers of sheep are increasing, as discussed in Chapter 7. According to the FAOSTAT statistics for all kinds of wool, other big wool producers are: the UK, Iran, Morocco, former Sudan, Argentina and Russia.

After wool and hair, a third category of animal fibres is made up of silk, which is a rather special kind of production that is primarily operated in Asian cultures, although silk production is found in other parts of the world. Box 8.3 gives a glimpse from this field.

Box 8.3 Silk production

Silk in its traditional and most famous form is associated with the mulberry tree, from which cocoons of the mulberry silkworm are obtained for further processing into fine silk threads that later may be found in the most exclusive high quality fashion. China is the world's largest producing country of natural silk, but substantial production is also found in, for example, India, Brazil, Viet Nam and Thailand. About 8 million Indian farmers, of whom 80 per cent belong to the rural poor, are said to be partly dependent on production of natural silk; either as silk farmers and/or in small-scale industries at village level.

Source: FAOSTAT and Patil *et al.* 2009.

Hides and other by-products of animal production

Except for fibres, farm animals also produce other kinds of non-foods, such as hides and other slaughter by-products. As this part of livestock production includes slaughter, flaying and handling of entrails, it has a mentally and culturally complicated character. In the words of Leach and Wilson (2009: 1), who refer to animal slaughter in what they call backyard situations, 'Hides and skins are often thought of as intrinsically unclean and end up being discarded or wasted.' Still, each slaughtered animal means a hide and a carcass to deal with.

In spite of the fact that the subject matter can be something of an invisible grey zone, hides and skins are of great importance for the production of shoes and other leather products for billions of people. Similarly, numerous by-products of animal origin are widely used in industrial production, for example gelatine in industrial food processing. In addition, high quality hides can be a source of income to the farm economy, although often of marginal character.

With reference to the aforementioned problems, it is reasonable to expect substantial discrepancies between numbers of animals and numbers of hides, which among other things mean waste and eventually hygiene and environmental problems too. It is thus not surprising that there are difficulties in quantifying the global production of hides and skins. According to estimates by FAOSTAT, cattle and buffaloes provided 71 per cent of global production in 2009, and sheep skins (without wool) and goat skins 15 and 9 per cent, respectively.

By-products from animals are subject to substantial interest from the authorities and thus subject to specific rules and regulations that are widely applied, although not everywhere. A cautious approach is motivated by the risks of hygiene problems and the spread of diseases that are embedded in materials of animal origin. You will read more about these aspects in Chapter 21, which deals with food safety.

Cut flowers and other non-food farm commodities

Farming resources are also used for a diverse mix of other products. Natural rubber, tobacco, medical plants, spice crops and cut flowers are some examples. According to FAOSTAT, natural rubber was produced on about 9 million hectares in 2009. Thailand and Indonesia are major producers of natural rubber, but also Malaysia, India, Viet Nam, China, Côte d'Ivoire, Nigeria, Sri Lanka, the Philippines and Brazil among others. In the case of tobacco, China is the world's leading grower, followed by Brazil, India and the US, but Malawi, Indonesia and Argentina are also large suppliers of tobacco, which in 2009 was cultivated on nearly 4 million hectares in total.

In recent years intercontinental flows of cut flowers have boosted. In Kenya, for example, roses and carnations are grown, wrapped in plastic and instantly flown to customers at the other side of the globe. This kind of floriculture (Figure 8.2) may be problematic because of high use of water, energy and other resources, but is at the same time an important source of income for many people and of export revenue. Other cut flower exporting countries are Colombia, Ecuador, Israel,

Figure 8.2 Cut flowers for sale thousands of kilometres away from the place where they were grown.
Photo: Anton Martiin and Ola Carlsson-Fredén.

Zimbabwe, Zambia and Uganda, among others. Large amounts of cut flowers are exported to Europe, but floriculture is also important in many European countries, with the Netherlands as an outstanding representative of the present and historical production of flowers. The survey of non-food products from farming will now continue with a discussion about recycling, after which we will discuss different kinds of services, followed by a final section on bio-energy.

Recycling for continued production

Recycling of as many nutrients and organic matter as possible is originally a fundamental part of farming and a prerequisite for being able to farm in the long run. Without it, the soil will become increasingly impoverished and the yields reduced, threatening the farming unit as well as the supply of food. When by-products such as straw, other crop residues and animal manure are recycled back to the land we can understand this as production of non-food by-products that serve as inputs for further production.

The principle of recirculation is valid for all kinds of farming, but in market oriented farming, with the possibility of purchasing crop nutrients, the need for recycling may be given less attention than in subsistence oriented farming, where recycling generally is a major alternative to maintain the fertility of the land. We will get back to and explain these matters further on, in Chapter 12. Most commonly, recycling of crop and animal residues takes place at the producing unit. By that means the same piece of land that delivered the crops and the animal feed will benefit from the returned nutrients. Some trade or barter with residues can, however, also occur, for example in the Netherlands and other regions where animal farming is so intensive so that it is difficult to find areas where manure can be spread in relevant quantities.

Recycling of urban waste is another form of recycling. Gigantic amounts of urban waste are constantly generated; waste that includes resources from near and far. The biomass fractions can thus include nutrients that are exported from agricultural areas in one part of the world to areas somewhere else, which is also pointed out in Chapter 12. This kind of recycling is a matter of recycling as such, rather than of recycling to the place from which the nutrients were obtained.

Farmers' engagement in different kinds of services

Farming can give access to a number of resources such as labour that now and then might be available for other kinds of activities than ordinary farming. The possibilities of taking on these kinds of extra activity differ widely between the world's farmers and depend on factors such as size of the holding, methods of production and access to labour. It is also necessary to consider costs and revenues, risks, and how eventual undertakings can be combined with ordinary farming. The opportunities naturally vary over time, between countries and regions, and from season to season. As an example, expensive and seasonally underutilized tractors and labour may be used for road building for some months; or a surplus building may be rebuilt and hired out to visiting tourists. A third example is when land is let out to private solar panel or windmill companies. The following list exemplifies a number of farm resources that, depending on the situation, might be able to be used for different kinds of services:

- Surplus labour
- Surplus machine capacity
- Surplus tools and other equipment
- Farm animals, for grazing of conservation areas
- Draught animals, or animals for riding
- Surplus buildings
- Marginal land (e.g. shrubby wetlands)
- Skills and experiences in practical management of land, water, soils, vegetation and animals
- Local knowledge with reference to geography, ecology, climate, traditions, etc.

In the following we will discuss three different examples of farmers' engagement in services: transportation and similar jobs, so-called ecosystem services and so-called agro-tourism.

Transportation and similar kinds of services

In many cases exchange of manual labour between farms is a natural part of life. Hire of manual labour can also be of a more formal kind, within and outside farming, for example occasional work at a big farm or in road building. It is also common that tractors, draught animals or mopeds are engaged for transportation or other jobs. A third variant in this category of farmers' engagement in services is when the farmer and his/her tractor, harvester or other kind of machinery are hired out for operations at neighbouring farms, or for other kinds of work, such as the building of roads, airports and other plants.

Ecosystem services

In recent years farming has increasingly become formally engaged in so-called ecosystem services, albeit to varying extents in different parts of the world. Simplified, the idea is to pay farmers for activities and arrangements that can counteract environmental problems and even improve the situation. As an example, farmers in some countries may be paid to maintain vegetation that favours endangered bird species.

Ecosystem services can be organized and paid for by governments, organizations or, with the European Union as an example, by supranational organizations. The payments usually cover part of farmers' costs, but can in some cases reach full compensation. Ecosystem services can refer to problems caused by external actors, for example carbon sequestration, but can also deal with problems caused by farming activities. A farmer might, for example, be offered economic support for investments that aim at reduced nutrient leakage from animal manure to an adjacent watercourse. Box 8.4 gives examples of a number of potential ecosystem services with varying relevance for different kinds of farming.

The term ecosystem service is comparatively new and reflects increased worries about the environment. Parts of world farming have, however, supported ecological processes since the early emergence of agriculture, such as serving as a carbon dioxide sink, and supported the kind of biodiversity that is associated with farmed landscapes. The often specific vegetation and fauna in permanent meadows and pastures is one example and pollinating insects another (see Box 8.5). The environmental advantages of farming have, however, also been accompanied by drawbacks, some of ancient origin and others of later date, such as overgrazing a overuse of agro-chemicals.

Some kinds of ecosystem services are operated as integrated parts of farming, for example altered tillage methods in order to reduce soil erosion. Other kinds of services require separate activities, for instance more or less large-scale projects for the restoration of wetlands. The undertaking of ecosystem services requires realistic expectations from all the actors involved. It is important to be realistic

> *Box 8.4* Potential ecosystem services, some examples
>
> - Carbon sequestering in order to counteract climate change
> - Counteract greenhouse gas emissions from farming operations
> - Prevent soil erosion
> - Prevent nutrient leakage and promote nutrient recycling
> - Prevent acidification of soils and waters
> - Promote water quality
> - Improve irrigation efficiency
> - Letting of land for renewable energy, e.g. solar panels, windmills and biogas plants
> - Promote pollinators
> - Promote biodiversity: plants, animals, insects, etc.
> - Wildlife habitats, e.g. via wetland restoration
> - Promote landscapes and cultural heritage

as regards possible results and how ecosystem services should be combined so that ordinary farming is not hampered. Moreover, it is worth noting that ecosystem services mean that the farm gets involved in other kinds of economies than in ordinary farming, which can mean extra accounting and controls, but also opportunities to learn and to discuss agriculture from other perspectives than farming.

Agro-tourism

The expression agro-tourism refers to tourist activities that are arranged in close connection to farming, such as: light versions of farm work in the UK or India; wildlife arrangements in Australia; horse trekking in Argentina; elephant trekking in Thailand; or picking grapes in French vineyards. Like ecosystem services, tourism links the farm to another kind of economy, which can reduce the risks involved in a one-sided dependency on farm production.

> *Box 8.5* Pollinators are of vital importance for food production
>
> Insects, birds and mammals serve as pollinators and are of crucial importance for the reproduction of wild and cultivated plants. Approximately two-thirds of all plants that are used as food are considered to be more or less dependent on pollinators. However, the number of pollinators is declining, which indicates emerging problems, problems that may reach a magnitude that, according to experts in the field, has not yet been fully understood.
>
> Source: FAO 2005b (accessed 14 September 2011).

Successful agro-tourism requires good planning and plenty of time so that the guests can be welcomed and supported without disturbing the ordinary farming. There are also needs for practical arrangements in terms of accommodation, water, food, transportation, payment and marketing. Cherry-picked case studies, so-called good examples, are often used as a way to back up projects of this kind, as well as ecosystem services. Examples are valuable, but might in some cases be too enthusiastic, forgetting to tell us about lessons learned along the way. As the last point in this chapter about non-food production we will now turn our attention to matters of bio-energy and to the abundance of sun that shines on agricultural areas.

Conversion of solar energy to bio-energy

From the perspective of energy, agricultural areas can be looked at as enormous solar panels. Farmland and farm crops receive enormous amounts of solar energy, which render farming a key position in matters of bio-energy. In the words of E. A. Wrigley, all economies that do not have access to fossil fuels depend

> exclusively, or almost exclusively, upon their ability to capture some part of the flow of energy reaching the earth in the form of insolation, and to pre-serve a favourable balance between the energy spent in this pursuit and the energy made available by it.
>
> (Wrigley 1988: 50f.)

Understanding the relationship between the sun and the farmer, in his/her role as supplier of bio-energy, requires a brief description of the process of photosynthesis and the terminology.

Solar energy generates biomass in the form of green plants where the energy is captured and stored, together with nutrients and other components. When we eat, the energy content in the food, measured in joules or calories, is made available for our varying needs, such as metabolism, muscle energy or body fat reserves. The same goes for animals that are supplied with energy via various feed stuffs. Figure 8.3 illustrates how energy is converted: from solar energy to energy in green plants (biomass), and in some cases further to energy in bio-fuels, from which bio-energy can be obtained. The process and the terminology are further explained below the figure.

E	E	E	E
Insolation + CO_2 + water ⟶	Biomass + O_2 ⟶	Bio-fuel ⟶	Bio-energy
Chlorophyll			

Figure 8.3 Energy from the sun is captured in the biomass of green plants, and is then in some cases converted into bio-fuels, from which bio-energy can be obtained.

Note: The letter E stands for energy, which is found in all stages, CO_2 stands for carbon dioxide and O_2 for oxygen.

Step by step, Figure 8.3 illustrates how solar energy, carbon dioxide and water are captured by green plants that continue to grow and release oxygen. The biomass content of energy can then be converted into some kind of bio-fuel, for example ethanol, that serves as a so-called energy carrier from which bio-energy can be obtained and used for heating, electricity or transportation. As you can see, all stages in Figure 8.3 include energy, E, although in different forms: solar radiation, biomass, bio-fuel and bio-energy, in accordance with the first law of thermodynamics, which states that energy can be transformed, but neither created nor destroyed.

At the same time as Figure 8.3 illustrates the process of photosynthesis it is also demonstrating a bio-energy chain, which can be seen as an extended version of the process of photosynthesis. In conclusion, you can see the sunshine as the beginning of the chain and the sunlit green field and the cultivating farmer as a second stage. Further on you find the processing into bio-fuel, also called agrofuel when it is extracted from agricultural main or by-products. Thereafter the energy content in the particular kind of bio-fuel is available for various uses. Box 8.6 shows some examples of simplified bio-energy chains. Each row in the box shows one kind of biomass, for example maize used as animal feed. The energy content in the maize provides farm animals with energy that is used for the animals' metabolism, muscles, other body functions and eventual production of milk or eggs.

All kinds of green plants contain energy, but the amount varies. Still, categorization in terms of so-called energy crops is chiefly due to how a certain crop is currently used. Maize (Figure 8.4) can, for example, be an energy crop, a feed crop or a food crop, depending on the purpose of its cultivation. The following list gives examples of different kinds of energy sources from the agricultural sector:

- Sugar and starch-rich crops, e.g. sugar cane, maize, grains
- Oil crops, e.g. rapeseed, palm oil, jatropha
- Other kinds of energy crops, e.g. willow, switchgrass and other kinds of grass
- Crop by-products, e.g. straw and leaves

Box 8.6 Conversion of energy, some practical examples

- Human food – human metabolism – muscle energy – carrying, walking, running
- Animal feed – animal metabolism – muscle energy – draught power, growth, milk
- Firewood – burning – heat
- Animal manure – anaerobic digestion – biogas – electricity
- Energy crops – fermentation – distillation – ethanol – bio-energy – transportation

Figure 8.4 Maize is a multifunctional crop that is grown for bio-energy, feed, food and as raw material for various kinds of industrial use.
Photo: Carin Martiin.

- Animal manure for biogas production
- Dried animal manure for heating
- Body heat from farm animals
- By-products generated at later stages of product chains

The amounts of energy that can be obtained depend on factors such as energy content in the crop, crop yields per hectare, and how much energy that is put into production, processing and distribution along the production chain. Ideas on optimal solutions have rapidly replaced each other in recent years.

Bio-energy from farming has been continuously utilized over the millennia. Crops fed to draught animals can be seen as a source of bio-energy, as is dried dung when it is used for heating. Recent enthusiasm, and doubts, about increased use of bio-energy refers primarily to altered perspectives in societies where fossil

Box 8.7 The jatropha

The jatropha has recently been highlighted as a potential large-scale bio-fuel alternative. The oilseed bearing tree is grown in the tropics and subtropics, where the oil is traditionally used as medicine and for lighting. With the newfound global interest in bio-fuels the jatropha has sometimes been pointed to as a kind of panacea. Among its pros is the deep root system that is able to supply the tree with water and nutrients from deep levels in the ground. Moreover, the oil can be used without processing. Some disadvantages are, however, also at hand: many jatropha varieties are poisonous; the trees have difficulty withstanding frost and water logging; the plants may spread to other fields, where they can become a hard-to-control weed; and the jatropha may serve as a host for cassava diseases. In 2008 jatropha was planted on around 900,000 hectares globally, but the area is supposed to be expanded. About 85 per cent of the area was found in Asia, and around 13 per cent in Africa. Some areas planted with jatropha are also found in Brazil.

Source: Brittaine and Lutaladio 2010.

energy sources dominate. At the same time as environmental considerations may call for bio-fuels, ethical doubts might point in the opposite direction. In the shadow of almost nine hundred million undernourished people and continuous population increase, it is questionable whether arable land, nutrients, water, energy, etc. should be used for fuel instead of bread. Increased interest is, however, currently being paid to so-called energy grasses and other kinds of vegetation that does not compete directly with food crops. The jatropha (see Box 8.7), for example, has now and then been put forward as a potential alternative for some parts of the world.

Summary

A multiplicity of non-food production is conducted in world agriculture. The field of non-food production highlights the multifunctionalities in agriculture and in part reflects other perspectives than those usually associated with farming. The chapter gives attention to traditional non-food products such as natural plant fibres, among which cotton is the dominant fibre. Animal fibres include a variety of wool and hair from different farm animals. Hides and other by-products of animal production are also discussed, although these matters may form a grey zone that is problematic from ethical, cultural and hygiene points of views. Furthermore, recycling of organic matter back to farming is considered as a kind of non-food production. Services form a third category, according to the wide understanding of non-food that is applied in this chapter. Farmers' undertakings in different kinds of services can be a strategy to make use of otherwise underutilized resources, such as machinery, marginal land or labour. These kinds of activities are exemplified by engagement in transportation, ecosystem services and agro-tourism.

A fourth and increasingly highlighted category is the bio-energy sector, in which agriculture holds a unique position because of the gigantic insolation on the land. Attention is paid to the basic connections between sun radiation and bio-energy, including the process of photosynthesis, in order to clarify how solar energy is converted to energy in crops and animals, and then can be further processed into bio-fuels that are carriers of the bio-energy. Various kinds of bio-energy chains are also exemplified and briefly discussed.

Next

The non-food production chapter ends Part II, which also gave accounts of population, areas, crops and animal farming in large-scale, often global perspectives. In Part III we will turn to matters of land, the focus of three different chapters which successively become more practical, leading to the even more practical perspectives in Part IV. The next chapter, Chapter 9, highlights farmers' access to land, which is decisive for almost all kinds of farming. You will, among other things, study different kinds of land rights, and consider ownership versus other kinds of user rights.

To discuss:

○ Compare three kinds of natural plant fibres as regards production, use and special characteristics.

○ Compare three kinds of natural animal fibres as regards production, use and special characteristics.

○ Give examples of some by-products of animal production that are not taboo in your culture.

○   Reflect on eventual differences between market and subsistence ori-
    ented farmers' possibilities of engaging in the various kinds of services
    that are discussed in this chapter.

○   Find out about some ecosystem services that are carried out by farm-
    ers, as close as possible to where you live.

○   Imagine some cases of agro-tourism, located at different types of
    farms, and consider pros and cons from the perspectives of the farming
    household and of the tourists.

○   Reflect on the forecasted increases in population and food consumption
    in combination with ambitions to replace some fossil fuels with bio-
    fuel. What are the pros and cons? What are your ideas for the world's
    future energy supply?

Part III

In need of land and soil

9   Access to farmland

Access to land is a key factor in the ability to practise farming. Getting hold of land is hardly something that goes without saying for the many people who are engaged in farming around the world. Matters of access to land are on the one hand rather concrete, for instance a certain farmer's difficulty in safeguarding his/her long-term access to an area. In broader perspectives land rights are highly decisive for how food is produced; for how farming resources are used; for rural societies at large; and for national and global food security.

This chapter highlights land rights in terms of farming, but neither urban expansion nor other competing interests for land. Before going deeper into these matters, we will pay some attention to the specific characteristics that make agricultural land a unique asset. You will then get introduced to land rights in general and to the main types of land rights: ownership, leasehold and customary land rights. We will discuss different categories of landowners, and the advantages of ownership in comparison with other ways of getting access to land. As regards leases, you will read about varying forms and learn that rented land is a widespread and far from unproblematic phenomenon in many kinds of agriculture. Moreover, you will read about the efforts of poor landless households to get at least temporary access to land, in rural as well as urban areas. Your attention will also be drawn to land reforms, which are a typical and widely discussed topic in the field of land rights. At the end of the chapter you will find a discussion about the price of land, which is an important and crucial factor in the ability to get access to land.

After this chapter you are expected to:

- Be able to discuss some unique characteristics of agricultural land
- Be aware of the importance of safe land rights, for farmers and world food security
- Be able to describe and compare the main forms of access to farmland
- Know the main categories of different landowners

- o   Be familiar with various ways of arranging the lease of farmland with respect to agreements, payment and the risk of arbitrariness
- o   Be able to describe the main characteristics of customary land rights, including ongoing changes
- o   Be familiar with the term land grabbing as it is used in current critical discussions
- o   Be familiar with grey zones in access to land, with regard to small-scale rural and urban farming
- o   Know the main characteristics of varying types of land reforms
- o   Be able to distinguish factors of importance for the price of land

Key words

Land rights, land ownership, leasehold, leasehold arrangements, fixed rent, shared rent, customary land rights, land grabbing, landless, urban farming, land reform, land price, capital asset.

Land is a unique asset

Land is special. Each piece of land is a unique piece of the earth's surface; a specific combination of local geography, climate, soil and ecosystems. Moreover, the land is influenced by human activities and, indirectly, also by economic, political, social and cultural conditions. We will not examine all these aspects but rather draw your attention to four specific characteristics of importance to matters of access to land.

First, farmland is a limited and geographically fixed resource that can be subject to competing interests, such as expanding cities, industries and road networks. Moreover, the fixed area means that one way of using it generally excludes simultaneous use for other purposes. Land use decisions are thus important. Cultivation of cotton excludes cultivation of wheat on the same area during the same season, and road building excludes farming totally (also see Chapter 17, Figure 17.4).

Second, farmland is at the same time a production resource and a capital asset. The combination is both favourable and problematic for farmers, who may benefit from capital growth but on the other hand can have difficulties coping with land prices higher than the production value. This kind of problem is most significant in areas with many competing interests in the land. You will read more about land prices by the end of this chapter.

Third, land areas can be special in terms of history. A particular area may, for example, reflect political history, colonial influences, socioeconomic hierarchies, religious and traditional values, and bear witness to the past history of agriculture.

Depending on the character of such tracks from the past, history may be a source of conflicts that hamper farming in some regions. At the individual level, land areas can be charged with strong emotional values. This can serve as a driving force that takes the farming business beyond simple economic rationality, but may on the other hand be a complicating factor if continued farming is threatened, for one reason or another.

The fourth of the farmland characteristics mentioned here connects to the previous one by referring to public interest; to the fact that land can be privately owned, at the same time as the area belongs to a country's territory and is subject to public interest. With differences between countries, the state may have the final say about how the land can be used, and may even be able to expropriate or confiscate land, for instance in favour of industrial expansion at the expense of farming.

The coincidental, sometimes contradictory public and private interests in agricultural land are to a greater or lesser extent handled on the basis of formal and informal laws and regulations that set the rules for how different actors are supposed to behave. This means that matters of access to farmland theoretically can be understood in terms of formal and informal institutions, which, for example, can be used as a way to understand the relations between the state and farmers

Figure 9.1 Land is a unique asset. West Cape Province, South Africa, 2011.
Photo: Viktoria Olausson.

Box 9.1 Farmland from the perspective of formal and informal institutions

The term institution may be abstract, but is useful for helping to grasp relations between different kinds of actors in local, national and international contexts. The Nobel laureate Douglass North has explained matters of institutions in a pedagogic way. Simplified, North compares institutions to playgrounds where the actors are expected to act in line with formal and informal laws and regulations (North 1994: 361). In football, for example, the football field can be seen as the institution, the framework within which the game takes place and where the players have to act in line with the set rules.

In the case of farmland the idea of the institutional playground can be understood as formal land laws and regulations plus informal rules, such as local norms and beliefs about rights to land and appropriate land use. Farmers and other interested parties, such as interest organizations and agri-business companies, are supposed to act in line with this framework, with landowner–leaseholder relations as a typical example.

across the country. With the state perceived as an institution, the farmers can be seen as actors who are supposed to operate the land in accordance with the frames and limitations that are set up by the state. The so-called institutional framework is applied to societal questions at large, and can in agriculture, for example, apply to land rights and numerous other questions such as farming and environmental issues or hygiene requirements on food of animal origin (Chapter 21). You will find more about formal and informal institutions in Box 9.1

Land rights, a key to farming

Rights to farmland generally take the form of ownership, leasehold or customary land rights. Some farmers are the fortunate owners of all land within the farming unit and their ownership is formally registered and well respected. Others cultivate plots to which the user rights are diffuse, based on oral permissions and that may be taken back at almost any time. Still others get access to land through customary land rights that are based on membership in a certain community, but may be threatened by external interest in the area.

A large number of the world's farming units are based on more than one of these categories, such as combinations of ownership and leasehold. The reasons for these combinations vary from case to case but may reflect processes of structural rationalization, for example in Europe and North America, where many previously independently operated farms have come to be incorporated in bigger farms in the form of an additional lease.

The forms of land rights and how these are practised are highly decisive for how a farm is managed with respect to methods of production, investments and the planning horizon. Safe and long-term access to a well-defined area is of great importance for proper and sustainable use of soils, grasslands and water resources. Land rights can, however, be problematic, in market as well as subsistence oriented farming. Poor smallholders in particular are highly exposed to, and are also more vulnerable to unsafe access to land. Land related troubles hamper individual farming and are stressful for the family, especially if they live with the impending risk of having to leave the farm. In addition, unfair or unreliable access to land may generate social unrest in rural areas, especially in countries where a large proportion of the total population lives in the countryside. The cumulative effects of the farmers' problems are also severe, because holding back individual farming results in underperformance at large, and consequently in reductions in the total production of food.

Forms of access to land

The possibilities of getting access to farmland at all, and under what conditions, are, among other things, influenced by individual economy and family bonds, with differences between varying parts of the world. Women risk being disfavoured in many countries, due to barriers to women's access to land, for instance through inheritance. The major ways of getting access to land are:

- Purchase of land
- Lease of land
- Transfer of land rights, within families or in other ways
- Membership in a community that holds customary land rights
- Distribution via land reforms or similar interventions

You will read about the points on the list in the following parts of this chapter, where particular interest is paid to lease of land, which is widespread and is applied in various forms. The importance of individual connections should not be underestimated in matters of land. Both purchase and lease are often achieved via personal contacts and informal networks, such as relatives and neighbours. In some countries retiring landowners may support a preferred successor through a reduced price and other favours, which reflects the aforementioned emotional bonds between farmers and land.

Land ownership

Ownership is usually the safest way to get access to land, assuming that the area is thoroughly specified, registered and well respected. Land ownership can be understood as the right to use a specific area, to sell it, lease it out, leave it to family members and use it as collateral for loans. The exact understanding of the term land ownership varies between different countries and can be more or less complete. It should be remembered that owning land never can be the same as being the owner of a thing, a thing that can be moved and used in line with the owner's preferences. In addition to the great value for the ability to farm, owner-ship can improve one's status and respect in the local society and can in many countries serve as door opener to societal influence.

We find landowning farmers in large-scale market oriented farming as well as in smallholder farming for subsistence purposes, and it is safe to say that most farmers would be happy to be included in the landowner category. The landowner is often but not always an individual person. In brief, the landowner category includes:

○   Active private landowners: individuals or families who farm the land themselves
○   Passive private landowners: individuals or families who let out the land for others to farm
○   Legal entities, such as commercial companies, cooperatives and non-profit organizations, with various motives for owning agricultural land
○   States that own land for different reasons

Among private proprietors of big farms some are deeply involved in practical and managerial operations, while others leave most or all of this to employees. Increasing numbers of the world's big farms are registered as family owned companies, often explained by the need to separate the private economy from the farming business. The group passive private landowners is diverse and include categories such as: retired owners of large areas; elderly poor smallholders who are unable to operate the land; smallholders who are away on off-farm work for longer time periods; and wealthy owners who are more interested in a comfortable country life than in practical farming. When it comes to landowning companies, some choose to organize practical farming using employees, while others let out the land for leaseholders to farm. These strategies are also applied when the land is owned by the state.

Leasehold and other user rights

Leasehold is a common way to get access to arable and pasture lands. In many countries the total leased area exceeds the acreage operated by the owner. The leasehold share varies, and is comparatively low in Latin America but high in the US and in many European countries, for instance in Belgium and France. Substantial proportions of all agricultural land are also farmed on lease on the Indian subcontinent and in the Philippines. In contrast to our definition of land-owners as active or passive, all kinds of leaseholders are here supposed to be active farmers. The leased property can be distinguished as:

○   Whole farms, including acreage, buildings, eventually with machinery, live-stock, etc.
○   All the land that is operated within a particular farming unit
○   Additional land that is farmed in parallel with the owned acreage

It is difficult to generalize about the status of ownership and leases even though a majority of the world's leaseholders may experience economic disadvantages and lower social status in comparison with landowning farmers.

A wholly or partly leased farm can, however, be the same size as a fully owned unit, and in Scandinavia, for example, farmers of wholly or partly leased farms are often as highly respected as those who just cultivate their own land. The second category on the list above includes the widest range, from relatively well-to-do farmers who operate big units, to utterly poor leaseholders who cultivate the smallest imaginable plots in unsafe conditions. The third category, lease of additional land, includes farmers with some but not enough land of their own, who enlarge the business with help of leased land. This strategy is common in some parts of the world, not least in many European countries, and can be explained by a higher supply of land for lease than for sale, and by difficulties in coping with high land prices. In addition to the categories outlined, the real world includes several alternatives, for example the Chinese structure of user rights to land, which you get an outline of in Box 9.2.

Leasehold agreements

Leasehold is a matter of mutual agreement between the landowner and the lease-holder, an agreement that is accompanied by rights and obligations that have to be relevant for both parties. If not, the landowner may back out of the deal, which reduces the supply of land for rent; or the leaseholder may find him/herself trapped by impossible leasing conditions. Ultimately, the landowner and the leaseholder are on good terms with each other and manage to make a deal that is functional for both parties. Apart from practical matters about rights and obligations, for

---

Box 9.2 Access to farmland in China

According to the Land Administration Law of the People's Republic of China, land in China is basically owned by the state, but is at the same time also considered to be under peasants' collective ownership, managed via local village committees. Once a farmer has obtained the right to land, the farmer is responsible for the area and for its proper farming. The user right is strong enough to entitle the farmer to economic compensation if the land is acquisitioned for urbanization or other reasons. Changes in land use and eventual transition of the user right shall be handled via the village committees. The time period for lease is long. According to Article 14 in Chapter 2 of the Land Administration Law, village farmers have thirty years' access to the land for cultivation, animal farming, forestry and fish farming.

Source: Land Administration Law of the People's Republic of China. Adopted 25 June 1986 and amended in 1998 and 1999 (accessed in December 2011).

example about water for irrigation and maintenance of roads to the fields, the landowner and leaseholder have to agree on the following:

○   Time period
○   Written or oral form of agreement
○   Form of payment

The first point highlights the importance of a specified and relevant time of disposal. This is necessary for the leaseholder to be able to operate the land in a sound manner. Long-term access to the same area makes it possible for the farmer to get to know the soil and the detailed local climate. Moreover, it becomes possible to choose between different crops and grow them appropriately with respect to fertilizer, weed control, maintenance of drainage and terraces and prevention of soil erosion. Formal time periods for a lease can range from a year, or even shorter, to several decades, as in the Chinese example in Box 9.2. Yet, many leaseholders are at the mercy of the landowner and do not know for how long they will be allowed to stay on the land.

Despite the recommendation to seek a written agreement, verbal agreements seem to be the most common, though they are generally less safe and often favour the stronger party at the expense of the weaker. The validity of a verbal agreement should not be underestimated, however, as face-to-face agreements can be well respected in many cultures and may even be legally valid. Still, oral agreements risk being ignored; for instance if the land is sold, or if external actors such as international exploiters have their eye on the area.

Third, forms of payment have to be thoroughly considered and agreed. Leases are generally paid as so-called fixed rent or as shared rent, with a number of modifications. In case of fixed rent, the leaseholder pays a specified rent irrespective of costs and revenues. The shared rent model briefly means that landowners and leaseholders share costs and revenues. In this case, both parties share the risk of harvest failures as well as the gains from good yields and high prices for the crop.

Shared rent has often been thought of as hampering farmers' interest in improvements because the gains would have to be shared with the landowner. Obstacles like that may, however, be overcome through modified agreements that neither disfavour one of the two parties nor hamper progress in methods of production. Shared rent is practised in both market and subsistence oriented farming, for example as described in Box 9.3, which refers to large-scale market oriented farming in Ohio, US.

Being a leaseholder, pros and cons

It is no secret that landlord–leaseholder relationships can be complicated, often with the tenant farmer as the weaker party. The landlord can, for instance, be more or less distanced from practical farming and the leaseholder's situation. Or, the landowner is a more or less unidentifiable company with which the leaseholder has difficulties communicating. In some cases the landowner controls

Box 9.3 Fixed and shared rent, examples from the US

Leasehold on the basis of a fixed cash lease means that the tenant pays a fixed sum each year, based on the area. Principally, the leaseholder is free to cultivate or graze the land, within the restrictions laid down by the land-owner or by formal or informal institutions. The fixed rent principle is uncomplicated in that the two parties are relatively independent and do not have to be in continual contact about the practical farming. As the whole risk lies with the leaseholder, the owner can count on a specified payment irrespective of production costs and revenues.

Alternatively, still with examples from the US, the lease can be arranged as a so-called flexible cash lease. The rent is then influenced by yields and selling prices, and eventually also by some costs of production. In this case landowners and leaseholders share some risks plus the eventual benefits of favourable harvests and good prices.

A third example is a so-called crop-share lease, which is closely linked to production. According to this principle, the rent is paid as a share of the actual yield. The owner and the leaseholder may also share some costs of production, such as fertilizer and post-harvest handling of the crop. This alternative requires that the landowner and the leaseholder communicate about decisions and practices throughout the season.

Source: Stoneberg 2011.

many parts of the food chain, such as money transactions, sale of fertilizer and sowing seed, and purchase of the harvest, which leaves the leaseholder almost totally in the hands of the landowner. Conversely, there are situations when the leaseholder is the stronger party, for example a large-scale farmer to whom an elderly smallholder lets the land because he/she is unable to cultivate it. This is in contrast to the general rule that landlords are stronger than leaseholders, and has tellingly been termed 'reversed tenancy'.

Among the problems that can burden the leaseholder and cause difficulties for practical farming are: unsafe time periods, nonexistent terms of notice, high costs and arbitrary leasehold conditions in general. In spite of these negative aspects, leasehold alternatives may have advantages too. A lease can be the only way to expand an existing holding if land is offered on a lease but is not for sale. In addition, purchase can be too risky from an economic point of view. Furthermore, leasehold can be a good way to get into farming. For young people leasehold is less risky than purchase, which it can be almost hopeless to finance if the farm is meant to be a full-time market oriented business. Regarding young people's opportunities, Box 9.4 describes the sharemilking system as it may be operated in New Zealand.

Box 9.4 New Zealand sharemilking

The New Zealand sharemilking system is often considered to be a win–win concept that makes it easier for young people to develop farming gradually, at the same time as it gives established dairy farmers opportunities to wind down in stages before retirement. The system is based on a contractual agreement between the young sharemilker and the landowner, who are operating two parallel but principally separate businesses on the same farm. Usually the sharemilker focuses on the dairy herd while the landowner cultivates the land, and pays for the land and other fixed costs. Gradually the sharemilker builds up his/her dairy herd, develops skills and experience, and is able to invest in machinery without being heavily indebted from the very beginning of their career as a dairy farmer. Later on the sharemilker may move his/her herd to another farm with sharemilking, but sooner or later he/she may be able to fulfil the dream of owning a farm. Sharemilking is reported to have been operated on approximately one-third of all New Zealand dairy farms by the end of the first decade of the twenty-first century.

Source: Gardner 2011.

Customary land rights

The term customary land rights refers to land that belongs to and is controlled by a local community whose members have access to the land. This category of land should not be confused with open access, which means that the land is available for anyone to use. Customary land rights are found in many parts of the world but are coming under increasing pressure from external interests. This has brought about ongoing changes such as individualization of the land rights; letting in other people than members of the community, for example urban residents in need of a plot for cultivation; or even selling or letting the land on a long-term lease.

Generally speaking, customary land rights are based on traditional thinking about land and other natural resources and are, because of their traditional character, seldom recorded on paper. The access may be respected within the local society but can, as mentioned earlier, be hard to defend if other actors claim rights to the area on the basis of written documents. Several examples reveal how external interests have managed to acquire land from the original right holders, whose livelihoods have thereby been more or less ruined. Intrusions like these can also affect eventual holders of informal secondary rights such as the rights to make use of marginal grazing resources.

Customary land rights are more or less clearly subordinated directly to the state, even though their traditional origin often has a longer history than the particular state. Representatives of the state might therefore be able to promote the individualization of land rights, and eventually also to transfer the land to other actors. In some cases external interests have, however, also been welcomed by representatives of the local community who may be engaged in 'Borrowing, pledging, renting and selling' (Atwood 1990: 661–2). The quotation may have relevance for a variety of land right transfers, of which some may be perceived as grey areas of land acquisition, the so-called land grabbing that is dealt with in the next section.

The land grabbing problem

The expression land grabbing has lately come to be used for the growing trend of foreign engagement in farming. Typically, domestic or overseas companies acquire land at the expense of local farmers, with the purpose of creating large and highly productive farms. The initiatives are sometimes welcomed by national and even local authorities, who may support the formal process of land acquisition. Advocates of this kind of business have referred to expected increases in agricultural productivity and to the companies' promises of investments in schools, hospitals and infrastructure.

The land grabbing phenomenon has, however, been intensively criticized for questionable negotiations, mismanagement and broken promises. Smallholders are deeply betrayed; having been persuaded or forced to give up the land, but without seeing much of the promised investment and without much chance of even being employed on the new farm unit that is being established on their former acreage.

The problem is, among others, accomplished by companies from Japan, China, South Korea and Saudi Arabia, which chiefly are engaged in Sub-Saharan Africa, for example in Ethiopia, Kenya, Madagascar, Nigeria and Uganda. We may understand so-called overseas land grabbing, or overseas farming, as a reaction to increased global demand for food in combination with volatile markets, which spurs investors into action and causes concern to governments in countries where land is scarce in proportion to the current and expected population.

Grey areas in small-scale rural and urban farming

A different phenomenon to that of land grabbing, with poor individuals as initiative takers, is the widespread and significant small-scale use of marginal plots that takes place without formal permission. You may have seen or even been engaged in crop cultivation on remote plots somewhere in the forest, or found grazing cattle and goats on any imaginable site in the landscape. This grey area of small-scale farming supports the livelihoods of millions of otherwise landless people for whom any kind of access to land is vital to survival, and is also contributing to intensive utilization of densely populated rural areas in some parts of the world.

Similar efforts are widely practised among poor inhabitants in urban areas in many parts of the world. Millions of people in the rapidly expanding urban areas in Africa, Asia and Latin America are engaged in small-scale crop and animal farming, on all imaginable pieces of land that have not yet been asphalted over or built on. You can read more about urban and peri-urban farming in Box 9.5, which highlights urban farming among poor people, while you are referred to other sources for studies of more experimental and trendy forms of urban farming.

Box 9.5 Urban and peri-urban farming

Urban and peri-urban farming is widely operated by the urban poor; in the outskirts of urban areas as well as closer to the centre. Cows are tended along highway roadsides, and pigs and chickens may be found almost anywhere, not least in many Asian cities. Substantial amounts of vegetables, berries, meat, milk, eggs and fish are being produced on the basis of all imaginable resources that can be found and utilized within urban areas. This kind of food production provides millions of people with fresh nutritious food that otherwise would be hard to afford. In addition, the produce can generate a cash income for the household, through street sale and local markets, and deliveries to restaurants and hotels that appreciate fresh deliveries to the door.

Figure 9.2 Urban farming is important in providing poor households with fresh fruit and vegetables, and in generating an income from small-scale sales.
Photo: Anna Martiin.

Land reform

Land reform is a widely discussed subject that has engaged agriculturalists and economists for centuries and, like land right issues in general, has later also been analysed by scholars and debaters in rural sociology and development studies. The term land reform refers to redistribution of farmland, and often refers to efforts to split large farms into smaller units in order to support smallholder farming. The development economist Michael Lipton writes:

> To over-simplify, land reform comprises laws with the main goal of reducing poverty by substantially increasing the proportion of farmland controlled by the poor, and thereby their income, power or status.
>
> (Lipton 2009: 1)

Many Latin American countries, for example, have over time been subject to numerous land reforms in order to develop fair and small-scale structures and greater social and economic equality in rural areas. In spite of initial enthusiasm and hard work, the results have, however, not always been successful.

Alternatively, land reform can be accomplished in order to create larger units of production. Agricultural history includes numerous examples of efforts in this direction. Land reform may also be initiated with the purpose of restoring previous land structures, which has been accomplished in parts of Eastern Europe since the political shift that began in 1989. Portions of previously confiscated farmland have since then been returned to the families that formerly owned them, traced back to the early twentieth century. In this way, some of the previous gigantic state-owned farms have been converted back to private ownership. Other structures have emerged as well, and the outcome of the redistribution varies from country to country.

Land reforms have often been strongly political and more or less dramatic processes. Through history, initiatives have been taken by varying kinds of interest groups and movements, but also by colonial powers, domestic governments and even by innovative landlords. It is not surprising that land reforms are multifaceted, and still widely debated. Lessons have, however, been learned and current debaters are recommending, among other things, less simple models and greater emphasis on the entire context in which the reform takes place. Increased attention seems to be paid to supporting farmers in the altered situation with respect to the accompanying need for investments, improved communications and well functioning channels for sale of the product. More emphasis is also put on the need to compensate the former landowners, in order to reduce the risk of troublesome tensions between old and new land right holders, and support the long-term survival of the reforms.

A more administrative kind of land reform is that of land titling and land registration, which aims at the formalization and individualization of previously informal land rights. We touched on these issues earlier in this chapter, in terms of farmers' need for safe access to land. Among others, the economist Hernando de Soto has claimed that formally registered land rights are decisive for poor smallholders. By this means, de Soto argues, diffuse rights are turned into a capital asset that can be used as collateral, which in turn would open the door to investments and improvements in smallholder farming. Like land reforms in general, matters of land titling and registration are debated. On the one hand, they are criticized because of high costs, the risk of individual conflicts and practical difficulties; on the other hand, formally documented land rights are most often put forward as necessary for the future safeguarding of smallholders' land rights and for the development of agricultural productivity.

The price of land

The price of land is a classic discussion in agricultural economics, well known from works by late eighteenth and early nineteenth century British economists, such as Adam Smith, Thomas Malthus and David Ricardo. Their reasoning focused on land and the costs of land in relation to demographic changes, food supply, productivity, land rent, landlords and farm labour. Some, but not all, of this is still relevant, which gives agricultural economics an honourable position in economics in general.

The price of land combines complex economic theory and the specific characteristics of agriculture. We will, however, leave the theoretical aspects of price formation for other studies, but mention that land values, among other things, take account of present values of expected future earnings of production, and the attractiveness of agricultural land as an investment in comparison with alternative investment objects. In the following we will concentrate on factors of importance for the price of purchased farmland, but add some aspects on the price of leasehold land at the end.

One of the factors influencing price is whether the land is sold on the open market or within the family or to other preferred buyers. If the latter, we can expect that the price is reduced in order to facilitate the transfer, for example to the younger generation. The price may also be reduced if the land use is put under some kind of constraint, for example by upper limits on animal production, or by building restrictions. Moreover, the price of land depends on the categories of potential buyers. If an area is of interest for farming only, the price is generally more closely related to the value of production than if non-farming interests are involved, such as actors searching for land for urban expansion. Below, we will focus on land values in terms of farming and address investment aspects later.

Land values in terms of farming

Land is a capital asset, for landowning farmers and for landowning investors of varying kind, but although farmers may benefit from land as a capital asset. We can assume that farmers primarily consider land values in terms of factors that are important for farm production, such as:

- Land category: arable or pasture land
- Location with respect to climate and other nature related factors

- Location in view of economic and social conditions
- Location of the particular area, in case of purchase of additional land
- Soil fertility
- Field forms
- Eventual irrigation possibilities
- Roads, drainage, terraces, fences and other facilities
- Eventual subsidies or other payments linked to the particular acreage

Generally speaking arable land is more expensive than permanent pasture land, although the ratios vary. The geographic location is particularly decisive, but communications and physical distances can be important as well, in view of sale of the product and access to services, labour, schools, hospitals, shops, cultural events and daily social contacts. Box 9.6 illustrates these aspects with an example that compares prices of remotely and centrally located farmland.

In addition to differences between arable and pasture land and where the land is situated, the exact position of a field can be of great interest to already established farmers who are looking for additional land. Further on the list of price influencing factors, the quality of a specific field is of central importance: the natural soil fertility, field forms, irrigation opportunities, terraces, ditches and other investments that have been made in the particular piece of land. You will read more about these aspects in Chapters 10, 11 and 12. Besides, fields that enable cultivation of special crops, such as grapes or vegetables, can achieve comparatively high prices.

Box 9.6 The price of land and geographic location

In 2010 arable land cost approximately ten times more in the very south of Sweden than far up in the north. The enormous gap is to some degree explained by the more favourable farming conditions in the warmer south, which is reminiscent of Denmark and in part is influenced by Danish land price levels. The difference in price between southern and northern Sweden is, however, also explained by the pressure on land resources down south, where urban expansion and intensive farming compete for the same areas of fertile land. The situation is more or less reversed in the remote north, where the supply of farmland exceeds the demand for farming and where other competing interests are few. A farmer with ambitions in dairy farming, almost the only relevant kind of full-time farming in the north, can thus expand the acreage at a reasonable cost. In addition, it is common for active farmers in the north to be offered land on lease for almost nothing. Still, long cold winters and short intense summers pose special requirements for methods of production, and for the farmer's ability to manage the challenges that come with living and farming in the north.

The final point on the list refers to situations when there are farm subsidies which are coupled to the possession of land, which may be reflected in the price of land, for example in the EU. Where several farmers are interested in the same piece of land the price may, however, exceed what is motivated in view of production. Still, tendencies towards overpricing are primarily due to purposes other than farming.

Farmland as investment

The fact that farmland has double roles, as a necessary resource of production and a capital asset, means that farmers may have to compete with investors who are prepared to pay more than the potential value of production. The pressure from other interested actors is influenced by the relative attractiveness of land in comparison with other available investment objects – although agricultural land is a more complicated asset than those in electronic format only.

The many practical requirements that come with land ownership seem to have served as a shelter against widespread speculation in land, but current tendencies indicate that farmland is becoming more attractive, which, among other things, is illustrated by the previously discussed so-called land grabbing.

In a particular case, the attractiveness of the area is decisive for the price, which can be pushed to unprecedented heights when the land is of interest for urban expansion, infrastructure or tourism. You can see this all over the world, where suburbs, road networks, factories and airports are spreading out on fertile agricultural land at high speed.

Furthermore, the price of agricultural land is impacted by financing and interest rates. Generally speaking, we can assume that farmers have limited assess to capital and have to manage the costs of land within the farm budget, which has to be balanced from season to season irrespective of eventual long-term capital gains. In contrast, investors with other financial situations and aims for the land may apply other strategies and have other funding opportunities.

Prices for the lease of arable and pasture lands

Many of the aforementioned price influencing factors are relevant for the lease of farmland too. Leases do, however, require more caution, compared with purchase. While the buyer can benefit from both production and capital gains, the costs of a lease generally have to be in direct proportion to what it is possible to earn from production. The close links between the costs of a lease and revenues from production may be apparent. Bad payments for beef may, for example, be directly mirrored in lowered costs for the lease of pasture land, presuming that the fee is not fixed.

The leasehold market can, however, also, like the market for sale, be exposed to competition, albeit chiefly between farmers. Due to this competition the price level can sometimes be surprisingly high, especially when several neighbours compete for the same strategically located area. For similar reasons remote districts can experience the opposite situation, where land may be for rent almost for free, for example from retired farmers who are not prepared to sell but wish to see the land actively farmed.

Summary

Land rights and how these are practised are highly decisive for farming practices, such as methods of production, investments and planning horizons. Moreover, the forms under which farmers have access to land are key factors for the global and national use of land, and for the global production of food and other farm products. Land rights can be problematic, in both market and subsistence oriented farming, but poor smallholders especially are frequently exposed and most vulnerable to unsafe leases, based on short-term and unreliable oral agreements.

Agricultural land is generally accessed through ownership, leasehold or communal land rights, sometimes in combination. The landowner category includes active or passive private landowners, but also various kinds of companies. Leasehold is common in both market and subsistence oriented farming worldwide. We find large, complete farms on leases; leasehold land that is operated in addition to an established farm; and rented small plots for subsistence production. The two main principles for the payment of leases are fixed or shared rent, both practised in various kinds of farming. Customary land rights belong to and are controlled by a local community whose members, generally speaking, have the right to utilize the land. Due to the traditional character of customary land, the rights are seldom recorded in written documents and are currently decreasing almost day by day.

We have also discussed problems with so-called overseas land grabbing, and given attention to poor, almost landless, people's use of land without permission in rural as well as urban areas. Furthermore, matters of access to land are considered from the perspective of land reforms, which often aim at improved livelihoods in the countryside through the splitting of large farming units into smallholdings. The final topic in this chapter deals with the price of land. Farmland prices are discussed in terms of farming and the fact that land is a capital asset too, but also in terms of the costs of land on lease.

Next

In Chapter 10 we will move from legal and economic perspectives on farmland to concrete physical land areas at farm level. As a point of departure you will read about the number of the world's farms and their acreage, and about how the term farm can be defined in various countries. The reasoning then continues with more detailed aspects about field forms, farm structures and the location of fields, buildings and other facilities within a farm. These aspects are fundamental and vital parts of the running of a farm and of everyday life at the holding.

To discuss

- Reflect on the differences between farmland and other assets, such as a suburban house and a brand new car.
- Compare the pros and cons of land ownership and leasehold, with the help of additional sources and interviews with farmers, if possible.
- Imagine two different farms with land on lease and discuss whether fixed or shared rent seems to be the best form of payment.
- Study customary land rights in a Sub-Saharan African country of special interest to you, with special attention to current trends and problems.
- Discuss so-called land grabbing from the perspective of local small-holders in an area that has attracted an international farming company.
- Look for examples of urban farming, of the kind described in this chapter, in the real world or with the help of electronic resources.
- Choose a region where some kind of land reform has taken place, recently or in earlier times. Try to find out as much as possible about the character of the land reform, motives, the actors involved, and short- and long-term results.
- Study the market for agricultural land by comparing character, supply, prices, areas, buildings and more specific kinds of information on the websites of some estate agents in different countries.

10 Farms and fields

This far we have been talking about arable and pasture lands in terms of aggregated areas without reflecting much about what farms and fields look like in reality. This chapter has a more detailed perspective on these matters, although it starts with the approximate number of farms around the globe. We will also discuss farm sizes and differences between large-scale farming and so-called factory-like agricultural production.

Your attention will then be turned to the farm level. We will give attention to hectares and acres, and to the fact that the same number of hectares can have the most varying shape with respect to slopes, field forms and number of separate fields or plots. These kinds of conditions are important for how the individual farm is organized and for what the daily work looks like. If different parts of the farm, such as arable fields, grazing areas, water and storage, are spread out, a lot of time may be spent on transportation and walking, which hardly contributes to productivity as such. Finally, we will take a look at the organization of two different farms, one highly market oriented Danish farm and one mainly subsistence oriented smallholding in Uganda.

After this chapter you are expected to:
- Be familiar with the approximate number of farms around the world
- Be familiar with the approximate number of farms of different acreages
- Be able to discuss agricultural production in terms of large-scale farming versus so-called factory-like agricultural production as defined in this chapter
- Be aware of current tendencies of increased polarization between very small and very big farming units
- Be able to define hectares and acres
- Be able to give examples of various types of irregular field forms and reflect on the practical impact on how the farm is operated
- Have a fair idea of how a farm can be organized in terms of spatial distribution of fields and other essential features, preferably by studying detailed maps

Key words

Farm size, smallholding, large-scale, factory-like, polarization, hectare, acre, field forms, field distribution, spatial organization.

Approximately 0.5 billion farm holdings around the world

Counting the world's farm holdings is a challenge that at best can result in estimates. You have already, in previous chapters, been reminded of the difficulties in transforming the reality of world farming into comparable statistical figures. As discussed in Chapter 9, many farms are based on combinations of ownership, leasehold and other kinds of land rights, of which some are registered, some not. This makes it difficult to know the exact number of farming units and, even more, the acreage utilized and the number of farm animals, albeit some countries have access to quite reliable national statistics.

New problems arise when national statistics are to be put together into comparable international figures. One of the problems is that the statistical definition of the term farm holding differs from country to country, not least when it comes to minimum requirements to be counted as a farm. This means that international summaries include smallholdings that are perceived as farm units in some countries but not in others. It is, however, important to state that even estimates are useful and serve as valuable tools, albeit sometimes more indicative than exact, for our understanding of the world of agriculture.

We will return to this discussion later on and study some examples of different ways of defining a farm (Box 10.1), but before that it is interesting to get a general idea about the approximate number of farm holdings and their acreages at an aggregated global scale, as shown in Table 10.1. The table derives from an often referred to study, presented by the International Food Policy Research Institute (IFPRI) and the former head of the institute, Joachim von Braun.

Table 10.1 shows a polarized world of farming, a world where smallholdings with less than two hectares dominate totally in numbers, whereas comparatively few farms are found in the upper categories. According to the table, as much as 85 per cent of all farm holdings in the world have less than two hectares of land and almost 97 per cent have at most 10 hectares. Even though our perception of small and big farms differs with the context, the table clearly demonstrates that most of the world's farmers are smallholders. In contrast, less than 3 per cent, or about 14 million, have between 10 and 100 hectares, and only 0.6 per cent more than 100 hectares.

Most likely the many smallholdings are highly subsistence oriented and thus have difficulty managing expenditures for production. We can therefore assume that a majority of all farms in the world are operated with the help of much manual labour but few or even no purchased input resources. In contrast, the relatively

Table 10.1 Number of farm holdings in the world and their acreage

Land area per farm	Approximate number of farms in the world	Share of all farms in the world, %
0.1–2 hectares	451	85
2–10 hectares	62	11.7
10–100 hectares	14	2.7
More than 100 hectares	3	0.6
Approximate total number of farms in the world	530	100

Source: Adapted from von Braun 2011: 9.

few large farms can be expected to produce for the market, with high yields and on the basis of high or relatively high flows of purchased resources such as fertilizer, seed, agro-chemicals and farm machinery. So, the few large farms account for large shares of all commercial input resources in agriculture and produce comparably large proportions of global production. It is also safe to suggest that the farms in the upper categories provide major amounts of the nationally and internationally traded quantities of food, fibre and bio-energy. Most of the food that is supplied to non-farming food consumers is thus likely to have been produced by relatively few producers.

The large number of smallholders should obviously not be understood as if small-holding farming dominates world agriculture in each and every aspect. Large-scale farming impacts the global and national agricultural sectors heavily, operates over large areas, produces high yields per hectare and animal, and dominates supermarket shelves across the world. Still, according to Joachim von Braun, 'Large farms are a minority, both in numbers and in coverage of land area' (von Braun 2011: 9).

The enormous number of farms means that even more people are more or less intensively engaged in farming and food production. Roughly, very roughly, the more than 0.5 billion holdings might be home to more than two billion people. As you will see from Box 10.1, many of these households can hardly be expected to survive on farming, but rather have it as a basis, or even just a complement to other ways of making a living. Even though we are talking about poor households it is worth reflecting on the global situation from a somewhat reverse perspective, namely that about two out of every seven people have some access to home pro-duced food, while the remaining five are totally dependent on food via the market.

Farms: a plethora of definitions

In the following we will take a closer look at the many different ways of defining farms in various parts of the world. The reasoning is based on information from the *2000 World Census of Agriculture*, which is an important source of informa-tion for global agriculture. The census has been conducted by the FAO since 1950, and has since then been published every decade. The material is frequently used and is, for instance, referred to as the underlying source for Table 10.1.

The most recent report, *2000 World Census of Agriculture* (FAO 2010a), was published in 2010 and includes agricultural statistics collected between 1996 and 2005. Some figures may thus be ten years older than others. The census includes information from 114 of the world's around double that number of countries and is thus not complete. Still, the material provides fascinating information about fields, livestock herds and people. Among other things, you can study country reports about numbers of farm holdings and, in most cases, also about the distribution of farm sizes. Most of the contributing countries define a farm on the basis of a minimum area and/or other minimum criteria, such as lowest numbers of farm animals, although with wide variations. In Box 10.1 you can see some of the minimum requirements for to be counted as a farm in the *2000 World Census*.

Box 10.1 What is a farm? Some country examples as defined in the *2000 World Census*

Canada: a 'census farm was defined as an agricultural operation that produces at least one of the following products intended for sale: Crops (hay, field crops, fruit or nut trees, berries or grapes, vegetables, seed); Livestock (cattle, pigs, sheep, horses, game animals, other livestock); Poultry (hens, chickens, turkeys, chicks, game birds, other poultry); Animal products (milk or cream, eggs, wool, furs, meat); Other agricultural products (Christmas trees, greenhouse or nursery products, mushrooms, sod, honey, maple syrup products).'

Egypt: 'Holdings with land must have at least 12 Sahm (87.5 square meters) land used wholly or partly for agricultural production (i.e. plants, livestock, poultry and fisheries).' 'The land could be under any tenure form. It includes livestock, un-reclaimed areas (waste land), buildings and aquacultures.' 'Holdings without land are considered as holdings if they have a minimum of one head of cattle, buffaloes or camels; or five heads of sheep or goats, or a combination of them; or hundred poultry; or ten beehives; or one fishery cage; or the ownership of one agricultural machine, or sharing it, used in agriculture. Units possessing only pigs or draught animals such as donkeys and mules are not considered as agricultural holdings.'

Germany: holdings 'with an area used for agriculture of two hectares or more or a minimum stock of animals (8 bovines, 8 pigs, 20 sheep, 200 laying hens/broilers/geese) or producing special crops (0.3 ha of vineyards/hops/tobacco/tree nurseries/outdoor flowers/market gardening and cultivation under glass cover/medicinal plants); holdings with a wooded area of at least 10 ha.'

India: 'Operational Holding (the statistical unit): is defined as all land wholly or partly used for agricultural (crop) production and operated as one technical unit by one person, alone or with others, without regard to title, legal form, size or location.'

Indonesia: 'Household Agricultural Holding: A household [is] categorized as an agricultural holding if one or more of the members of household do at least one of the following activities: cultivates crops (rice, secondary crop, horticulture crops, and estates crops), cultivates forest tree, breeds wild-life animals, livestock/poultry, cultivates fish, collects forest product and/or captures wild animals, and renders agricultural services.'

Iran: 'Holdings covered in the census satisfied at least one of the following conditions: Having/operating: 400 m^2 of land under temporary crops; or 200 m^2 of horticultural and permanent crops; or 2 head of sheep or goats; or 1 head of cattle or camel; or 10 head of poultry; or a greenhouse of any scale; or Silk worms keeping (sericulture) of any scale; or Honey bees keeping (apiculture) of any scale.'

Italy: 'The census unit was defined as a technical-economic unit of agricultural production including forestry and livestock production, consisting of one or more plots of land, even non-contiguous or located in different municipalities, consisting also of agricultural machinery and/or buildings for agricultural production, operated by a holder (physical person, company or public body) assuming the risk of management, alone or together with others.'

Jordan: 'For census purposes, an agricultural holding is enumerated if reporting an area of at least one dunum (1000 square meters). Holdings without land are also considered for census purposes, if reporting at least one of the following: Ten sheep; Ten goats; One head of cattle; Three camels; Five beehives.'

Mongolia: 'Livestock holding is any household or enterprise with livestock for agricultural production. No threshold is applied.'

Nicaragua: 'Agricultural holding (Explotación Agropecuaria, EA) is all land totally or partially exploited inside a municipality as a techno-economic unit of agricultural production under single management, regardless of size, title or legal form. An agricultural holding could be a landless holding, either located in rural or in urban areas.'

Tanzania: 'The agricultural holdings were restricted to those meeting one of the following conditions: – Having or operated at least 25 sq. metres of arable land; – Owning or keeping at least one head of cattle or five goats/sheep/pigs or fifty chickens/ducks/turkeys, during the reference year.'

Venezuela: 'Agricultural holding was defined as an economic unit of agricultural production under single management, comprising all livestock kept and all land used wholly or partly for agricultural purposes, without regard to title and legal form. Places with less than the minimum size, abandoned holdings and those used only for recreation, were not considered as agricultural holdings.'

Source: FAO 2010a.

The quotations are word for word but the text has been restructured for practical reasons. As you can see, the definitions give exciting glimpses of what farming looks like in the countries referred to.

According to the colourful mixture in Box 10.1 the minimum acreage to be defined as an agricultural holding varies widely, from 25 square metres or less, up to a minimum acreage of two hectares. Farms with less than 0.1 hectares are, however, not included in the number of farms in Table 10.1. Moreover, Box 10.1 gives you an idea about the number of different farm animals that you can expect to come across on a smallholding in the countries illustrated. In addition, the descriptions highlight more specific characteristics, such as Christmas trees, maple syrup, medicinal plants, wildlife, silk worms, beehives, urban farming and the exclusion of holdings used for recreation.

Statistical information cannot, however, cover all characteristics. Even neighbouring farms can in fact be expected to differ in one way or another, even if they may seem identical at first glance. If you are going to work with an advisory service, as a veterinarian or in another kind of job that includes visits to many farms, you will probably find that there are hardly two identical farms, or farm systems (see Box 10.2), and thus come to come to agree with the following quotation that claims that

Figure 10.1 Smallholding with poultry and some household gardening. Greece, 2008.
Photo: Carin Martiin.

Box 10.2 Farms can be seen as systems

A farm can be understood as a system that is organized in order to produce food, fibre, bio-energy and/or other non-foods. Farm systems are considered differently by various authors but can be described as the sum of a number of elements: arable fields, pastures, forest land, farm centre with varying kinds of houses and facilities for people and farm animals, outdoor storage facilities, wells, ponds, ditches, fences, pathways and arrangements for energy supply.

A holistic approach also includes impact of nature, resource flows, social, economic and political aspects, and various forms of interactions. See also Figure 17.1 in Chapter 17.

Each individual farm has its own specific characteristics arising from variations in resource endowments and family circumstances. The household, its resources, and the resource flows and interactions at this individual farm level are together referred to as a *farm system*.

(Dixon *et al.* 2001: 8)

Matters of farm sizes are in part relative

How about small, medium-sized and big farms? A general answer to this question is almost impossible, at least at the global scale. Even though acreage and herd sizes provide some guidance, we have to consider where the farm is situated before it is possible to get a fair idea of the situation. Matters of farm sizes can thus in a way be understood as relative; with differences between countries and regions, and over time as well. A five hectare holding can be seen as fairly large in many countries south of the Sahara, whereas the same area may be deemed much too small for professional farming and may instead serve as a hobby farm in, for example, the UK, where full-time farmers often operate hundreds of hectares. In the latter kind of countries smallholdings have long since lost their former functions as food producing units, and either been included in expanding neighbouring farms or been rebuilt to create attractive country dwellings. We can also find intermediate alternatives as in the Romanian example in Chapter 3, Box 3.4, where seven hectares of arable land, plus pastures and livestock, were said to contribute to substantial parts of the household economy, at the same time as it was necessary to have additional income from off-farm work.

In spite of the previous argument for farm sizes being relative there is no doubt that farms with hundreds or thousands of hectares can be understood as big. Large or very large farming units are found on all continents, although large-scale

Box 10.3 Big landed properties

Large farm units can have the most varied backgrounds, for instance in European estates from medieval times; huge ranches in North America and Australia established during the nineteenth century; Latin American haciendas and plantations in Africa and Asia, deriving from colonial times. In the US and many parts of Europe previously modest-sized farms have been enlarged through additional purchase or lease. Recently large-scale farms are also being created in other ways, such as the previously discussed land-grabbing phenomenon in Sub-Saharan Africa, and in Russia, where international conglomerates for large-scale farming invest in land that previously was operated in the form of kolkhozes, the large-scale collective farms in the former Soviet Union.

farming is more common in some parts of the world than in others. You can read a little more about big farms and their various backgrounds in Box 10.3.

Factory-like agricultural production

In connection with large-scale farming some words should be said about the expressions industrial farming and factory farming. Both terms are frequently heard in critical discussions about methods of production, food quality, animal ethics and environmental impact. Large-scale farming as such is often perceived as the same as industrial or factory farming, but in this book a distinction is made between these and large-scale farming. Moreover, the longer term factory-like agricultural production is preferred instead of just industrial or factory farming.

As a point of departure for our definition, we will consider whether or not the production is connected to adjacent land. It is suggested that the term large-scale farming is used when the production is dependent on land nearby, and therefore also on the sun, rain and other natural forces that impact the surroundings. This is the case when a large-scale farm combines the production of tens of thousands of hogs with thousands of hectares that provide at least part of the feed, and to which manure from the animals is recycled. According to our point of departure, the same kind of hog production would be considered as factory-like if the animals were only fed on purchased feed that is transported to the hog plant from else-where. You may also come into contact with combinations of large-scale arable farming and factory-like production in one place, if all crops are sold while the animals are supplied with purchased feed from the outside, often in the form of ready-made feed from a feed processing plant.

The factory-like production plant can thus be located almost anywhere, and production can go on virtually irrespective of the weather and crop growth just outside the stable. According to the suggested definition, the term factory farming can hardly be applied to arable farming, but rather to intensive production of tens or hundreds of thousands of hogs or chicken, of eggs, and to gigantic plants for fish farming and greenhouse cultivation.

Big farms are getting even bigger

Farm units that are already very large often continue to grow. Many individual farmers as well as farming companies find their acreage is insufficient to manage increasing costs of machinery, labour, energy and other inputs at the same time as prices paid per kilo for grain and meat have, generally speaking, decreased over time. The solution is in many cases found in economies of scale, in additional land areas and in enlarged numbers of livestock. Tendencies like these have a long history in, for example, Western Europe and North America, where the changes should be seen in the light of industrialization and urbanization that called for increased productivity and efficiency. Consequently farms that were previously tens of hectares have successively become hundreds and thousands, at the same time as the number of farmers has drastically reduced.

In parallel with the enlarged acreage of some farms, almost all smallholdings have more or less disappeared as economic units of agricultural production and mid-sized farms have become increasingly rare. At the same time the rural landscape has often become more monotonous, and the distances between farm centres and people engaged in farming have increased. You may have observed these processes yourself and/or heard the issue discussed by older generations, at least if your major point of reference applies to societies like those described above. Globally, quite the reverse changes are also occurring. If you are more familiar with smallholder farming for a living, you may instead have observed that already smallholdings are being divided into even smaller units, with areas that are only a fraction of a hectare.

The fact that already big units are getting bigger while already small ones are getting even smaller can be said to be typical of the present changes in the global agricultural landscape. As a result we have bigger differences than ever between the world's farmers. You will find more about differences in practices and outcomes in Part IV, where practices in crop and animal production are discussed. In the following we will study what farms can look like in terms of areas and spatial organization. Much of the reasoning is valid irrespective of size, but you will not have any problem applying features such as field slopes and distances between fields or parcels to either big or small units. First, we will pay attention to ways of measuring land.

Hectares and acres

The term hectare has already been used innumerable times in the previous chapters, not least in Chapter 6, where global and national areas of arable and pasture land were discussed. Although you have already got used to the term, some special attention to these matters may be helpful.

Figure 10.2 Harvester in a landscape that was previously divided between several mid-sized units. Sweden, 2011.

Photo: Carin Martiin.

The hectare (ha) serves as the international unit for land area. It is easy to state that a hectare is 10,000 square metres, but it can be less easy to transfer the figures to reality. If the field is regular it is useful to know that a hectare is the same as a quadrangle with 100 metre sides. Another common unit of measurement is the international acre, which is the same as 4,047 square metres, or 0.4047 of a hectare. The two units of measurement are demonstrated in Figure 10.3, which also gives a hint about the proportions between the two, although the scale is not exact.

If the square A in Figure 10.3 is transformed into an area of 100 hectares we have to do with a square with 1,000 metre (one kilometre) sides, or four kilometres circumference. Moving to B, the circumference means about 2.8 kilometres walking around the outer edge.

Figure 10.3 One hectare, theoretically a square of 100 × 100 metres, compared with one acre, illustrated as a rectangle of 100 × 40.47 metres. The scale is indicative but not exact.

As you can see in Figure 10.4 below irregular fields mean longer outer edges and are harder to estimate in terms of hectares and acres, or other ways of measuring land, such as the chinese mu or dunum in the Jordan example in Box 10.1. A lot of information in agricultural matters is given in hectares, such as:

* Yields per hectare
* Recommended quantities of sowing seed, fertilizer and pesticides
* Farm machine capacity
* Irrigation
* Payment for some kind of work, such as manual weeding
* Payment of a lease
* Comparisons of land prices, as in Chapter 9, Box 9.6
* Several questions in matters of land, for instance carbon sequestration in pasture lands

Irregular farmland

Regular fields like those in Figure 10.3 certainly exist but a great deal of the farmed areas around the world are irregular in one way or another. While some farmers cultivate almost endless fields with neither slopes nor irregularities, many others have to navigate along terrace edges and ditches, between trees and bushes, and up and down steep hillsides. This requires more experience and takes time, which means more labour, traction and energy.

Figure 10.4 illustrates some irregularities seen from the side: slopes, ditches and terraces.

Figure 10.4 A piece of arable land seen from the side. A. plain field. B. steep slope. C. open ditch. D. terraces.

The plain surface A and the slope B in Figure 10.4 can generally be assumed to mirror natural conditions, even though human activities may have made the field even plainer. Moreover, stones, trees and holes may have been taken away, and previously open ditches may have been covered, with these changes accomplished at one time, or little by little by generations of farmers. In contrast to such clearing efforts, the ditch C and the terraces D are constructions made in order to support farming, for example the need to regulate water (see Chapter 12) or to make it possible to cultivate slopes.

In Figure 10.5 you can see some irregular forms from above. Irregular field forms are, among other things, framed by the surrounding terrain, water streams, roads across the field, fences, etc. You may, for instance, also find bushes, trees, ponds, stones, open ditches, buildings or windmills in arable fields. All this is not illustrated in the figure, which has a comparative approach, with an emphasis on differences due to field forms, scattered fields and the presence of various elements within arable fields.

The letter A in Figure 10.5 shows the total area as one regular field, which offers optimal rationality with regard to tillage and other practical operations. The farm centre, x, is comfortably located, surrounded by the land. Moving on to farm B, you find approximately the same acreage but with more irregular form and crossed by a road, which in practice means that the area has to be cultivated as two separate parts. Alternative C shows how the same total area is spread out in four places. The grey mark inside the field top right illustrates some kind of element that not is part of the cultivation, for example a pond, and the field bottom right includes two open ditches, which in practice means three separate areas. The farmer of C thus has six irregular fields to manage, which, as mentioned, brings about notably more work and other costs of production in comparison with alternatives A and B. The examples in Figure 10.5 refer to a total area of one hectare, typical of many smallholdings, but the same principles can be applied to larger areas too, although the impact decreases with increased area.

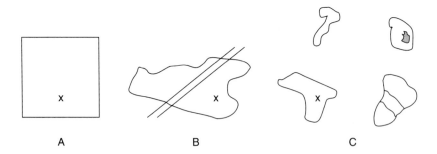

A   B   C

Figure 10.5 A, B and C all illustrate the same total arable area, although they differ with respect to number of fields, field form and the presence of other elements. The total area is thought of as one hectare per farm, but could be ten or hundreds of hectares. The impact of complicating field forms can, however, be assumed to decrease with increased area. The letter x indicates the farm centre.

According to the *2000 World Census of Agriculture*, a few parcels or fields is the most common alternative, but many countries report around ten parcels or more, for example the Philippines, Turkey and Chile. Portugal specifies the number of holdings with twenty parcels or more, and Spain and Cyprus have separate categories for farming units with as many as fifty parcels or more. Remembering the often diffuse forms for leasehold (Chapter 9), we can assume that many farmers operate additional fields that are not reflected in the official statistics.

In spite of the practical disadvantages of scattered farm structures, there are also some advantages. Having the fields spread out, with, for example, forest land in between, can reduce the risk of the spread of weeds, plant diseases and harmful insects. It can also be favourable to have fields or plots at slightly different sites in the landscape. As we will discuss further in Chapter 11, soils and other natural conditions can differ locally, for example with regard to soil fertility, exposure to soil erosion and the risk of frost. Depending on the character of the landscape, irregular and relatively small fields can also be positive in terms of biodiversity and beautiful, small-scale agricultural landscapes.

The spatial organization of a farm

Where fields are situated and livestock kept, how storage is arranged, and where the people engaged in farming are living is enormously decisive for the organization and efficiency of daily work, for production, and for the total result. Scattered structures and bad organization bring about a waste of time that otherwise could have been used productively. The time used for driving around or walking long distances between the farm centre and fields that are spread out in the landscape can differ greatly between farms, and can make a considerable difference in terms of total working hours and costs of tractor and animal traction. This reasoning is also valid for the spatial organization of functions such as water sources, tools, machinery and the storing of animal feed and manure.

The spatial organization of a holding is also important for communication between people and for the ability to keep a close eye on all parts of production. It is also interesting to consider where the farm is situated in relation to the surrounding local society. How long does it take to get in touch with neighbours, and what are the distances to schools, health care, local markets and different kinds of farm service? As a summarizing final part of this chapter, we will study the spatial organization of two fictitious farms, one highly market oriented Danish farm (Figure 10.6), and one primarily subsistence oriented Ugandan smallholding (Figure 10.7). The first example shows a farm with more than 200 hectares of arable land and intensive pig production, situated just outside a small Danish town.

As you can see from Figure 10.6, the Danish farm cultivates both owned land and areas on lease. The farm structure shows the last decades' successive expansion during which the total arable area has been tripled. Area B used to be a separate farm that was operated by a relative, but was then added to this farm.

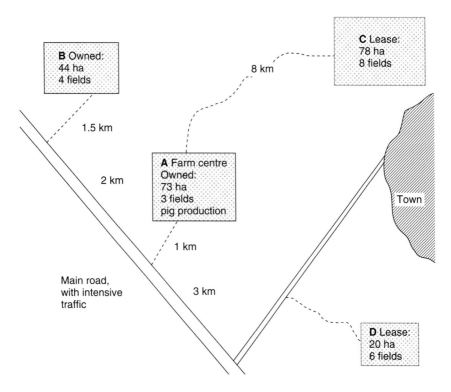

Figure 10.6 A 200 hectare Danish farm with the farm centre A and arable land situated at A, B, C and D. The dotted lines indicate small roads and the double lines show main roads. The farm is not drawn to scale.

The house and a horse paddock were sold as a hobby farm, which helped finance the purchase. At 8 kilometres distance from the farm centre A, area C marks 78 hectares that are leased from an organization that is primarily interested in the land as a long-term inflation-proof investment. The location close to the town makes the area attractive for urban expansion, which worries the farmer. The lease is for two-year periods only and may not be extended. Area D is less risky, as the owner is an old retired friend who would never see his land asphalted over. Today 215 hectares of arable land are cultivated, spread out over 21 fields in the flat Danish landscape. The relatively long distances make transportation and planning a central issue in the organization of daily work, which is conducted by the husband and a part-time employee, while the wife works as an architect in the nearby town. Many of the fields are almost regular, with areas between 30 and 40 hectares on which wheat, barley, rape seed and sugar beets are grown. Much of this is sold, but some is used for the intensive pig production that used to provide a substantial part of the total farm income, but recently has been troubled by falling prices.

The pigs are also problematic because of the difficulty of spreading manure close to the town, from which negative comments are heard now and then. Still, the nearness to town is appreciated, as it offers schools, sports, shopping, health care, amusements and off-farm employment opportunities for members of the family.

Moving from Denmark to Uganda and the smallholding in Figure 10.7, you will encounter another reality but also some shared similarities, such as a farm structure with the fields spread out at varying distances from the farm centre.

The Ugandan smallholding in Figure 10.7 consists of a total of 3/4 hectare, which is structured as four cultivated parcels that are spread out at various distances from the farm centre. It is also possible to utilize the grove, top left, for grazing animals and collecting firewood and other edible and non-edible resources. The landscape is beautiful, with hills and valleys, and intensively cultivated slopes along the hillsides. The land is operated individually, but not individually owned. Each parcel includes a number of even smaller plots where, for example, beans, maize, bananas and potatoes are grown. The distances between the parcels are comparatively short but plot 4 in Figure 10.7 is located about one kilometre uphill, which involves carrying seed, manure, tools and harvested crops this distance. In addition, children who cannot be left at home and are not yet able to walk may be carried, mostly by women. Almost all products are consumed by the household, such as cassava, sweet potatoes, maize, beans, groundnuts, bananas, vegetables and fruits, plus products from a cow, about three goats and some poultry. Production is not sufficient for the approximately seven members

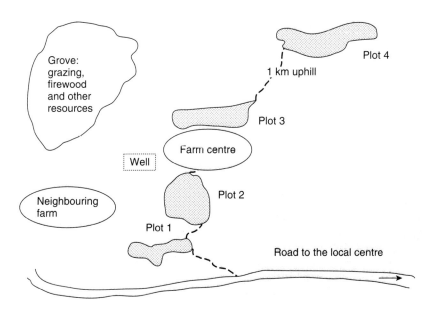

Figure 10.7 Outline of the structure of a Ugandan smallholding, including the farm centre, four plots of arable land and connecting paths. The farm is not drawn to scale.

of the household, not even during the most favourable years. Occasional surpluses can be sold, but the main cash income is the money that is sent back home from relatives who have emigrated to England. Compared with the relative lack of farming neighbours in the Danish example, the Ugandan family is surrounded by farming neighbours of all ages. It is only some 100 metres from the small farmhouse down to the road that leads to the primary school, the small medical station and some shops nearby. The nearest town is situated about two hours' walk away. There is also a bus, at least seasonally, as the road is difficult to use during the short rains, March to May, and the long rains, September to November.

Summary

There are enormous differences in farm sizes. The area ranges from fractions of a hectare to tens of thousands of hectares of arable or pasture land. Most of the world's approximately 0.5 billion farm units are very small, and at best able to supply the household with part of its annual needs. The enormous number of smallholdings can in part be explained by generous definitions of the term farm. In this chapter we have also discussed the fact that farm sizes in part can be seen as relative, depending on the context in which the farm is operated. Moreover, this chapter suggests a definition of factory-like agricultural production as being operated on the basis of resources delivered from elsewhere, without being dependent on the surrounding land. As regards farm sizes, current global trends point to increased polarization: smallholdings are getting even smaller and big ones are getting even bigger. The second half of the chapter focuses on arable and pasture fields at farm level. Hectares and acres are explained and examples given, with special attention to irregularities and how fields and plots are distributed within the farm unit. As a final point, the spatial organization of two fictitious examples has been demonstrated: a large-scale Danish farm and a smallholding in Uganda.

Next

In Chapter 11 you will be introduced to the world beneath the land's surface, to the soil. The reasoning will be relatively detailed and you will learn, among other things, how soils are structured and their functioning.

To discuss

○ Study national farm statistics for a certain country, for example where you live, and compare how the term farm is defined and what this looks like in comparison with your general view of typical farms in this country.

○ Study the *2000 World Census* in more detail than has been possible in this chapter. Focus especially on differences between the countries as regards the reported categories.

○ Consider current tendencies of polarization of farms into very big and very small units respectively. Does this seem to be valid for regions that you are familiar with? Discuss this with someone from an older generation.

○ Study the number of farms in Table 10.1, together with the farm definitions in Box 10.1, and discuss what the situation may look like in the future, in view of ongoing urbanization and population increase.

○ Practise your eye for areas, for example guessing the size of areas in the surroundings, such as arable fields, parks, gardens, parking areas in and other areas by the university or elsewhere.

○ Study field sizes, forms and distribution on some farms with the help of large-scale maps and/or in the real world.

11 Soils, the world beneath the surface

Soil is a key factor in farm production: to be able to grow at all; for the kind of crops that can be grown at different sites, for the methods of production and for the potential yields that can be expected. Furthermore, soils are essential for recycling of water, nutrients and organic matter. Because of these fundamental roles it is hardly possible to grasp matters of farming and the world of agriculture in general without at least some familiarity with soils. You will find that this chapter is more detailed and rich in facts than the previous ones in this book. You might even find some parts a little complicated, but at the same time you will be given the opportunity to get a glimpse of what more specific studies in agriculture may deal with. You will be introduced to a fascinating world beneath the surface, a world that can be seen as a kind of melting pot where air, water, minerals and living organisms meet and interact.

After this chapter you are expected to:

- ○   Be able to account for the main soil functions
- ○   Know the main parts of the soil ecosystem
- ○   Be familiar with the main soil formation factors and the movement of material, water and air within the soil
- ○   Be familiar with the terms soil texture and soil horizon
- ○   Have a fair idea of the main characteristics of sandy soils, loam and clays

Key words

Soil functions, soil ecosystems, mineral and organic matter, soil water, soil air, soil parent material, soil transformation, soil texture, soil horizon, soil colour, sand, silt, clay.

Soils serve numerous vital functions

In contrast to their unpretentious appearance soils are fulfilling many functions of vital importance for all kinds of farm production and for the circulation of resources, such as the global hydrologic cycle and recycling of carbon, oxygen, nitrogen and phosphorus. In this context the soil can be seen as a kind of melting pot where the various spheres meet: air from the atmosphere, water from the hydrosphere, minerals from the lithosphere and living organisms from the biosphere; all meeting in the soil, which is termed the pedosphere. In more detail, soils:

- Serve as the fundament for plants and root systems
- Serve as the medium for physical, chemical and biological processes
- Serve as a habitat for soil organisms, as a kind of playground for soil biodiversity
- Serve as a pool for plant nutrients
- Supply root systems with water
- Supply plants with crop nutrients
- Filter, regulate and store water for plants and other purposes
- Neutralize eventual harmful substances in the soil

The many soil functions on the list have their point of departure in the soil ecosystem. The outcome, in terms of production and recycling, is largely dependent on the type, character and vigour of the ecosystem, which is described in what follows.

Soil ecosystems are full of life

Soils are full of life. Each hectare of agricultural land contains tons of living organisms that have various functions in the soil ecosystem. The Swedish author and Nobel laureate Harry Martinson highlighted the soil ecosystem with a poem about the earthworm, 'the grey little farmer', who constantly and tirelessly works the soil, and thereby improves its fertility and production potential. To understand this kind of relationship between soil organisms and farm yields, you need to know the four main constituents of the soil ecosystem: mineral and organic substances, and soil water and soil air. Figure 11.1 shows the principal construction of the soil ecosystem in the form of a small soil segment, where 'the grey little farmer' and other living organisms are included in the term organic substances.

The share of organic material is usually much smaller than the mineral share. According to an example given by Brady and Weil (1999: 15), loam in good condition may include about 45 per cent mineral and 5 per cent organic matter on the basis of volume. In this case approximately half the volume is solid matter, whereas approximately 20–30 per cent is water and 20–30 per cent is air. The proportions between water and air change in line with the actual water conditions; if there is a lot of water in the soil there is little room for soil air, and vice versa.

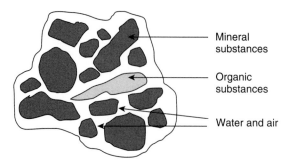

Figure 11.1 Main soil constituents of the soil ecosystem: mineral substances (dark grey), organic substances (light grey), and pores with water and air in varying proportions.

To simplify, the mineral fraction consists of material from the local bedrock, from which minerals are weathering. The weathering is generally a slow process, which successively supplies the soil with dissolved ions. The degree of weathering is thus of great importance for the nutrient supply capacity, although highly weathered soils can be a problem, for example in the humid tropics.

The organic fraction includes living and dead organisms. A single hectare of fertile arable or pasture land includes several tons of living macro and micro organisms. In the upper layers you will find nematodes, mites and earthworms, and further down large amounts of fungi, bacteria, protozoa and actinomy-cetes. You may know of some of these but may not be familiar with the actino-mycetes, which provide the special scent of soil that appears after short rains. An example of the dead organic matter is the more or less completely decom-posed leaves that may be visible to the naked eye during the early stages of decomposition. The final residual fraction that remains after the process of decomposition is termed humus, which is a relatively stable often dark coloured matter of vital importance to the vitality and functioning of the soil ecosystem. The photo in Figure 11.2 shows a piece of soil with some clearly visible mineral and organic substances.

Going back to Figure 11.1, you can see it shows water (soil water) and air (soil air) that fill the space that is not filled with solid matter. The water supplies the soil ecosystem with valuable dissolved nutrients, whereas the soil air provides neces-sary oxygen and other important gases to the system. At first the pores and chan-nels between the mineral and organic particles are filled with water, while air flows into the remaining space. When rain or irrigation increases the amount of water the proportion of air is reduced, as mentioned earlier; and if the soil gets dry a larger share of the pores and channels will be filled with air. The proportions of water and air, not too little and not too much, are crucial for the vitality of the soil ecosystem, for the soil temperature and for the soil formation processes described later. If the soil is drenched with water, all pores will be filled with water, while

Figure 11.2 Close-up photo of a mineral soil with some straw in the early stages of decomposition.
Photo: Carin Martiin.

lack of air soon will be acute, and if an arable field is compacted by heavy machinery, pores and channels will be damaged.

In addition to continuous interaction between the constituents of the soil ecosystem, the system is involved in so-called soil formation processes, through which the soil is continuously shaped and reshaped. In the following you will be introduced to the soil formation processes, which have been going on for millennia and are of the greatest importance to present and future agriculture.

Tens of thousands of soils

A glance at the more than 900-page thick *Keys to Soil Taxonomy* (USDA 1999) from the United States Department of Agriculture (USDA) and Natural Resources Conservation Service reveals that the world's land surface is covered by tens of thousands of different kinds of soils, or even more. You will not be asked to grasp this enormous variety, but rather to be aware of the diversity as such and to learn some basics behind the many nuances.

The diversity in soils means that farmers around the world operate land with the most different potential for production. The variety can be substantial even at local level, where one field may produce twice as much as another within walking distance. The details are often best known by practitioners who have observed and worked with a specific piece of land for many years, experiencing different weather, methods of production and yield levels.

Among the reasons behind the diversity of soils is the fact that soil-forming processes take place in an infinite number of different ways. The processes are based on five main soil-forming factors, which you find illustrated in Figure 11.3.

The first soil-forming factor in Figure 11.3 is the parent material (1), which usually is the local rock and its content of minerals. Alternatively the mineral parent matter consists of deposits that have been transported to the site by water or wind, such as eroded sand, loess and volcanic ash. Clay made of glacial drift far back in the Earth's early history is another example. The parent material can, however, also be of organic origin, which is the case for peat and muck where the organic share is so high that, when the soil is classified, it is considered a parent material constituent, rather than a complement to the minerals.

Second, the many organisms (2) in the soil are important for the character of the soil at large, and impact the soil structure, the content of nutrients and humus, and the ability of soil to store air and water. In arable land the content of organic matter is favoured by recycling of animal manure and crop residues. The added biomass can be expected to encourage the soil biodiversity that in turn is beneficial for continued decomposition of the organic matter. The importance of caring for and even increasing the amount of organic matter in soils is currently highlighted as one of the great challenges for increased sustainability in the management of soils around the globe.

As regards the climate (3), rain, snow and temperature are the most influential features. Proper humidity in combination with high temperature stimulates weathering and the decomposition of organic residues, whereas dry conditions mean slower changes in the soil. Differences like these contribute to different soil characteristics, for example to varying proportions between mineral and organic substances.

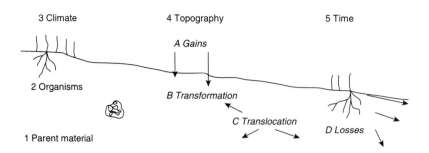

Figure 11.3 Overview of the soil-forming processes. Nos. 1–5 show the main soil-forming factors: parent material, organisms, climate, topography and time. The letters A–D and the arrows indicate movement: gains from the surface, transformations and translocations within the soil, and losses. To the right of parent material and organisms you can see a reduced, albeit still oversized, version of Figure 11.1, which thereby connects Figures 11.1 and 11.3.

Furthermore, the topography (4) has to be considered. Topography impacts local temperatures, humidity and wind, and can be of decisive importance for the local farming. Fine soil particles tend to be moved downwards, especially when the soil is laid bare. Thus the fine and usually more fertile soil material accumulates in valleys, while coarser material remains on higher sites. This kind of process increases if the land is exposed to strong forces of erosion, for example if permanent grasslands are grazed too intensively.

The time factor (5) can be a matter of relatively rapid changes, such as soil erosion which can be visible from one year to another. Generally speaking, however, soil formation processes are extremely slow processes of change, such as bedrock weathering. Before we move on to the different kinds of movement of soil matter, the soil formation processes should be summarized through the following quotation:

> At each location on the land, the earth's surface has experienced a particular combination of influences from the five soil-forming factors, causing a different set of layers (horizons) to form in each part of the landscape, thus slowly giving rise to the natural bodies we call **soils**.
>
> (Brady and Weil 1999: 65)

Further, the letters A–D in Figure 11.3 also illustrate how material is added to the soil from the surroundings, transformed and translocated in the ground, and lost through leakage or in other ways. Material is gained (A) by the soil through the adding of material to the surface, for example straw and animal manure (Figure 11.2), and through processes in the ground. Through weathering and decomposition the mineral and organic substances are transformed (B) and successively translocated (C) to other parts of the soil. In some cases the processes include accumulation, but further movement in others, often in the form of leakage to the ground water, rivers or the sea (D). Some of the outflows from the soil ecosystem are natural parts of the water, nitrogen and phosphorus cycles, but present large-scale losses of crop nutrients are a big problem for farmers, who lose valuable crop nutrients, and, not least, from the environmental point of view.

Remembering the Danish and Ugandan examples in Chapter 10, it is easy to understand that the temperate climate and flat landscape in Denmark mean different kinds of soil-forming processes than in the tropical climate and hilly terrain in the Ugandan example.

Systematizing soils

How is it then possible to grasp thousands of different soils? Soil science classifies soils systematically in six levels, from orders down to series, which is reminiscent of the Linnaean taxonomy of the eighteenth century. Classification of soils is to a large extent based on observable attributes, such as the soil texture, the so-called soil horizon and the colour of the soil. There is more than one system, among them the World Reference Base for Soil Resources (WRB). The systematization includes practical field work in the form of digging, testing of the soil texture between the fingers and examination of different soil layers and their colour nuances.

Soil textures

The examination of soil textures focuses on the proportions between clay, silt and sand in a particular soil. The term clay is used for the finest mineral particles, silt for medium-sized particles and sand for relatively coarse particles. The particle size is of great importance for the soil characteristics, such as water holding capacity and response to drought. The finer the particles and the larger the share of fine particles, the higher is the capacity to hold water and nutrients, whereas water and nutrient leakage can be high in soils with large proportions of big particles. These relationships are logical and easy to grasp if you go back to Figure 11.1 and imagine that the big mineral particles are replaced by many small ones with small pores and channels in between.

All soils include greater or lesser quantities of clay, silt and sand; loam soils, for instance, contain combinations of 7–27 per cent clay, 28–50 per cent silt and less than 52 per cent sand. The proportions of clay, silt and sand can elegantly be determined with help of the so-called soil texture triangle, shown in Figure 11.4. The figure shows a simplified version, without the many details that are found in more detailed versions of the triangle.

It is relatively easy to get an approximate idea of the type of soil, simply by feeling the soil in the palm and between the fingers. In brief, wet clays are sticky and easy to mould into rolls. The thinner the roll the finer are the particles. Silty soils are coarser and reminiscent of flour; whereas sandy soils have large shares of coarse grains that are big enough to be visible to the eye. In Box 11.1 you can

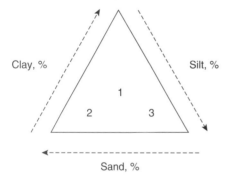

Figure 11.4 Simplified version of the soil texture triangle. The percentages of clay, silt and sand, respectively, are represented by a point in the triangle. In this example 1 shows clay loam, 2 sandy loam and 3 silt loam.

Box 11.1 Clays can be both favourable and tricky

The large share of small mineral particles in clays means that the total surface area is enormous, of the order 100 m^2 per gram. The large specific area promotes chemical weathering, and thereby the release of potassium, magnesium, calcium and other crop nutrients to the growing crop. This makes clays potentially fertile (provided that the kinds of minerals they contain are susceptible to weathering). Another specific feature of clayey soils is that several small clay particles generally are organized in larger structural units called aggregates. By the formation of aggregates, large pores are created too, pores that are of fundamental importance to the fertility of a clayey soil, because larger pores enhance the movement of water and air in the soil.

Most importantly, however, clays are heavy to work compared with silty and sandy soils, and ploughing can be impossible without access to tractor power. Clays shrink and swell, and in times of drought the clay can become as hard as brick and may be difficult to restore. Obviously, clays are complicated and can behave rather differently, which highlights the value of local knowledge and practical experience.

read more about clays, which may contain many nutrients and water but can be tricky to cultivate.

Soil horizons and colours of soils

Valuable information about the soil can also be obtained through looking at so-called soil horizons (soil layers), which you can see if you dig a pit 0.5–1 metre straight down into the ground. The horizons you may observe differ from each other in one or more respect: texture, colour and structure (aggregation). Typically the uppermost horizon is a brownish one, due to its content of more or less visible organic material in various stages of decomposition, root systems, and parts of the macro and micro soil organisms. Further down the soil profile it is common to find horizons characterized by the accumulation of migrating clay minerals and/or precipitates of rust, which may generate layers in brighter or more colourful hues. Further down the material shows fewer visible signs of the soil-forming processes.

Like the soil horizon, the soil colour mirrors the processes of soil formation, and serves as a beneficial tool for classification of soils. A close look at the farmed landscape reveals a fascinating palette, with shades of red, brown, yellow, greenish, almost black and lightest grey. All soil-forming factors may impact the colour: the parent material, organic content, climate, topography and time.

Summary

Soils are part of vital physical, chemical and biological processes. The soil serves as a habitat for soil organisms, regulates water and supplies plants with nutrients. The soil ecosystem is based on four main constituents: mineral and organic substances, soil water and soil air. Although invisible to the untrained eye, soil is dynamic and constantly changing, which results in tens of thousands of different kinds of soils. The formation of soils is influenced by five soil-forming factors: the parent material, organisms, climate, topography and time. Further, materials are added, accumulated and transformed, and successively translocated to other layers underground, but also lost through different kinds of leakages. The classification of the many thousands of soils is to a large extent based on observable characteristics such as the proportions between clay, silt and sand; observations of the so-called soil horizon; and the colours of different soils and soil layers.

Next

Chapter 12 is a continuation of the topics in this chapter, in that it highlights water and plant nutrients. Both are primarily found underground and can more or less be seen as parts of the soil. You will read about the necessity of water and about drainage and irrigation. Plant nutrients and fertilizing are accounted for in more detail, but also principally in terms of recirculation and strategies for plant nutrient supply.

To discuss

- Go outside and take some soil samples at a place where this is appropriate, if possible from different sites. Try to make rolls, and feel the material between your fingers. Does the soil seem to have a rich content of clay, silt or sand? How about the colour of the samples? How much water can your samples absorb?
- If possible, dig a pit 0.5–1 metre deep and study the soil horizon with the help of supplementary literature.

- ○ Study a soil map with a focus on two or more regions that you are familiar with. What kind of soils can you find? (The terminology can be complicated but you may be familiar with some of the denominations.)
- ○ Compare a soil map with a topographic map of the same region. Do there seem to be any connections between the topography and the different kinds of soils?

12 Water and plant nutrients

Like Chapter 11, this one is comparably rich in details and facts. Focus is here concentrated on the roles of water and nutrients for farm production. Neither of these aspects is controversial, especially not from an environmental point of view. You will learn that plants are threatened by surpluses as well as shortages of water. Attention is given to drainage of excess water, which it is necessary to consider in both rainfed and irrigated fields. Irrigation is in part discussed in wider perspectives, such as water as a common pool resource, but also from practical points of view. The second half of this chapter deals with plant nutrients. We will examine nutrient needs in general and the so-called macronutrients and micronutrients that are necessary for managing crop farming in the long run. A variety of plant nutrient sources are highlighted, ranging from purchased inorganic fertilizers to crop residues and waste, which reminds us of market and subsistence oriented farmers' different farming opportunities.

After this chapter you are expected to:

- Be able to account for the main water functions in plants
- Be familiar with soil drainage and explain why drainage is important
- Be familiar with different kinds of farmland irrigation
- Be able to discuss the pros and cons of crop irrigation from different points of view
- Be able to account for the main factors that impact the need for crop nutrients and understand why farming requires continuous care of the crop nutrient situation
- Know the main categories of macro- and micronutrients
- Know the main kinds of inorganic and organic fertilizers
- Understand why market and subsistence oriented farmers often have different strategies for crop nutrient supply
- Understand the importance of nutrient circulation, for practical farming and long-term sustainability in global agriculture

Key words

Water uptake, excess water, drainage, humidity, drought, irrigation, inorganic fertilizer, organic fertilizer, macronutrients, micronutrients, manure, crop residues, waste, nitrogen fixing plants, green fertilizer, liming, pH, recirculation.

Water for plant growth

Water is of direct vital importance to the individual plant and to all kinds of crop farming and animal grazing, even though the requirements differ according to soil, plant and season. As the precipitation finds its way through the soil, part of the water is absorbed by the root system and transported further up the plant and then transpired out to the atmosphere via open- and closable stomata in the leaves. These losses make up major parts of the total amount of water, while only a minor share of all water that falls on the ground is utilized by the plant. Still, in spite of the losses, approximately 60 to 90 per cent of the green plant consists of water, with extremely high shares in, for example, melons and cucumbers. The water fulfils a number of essential functions for the plant, such as:

- Maintaining the turgidity in the plant cells, without which the plant will collapse
- Serving as a solvent for nutrients and other vital elements
- Contributing to processes in the plant, such as photosynthesis
- Contributing to seed germination, plant growth and maintenance of the plant, which is discussed in Chapter 13

Patterns of precipitation differ globally, regionally and locally with respect to total yearly amounts, intensity and how the rains are distributed over the year. Farming in a region is generally adapted to normal access to water, but more or less normal years are accompanied by years with extreme water conditions. While some farmers worry about never-ending rains, others suffer from a dearth of precipitation (Box 12.1). The next year previously flooded fields can suffer badly

Box 12.1 Water stress, for plants and farmers

In case of drought plants can react with so-called water stress. In order to survive, the plant reduces the loss of water by closing the stomata in the leaves, which, however, hampers photosynthesis (see Chapter 12) and reduces the growth of green leaves, while the root system is less affected. Despite these efforts the plant may reach wilting point and is thereby lost. If all plants wilt, all farm work and expenditures for the crop are wasted and the land may not be able to produce until next year, which hopefully will be better.

Box 12.2 Absent rains hit soils in similar ways but hurt people differently

In the world as it looks today, drought in Australia or in the US has different consequences from drought in the Horn of Africa. Water scarcity as such can hit soils in similar ways, with wilting plants and terrible cracks in the ground, and all kinds of farmers are troubled in cases of drought. Likewise, grasslands can turn yellow and brownish everywhere, leaving nothing for the livestock to eat. In both market and subsistence oriented agriculture the farmer can suffer losses of harvests and herds, but there the similarities end. The Australian farmer may be forced to sell the farm and move – to another kind of job, other schools and other neighbours. Life will no longer be the same, but it will go on. Neither the farm household nor those in the region will starve, and imports will probably make sure that the supermarket customers in Sidney can enjoy the same selection of food as usual.

Comparisons with the drought in Somalia and parts of Ethiopia and Kenya in 2011, and before that, highlight terrible consequences and human tragedies on another scale. Reports of famine and hundreds of thousands of victims revealed this to the world through pictures of dying children and cattle skeletons. This kind of catastrophe spreads acutely to large parts of the population, and remains for a long time in the form of difficulties re-establishing crops and herds, personal traumas and long-lasting health problems, not least among children. In many cases, the catastrophic consequences cannot solely be explained by drought, but rather by combinations of drought and military conflicts or other crises.

from drought and vice versa. Moreover, the frequency and severity of flooding and/or drought are greater in some areas than in others, and the consequences are more brutal for some farmers than others, as discussed in Box 12.2.

All kinds of farming, except greenhouse cultivation and indoor livestock systems, are exposed to more or less capricious rainfall conditions. A number of efforts have been made in order to manage surpluses, scarcities and other water related problems as well as possible. Tillage methods and choice of crops can be helpful, but the major specific tools are drainage and irrigation, which are discussed in what follows.

Drainage of excess water from the land

Soil drainage, to remove excess water from the ground, is an important part of land management that may, however, be overshadowed by more visible and obvious problems with water scarcity and irrigation. As a matter of fact, irrigation requires drainage. Badly drained soils yield poorly, which is a waste of land, sowing seed, crop nutrients, labour, energy and other resources that may have been put into the land. Drainage is most common in arable fields, but can also be arranged in valuable and intensively used pasture lands.

Ideally the soil is naturally self-draining and allows excess water to drain downwards without any specific drainage arrangements. Most often, however, sufficient control of the water table calls for man-made drainage systems through which the water content can be balanced. As soils can be dry on the surface but harmfully swampy further down, it can be difficult to assess the need for drainage at first sight. As previously discussed, the need for drainage varies with soil characteristics, but also with the natural water table and local patterns of precipitation.

Drainage is a matter for both rainfed and irrigated farmland. The need to combine irrigation with drainage may seem strange, but is explained by the importance of draining surplus water away from the root system level. If this is not done, accumulated irrigation water will displace the soil air and can actually suffocate root systems and plants, instead of supporting their growth.

There are two main principles to arranging the drainage of farmland: (1) on the surface, via open ditches, ridges or furrows; and (2) as subsurface systems in the ground. Through open ditches or channels surplus soil water can be directed further on to rivers and lakes, driven by natural gravity or pumping systems. Rice cultivation can include temporary arrangements of basins and gates through which the water level is regulated. The second alternative, drainage in the ground, is often arranged in the form of pipe-systems that lead the water further to open water, such as streams and rivers. This kind of drainage requires careful arrangements and often professional assistance. Underground pipes require greater investment than open ditches, but have many advantages, such as improved field structures, as was discussed in connection with Figure 10.5 in Chapter 10. Both ditches and pipes require regular control and maintenance; to what extent depends on the kind of soil, the weather and the quality of the original work. As previously stated, proper drainage is a prerequisite for appropriate and successful irrigation.

Farmland irrigation

The irrigated area has more than doubled since the early 1960s and currently covers approximately 20 per cent of the global area of arable land. The irrigated area accounts for about 40 per cent of the total crop production, all according to figures from 2005/07 in *The State of the World's Land and Water Resources for Food and Agriculture* (FAO 2011b), in the FAO's State of the World report series. A major part of all irrigated land is found in Asia, and the share is relatively high in the US too. In contrast, the irrigated area is rather low in Sub-Saharan Africa. According to the same report, irrigated land in developing countries may yield more than twice as much as rainfed land, although the differences may be due to a complex of technologies, such as irrigation, seeds and fertilizer.

Much irrigation is operated as a regular part of the cultivation, as in paddy rice farming. Another alternative is when irrigation is operated occasionally, as a way to manage more or less frequently occurring periods of drought. This kind of strategy can, for example, be found in large-scale potato cultivation in temperate parts of the world. Substantial numbers of all farmers lack, however, any possibility to compensate for insufficient precipitation with irrigation. In recent years livestock farmers in Australia and Argentina, among others, have suffered from disastrous droughts, without being able to do much more than wait for the rain to come and turn the vast grasslands green again.

Practical and economic considerations

Farmland irrigation requires several practical and economic considerations. First and foremost, water must be available, in sufficient quantity and with decent hygiene quality. And, not least, the farmer must have the right to use the water. Many different kinds of water sources are used for irrigation purposes, such as: rivers and lakes; temporary reservoirs aimed at irrigation purposes; excess water from drainage systems; groundwater from wells; waste water; and desalinated water.

Second, a number of practical arrangements have to be taken into account, such as: distances to the intended water source; areas, field forms and how the fields are distributed; irrigation technology and energy supply; and access to labour for the daily management of the irrigation system. Many types of irrigation equipment require access to electricity or diesel, which is likely to limit many smallholders to manual systems. Box 12.3 gives a few examples of irrigation systems.

Third, as previously stressed, irrigation requires accompanying drainage arrangements that prevent harmful accumulation of the percolated irrigation water. Without sufficient drainage, the irrigation water can threaten the crop and soil ecosystem because of waterlogging and problems with salinization.

Box 12.3 A wide variety of irrigation systems

World farming includes a wide variety of irrigation systems, such as manual direction of surface water and electronically controlled trickle irrigation. We find arrangements for periodical flooding, with water harvesting, basins and channel networks; all gravity-fed and in many cases built upon collaboration between many farmers in the area. Open air sprinklers are common, but cause high losses of water into the atmosphere, whereas just a limited share is utilized by the plant. Among the most sophisticated systems are those that combine irrigation and recirculation of drainage water in underground precision systems, which also are constructed for the exact supply of plant nutrients and agro-chemicals in line with detailed analysis from automatic control systems.

Figure 12.1 Dry clay in a rainfed area, 2011.
Photo: Carin Martiin.

A fourth point to be considered is economic aspects. Irrigation projects often require a high level of investment in equipment and/or in labour. Moreover, annual operating costs for energy, labour and maintenance of the equipment have to be taken into account and balanced against risks and expected revenues. The economic aspects of irrigation differ between countries and from case to case but it is, generally speaking, best for high yielding, sensitive and comparably high-earning crops, such as some vegetables, fruits, berries and flowers, while the costs may be irrelevant for grains and, even more, for vast pasture lands.

Social and environmental concerns

In addition to the practical and economic aspects of irrigation and other kinds of water regulation, attention has to be paid to social and environmental issues. Matters of irrigation have a social side due to water's character as a so-called common pool resource. Access to water does not automatically follow with access to land, which is a natural consequence of the fact that water is part of the hydrological cycle – the water moves through the landscape and if one person withdraws water from the system, to his/her fields, everybody who lives downstream will suffer from less or almost no water at all. Numerous examples, from India and Bangladesh among others, reveal how poor smallholder farming has come to suffer from large-scale irrigation projects further up in the water system. Obviously, farmland irrigation is not a matter of individual decisions only, but also about communities and institutional frameworks, such as water legislation and local collaboration. In this context the Nobel laureate Elinor Ostrom should be mentioned, as she highlights the value of local organization and management of common pool resources, such as irrigation projects.

Environmental drawbacks associated with irrigation, such as overuse of water, use of fossil water, salinization of soils and degradation of soil ecosystems, are gigantic global problems that pose a threat to soils, drinking-water resources and other vital prerequisites for our existence. In addition, these problems collide with current and future pressures from population growth and the need for increased global food production.

Intensified production on existing areas is generally suggested as a way forward, and parts of this intensification are assumed to be achieved through more efficient methods of irrigation. Alternatively formulated, the idea is to make each hectare yield more on the basis of less irrigation water. This challenge primarily has to be handled by farmers, in collaboration with agronomists, hydrologists, engineers and others who may be engaged in the practical design. There is also a need for support from other parts of society, such as regulations and other institutional frameworks, financing and education. Another challenge in a similar global context refers to crop nutrient supply, which is the focal point in the remaining part of this chapter.

Crop nutrients, a prerequisite for plant growth

Just as humans must have food and animals feed, plants must be supplied with nutrients to be able to grow and for continued maintenance. This is true for both wild and domesticated plants; but while the wild, by definition, are left to adapt freely to the available nutrient levels, the idea of agriculture as an organized way to produce means that the crop nutrient situation has to be cared for. Balancing the plant nutrient status has been a challenge ever since the beginning of agriculture, as discussed in Box 12.4.

Shortage of nutrients is inevitably reflected in production, which will be reduced year after year. As crops, and the nutrients included, are withdrawn from the field, the nutrient losses have to be compensated for – what has been taken away has to be added back in. Each farmer must thus have an active crop nutrient strategy for how to manage losses, next year's needs and long-term supply. At the same time as plant nutrients are necessary and, therefore are matters of economizing and planning at farm level, they are also associated with problems. World agriculture wrestles with severe problems associated with crop nutrients such as: over- or underuse; volatile prices of marketed fertilizer; and problems with harmful nutrient leakage into the sea. In terms of production the primary question is how to cover nutrient needs and, as a beginning, to identify the needs. The farmer, eventually in collaboration with an expert adviser, thus has

Box 12.4 Scarcity of crop nutrients is a classic problem

The challenge of maintaining crop nutrient levels in soils is a classic dilemma that has followed humankind since the invention of agriculture. The problem was highlighted by the classical economists, such as Thomas R. Malthus (1766–1834) and David Ricardo (1772–1823), who, to simplify, argued that high yields were harvested at the expense of soil fertility and therefore soon would have to be paid back through reduced future yields.

The pessimistic classical approach was modified by some improvements, such as crop rotation and increased use of nitrogen fixing leguminous plants. The big leap came, however, with the development and spread of industrially based inorganic fertilizers, which made it possible to purchase concentrated nutrients and to transport them to the farm from far away instead of from the surrounding land. By this means, market oriented farming could be more or less decoupled from the necessity of managing the crop nutrient supply within the farming unit. Still, farmers without the possibility of paying for fertilizer are forced to economize thoroughly with all possible resources and to recirculate them as much as possible.

to assess the need for crop nutrients in each specific case. The need is primarily influenced by:

- Kind of soil and its natural content of nutrients
- Kind of crop
- Expected yield level
- Specific aims as regards protein content or other qualities
- Need to compensate for previous yields
- Degree of recirculation of crop residues
- Need to compensate for abnormal losses, for example because of heavy rains

It is difficult to know the detailed status of a soil without tests and analyses, even for an experienced farmer or adviser. Soil analyses can, for instance, provide information about soil texture, percentage of organic matter, soil acidity and the content of different kinds of nutrients. This kind of information is of great value for the ability to avoid over- or underuse and to reduce nutrient leakage. It may be difficult for poor smallholder farmers to make use of analyses although they are sometimes subsidized by governments or organizations with ambitions to support smallholder farming or to prevent nutrient leakage into lakes and along coastlines. In addition to the usefulness of technical tests, the value of farmers' 'green fingers' should not be ignored. The expression is used to describe a person's ability to observe, understand and act intuitively and on the basis of practical experience, for example to understand the interplay between soil, water, nutrients and plants.

Table 12.1 The macro and micro crop nutrients

Macronutrients		Micronutrients	
Large quantities	Smaller quantities		
Nitrogen (N)	Calcium (Ca)	Iron (Fe)	Molybdenum (Mo)
Phosphorus (P)	Magnesium (Mg)	Manganese (Mn)	Boron (B)
Potassium (K)	Sulphur (S)	Zinc (Zn)	Cobalt (Co)
		Copper (Cu)	Chlorine (Cl)
			Nickel (Ni)

A variety of macro and micro crop nutrients

The most important crop nutrients that have to be compensated for are nitrogen (N), phosphorus (P) and potassium (K), which are used in large quantities, ranging from tens to hundreds of kilos per hectare. Table 12.1 presents fifteen elements of great importance as crop nutrients. To the left you find six so-called macronutrients, divided into two columns, one for elements used in large quantities per hectare and one column for elements that are used in smaller volumes. To the right you can see nine micronutrients, also called trace elements.

As previously discussed, the level of various elements in the soil is strongly impacted by the parent rock, for example by its level of calcium, magnesium, sulphur and micronutrients. This means that farmers who, for instance, happen to live in areas with phosphorus-rich bedrock benefit from high natural phosphorus levels in the soil and thus will have fewer problems with phosphorus compensation in comparison with farmers who cultivate phosphorus-poor soils. Similar reasoning can be applied to the other elements, such as zinc, which, among other places, is lacking in parts of Turkey and India, but may be sufficient in other parts of the two countries.

It is important to remember that plant nutrients are not created, but rather transformed, recirculated and moved along the food chain, in crops as in Figure 12.2, and in the food we eat. This reminds of the character of energy and water, which are not produced but circulate in different forms, such as snow, water and vapour. You can read more about the circulation of nutrients in Box 12.5.

Inorganic and organic crop nutrient sources

Thus far you have been introduced to the reasons behind the need to fertilize farmland, and to the different elements that have to be cared for. In the following we will discuss different ways of managing the nutrient supply in arable farming through inorganic and organic fertilizers.

Inorganic fertilizers can briefly be described as industrially processed raw materials that are marketed and sold by fertilizer companies. Different kinds of macro and micro elements are supplied either separately, for instance nitrogen (N), or as multi-nutrient fertilizers, such as NPK, which includes nitrogen (N),

Figure 12.2 Without access to a variety of macro- and micronutrients, it is not possible to cultivate in the long run. South-East Asia, 2010.

Photo: Anna Martiin.

phosphorus (P) and potassium (K). You find these abbreviations on sacks with fertilizer and in tables with information about nutrient content and fertilizer prices. The abbreviations are often accompanied by information about the nutrient content as a percentage of the total weight, such as NPK 20. The different

---

Box 12.5 Moveable plant nutrients

A common misunderstanding in matters of agricultural production is that nutrients can be created, for example by farm animals. The correct understanding is, however, that the nutrients that are found in animal manure derive from nutrients in the feed, which in turn have been taken up from the soil. Another example of plant nutrient chains is when nitrogen in the soil is taken up by grass that is eaten by a dairy cow that synthesizes the nitrogen to protein, which then is consumed by a human being, who utilizes some of the nitrogen for body maintenance, while the rest in the best case is recirculated back to the land.

If consumption takes place close to the place of production at least some of the nutrients may be recirculated back to their place of origin. The nutrients are, however, often transported far away as food or feed. This means that farming areas risk increased nutrient scarcities, whereas highly urbanized regions will be burdened by nutrient accumulation. Plant nutrients travel globally more than ever before (for example, in the form of the globe-trotting biscuit in Chapter 4), and this moveability of nutrients is undoubtedly one of the key problems for long-term sustainable agriculture.

combinations are numerous and can be designed in order to fit specific crops and/or common needs in a certain area.

As access to inorganic fertilizers is constrained by high costs, these are primarily used in market oriented farming, although small amounts of inorganic fertilizer can be found in primarily subsistence oriented farming too. Over time the use of inorganic fertilizers has now and then been supported, for example recently in Malawi, where much-debated government subsidies have made inorganic fertilizers more easily available to smallholders.

Most organic fertilizers are by-products such as animal manure, crop residues and household waste. In addition, various kinds of green plants, green fertilizers and nitrogen fixing plants are utilized. Some of these materials are processed or composted before being spread. Manure and compost require storing and handling, and have to be sheltered from rain in order to maintain the nutrients and avoid leakage. Strategies like these can primarily be seen as matters of recirculation of biomass, which contains a number of valuable elements and organic substances. Utilization of organic matter for fertilizing is thus of a different character from fertilizing on the basis of manufactured inorganic fertilizer purchased and transported to the farm.

Although organic matter can be rich in terms of diversity with respect to the presence of different macro- and particularly micronutrients, the total content is poor when counted in kilo nutrients per ton of manure, compost, etc. The total effect can, however, be more beneficial than the nutrient content indicates, which may be explained by factors such as added organic matter and positive effects on the microbial life and the entire soil ecosystem.

Market oriented farming makes use of organic matter too, in the form of manure and crop remnants left in the field. In addition, the commercial fertilizer market processes organic fertilizers that sometimes are used in certified so-called organic production (which should not be confused with the more general term organic as it is used in this book). You can read more about the major types of organic fertilizer in Box 12.6 and in Table 12.2, where the characteristics of inorganic and organic types of fertilizers are compared.

Fertilizers from an environmental point of view

Like irrigation, crop nutrients are a complicated issue: on the one hand they are beneficial and necessary, but on the other hand they can have severe

Box 12.6 Main categories of organic crop nutrient sources

Animal manure is the major plant nutrient source on many farms world-wide, in some market oriented farming, but even more in subsistence oriented farming. Manure has a rich and diverse content of both macro- and micronutrients, plus valuable organic matter. The content reflects the feed and type of animal, and thus differs widely. As an example, intensively fed chickens produce highly concentrated dung compared with manure from sparsely fed sheep. Generally speaking, phosphorus and potassium levels are comparatively high and stable, while the nitrogen content is relatively low compared with artificial nitrogen fertilizers.

Crop residues, such as straw, leaves and root systems, are utilized in both market and subsistence oriented farming. Some of the residues are left in the field, typically the root systems, while most of the straw may be utilized in animal husbandry before being brought back to the field in the form of manure.

Household waste can be recycled back to the land at household level, or as large-scale deliveries of sludge from urban areas. Recycling from town to country is logical but is accompanied by the risk of spreading toxic substances and contagious diseases (see Chapter 21). This kind of nutrient recycling can thus be seen as a public concern that requires thorough planning and handling all the way from consumer level back to the field.

Green fertilizer, also called green manure, is a term used for crops that are grown with the purpose of ploughing them down into the soil in order to provide the soil ecosystem with nutrients and organic matter. This kind of production is thus a kind of non-food production. Parts of the crop may be harvested before the biomass is turned into the ground. We may also add the spreading of collected green plants to this category.

Nitrogen fixing plants have the ability to make use of air-borne nitrogen, via the soil air. By this means agriculture is supplied with nitrogen without extra work or expenditure. In addition, nitrogen fixing trees and plants (such as alfalfa and beans) may be intercropped, for example with maize. It should, however, be remembered that the other nutrients still have to be supplied.

negative side-effects. A crucial problem with inorganic fertilizers is that they make use of non-renewable natural resources, whereas organic fertilizers are both renewable and actively recycled. Phosphate mining and processing is energy intensive and consumes non-renewable resources, and even though air-borne nitrogen is available in large amounts, processing it into nitrogen fertilizer requires a lot of energy. On the other hand, inorganic fertilizer is a labour

---

Box 12.7 Liming

Lime sometimes has to be applied in order to reduce soil acidity. The natural soil acidity level is often just below the neutral point, pH 7. Some soils are naturally more acidic than others, but acidity below natural levels is a problem for many farmers, as this disturbs the soil ecosystem and can reduce the effect of the applied fertilizers. Soil acidity can thus be a reason for low crop yields. Problems with acid soils are, among other things, caused by fossil fuel emissions that cause acid rain, and by so-called nitrification processes in the ground, which increase with the use of some nitrogen fertilizers. Depending on local circumstances liming may have to take place more or less frequently, which adds the costs of liming to the fertilizer budget.

---

saving technology at farm level, compared with manure and compost, which is more bulky, heavy and time consuming to handle. Another advantage of commercial inorganic fertilizers is the declared nutrient content, which makes it possible to apply the nutrients more exactly in comparison with spreading unanalysed organic fertilizers.

As mentioned earlier, fertilizer, both inorganic and organic, brings about problems with nutrient leakages. The leakage patterns are complicated but are, among other things, related to type of soils, precipitation and eventual overuse of fertilizers, at levels above what the plants are able to absorb. Fertilizer may thus generate negative side-effects. There are also reverse situations, when farmland is exposed to environmental damage, such as acidification of soils because of harmful emissions, for example from road traffic and factories. The problem may be handled with the help of liming, which is briefly discussed in Box 12.7.

Pros and cons of inorganic and organic fertilizer

For a complete picture of the pros and cons of inorganic versus organic fertilizer we would have to consider the entire chain of each kind of fertilizer; from environmental and production perspectives, and from many other points of view. We will not go that deeply into the subject, but instead summarize the previously discussed crop nutrient sources in a comparative overview that is shown in Table 12.2. The table will not be further commented on here, as the analysis is left to you in the 'To Discuss' section at the end of the chapter.

Table 12.2 Summary comparison of major characteristics of inorganic and organic fertilizers

Crop nutrients sources and overview

	Inorganic		Organic				
Origin	Mining and extraction of raw materials	Airborne nitrogen	Animal manure	Crop residues	Household waste	Green fertilizer	Nitrogen fixing plants
Nutrient elements	P, K, Ca, Mg, S and the micronutrients	N	Mix of many elements	Mix of many elements	Mix of many elements	Mix of many elements	N
Renewable	No	Yes, N	Yes	Yes	Yes	Yes	Yes
Process of production	Industrial	Industrial	Animal farming	Crop farming	Households, urban or rural	Crop farming	Crop farming
Energy needs for production	High, often non-renewable	High, often non-renewable	Not specifically for the fertilizer	Not specifically for the fertilizer	Not specifically for the fertilizer	Muscle or fossil energy for cultivation	Not specifically for the fertilizer
Cash expenditures	Can be high	Can be high	Generally no	Not specifically for the fertilizer	Generally no	Cultivation costs	Not specifically for the fertilizer
Applied in market or subsistence oriented farming	Primarily market oriented	Primarily market oriented	Market and subsistence oriented	Market and subsistence oriented	Primarily subsistence oriented	Market and subsistence oriented	Market and subsistence oriented

(*continued*)

Table 12.2 (continued)

Crop nutrients sources and overview

	Inorganic		Organic				
Availability	Unlimited market supply	Unlimited market supply	In relation to type of livestock and feeding intensity	In relation to arable production	Varies	Depend on cultivation and collecting	In relation to cultivation of these crops
Known nutrient content?	Declared	Declared	May be analysed	Generally no	Generally no	Generally no	Generally no
Labour	Labour saving in comparison with organic alternatives	Labour saving in comparison with organic alternatives	Labour intensive	No extra labour for residues in the field	Calls for careful handling	Labour for cultivation Collecting is very labour intensive	No extra labour
Risk of contaminants in the material	Heavy metals and contaminants can occur		Risk of contagious diseases		Risk of contagious diseases		

Opposite strategies for crop nutrient supply

Generally speaking, and overlooking the fact that many inorganic fertilizers are limited resources, the market supply of inorganic fertilizers is unlimited for a farmer who is willing to pay, whereas the supply of organic fertilizers is proportionate to livestock, crops and other organic resources at the farm. We may understand this as two contrasting strategies, of which the first is output driven and the second is input driven in that it is limited by the available supply of crop nutrients. The two alternative strategies can be summarized as follows:

- An output driven strategy with its point of departure in expected yields (output), for which the approximate nutrient needs are calculated and purchased. A high flow of nutrients into the production creates the likelihood of high yields and high flows of nutrients out from the farm. This strategy is widely applied in highly market oriented farming.
- An input driven strategy with its point of departure in limited access to plant nutrients that can be put into production, and that often have to be obtained with no or a minimum of cash expenditures. This generally means organic fertilizers from the farming unit, which consequently sets the upper limit for what it is possible to produce. This strategy is characterized by low flows of nutrients into and out from the field, and is widely applied in highly subsistence oriented farming.

The situation in the second alternative may serve as a trap that reminds us of the previously described classic dilemma of maintaining nutrient levels year after year (Box 12.4). In reality, the two fertilizer principles are often combined. Highly market oriented farmers with combined crop and animal farming will typically include the manure in their calculus and be happy to be able to reduce the purchase of fertilizer. Even mainly subsistence oriented farmers may be able to combine nutrients from the farm with small quantities of purchased fertilizers, which can result in substantially increased harvests.

Closing the circle

In Chapter 4, where you read about the food chain concept, crop nutrients and other input resources were shown as the initial stage of the food chain, from farm to fork. It was also mentioned that the ideal chain should be seen as a circle where nutrients and other resources are recirculated and again made available as inputs for continued production. In Figures 12.3 and 12.4 you can see modified versions of Figure 4.4 in Chapter 4, with Figure 12.3 representing the abovementioned output driven strategy and Figure 12.4 the input driven alternative.

According to Figures 12.3 and 12.4 the output driven strategy is characterized by large resource flows, exemplified by purchased inorganic fertilizer and high production, whereas the input driven strategy typically is based on rather limited flows of resources into and out from the farm holding. The first of the two figures

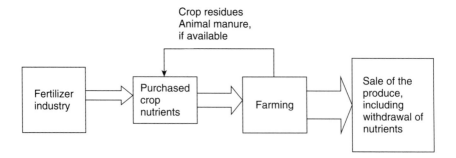

Figure 12.3 Output driven strategy, which means high flows of nutrients into and out of the farm.

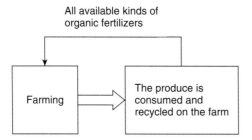

Figure 12.4 Input driven strategy, which in this example is shown as a complete internal recirculation of nutrients. In reality, however, leakages and incomplete recirculation make it difficult to close the circle. This figure is therefore more of a theoretical than reality based example.

indicates proportionally low degrees of recycling in highly market oriented farming, especially if the farm lacks access to manure. In contrast, the second figure points to proportionally high levels of recycling in mainly subsistence oriented farming, which, however, does not guarantee that nutrient supply and production are in balance.

Summary

This chapter has dealt with water in farming in terms of the basic functions of water for plant growth, and with regard to excess water and water scarcity. Excess water has to be drained away from the root system, which otherwise can be damaged and, at the very least, produce lower yields. Farmland is drained through open ditches and other arrangements on the surface, or in the form of pipe-systems below the surface. Thorough drainage systems are of particular importance in irrigated fields that are otherwise threatened by waterlogging and salinization. About one-fifth of the world's arable land is irrigated, and this is especially common in Asian farming. Farmland irrigation can be arranged in various ways, such as basins and channels for periodical flooding, sprinkler systems or sophisticated precision systems. Moreover, the chapter touches on irrigation from the perspective of economic, social and environmental aspects.

Plant growth requires access to macro- and micronutrients in appropriate proportions and quantities. These can be supplied with the help of different types of fertilizers, such as manufactured inorganic fertilizers and on-farm produced organic matter, which are discussed and compared in this chapter.

Matters of plant nutrients are also central in the recirculation of nutrients in general, and are thus of concern to global society at large. The final pages of this chapter distinguish two principally different strategies for nutrient supply in farming: output and input driven, which, generally speaking, can be referred to as market and subsistence oriented farming respectively.

Next

This chapter ends the reasoning about land and soils, and will now be followed by Part IV, which deals with crop and animal farming in practice. Beginning with Chapter 13, you will study different stages of the growing season, including decisions and practical operations throughout the season.

To discuss

○ Give examples of regions that have been hit by severe drought in recent years, and try to find out if these regions seem to be dominated by big market oriented farms or vice versa, for example with help of the *2000 World Census of Agriculture* (FAO 2010a), which was described in Chapter 10.
○ Take a look at some different kind of irrigation equipment on the market.
○ Discuss economic, social and political aspects of farmland irrigation, on the basis of varying kinds of supplementary sources.
○ Examine Table 12.2 and reflect on the different types of plant nutrients in the light of agricultural production.

Part IV

The many faces of farming

13 The growing season

Practical crop farming is the centre of attention in this chapter and Chapter 14, which are characterized by farm level perspectives. In brief, you will read about what to grow and how to do it. This chapter is built up around the growing season, which is described in general terms in order to be applicable to many kinds of crop farming around the world. The practical work begins with soil tillage, fertilizing and other preparation before seeding and emergence. Thereafter follows a long phase of vegetative growth when the plants are assumed to develop into a luxuriant crop before maturity and harvest. In parallel with the main parts of the growing season, we will address some related questions, such as various tillage methods and practical aspects of fertilizing, although other crop farming issues follow in Chapter 14.

After this chapter you are expected to:

- Be aware of the many factors that influence farmers' decisions about what to grow
- Be capable of giving a short overview of the principal parts of the growing season
- Bc familiar with the operational stage before seeding
- Have a fair idea of relevant fertilizer levels
- Be familiar with the stage when the field is sown and the seed emerges
- Be aware of tasks and problems that may occur during the vegetative phase of the growing season
- Be able to point out some key aspects that the farmer has to consider as the crop ripens and it is time for harvest

Key words

Growing season, planning, soil tillage, fertilizer rates, seeding, emergence, vegetative growth, crop maturity, harvest.

What to grow?

At the beginning of this book you read about a number of fundamentals that were said to characterize agriculture (Chapter 2). Three of these fundamentals deserve to be particularly emphasized in the context of arable farming. First, crop cultivation is a meeting between nature and humans. Second, to grow crops is to be heavily bound to weather, seasons and biological rhythms (see Box 13.1). Third, crop cultivation is in part an unpredictable activity. The close dependence on forces of nature can greatly influence a farmer's decisions on how to use the available acreage. The key factors to consider when deciding what to grow can be summarized as follows:

- Which crops are relevant, with respect to climate, soil and biology?
- Which crops are needed, in terms of food and feed crops for internal use at the farm?
- Which cash crops are demanded and relevant?
- How about costs of production for various crops?
- How about financing possibilities?
- Do any of the relevant crops entail high risks of harvest failure?
- Can the final use of the crop, as food, feed or cash crop, be decided later, when the outcome of the growing season is known?
- What access is there to the seed that would be needed?
- What are the peaks and needs for extra labour?
- Is there a need for special farm machinery or other equipment?
- Is there a need for special storage facilities?

Box 13.1 Weather, a factor of uncertainty

Weather is a key problem in farming. Crop cultivation is highly dependent on regularity and normality as regards precipitation, temperature, light and length of the seasons. Normal weather should not be understood as perfect weather, but rather as an interval in which the weather is expected to vary. This interval can be supposed to be manageable, at least by the experienced farmer, even though the yields will be below average.

Farming is by necessity organized in line with what are considered to be normal weather conditions at each particular place, but if the normal patterns are replaced by extremes, farming and food production get into trouble. The beginning of the growing season can, for instance, be delayed by long-lasting drought, which puts at risk the remaining season and thereby the harvest. Protracted monsoon rains and unexpected harsh night-time temperatures are other variables, but the list can be made longer.

- What are the competence, ambitions and previous experiences of a particular crop?
- Are there constraints due to land tenure, such as short-term lease or specific limitations?

Once the farmer has decided what to grow, the planning goes on with respect to seed, nutrients, equipment and other economic and practical matters. Moreover, the field has to be frequently observed in order to find the optimal day to begin, when temperature and soil moisture permit the soil to be tilled and seeded.

The growing season in general

The growing season can be studied as four different stages: preparation before seeding; seeding and emergence; plant growth and further development; ripening and harvest. The details differ depending on crop, climate and methods of production, but the basic principles remain. This is also true where the particular crop has a growth cycle that is shorter or longer than one growing season. The following alternative crop cycles can be distinguished:

- The crop is sown by the beginning of the season and harvested by the end of the same season. Examples: maize, rice, barley, soybean, tomatoes.
- There are two or more yields per season. Examples: grass, spinach and many crops in greenhouse production.
- The crop is sown one season and harvested the next year. Example: winter wheat which is sown in the autumn of year one and harvested in summer–autumn of year two.
- The crop is sown or planted several years before the first yield. Example: permanent crops such as coffee, grapes, citrus and oil palm.

As previously stated, the following account of the growing season is a generalization that principally is valid for a wide range of farm crops. The more detailed reasoning in the following account of the four main stages of the growing season will, however, refer primarily to spring-sown cereals such as maize, rice and spring wheat. Figure 13.1 shows the general stages of the growing season.

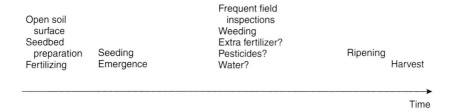

Figure 13.1 The growing season, including practical field work and plant development.

Stage one: preparation before seeding

The first operational task at the beginning of the new season is to prepare the land for the new crop. The aim is to provide the best possible conditions for seed germination and for the plant to develop into a luxuriant crop. The concrete work largely consists of varying kinds of soil tillage, which takes various forms depending on the kind of farming, soil, climate, crops, technology and individual strategies. Differing soil tillage practices are discussed later, but before that some basic principles will be described.

The purpose of soil tillage is, generally speaking, to chop and incorporate stubble and crop residues from the previous harvest into the soil, to break clods, fight weeds, level the field and to create a fine tilth that is favourable for seeding. The field may have been stubble cultivated and/or ploughed or hoed after the previous harvest. In other cases the season generally begins with ploughing or hoeing. Furthermore, stones and debris may have to be taken away from the field. Depending on the character of the previous crop, and on natural processes and the tillage since harvest, some stubble may still remain and need attention.

The field may have to be harrowed several times before it is ready for seeding. The final harrowing should focus on the creation of a favourable seedbed, with a fine but not too fine tilth that is humid and airy and thus provides the best possible conditions for the new crop. One of the challenges is to balance the need for tilling, which dries out the surface, and the need to maintain soil humidity. As explained later, water is a key factor without which the seed germination processes will not get started. Figure 13.2 illustrates the initial stage of the growing season, a field that is ready for seeding.

Soil tillage practices differ, as mentioned, and range from intensive ploughing and harrowing to slash-and-burn strategies, to give the extremes, plus various alternatives in between. The type of soil can be decisive, together with technology, the local climate and various kinds of crops. Potato planting, for instance, requires different forms of tillage to the sowing of small rape seeds. On the individual farm, the farmer's strategies and experiences can play an important role as well, although one should not underestimate the impact of the neighbourhood, which can provide valuable long-term experience. In addition, common behaviour in farming practices can be seen as a kind of shared risk, in that one will not be alone if the harvest fails. Still, there are regions where some farmers plough the land every year, whereas neighbours with similar soils, climate and crops strive to reduce tillage and avoid ploughing as much as possible.

Large-scale market oriented farming can have access to a number of cultivators and harrows with special properties. In contrast, the low or non-existent investment opportunities in subsistence farming mean that soil tillage has to be conducted with simple sets of tools, for draught animals or manual work. Highly mechanized tillage methods are advantageous in many ways, as regrads tillage efficiency, but can pose risks of harmful soil compaction. Frequent driving with heavy machinery, especially on wet soils, can reduce the soil pore space and soil aeration, and hamper water movement in the soil (Chapter 11).

Figure 13.2 Harrowed land ready for seeding. A newly sown field is a beautiful sight that signals work completed and hope. Many things will, however, have to be considered throughout the growing season and much can happen before the crop is harvested and safe.

Photo: Carin Martiin.

It is therefore valuable to reduce driving as much as possible, for example through combinations of more than one function, such as final harrowing, fertilizing and seeding. This can reduce the pressure on the soil, and save fuel and working hours, provided that the combined equipment is not too heavy in itself. A number of alternatives to ploughing have been developed and are increasingly applied, among which you can read about so-called reduced tillage farming in Box 13.2.

Fertilizer rates

Fertilizing may take place some time before seeding, at almost the same time as the field is sown, but also later during the growing season. You are already familiar with the subject matter from Chapter 12, although no attention was paid there to the practical application of fertilizers or to rates per hectare. Before continuing, it should be said that the rates that are applied in reality range from several hundred kilos of nitrogen, phosphorus and/or potassium, in highly market oriented farming, to just a few or tens of kilos in farming with a high degree of subsistence orientation. Moreover, it should be remembered that the effects of crop nutrients are not linear, which is discussed in Box 13.3.

Box 13.2 Reduced tillage

The importance of preserving soil moisture is one of the driving forces behind the idea of reduced tillage, which also reduces problems with soil compaction and improves the content of organic matter and benefits the soil ecosystem as a whole. In addition, the fact that the surface will not be laid bare reduces the exposure of soil to erosion and nutrient leakage.

There are, however, also a number of disadvantages that may be of vital importance for the decision on whether or not to apply reduced tilling methods. In particular, the pressure from weeds can be expected to increase. Moreover, greater amounts of crop residues in the field may increase the risk of plant pathogens. Reduced tillage may also bring about practical problems with bulky manure and crop residues that hinder the sowing procedure. Reduced tillage can take various forms, such as no tillage at all, stubble cultivation only, or alternating between the methods from year to year.

As regards fertilizing practices, organic fertilizers are more or less bulky and need to be worked into the soil before seeding. The decomposition is complicated but from a practical point of view it is beneficial to apply the organic matter early, even directly after the previous harvest. Inorganic fertilizers are easier to handle and can easily be applied, at the same time as seeding or later on during the growing season. Topdressing of the growing crop with extra nutrients is more or less frequently practised, either as a regular strategy, or if the plants seem to suffer from some kind of nutrient deficiency.

Not even almost exact application of fertilizers guarantees the final output of grains or other crops. You may remember the list in Chapter 12, where soils, weather and other factors were shown to impact the need for crop nutrients, and that makes it clear that fertilizing involves several uncertainties that depend on

Box 13.3 Diminishing marginal returns of fertilizers

Fertilizers generally give diminishing marginal returns, especially at high quantities. This means that adding one more kilo of nutrients will result in decreased marginal output, other factors being held constant. The marginal returns can, however, be high in sparsely fertilized fields. For example, an increase from 20 to 40 kilos of nitrogen per hectare is likely to generate a higher increase in potential yield, compared with an increase from 230 to 250 kilos per hectare.

complex interactions between farmers and the forces of nature. Still, farmers have to strive for the best possible nutrient conditions, which otherwise can be the weakest point in this interplay. As mentioned earlier, soil analysis is a beneficial tool for this, and so are guiding principles and recommendations from experts in the field.

Practical considerations, not least the economic situation at the farm, may, however, hamper the ability to follow the recommendations. The actual situation may therefore be a matter of compromises between the ideal level of nutrient supply and what is considered economically possible in view of the liquidity situation at the farm and with respect to possible yields, risk of failures, and the relationship between fertilizer costs and expected revenues. This kind of situation can be exemplified by a study of British farming conducted by the Department for Environment, Food and Rural Affairs (Defra 2011). According to the study the average use of phosphate per hectare tillage crop fell from 55 to 30 kilos per hectare from 1997 to 2010. At the same time the average application of potassium was reduced from 67 to 38 kilos per hectare, whereas the average use of nitrogen was maintained, at 149 kilos per hectare in both 1997 and 2010. We may understand the changes as a sign of economic difficulties or other economic considerations. As mentioned in Chapter 12, inorganic fertilizer includes specific percentages of nutrients. If a commercial fertilizer includes, for example, 20 per cent nitrogen and the farmer aims at 100 kilos of nitrogen per hectare, he/she has to buy and spread 500 kilos of the fertilizer per hectare.

Fertilizer levels are often higher in irrigated than in rainfed fields in a similar area, which is logical given the higher potential yield when the risk of water scarcity is reduced. For example, an Indian study found about 50 per cent higher nitrogen rates in irrigated than in rainfed cotton production, but the differences may be lower or higher in other cases. Questions like these are associated with aspects of the so-called Green Revolution that are due to packages of fertilizer, improved seeds, agro-chemicals and irrigation (see Chapter 14).

As regards organic fertilizers, for example manure, it is possible to have the nutrient content analysed, although this can be assumed to be more common in market oriented animal farming than among the world's many smallholders. Except for aspects of availability and costs of analysis, the many small and different quantities of manure, compost, waste, etc. complicate the situation.

From a practical point of view, organic fertilizers are bulky and less concentrated in comparison with the inorganic fertilizers that are purchased in sacks. It is hardly possible to apply similar nutrient levels through organic fertilizers. Despite this, organic fertilizers can, however, contribute to relatively high yield levels, which is primarily due to the content of macro- and micronutrients and valuable organic matter.

Stage two: seeding and emergence

As a second stage of the growing season the field is seeded, which traditionally is one of the central moments of the season. The seed itself plays a key role and it is important to consider that bad and good seed use the same land area, working hours and other resources, but pay back less. We will pay attention to matters of seed quality, ways of getting hold of seed and plant breeding in Chapter 14. In the following we will concentrate on seed rates, different seeding methods and the germination process.

Seed rates are relatively equal for the same crop species, despite differences in the final yield. This means that the ratio between seed and final yield differs significantly and that the seed accounts for a comparatively low share of the costs if the yields are high, and vice versa. Various kinds of crops, however, require quite different amounts of seed per hectare. According to estimates for Northern Europe, about 20 kilos per hectare is common for grass seed, about 200 kilos per hectare for barley and about ten times that for potato seed. In more detail, the recommended seed rate per hectare is influenced by the kind of crop and the crop variety, germinability, seeding method and the need to adjust the rate in line with specific local circumstances, such as high risk of drought. The term germinability expresses the ability to germinate; if 80 per cent of the seed germinates the germinability is 80 per cent. If only 60 per cent germinates, it may be possible to compensate for this through a corresponding increase in kilos per hectare, provided that other qualities are equal.

Seeding methods

Farm crops are sown or planted on the surface, in furrows or on ridges, with variations according to crops and the available technologies. Small seeds, such as oil rape, require slightly different seeding strategies compared with the sowing of large beans. Quite different methods are applied for potatoes and cassava, which are propagated vegetatively, as seed potatoes or parts of a cassava mother plant. Moreover, cereals can be sown quite differently. While wheat is sown directly in the field where it will grow and ripen, rice is usually established as a two-step operation. Special attention is give to rice in Box 13.4.

Seeding methods impact seed rates, germination and emergence, among other things. Precise seeding improves germination and saves seed, compared with seeding in rows and broadcasting. So-called precision seeding is a high-tech alternative that includes advanced electronic equipment for the detailed register-ing of sowing depth, soil humidity, temperature and other kinds of information. Seeding in poor smallholder farming can also be rather precise, although techno-logically simple, labour intensive and merely registered by the human eye. In this kind of seeding, sometimes termed dibbling, each seed is dropped manually into a small hole.

A less precise technology is drilling, where the seed is sown in long rows, at a depth of a few centimetres. You find drillers in many different kinds of farming, such as advanced drillers in highly market oriented farming, cheaper alternatives for tractor or animal traction and simple hand driven alternatives as well. The least precise method, and therefore the one that uses most seed, is broadcasting,

---

Box 13.4 Rice cultivation in different worlds

The rice on your plate can derive from the most different kinds of production. Much of the rice on the world market is produced by large-scale farming, but some quantities have found their way to the international stage from smallholder farmers who have managed to produce some surplus for sale.

The first alternative may involve seedbed preparation and seeding with the help of electronic information, fertilizing by aeroplane, and thorough irrigation and recirculation of drainage water. As the crop ripens and gets ready for harvest, this is conducted with large electronically equipped combines that harvest the rice at the ideal moisture content and with minimal losses, in the field and during post-harvest handling.

In contrast, the smallholder produced rice has involved many hours of manual work, from seeding to harvest and post-harvest handling. Seeding generally takes place in small nurseries, from which the seedlings are manually transplanted to fields or bigger plots some weeks later. Throughout the growing season the crop is irrigated and drained several times, through gravity or pump driven systems. Each parcel of land will be manually weeded a number of times during the season. At harvest time extra labour may be called for, and the work may all be done manually, or with the help of small mobile or stationary harvesters. After threshing the rice may be dried under the sun, turned over occasionally, and winnowed in order to separate chaff and similar matter.

---

which means that the seed is simply spread on the soil surface, often by hand. In reduced tillage systems (Box 13.2) the equipment has to be adjusted so that the sowing, often in the form of so-called direct-seeding, can be managed in different conditions. Irrespective of method, it is important for the seed to be covered with soil and slightly compacted in order to prevent soil moisture loss, but without hampering soil aeration.

Germination and emerging seedlings

Depending on the crop, seeding method, precipitation and temperature, the field can generally be expected to be shaded in green within a few weeks. Soil humidity is a key factor in setting the germination process in motion, together with temperature and an appropriate content of soil air. For example, germination of some maize varieties requires a moisture content of about 30 per cent and a temperature of at least 10°C. The germination process is in some cases accelerated through soaking in water or by treatment with chemical substances, for instance in intensive production of vegetables.

Initially the germinating seed is totally dependent on stored resources in the seed, such as energy-rich starch. Gradually the seedling makes increased use of resources outside the seed. In order to ensure the water and nutrient supply, thin seedling roots may develop before the first green shoots start growing. Still, the young seedlings are especially susceptible to stress during this period of transition, such as that caused by drought, frost or hard winds, but also to manual and mechanical weeding. The second stage of the growing season is thus a dramatic phase during which the sown seed is expected to manage both germination and emergence. What happens next determines what the continuing season will look like.

Stage three: vegetative and reproductive development

The third phase of the growing season in Figure 13.1 is the long time period when the seedlings develop into fully grown plants, and get ready to ripen. As you probably know, vegetative growth is driven by the process of photosynthesis, without which no green matter would be able to grow. Box 13.5 briefly describes the process, also shown in Chapter 8.

Gradually stems and leaves develop, and the field gets greener and greener. The progress of each particular kind of leaf and of the so-called internodes at the stems provides valuable information that helps the skilled farmer and adviser

---

Box 13.5 The process of photosynthesis

Green plants are utterly dependent on the photosynthesis process that creates almost all dry matter. Through photosynthesis green plants are able to synthesize carbon dioxide and water into carbohydrates in the plant, with oxygen as a by-product. The process also means that solar energy is transformed into chemical energy, which is supported by the green pigment chlorophyll. Simplified, the process can be expressed as follows:

$$\text{Energy} + \text{Carbon dioxide} + \text{Water} \xrightarrow{\text{Chlorophyll}} \text{Carbohydrate} + \text{Oxygen}$$

Obviously the process of photosynthesis is able to produce food crops and other plants on the basis of the soil and carbon dioxide from the air, free of charge. Carbon dioxide, which is one of the drivers of climate change, is thus playing a positive key role in all kinds of vegetative growth. Moreover, the constant capturing of carbon dioxide (conducted with the help of leaves' stomata, as mentioned in Box 12.1 in Chapter 12) means that green plants also have an important role in carbon sequestration.

---

decide on measures such as additional fertilizing, weeding and eventual pesticides. It is also important to make frequent field inspections in order to watch out for potential threats from insects and plant diseases.

If irrigation is available this will most likely be utilized during the long period of vegetative growth, although some crops may be irrigated any time from seeding to harvest. As regards irrigation, it is important to use water economically, while also ensuring that the water benefits the crop as much as possible. Attention should thus be paid to amounts of water, irrigation frequency, sun radiation, winds and natural air humidity. It can, for example, be pointless, and even damaging to the crop, to use open air sprinklers in the middle of the day when the sun is most intense, or when the water may be blown away by strong winds.

Sooner or later the plants reach a point when the focus turns from the production of green matter to the production of flowers. At this point the reproductive stage has been reached. Oilseeds, cucumbers and plenty of other crops have beautiful flowers, while many farm crops have quite modest flowers that can be difficult for the untrained eye to recognize. Grains generally have well-synchronized and short flowering periods, almost within a few days, whereas many other kinds of crops have protracted flowering periods, coffee for instance. During this stage pollination may be managed, for instance through wind pollination of maize and rye, and insect pollination of sunflowers. Many crops are self-pollinating but benefit from, for example, bee pollination (also see Box 8.5 in Chapter 8).

Stage four: ripening and harvest

The fourth and final stage of the crop season is the time period when the crop ripens and the harvest is approaching. Each kind of crop has its specific process of maturity and should be harvested with regard to optimal water content, colour and other specific qualities. Like the three previous stages, the last phase is here illustrated by grain crops that are cropped at full maturity. Some crops, however, such as spinach and grass for hay or silage, are harvested during the vegetative stage, and still others are harvested at the reproductive stage but before full maturity, for example many beans.

Returning to the ripening of grains, the seed-filling development is now taking place at the same time as the moisture content decreases, and the fields turn from green to different shades of yellow. The maturation process will directly impact the final crop yield. Poorly developed kernels will naturally yield less than well-filled ones, as will grains with high shares of husk in proportion to the nutritious endosperm. The detailed processes are complex and can, among other things, be affected by drought, which shortens the period of crop maturation and reduces the share of endosperm.

During the maturation process the moisture content of grains goes down significantly, to about 5–15 per cent. It is now possible to separate the seed kernels from the ear through mechanical or manual threshing. Synchronous

Figure 13.3 Wheat ready for the combine harvester.
Photo: Carin Martiin.

ripening, as in grains, can be seen as a prerequisite for the ability to mechanize the harvest. It would hardly be possible to use combine harvesters in an unevenly ripening crop. Figure 13.3 shows homogeneously ripened wheat.

The harvest of grains includes similar main steps, although technologies differ strikingly. The straw will be cut, gathered and threshed so that the kernels are loosened from the head. Grains also have to be winnowed in order to separate the kernels from chaff, dust and weed seeds. In addition, straw and other crop residues have to be considered. There the similarities end, however.

The highly market oriented farmer, or someone he/she hires in for the threshing, can be found sitting in a gigantic combine that is generously equipped with electronic control systems and a gigantic cutter bar that is able to clear several hectares per hour, including all the described operational stages. Combines are used for cereals, pulses, oilseeds, etc. In addition, a range of highly specialized machines have been developed, for example for roots, vegetables and berries. As an intermediate stage, for example at farms with only a few or some tens of hectares of grains, stationary threshing machines may be used, which simplifies the threshing, while most other steps remain.

The subsistence oriented farmer is hardly able to make use of costly technologies. Manual harvesting of a few hectares, or less, may take several days, and has to be accompanied by a chain of operations, principally the same as the combiner: cutting, gathering, threshing and winnowing. Apart from eye-catching differences in technologies, investment costs and working hours, it is important to bear in mind that time-saving methods reduce the time during which the ripened crop is exposed to the forces of nature. In contrast, the drawn-out manual process on many smallholdings around the world brings with it the risk that the harvest will be destroyed because of bad weather.

Irrespective of harvest method, the farmer has to watch the moisture content in the harvested crop. Even in dry and hot climates newly threshed grains have to be dried, although in these climates just a few days may be enough. In temperate climates grain crops often have to be dried for a longer period before they can be stored. Market oriented farmers' strategies for drying and storing differ between farmers, and are greatly influenced by energy costs, available storage facilities, and the prices paid for different qualities and at different times of the year.

Summary

In general terms, and with the point of departure as grains, the growing season can be divided into four stages. Their duration vary with the crop in question, but the basic principles remain. The initial period is characterized by soil tillage and other preparation for the seeding. The seeding can be seen as the key event during the second stage, during which germinating and emergence of the seedlings take place as well. Fertilizing is generally conducted before or at the beginning of the growing season, although different kinds of farming and varying economic opportunities mean that the crop nutrient supply differs greatly. The third stage of the growing season generally covers the longest time period, the stage when vegetative and reproductive development is taking place. Some crops are harvested at this stage, but grains, among others, generally have to reach full maturity before they are ready to be harvested.

Next

Chapter 14 is a direct continuation of this one. It contains discussion of weeds and pests, and about so-called crop rotation and fallow land. Attention is paid to various aspects of seeds, and the chapter ends with a summarizing discussion about different yield levels and the main factors influencing these.

To discuss

○   Look for fertilizer recommendations for various crops from a research institute or university, private expert advisers or fertilizer companies.

○   Select a vegetable that you eat fresh and outline the growing season for this crop (as an alternative to the spring-sown grain that serves as the point of departure for the reasoning in this chapter).

○   Try to find out what the grain season looks like for some farmers in the country where you live. If both market and subsistence oriented farming are common, try to compare these.

14 Weeds, seeds and other crop issues

Like Chapter 13, this one focuses on arable farming. We will take the previous discussion further and study some aspects in more detail. First you will read about farmers' problems with weeds, pests and plant diseases, including the use of pesticides and other ways to fight these problems. Sound growing conditions are also important and are among other things supported by so-called crop rotation. The crop rotation plan states the kind of crops that will be grown at a particular farm, and in what order they are to be grown in the fields during the crop rotation cycle, which may, for example, last five years. By this means the pressure from weeds, pests and plant diseases can be reduced, at the same time as the rotation provides other benefits too. Different kinds of fallow land are also discussed, before the focus is turned to matters of sowing seed, to which much attention is paid in this chapter. You will learn about several aspects of plant breeding and different breeding methods, but also worries about lost genetic diversity and genetically modified seeds. We will also discuss alternative ways to get hold of seed for the coming season. The chapter ends with a discussion about yield levels and includes a list of the main yield influencing factors, which serves as a kind of general summary of crop cultivation issues.

After this chapter you are expected to:

- Be aware of problems with weeds, pests and plant diseases in crop farming
- Understand the principle of crop rotation and its advantages
- Be familiar with various reasons for fallow land
- Be able to give examples of improvements that have been obtained through plant breeding
- Be familiar with the major forms of plant breeding
- Be able to discuss the pros and cons of various ways to get hold of seed for sowing
- Be able to suggest a number of factors that may contribute to differing yields per hectare

Weeds, insect pests and plant diseases

Throughout the season the growing crop is more or less intensively exposed to pressures from weeds, insect pests and plant diseases. Weeds can be defined as undesired plants, other than those that are supposed to grow in a particular field. Any kind of plant can thus be identified as a weed if it is found in a place where it is not intended to grow. The distinction between weeds and crops can thus be seen as part of the idea of crop farming as a matter of organized and controlled cultivation, in contrast to hunter-gathering systems.

The major problem with weeds is that they compete with the crop for nutrients, moisture, light and space. If the crop is harvested using a technique that does not clear away the weeds, these may reduce the quality of the final product. This can, for example, be the case with silage, where grass and weeds are not separated. A modest number of relatively harmless weeds can generally be accepted, in view of the work and other costs that are associated with weeding. Even so, weeds can be said to constitute a major problem in crop farming, in terms of pesticide use and almost endless hours spent on manual weeding. Insect pests may, however, cause more severe and sudden damage. While weeds make crops underperform, pests can destroy parts of the plants and may, in the worst case, ruin the field totally. Among the many kinds of pests and diseases that farmers have to deal with you will find harmful insects such as aphids, and plant pathogens such as infectious fungi, soil nematodes and molluscs. In addition birds and mammals may cause big problems, regionally and for individual farmers.

Ways of fighting the problems

As a rule, farming methods should be framed in order to favour the crop, but disfavour weeds and pests. This is a matter of qualified farming practices that, among other things, can include variations in soil tillage and good timing. Moreover, it is important to use healthy sowing seed and to avoid inappropriate handling of crop residues which otherwise may serve as pools for weed seed and as sources of various crop diseases. In addition to using prevention it is also necessary to be observant and detect even subtle signs of emerging threats throughout the growing season, instead of being taken aback by a sudden discovery, for example of rust of wheat in the field.

In smallholder farming weeding is generally a matter of labour intensive manual work that has to be done several times throughout the growing season. On higher acreages mechanical harrowing can be an alternative against the weeds, but on middle-sized and big farms chemical methods can be expected to dominate. The term pesticide is used collectively for, among others:

- Herbicides, against weeds
- Insecticides, against harmful insects
- Fungicides, against fungi or fungal spores

Before deciding on the use of pesticides it is important to understand the problem as well as possible. The farmer or his/her adviser has to identify the kind of weed or pest in terms of species, stage of development, approximate risks of expansion and estimated damage to the crop. It is important to study the crop, for example the number of leaves, stem development and eventual flowering, to make sure that the crop will be able to withstand the action while the weeds, insect pest or plant disease will not. On the basis of this kind of information the expert adviser may be able to assess whether the use of some kind of herbicide, insecticide or fungicide is motivated, and, if so, when and how this should be used. Alternatively the farmer is advised to observe the situation another day or two before deciding about the eventual pesticide. In some cases natural enemies to harmful insects are discovered and may be the best way of managing an acute situation. Considerations like these are necessary to manage the problems as well as possible, at the same time reducing the risk of negative side-effects. The use of pesticides varies greatly, in terms of application, substances and the number of treatments per growing season, which in turn are influenced by factors such as the following:

- The crop
- Pressure from weeds, harmful insects and plant diseases
- Severity of the threat
- Climate and other natural conditions
- Methods of production
- Marketing, agro-chemicals
- Consumer attitudes
- Laws and regulations

The use of pesticides is regulated in many countries, but substances prohibited in one country may be allowed in another. Some countries require certificates for the purchase and spread of chemicals, while handling of pesticides is more or less uncontrolled in others. Furthermore, we find differences from farm to farm, with some farmers following a detailed plan for preventive chemical treatment throughout the crop season, more or less irrespective of the situation in the field, while others limit the use to identified need. Still others do not use any pesticides at all, for economic reasons in poor smallholding farming, or for other reasons, such as the production of certified so-called organic foods.

Hormones

In addition to pesticides, parts of the market oriented agricultural sector make use of other kinds of substances, such as hormones. These are applied in order to regulate the growth and development of the crop, for instance to accelerate the process of germination, shorten the straw in grains, extend the flowering period and direct the ripening processes in tomatoes and bananas. As in the case of pesticides, the use of hormones in farm production is regulated and even forbidden in some countries. In addition, this kind of substance is sometimes also applied further along the food chain, for example to regulate the ripening process in fruits and vegetables that are transported from one part of the world to another.

Agrochemicals from wider perspectives

Access to agrochemicals has contributed to substantial increases in crop yields. The enormous increases in crop production that were shown in Chapter 6 are in part explained by the use of pesticides, together with fertilizing, irrigation and plant breeding. It is, however, well known that pesticides have a number of draw-backs due to their toxicity and potential risks to wells and rivers, soils, natural predators, surrounding ecosystems and people who come into contact with the chemicals. These kinds of problems have been known for a long time and were highlighted by the American biologist Rachel Carson, whose book *Silent Spring* (1962) has had a powerful influence on environmental concerns. Lately the FAO and several other organizations and actors have given increased attention to the drawbacks of overuse of pesticides, which is illustrated in the following quotation:

> Pesticides kill pests, but also pests' natural enemies, and their overuse can harm farmers, consumers and the environment. The first line of defence is a healthy agro-ecosystem.
>
> (FAO 2011: 65)

Crop rotation

As mentioned in the introduction to this chapter, problems with weeds, insect pests and plant diseases can be reduced with the help of sound crop rotation plans. The term crop rotation means that the cultivation of crops at the particular farm follows a plan that states the kind of crops that are to be grown, and how these should be rotated from field to field. The length of the crop rotation cycle varies, and can, for example, be four or seven years. The basic ideas behind crop rotation are to avoid cultivation of similar crops in the same field year after year, but instead organize a favourable rotation where next year's crop benefits as much as possible from the previous year's. Systematic crop rotation contributes to a number of benefits such as:

• Reduced problems with weeds
• Reduced pressure from some harmful insects
• Reduced risk of soil-borne crop diseases
• Economizing with crop nutrients
• Benefits to soil ecosystem and soil biodiversity

Figure 14.1 shows a five-year crop rotation at a dairy farm in Northern Europe, where the arable farming is characterized by feed production.

Field number 1 in Figure 14.1 is sown with winter wheat in year one, with barley in year two, oats in year three, and grass and clover years in number four and five. As the dairy production requires an equal supply of roughage each year, the rotation is organized so that the two small fields (5) grow the same kind of crop. This makes it possible to set up a crop rotation plan for five relatively equal areas. Grass and clover are favourable for the subsequent crop and therefore wheat, the most nutrient requiring crop in the example, is grown directly after grass and clover, before the less nutrient requiring barley and oats.

You will find some other examples of crop rotation in Box 14.1. Their length and character varies, and even though the examples have been related to specified countries, the combination of crops may not be the most typical. Moreover, the alternatives are numerous and the number of combinable crops is bigger in some parts of the world than others.

In addition to biological considerations, it is important to organize the crop rotation so that it fits the particular farm, for instance considering the priority of feed production in Figure 14.1. Similarly, it is of vital importance to plan for appropriate proportions of cash crops and food crops.

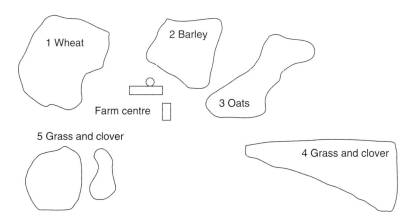

Figure 14.1 The principle of crop rotation, using the example of a North European dairy farm.

Box 14.1 Examples of crop rotation cycles

(The examples may not be highly typical for the country, and may be applied in many other countries.)

1   Northern Europe: winter wheat – barley – oats – grass and clover – grass and clover
2   UK: oilseed rape – wheat – barley
3   US: maize (corn) – alfalfa (north); or maize – soybean (south)
4   Ghana: maize – groundnut – sorghum
5   Nigeria: sorghum – fallow – millet – cowpea
6   Peru: potato – quinoa – barley – beans – fallow – fallow

Crop rotation has been considered as a key factor in the agricultural economic and social development of Western Europe from the late eighteenth century onwards. Together with increased cultivation of grass and clover, the idea of systematic crop rotation made it possible to increase production without impoverishing the soil. By this means farmers experienced a relief from some of the constraints of the so-called 'Malthusian trap', mentioned in Chapter 5. Today, the principle is as relevant for market and subsistence oriented farming, and rotation as such can principally be managed without expenditures.

Alternatives to monocultures

In addition to monocultures, where one crop is grown per field, you may also come into contact with so-called multiple cropping, where two or more species are grown together in various ways. The combinations are many, such as roots and permanent crops, or crops sown at the same time but harvested separately and at slightly different points in time.

The combination of different crops makes it complicated to mechanize this kind of crop farming but can be advantageous in other ways. Different plant height can create a welcome shadow for the lower vegetation, and various root system depths can make it possible to utilize nutrients at different levels in the soil. In addition, multiple cropping can be favourable in view of weeds and pests. It is, for example, easy to imagine the bigger risks of insect invasions in big monocultures compared with a piece of land where a row of cassava is planted next to a row of maize.

So-called cover crops

So-called cover crops should also be mentioned. The idea of cover crops is not to produce a specific crop for sale or consumption, but rather to provide a number of other benefits in terms of resources and environmental gains. Cover crops are not specific kind of plants, but crops that are suitable for a specific task, for example to reduce nutrient leakage from soils into water courses; improve the soil structure and soil ecosystem; fix air-borne nitrogen; promote carbon sequestration. Another purpose is the production of so-called green fertilizer, which was discussed in Chapter 12.

Cover crops are grown in different contexts: on fallow land; during a part of the year when the land would otherwise lay bare or untilled; during a growing season, together with the ordinary crop. If the cover crop is supposed to replace ordinary production in a field it is important to consider the effects of the reduced production, in view of long-term gains and the possibilities of managing short-term losses. Cover crops have recently been highlighted as a beneficial way to combine agricultural productivity and environmental politics as part of agricultural policy, for example the Common Agricultural Policy (CAP) of the European Union (EU).

Fallow land

The term fallow land refers to cropland that is not cropped during one or more growing seasons. The definitions differ, but the FAO suggests an upper limit of at most four years, after which the area might be considered as belonging to another land use category, such as permanent pasture (Chapter 6). We find fallow land in different contexts and, as discussed later, in various forms. Land can be laid faollow for different reasons:

○   As a way for the soil to recover from previous overuse
○   As a way to improve biodiversity
○   As a political strategy to regulate a country's cropped area
○   Due to difficulties operating the land because of a lack of labour or other troubles
○   As an active withdrawal of an area from farming for different reasons

The first motive, efforts to make the soil recover, is in line with the original idea of leaving land uncultivated in order to handle problems with soil fertility, weeds and pests. This kind of fallow, often seen as letting the soil rest and recover, is an active strategy in order to safeguard long-term farming. The second reason, fallow for environmental reasons, can be seen as a recent phenomenon, as a reaction to biodiversity losses and other worries about too-intensive and monocultural crop farming. Narrow strips of arable land can, for example, be laid fallow along river-banks in order to reduce nutrient leakage from crop cultivation. According to the third alternative, political strategies, fallow land is sometimes used as a buffer, a land reserve, which can be enlarged or reduced in line with policies, such as national attempts to avoid surplus production. This kind of fallow has occasionally been applied in the US and the EU. For example, the EU required a certain percentage of obligatory fallow on large and medium-sized farms in the early years of the twenty-first century. Fourth, land may be more or less temporarily abandoned because of difficulties in managing practical farming. Among the various reasons for this we may find migration to off-farm jobs, armed conflicts or natural disasters. The fifth suggested reason points to active withdrawal of land from arable farming, illustrated by speculation in land that is left uncultivated while waiting for more profitable alternatives, such as urban expansion.

Fallow land can look very different. You will find at least four alternative types of green or open fallow that reflect various degrees of activity or passivity of the landowner or leaseholder, and that may have positive or negative implications for future soil fertility:

- Initially open fields where weeds are left to grow and are eventually grazed, after which the land is actively tilled. This is a traditional strategy to reduce weed pressure.
- Green fields with some kind of cover crop. This alternative may improve later farm production as well as biodiversity and other environmental aims.
- Open and intensively tilled fields where weeds and pests are reduced through intensive manual, mechanical and/or chemical means. This strategy can be efficient in the case of severe troubles with weeds and pests, but the open surface poses the risk of nutrient leakage and soil erosion.
- Abandoned land that is gradually overgrown with weeds and bushes.

All the four alternatives can serve as land reserves, and the first three can be part of active arable farming. Except for alternative three, all alternatives can be combined with more or less intensive grazing. From an environmental viewpoint the second alternative is probably preferable, whereas the other alternatives can be accompanied by both positive and negative environmental aspects.

Our attention now turns to matters of seed, which is discussed from different angles, including an introduction to the idea of plant breeding, different kinds of plant breeding and farmers' ways of securing seed for sowing.

Seeds are carriers of genetic potential

The number of crop species in world farming is counted in the hundreds, and each species includes a number of varieties with more or less different characteristics. Thanks to this variety it is possible to grow, for example, potatoes and barley under very different conditions around the world (Figure 14.2). Other species, however, such as sugar cane, are concentrated in regions with similar climatic conditions. In addition to the natural diversity, humankind has tried to improve crops since the birth of agriculture. By selecting seed from the best plants next year's yields were supposed to be a little better, and gradually the farmed crops were improved, in quantity and quality, and adapted to various conditions around the world.

The changes have long been relatively modest, but since the latter part of the nineteenth century agriculture has benefited greatly from systematic plant breeding,

Figure 14.2 Barley, which is widely cultivated and highly adaptable to very different environments around the world.
Photo: Carin Martiin.

with field experiments, laboratory work and commercial interests. Plant breeding has contributed to the fact that many European and North American farmers, among others, are able to harvest five to ten times more per hectare, compared with their ancestors. There is no doubt that these means are one of the key explanations for the increased total production of food that was discussed in Chapter 6. Among the many improvements that have been obtained through plant breeding you will find:

- Increased shares of edible parts, while non-edible parts have been reduced, such as husks, peel and straw
- Shorter and stronger straw, which increases the plant's ability to manage heavy heads of grains, and to withstand pelting rain and winds
- Increased number of seeds, tomatoes, etc. per plant
- Shorter growing season, which reduces the risk of harvest failure
- Adaptation to different climatic and other environmental factors, thereby expanding the potential growing area for many edible species

- Synchronous ripening, making it possible to harvest the whole field at the same time, and to mechanize the harvest
- Improved resistance to drought or frost
- Increased resistance to pests, and lately to pesticides as well
- Improved qualities, such as energy and protein content

It is important to bear in mind that plant breeding is a matter of improved genetic potential, that also depends on other conditions to come to fruition. The fact that a new breed has a higher upper limit for what it is possible to produce is not the same as the concrete yield. Some breeds that are highly productive under favourable growing conditions but may produce badly under more harsh circumstances, where locally adapted varieties can be a safer choice. As you can see from the list of plant breeding improvements, some refer to higher yield potential while others aim at increased yield stability from year to year, such as resistance to various threats, which is important in all kinds of agriculture, not least in poor smallholder farming.

Various forms of plant breeding

As mentioned in the introduction to the plant breeding part of this chapter, improvement of farm crops has long been a matter of selection. In brief, this so-called selective plant breeding means that plants with desired, usually visible characteristics, are selected and saved to be sown the next year. The most luxuriant and high yielding wheat plant should thus not be used to bake bread but rather be saved as seed.

During the twentieth century farmers' selective plant breeding was accompanied by so-called cross breeding, which was conducted by professional plant breeders at universities and research institutes and by commercial companies. Cross breeding aims to combine traits from different plants. A high yielding wheat variety can be combined with a variety with excellent straw strength, and thereby result in a new variety that combines the high yield and the desired straw characteristics. Depending on reproductive strategy, some crops are able to maintain the obtained improvements generation after generation whereas others are not. Still other breeds are sterile, which requires deliveries of new seed, often from a specific company with patented rights to the variety in question.

In addition to selective plant breeding and cross breeding, other methods have been developed in recent decades. New technologies for the genetic modification of crops, so-called GMOs (Genetically Modified Organisms), take plant breeding to another, often criticized, level, beyond the selection and crossing of whole plants. The field is complex, but we may distinguish between two different strategies. To simplify, so-called transgenic modification means that one or more specific genes from another organism are added to the plant's genome, whereas so-called ingenic modification means that native but modified DNA is reinserted into the same plant.

From the perspective of production, genetic modification has, among other things, aimed at improved tolerance to drought, to some pest and plant diseases, and at increased tolerance of some pesticides. Moreover, the technology, also called genetic engineering, can be used for so-called biofortified foods, for instance with extra vitamins. The technology has also gained increased interest in sectors other than agriculture that see genetic engineering as a way of utilizing farm crops as a base for different kinds of pharmaceutical agents and a variety of industrial methods.

From the 1980s onwards crops such as tobacco, potatoes, tomatoes, cotton and maize have been subject to genetic engineering, and are now widely spread across all continents, with some exceptions. In particular, European consumers, and farmers, have been reluctant to accept the production and consumption of genetically modified plants. Doubts relate to, among other things: worries over the spread of modified genes to local ecosystems; the combination of genes from different species through transgenic modification; the development of crops that are highly tolerant to herbicides. On the other hand built-in resistance to some crop diseases might reduce the use of chemicals.

To conclude, the returns from plant breeding have been enormous. Through selection of the biggest, highest yielding and best surviving plants, farmers, and in recent times plant breeders, have contributed to gigantic increases in the supply of food. The tripling of the world's maize production and doubling of wheat and rice in the period 1970–2009, highlighted in Chapter 6, would hardly have been possible without plant breeding in combination with other inputs. Boosts in production took place particularly in areas where the so-called Green Revolution was established (see Box 14.2).

Box 14.2 The Green Revolution

The term Green Revolution usually refers to the large-scale increases in agricultural production made possible on the basis of new breeds, fertilizer and pesticides, plus irrigation, that took place during the second half of the twentieth century. The Green Revolution is generally associated with the introduction of so-called HYVs (high yielding varieties) in the 1950s and 1960s, initially in Mexico, followed by India and a number of other countries in Asia and Latin America; Africa was only marginally involved. The boosts in yields are the result of a package of interdependent resources that have to be brought to the farm to realize the potential of the new seed and the other inputs. The Green Revolution is thus a highly output driven concept. For example, the FAO has reported that the total use of NPK fertilizer in India grew ninefold from 1969/1970 to 1999/2000.

The Green Revolution has been applauded for its potential to relieve starvation, and its central figure, Norman Borlaug, was awarded the Nobel

Peace Prize in 1970. The appreciation has, however, been accompanied by intense criticism, pointing to overuse of water for irrigation, social conflicts and trouble for indebted smallholders with higher costs than revenues. Discussions about the Green Revolution in the 1960s and 1970s came to engage students and urban citizens in discussions on agricultural practices and the increase in world population, at that time less than half of the present population. Later the Green Revolution almost disappeared from the international debate, although it has recently returned as 'A new Green Revolution', now with Africa in focus, and again engaging voices for and against.

Ways of getting hold of seed for sowing

As seed is the key to next year's cultivation, farmers' livelihoods and world food production, the supply of seed for the next year is of the greatest importance. This is in part a matter of seed characteristics, as just discussed, but also about access to functional seed. There is much wisdom in the advice that 'It is false economy to sow anything but seed of high germination and vigour, whether purchased or home-saved' (Jellings and Fuller, in Soffe 2003: 82). The following reasoning focuses on different ways of getting hold of seed, and refers primarily to cereals, whereas perennials, for example, call for specific considerations. The following major strategies can be distinguished:

o   Farm-saved seed
o   Exchanges between neighbours and others
o   Purchase of commercially bred seed on the open market
o   Deliveries of a specific seed variety as part of so-called contract farming

Farm-saved seed has both pros and cons. The fact that home-saved seed saves the farmer from another bill is one of the pros, at least in the short run. Moreover, the seed is often well adapted to local growing conditions, a value that deserves to be emphasized. However, the internal circulation of seed within the farm involves the risk of seed-borne crop diseases. This risk generally increases with the number of seasons without fresh seed from the outside. Also, internal production of sowing seed means that the farm will not benefit from progress in plant breeding, and may also serve as an obstacle to the interest in trying alternative crops. The practice of saving seed on the farm is rather common, especially in poor smallholder farming, but also among some market oriented farmers. The strategy requires that sufficient quantities of last year's harvest are set aside, are thoroughly cleaned of weed seeds, husks and dust, are dried, and are appropriately stored so that germinating capacity and other qualities are maintained.

Informal local exchanges of sowing seed are often used as a complement to one's own farm-saved seed. Provided that the seeds are slightly different, this kind of exchange may at the same time contribute to minor changes in seed characteristics and reduce the pressure from certain seed-borne diseases. Local seeds can also be combined with occasional purchases, which means that the local pool of genes may be both advantageously and disadvantageously influenced by improved breeds.

In addition, farm-saved seed and local exchanges can have cultural and personal value in that the seed may be associated with the particular place and culture and, in some societies, can be inherited between generations. Box 14.3 discusses the value of local seeds in terms of plant genetic resources, which is highlighted by many organizations, both giants such as the Consultative Group on International Agricultural Research (CGIAR) and local NGOs.

Purchase of seed from the commercial market is the third alternative on the list of ways of getting hold of seed for sowing. Purchases can be assumed to increase with the degree of market oriented farming, which, as frequently mentioned in this book, makes it possible to buy input resources instead of being solely dependent on internal circulation. In doing so, the farmer gets access to the latest breeds, and can select crop species and varieties in line with his/her aims and specific needs, such as disease resistance and other characteristics. Still, the purchased seed has to be selected with respect to local growing conditions and other circumstances at the farm in question.

Box 14.3 Plant genetic resources

Although plant breeding has a number of advantages, cautious voices warn of losses of genetic variation. Genetic diversity is often highlighted as a matter of key importance for handling foreseeable and unforeseeable challenges in the future, considering food security, food safety and resource scarcity. Parallel to plant breeding, a large number of local varieties have been replaced by fewer bred varieties. In many cases this has benefited farm production, but at the same time it has reduced variety.

The problem is increasingly discussed by, among others, the FAO and large and local NGOs. Gene banks of various crops have been built up in, for example, Mexico, Peru, Syria, India, Nigeria and the Philippines. Among the crops in these gene banks are found varieties of maize, rice, wheat, barley, sorghum, beans, peas, potato and cassava. Seeds under threat of disappearing can also be cared for through active cultivation: in field trials, by hobby farmers and, not least, by smallholder farmers, for whom local varieties may be the most relevant alternative.

A fourth alternative way to get seed for sowing is when the farmer produces on contract, for example a certain kind of vegetable, for which the contracting company requires a specific, often patented, seed variety. The farmer is then supplied with the quantity, or the practical seed sowing may even be conducted by a third party.

The discussion of seed will now be followed by a short discussion of yield levels and yield influencing factors.

Yield levels

Yield levels are of substantial interest, to farmers, advisers, plant breeders, cereal traders, politicians and sometimes more generally, although primarily as a matter of figures and records. You read about global and some national yields in Chapter 6. Below we will instead focus on yields per hectare. Table 14.1 shows three-year average per hectare yields of maize in some countries in 2008–2010. As you know, maize is one of the world's three biggest cereals and is widely grown as a cash and food crop.

The main dissimilarities in Table 14.1 are explained by different natural given conditions, and by methods of production that also reflect various degrees of market orientation. The first two countries on the list, the US and France, are almost totally dominated by market oriented farming and are farmed using relatively similar methods of production (highly mechanized, and purchased fertilizer, seed, agro-chemicals, etc.), which, generally speaking, can be assumed to result in relatively equal yields at various farms. The yield per hectare can thus be assumed to be representative for many farms of similar character. The next countries in the table, China, Brazil, Peru and India, comprise varying degrees of market and subsistence oriented farming. The average yields of maize can therefore include both high and low yields. The last example, Uganda, has a comparably large share of subsistence farming of similar character, which is clearly illustrated by the low and probably relatively representative figure. The following list provides an overview of a number of the main influencing yield factors, most of which you are familiar with from the previous chapters:

Table 14.1 Three-year average yields of maize by country, 2008–2010

Country	Maize, average yield, kilos per hectare
US	9,592
France	8,896
China	5,460
Brazil	4,367
India	1,958
Uganda	1,543

Source: FAOSTAT 2010 (accessed 10 October 2012).

- Safe and long-term access to land
- Exposure to natural disasters
- Farm management
- Individual skills and ambitions
- Soil fertility
- Soil humidity and access to irrigation
- Crop nutrient situation
- Soil tillage and seedbed preparation
- Crop species and crop variety
- Germination capacity and other seed qualities
- Weather conditions during various stages of the crop season
- Machinery and other equipment, capacity and character
- Timing of operations during the growing season
- Problems with weeds, insect pests and plant diseases, and possibilities of managing the problems
- Process of ripening, in grains and other crops that are harvested at full maturity
- Organization of harvest and post-harvest handling of the crop

It is hardly possible to judge which of the many yield influencing factors are most critical. This differs between farms and regions, and the problems change throughout the season and between the years. It is, however, wise to consider the importance of identifying weak links, as it is often those that set the limits for the outcome.

Summary

Crop farming is more or less severely exposed to pressure from weeds, insect pests and plant diseases, which requires thorough observations throughout the growing season. The problems are handled manually, mechanically and chemically through various kinds of pesticides. Repeated cultivation of the same kind of crop in the same field increases the problems, and is also negative with respect to crop nutrient supply and other aspects. It is therefore beneficial to rotate the crops, in line with a crop rotation plan that decides the kind of crops and in which order they should be grown in each field. Fallow land may be, but is far from always, included in the crop rotation plan. We find fallow land in many different contexts, ranging from ambitions to improve the soil to short-term abandonment of a piece of land. Seed is a key element in crop farming. Through plant breeding the genetic potential of various kinds of seeds has been dramatically improved. By that means yields have been increased, and several crops are now able to be grown under various climatic conditions in different corners of the world. Improved seed is in part a matter of successive selective breeding at farm level, primarily in subsistence farming. Plant breeding is, however, also a big business that is conducted by seed companies, as well as institutes and universities. Cross breeding is a widely applied method that is increasingly accompanied by different forms of genetic modification. The so-called Green Revolution was based on a package with fertilizer, irrigation, pesticides and new high yielding breeds. The world's farmers get hold of seed for sowing by saving parts of the previous harvest, through local exchanges and, not least, through purchases. In spite of the many advantages of plant breeding there are also drawbacks such as the risk of reduced genetic diversity. Crop yields and yield influencing factors are also given attention in this chapter, which is the final one among the soil and crop related chapters in this book.

Next

In the two following chapters you will read about animal husbandry. Chapter 15 discusses livestock farming in terms of resource use and different strategies, and various kinds of animal farming. Attention is also paid to the life cycles of different categories of farm animals, such as dairy cows and chicken.

To discuss

- Study the websites of some agro-chemical companies and look at how herbicides, insecticides and fungicides are discussed and marketed.
- Discuss what you think are realistic ways to handle weeds, pests and plant diseases in different kinds of farming.
- What kind of combinations of crops seems to be common in rural areas close to where you live? Is it possible to distinguish typical crop rotation systems?
- Try to find some area in the neighbourhood that you would define as lying fallow, and try to explain the reason for this.
- Study the websites of some seed companies. Select one or two species and examine how differences between varieties of these species are discussed, in terms of yields, hardiness, etc.

15 Animal production, resources and strategies

If contrasts are big in crop farming they are least as large in animal production. You find striking polar opposites and uncountable variations in between with respect to land use, housing, technologies, feeding and levels of production. Just imagine the differences between the gigantic hog farming systems of factory-like character in North Carolina, US, family run dairy farming in Switzerland, pastoralism in Kyrgyzstan and backyard farming in Nigeria.

This chapter continues the large-scale outline of world animal production in Chapter 7 but has, like the two previous crop farming chapters (Chapters 13 and 14), a greater focus on farm level and practical issues. Initially we will apply a resource perspective on livestock production, by discussing animal farming on the basis of pastures, arable land and other feed resources. Like crop farming, animal production can be discussed in terms of output or input driven activities, which primarily refers to how the animals are fed and supplied with nutrients and other necessities.

This is followed by some reflections on differences in resource use due to the various life spans of an animal that is raised in order to produce meat only, or that produces milk, wool or eggs for many years. We will also pay attention to the motives behind farmers' decisions to work with certain kinds of livestock, which takes the chapter further to an account of different forms of animal production, such as mixed farming and different kinds of pastoral animal husbandry.

After this chapter you are expected to:

- Be able to discuss animal husbandry in terms of land use
- Be able to discuss livestock production with regard to how the animals are utilized during their life span
- Understand the principal differences between output and input driven livestock farming
- Give an account of farmers' considerations of what kind of livestock to keep

○   Be familiar with animal farming of various characters, such as mixed farming and pastoral animal husbandry

Key words

Pasture land, arable land, marginal resources, output driven, input driven, live animals, slaughtered animals, animals' life cycles, outdoors, indoors, mixed farming, backyard, pastoral, factory-like.

Resource bases for animal farming

The world of animal farming is based on a wide range of resources. As mentioned in Chapter 7, some of these would otherwise have been left unutilized, such as vast pasture lands with virtually no alternative use. The same is often true of the use of various by-products as animal feed, matter like straw from crop farming, household waste, and leaves and other forest resources. In other cases, however, the resources derive from arable land and may alternatively have been consumed by human beings, for instance maize, wheat and soybeans. The different strategies are further discussed below, but can be summarized as ways of:

- Making resources available, which it is not otherwise possible for humans to consume
- Refining resources that are already available for human consumption

Three main alternatives

The first alternative, pasture grazing, means that the animals transform nutrients in grass, herbaceous plants and other kinds of vegetation into protein-rich and otherwise nutritious animal foods for human consumption. If we recall, from Chapter 6, that about two-thirds of the global agricultural area and about one-quarter of the entire land area is categorized as meadows and pastures, there is no doubt that animal grazing is of great importance to world food supply and the utilization of natural resources. It should, however, also be remembered that the potential output of animal products per hectare of pasture is substantially below what can be produced from arable land.

Extensive pasture areas are often situated in remote regions with harsh climatic conditions, which means that the regional distribution of pastoral farming differs greatly. Vast expanses of pasture land are found in Central Asia, Africa, Australia and New Zealand, and parts of the Americas. Smaller areas are widely spread and, for example, used for grazing in so-called mixed farming, which we will get back to later in this chapter. In contrast to crop farming, in which the nutrient situation always has to be considered, pasture lands can be grazed year after year without active fertilizing, provided that the area is not too intensively grazed. It deserves to be repeated that without pasture grazing gigantic areas and huge amounts of organic resources would be almost unutilized, and many rural areas, economies and societies would look very different.

The second form of resource base is by-products and leftovers of various kinds. Food waste (preferably boiled to avoid the spread of diseases between humans and animals) may be used in large-scale farming, but is primarily utilized in poor smallholder farming. Depending on the types of animals, this kind of animal husbandry is typically supplemented by manual collection of feed from bushes and trees, and by grazing of small marginal pieces of land, such as roadsides. Also, this kind of animal husbandry means that nutrients that probably otherwise would have been wasted, or used for energy purposes, instead are made available for human needs. However, the level of production is generally low, due to difficulties in supplying the animals with enough feed, in terms of volume as well as nutrient content. And living conditions can be harsh for both farmers and animals. A further drawback is the hygiene problems inherent in the use of residues, especially food waste (see Chapter 21).

A third kind of resource base for animal farming is arable land. Feeding farm animals with crops can be seen as a way of refining arable products into more concentrated and nutritious animal foods. This kind of animal production is

Figure 15.1 People and farm animals are frequently seen in some landscapes. Cambodia, 2010.

Photo: Anna Martiin.

primarily applied in market oriented production of meat, milk and eggs. A pig, for instance, can be fed with large amounts of cereals, soybeans and other protein-rich feed, whereas the final pork includes only a limited share of these nutrients, although with higher nutritional and economic value. As previously said, wheat, maize, beans and other kinds of feed from arable land may alternatively have been eaten by a person. When the field is sown with clover or grass, it is, admittedly, not possible for us to eat this, but, at least theoretically, the field could have been used for other kinds of crops.

The three strategies outlined above are often combined, and applicable to most kinds of farm animal species, except for pigs and poultry, which are not able to survive on roughage only. For example, cattle may graze pasture land but also be given additional grain or concentrates. Generally speaking, all the three resource bases, pasture, marginal and arable, contribute to production of nutritious and in-demand products that play important roles in global food supply, farm households and rural societies around the world.

Farm animals may serve as a buffer

An additional aspect of livestock farming is that the animals can be utilized as various kinds of buffers. The animals can be used as a buffer between good and bad years, in that occasional surpluses of grazing or cereals can be fed to the animals, which can later be sold or slaughtered.

In addition to this kind of individual buffer, livestock can serve as a buffer for society at large, for which the stock of farm animals can provide a reserve that can be realized in bad times, for example when a society is hit by natural disasters or armed conflicts. In situations like this the supply of meat may rise initially, obviously not because of expanded production but rather due to increased slaughter because of the crisis.

Moreover, we may look at animal production on the basis of arable land as a way of maintaining a land reserve. By using the fields for production of feed, farms, production apparatuses, competence and land can, if necessary, rapidly be switched over to production of food for direct human consumption.

Output and input driven strategies

Animal production is greatly influenced by the resources that are put into the production, but also by other circumstances such as genetic potential, animal health and how the animals are cared for. The quantities and qualities of feed are of the greatest importance and are one of the key explanatory factors for the widely differing yield levels in animal production. If we limit the discussion to feed, livestock farming can, like crop farming, be understood in terms of output and input driven strategies.

In brief, output driven livestock production means that the animals are given all the feed that is needed to make them reach the set aims of production. Beef cattle can, for example, be fed in order to gain 1 kilo live weight per day, and dairy cows to yield 40 litres of milk per head and day. In the same way, farmers who run output driven pig production aim at quantities and qualities of feed that are as exact as possible, in order to obtain certain live weights and carcass qualities at a particular date. The typical farmer with output driven production is highly market oriented and prepared to supply the livestock with whatever feed they might need, including costly supplementary purchases, if the aims of production are achieved. Turning to input driven animal farming, this is typically subordinate to the available means of production. In reality this means that production is likely to be constrained by scarcity of feed. The farmer usually has no other choice than to use whatever feedstuffs can be found, while he/she will have to cope with whatever production this may give.

Continuous or one-time use of farm animals

With respect to utilization of feed, the efficiency rate differs between animal species, breeds and individuals. You will, however, find the largest differences in comparisons between production of meats, on the one hand, and milk and eggs, on the other. The main explanation for this discrepancy is that meat can be achieved one time per animal, is a one-time use, while milk, eggs and other products from live animals can be obtained again and again from the same animal. Alternatively formulated, a hen can produce eggs over a long time, but can only produce herself once. On the basis of this discussion three main ways of utilizing farm animals can be distinguished:

○   Regular daily use of live animals
○   Regular seasonal or yearly use of live animals
○   One-time use of the final products from slaughtered animals

The first point, regular daily use of the animals, refers to milk, eggs, manure and animal traction. Regular but not daily use means wool, hair, offspring and other products that are obtained from living farm animals more or less regularly over the years. The first two points are chiefly but not only relevant for cows, ewes, does (or nannies) and laying hens. The slightly provocative expression one-time use refers to livestock that are kept solely to produce meat, such as hogs, broilers and specialized beef cattle.

Many types of farm animals are kept for multiple purposes and thus combine the three alternatives. Dairy sheep, for example, produce milk on a daily basis, wool once or twice a year, lambs once a year, and later on mutton and sheepskin as final products.

In addition to resource perspectives, the ways in which we make use of farm animals have a wide-ranging impact in terms of farm economy, environment, animal ethics, and relations between humans and animals. Animals that are being intensively cared for and milked every day, year after year, are likely to be looked at as individuals, as opposed to animals that are slaughtered as soon as they have reached a certain age or body weight.

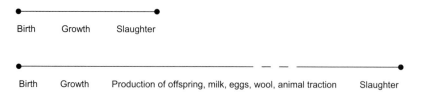

Birth   Growth   Slaughter

Birth   Growth   Production of offspring, milk, eggs, wool, animal traction   Slaughter

Figure 15.2 Differences in life cycles due to how the animal is utilized. The lower line
             illustrates the principal life cycle of female farm animals that deliver a variety
             of products before they are slaughtered. The upper line shows the generally
             shorter life span of animals that are used for meat production only.

The reasoning about daily, occasional and one-time use of farm animals is
shown in Figure 15.2, which is relevant for all main categories of farm animals.
The longer life cycle at the bottom outlines the first two alternatives. The short
upper line shows the alternative where the animal is used for meat only. Moreover,
the bottom line in Figure 15.2 demonstrates a situation where the costs
of production can be spread over a larger number of produced units, such as
hundreds of eggs or tons of milk, instead of one single product, the final
carcass, as in the upper line (see Figure 15.3). What is more, the long line
shows more diverse production in comparison with the upper line, where
the farmer is almost entirely dependent on one product, meat, and has to invest
in feed, labour and other resources long before any revenues or usable products
can be obtained.

Despite the many advantages of other kinds of animal production than meat, it
should be kept in mind that the framing of the individual farm's production
depends on what is relevant at each particular place with respect to nature,
economy, current structures and other circumstances. The influencing factors are
further discussed in the next section, which primarily refers to market oriented
animal production.

What kind of livestock to keep

In most cases questions about which kind of farm animal to keep seldom if
ever come up. Most farms are already adapted to certain types of livestock
as regards access to land, organization of the area, housing, feed crops and crop
rotation, farm machinery and equipment, and the farmer's competence and interest. The question may, however, arise in situations such as: generational shift;
a move to another holding; the start of a new business, weak profitability
and gloomy prospects for the present type of production; changes in rules and
regulations that question current production. In situations like these, the farmer's
decisions on future animal production are influenced by the following major
aspects:

Figure 15.3 Heifers of dairy breed that will soon enter their first lactation period, during which they may yield about 8,000–9,000 litres each.

Photo: Jakob Martiin.

- Current and expected future demand for the products
- Local climate and other natural conditions of importance for the animals
- Grazing and other feed requirements
- Access to water for the animals and cleaning
- Energy supply
- Specific outdoor or indoor requirements
- Accompanying investments
- Liquidity aspects, frequent payments or a few times per year
- Transportation and distances to a dairy or abatoir
- Harmonizing with eventual crop farming
- Harmonizing between peak periods in production
- Local traditions and cultural and religious attitudes to various farm animals
- Rules and regulations, taxes, subsidies
- Competence and interest

The last point should not be overlooked, as the farmer's interest and skills can be decisive for managing the complex business of animal farming, particularly in the long run. It is often easier to try a new crop than to expand ongoing animal production or even introduce a new type of animal onto a farm. With some exceptions, the response to altered prices and trade conditions can therefore be expected to be somewhat slower in animal than in crop farming. Still, a lot of changes are taking place, not least expansion and/or intensification of existing herds, which is discussed in Boxes 15.1 and 15.2.

Animal husbandry in different kinds of farming

The practical organization of animal husbandry naturally depends on where and in what kind of farming it is taking place. You find an overview in Table 15.1. In mixed farming both arable and animal production are operated within the same farming unit. The two kinds of production are often mutually dependent in terms of feed production, crop rotation and circulation of nutrients. The scale can be anything from thousands of hectares and livestock, to hundreds or tens, down to smallholdings with small plots and a few animals. The animals are kept in many alternative ways: outdoors and close to or at some distance from the farm centre; indoors all year round; outdoors and indoors in various seasons, or alternating between in and out during the day.

The second alternative in Table 15.1 is termed backyard farming. The expression is sometimes used for new waves of urban farming that are run at hobby level

---

Box 15.1 Expanding animal production

The recent expansion in the consumption of meat, eggs and dairy products in many parts of the world (Chapter 7) has in many cases been met by enlargement of existing herds and/or intensified production. In addition, some farmers have set up with livestock as a new branch on their farms or even established new plants for animal production. As a consequence, already large-scale production units have been scaled up even further, from hundreds to thousands of dairy cows; from thousands to tens of thousands of pigs; and to hundreds of thousands of chickens.

At the same time the previously mentioned tendency towards the fragmentation of already small holdings (Chapter 10) makes it reasonable to assume that there will be an increased number of small herds with a few animals. Parallel to these opposite movements, efforts are also being made to intensify poor smallholder animal farming, through better feed and a few animals more, in order to make it possible to generate some surpluses for small-scale sale. Accordingly, the world seems to face increased polarization in animal farming, with a few but increasingly large units of production on the one hand and a large number of very small units on the other.

Box 15.2 'Operation Flood', India's 'White Revolution'

The so-called Operation Flood programme in India was launched by the Indian National Dairy Development Board in 1970. Its purpose was to stimulate the many Indian smallholders to become dairy suppliers and thereby generate regular cash income, improve animal farming, and support livelihoods and rural societies in general. Gradually millions of producers have become members of small locally organized dairy cooperatives that in turn are linked to a nationwide milk grid, through which the milk is transported, processed, marketed and distributed for sale and consumption. In addition the programme has come to support animal health and nutrition and other aspects of animal husbandry. The programme has also been called the 'White Revolution', with reference to the 'Green Revolution' (Chapter 14).

Source: National Dairy Development Board, India, http://www.nddb.org/English/Pages/default.aspx (accessed 31 March 2012), and FAO Diversification booklet 6, 2009.

---

rather than from a need to get food. In this book, however, backyard farming is considered as a way for poor households to survive, in rural or urban areas. By definition, backyard farming is limited to the small area of a backyard, eventually supplemented by occasional grazing and gathering of some feed. There is no clear distinction between backyard farming and smallholdings with mixed farming, but backyard farming is more often run almost without land, by what may be called landless farmers, and is often a matter of animal farming. The practical arrangements vary but poultry, pigs, goats, sheep and cattle can be expected to be more or less closely interconnected with the household. You can find this kind

Table 15.1 Major kinds of farming with animal husbandry

	Outdoors		Indoors	Both outdoors and indoors
	Grazing	Pens and corrals		
Mixed farming	x	x	x	x
Backyard farming	x	x	x	x
Pastoral, stationary	x			
Pastoral, nomadic	x			
Factory-like livestock production		(x)	x	

of animal husbandry almost anywhere in Asia and Africa, and to some extent in Latin America; outdoors and indoors, and in rural as well as urban areas.

Pastoral livestock farming on a stationary basis is characterized by access to vast grassland areas where often gigantic herds of beef cattle or sheep are kept grazing almost all year round, eventually interrupted by moving, regrouping, wool shearing or sale. The land is usually privately owned and sometimes fenced, sometimes not. This kind of livestock production is well known from ranches in North America, Australia and Argentina.

Nomadic pastoral forms of animal husbandry are typically characterized by mobility and by customary land rights to the utilized areas. Stationary centres can, however, be part of the system, as well as combinations with some stationary husbandry and complementary cultivation, although meat, milk and other animal products from the pastoral herd dominate. As natural conditions can be harsh, or very harsh, the animals must be well adapted to long movements and scarce grazing and water resources. We find nomadic pastoral forms based on hardy local breeds of cattle, or other species such as yaks.

Factory-like livestock production contrasts especially with backyard farming and nomadic pastoral forms. According to how the term factory-like was defined in Chapter 10, this kind of animal production is conducted almost independently of the surrounding land and the local weather. You have probably seen photos of hogs, laying hens and chickens kept indoors in confined production systems; or of cattle kept indoors or in outdoor pens on a concrete surface. The animals may be moved between buildings or between plants, for example from hatcheries. The scale of the factory-like livestock production plant is generally gigantic, although the definition refers to its character. The factory-like plant is stationary, indeed, but differs from stationary animal farming in its dependence on inflows of feed and other resources from near and far, sometimes from the other side of the globe.

Summary

This chapter puts great emphasis on resource use in animal farming, which is a key factor for levels of production and is interesting in terms of global food production and resources generally. Three different resource categories are distinguished: pasture grazing, by-products and residues, and arable crops.

In addition to ordinary production, animal farming can be seen as a buffer between good and bad years, as a reserve for times of crisis or other needs, and as a way to maintain a land reserve that can be rapidly redirected to the production of food for direct human consumption. Like crop farming, animal farming can be discussed in terms of output and input driven activities: the first alternative means that the creatures are supplied with all the feed that is needed to reach a certain level of production; for input driven farming access to grazing and other feeds is one of the most important limiting factors. Furthermore, this chapter identifies different life cycles, depending on whether a farm animal is producing on a daily basis (eggs and milk), occasionally over the year (wool, offspring) or only after slaughter. Generally speaking, a long life cycle with continuous production means better resource economy, among other aspects. The kind of animals and the aims of production are, however, also influenced by many other factors, a long list of which includes nature, economy, competence and culture. The major kinds of farming with animal production are, in this chapter, categorized as mixed farming, so-called backyard farming, stationary pastoral farming, nomadic pastoral farming and, in contrast, factory-like livestock production.

Next

In the next chapter we will continue the discussion of farm animal production, but now in more detail and at an explicit practical level. Like this chapter, Chapter 16 gives much attention to feeding. You will read about the animals' nutrient needs for different purposes, ruminants and non-ruminants, water, animal health, housing and farm animal breeding.

To discuss

- Try to find out what kind of resources for animal production are utilized in the region where you live. What kind of resources are they, in terms of pasture, by-products, residues and arable?
- Study media reports about a region that has been severely hit by drought in recent years, and where the number of cattle, sheep or goats consequently was substantially reduced.
- Select a kind of animal food and study its origin in view of the alternative farm animal life cycle in Figure 15.2.

- ○ Study media reports (preferably with farmers' perspectives) about animal farming in a country of interest. Try to find out whether the livestock sector currently seems to be a sector in transition and, if so, how.
- ○ With reference to Table 15.1, what kinds of livestock farming are conducted in the country where you live? Which animal species are involved in the different forms?

16 Animal feeding, health and breeding

This chapter has a more practical approach than the previous one, and focuses directly on practical animal husbandry. Much attention is paid to the animals' nutrient needs and other aspects on the feeding of ruminants and non-ruminants. Similarly, you will learn about the importance of having access to sufficient water of good hygiene quality, for the animals to drink and for cleaning and other needs. Outdoor and indoor forms of animal farming were touched on in Chapter 15, but some attention is also paid to them here before the discussion turns to matters of animal health.

Keeping animals healthy is of key importance for levels of production, farm economy and animal welfare. Animal health can, however, be threatened by a variety of causes, and thus has to be continuously observed and managed by each person who works with the animals. You will then study matters of reproduction, animal breeding and different kinds of animal breeds. As something of a parallel to the list of yield influencing factors in Chapter 14, this chapter ends with a list of factors that impact the yields of meat, milk, eggs and other animal products.

After this chapter you are expected to:

- Know that farm animals' needs for feed can be understood in terms of body maintenance, growth and other requirements
- Have a fair idea of the main differences in the feeding of ruminants and non-ruminants
- Be able to give examples of different kinds of animal feed
- Be aware of the importance of fresh water in animal farming
- Have some familiarity with outdoor and indoor systems
- Be aware of the many factors of importance for farm animal health
- Have an idea of matters of farm animal reproduction
- Be able to give examples of some desirable traits for which various kinds of farm animals are bred
- Have a decent view on matters of animal breeds
- Know the main influencing factors of importance for levels of production in animal farming

Key words

Feeding, energy, protein, minerals, vitamins, body maintenance, growth, pregnancy, lactation, activity, ruminants, non-ruminants, water quantity, water quality, outdoors, indoors, animal health, reproduction, breeding, animal breeds.

Feeding the animals

Animal feed is a key factor in livestock farming in that it is highly decisive for what it is possible to produce, and represents a substantial part of the costs of production. It is important to provide the animals with sufficient amounts of energy, protein, minerals and vitamins, and to consider the different species' needs for various kinds of feed. In intensive dairy production, for instance, it is necessary to consider the proportions of roughage and cereals.

In poor smallholder farming, lack of feed can be a constantly pressing issue that reduces the yields and in severe situations even the number of animals as such. Feed supply can, however, also be seen as a problem among farmers in intensive animal production, who certainly can have problems with unexpectedly low yields or bad nutrient content, but just as often may be concerned about problems in making the animals consume enough to reach their production potential.

Nutrient needs for different purposes

Due to the crucial importance of animal feeding it is most valuable to adjust the feeding so that each animal, or category of animals, can be fed as optimally as possible. Both overfeeding and underfeeding are bad economically, due to underperforming animals, health problems, increased expenditures and lost revenues. Farm animals' needs for feed depend on the animal species and the individual animal. The individual animal's requirements are generally understood as the sum of needs for:

- Body maintenance: the need to maintain the body weight and fulfil basic physiological functions (similar to our basic daily need for calories and protein).
- Growth: required for animals that are not yet fully grown. Feeding for growth is often the major cost in the rearing of animals for meat production.
- Pregnancy, which naturally is relevant only for female mammals.
- Lactation, which also is relevant just for female mammals. Corresponding needs are to be considered in egg production. This is often the highest cost in high yielding dairy production.
- Activity, in the form of animal traction, riding or long distance movements over vast grasslands.

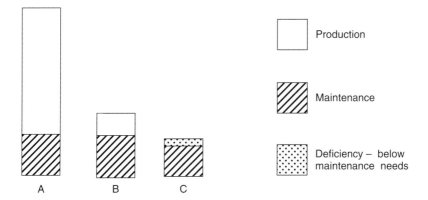

Figure 16.1 Needs for body maintenance and production at three levels of production. Bar A shows high production and B a modest level, while C illustrates low production by undernourished animals. The costs for body maintenance can be spread over more units of production in A than in B. In C the animal is underfed and is likely to produce on body reserves.

We may simplify the feed requirements as the sum of needs for maintenance and production, with production including growth, pregnancy, lactation and activity. The basic maintenance needs can be seen as a fixed cost that has to be managed irrespective of what the animal may produce. The other needs can be likened to variable costs of production. This way of thinking is illustrated by Figure 16.1, where the bars A and B illustrate different proportions between maintenance and production, while C illustrates a situation of feed scarcity and undernutrition.

Figure 16.1 can, for instance, be applied to milk. The high level of production in A then means that the fixed costs for body maintenance are spread over many litres of milk, for example 40 litres. The lower yield in B, 5 litres for example, means higher fixed costs per litre. In production of beef, pork, lamb/mutton and chicken production is concretized as body growth per day, week or month. Slow growth, B, means that the animals' basic needs have to be fulfilled during a long time period, while proportionally little growth is gained. The reasoning overlooks the fact that high levels of production may be obtained through more expensive feed and other costs, which means that the economic returns automatically cannot be assumed to be proportional to levels of production. The bar C illustrates a situation where the animal is underfed, due to acute feed shortage or lost appetite because of illness. As you can see, the animal is then not even supplied with enough to cover its maintenance needs. The individual animal can be expected to survive on body reserves for some time, and lactation will be reduced or will cease altogether.

Ruminants and non-ruminants

Whether an animal is a ruminant or not is largely decisive for the feeding strategy on a particular holding. While ruminants are able to digest and survive on grass and other herbaceous plants and vegetation, non-ruminants, primarily pigs and poultry, lack this capacity and thus have to be fed on more easily digestible matter, such as grains and maize.

Many of the world's farm animals are ruminants: cattle, buffaloes, sheep and goats, and even though camelids and horses differ, their digestion is more or less ruminant-like as regards the ability to utilize various kinds of vegetation. All these farm animal species are able to digest huge quantities of grass, straw, leaves, etc. and to transform them into valuable nutrients in the form of meat and dairy products.

Although ruminants and similar farm animals are able to produce human food without competing for cereals, there is no doubt that a great deal of the world's market oriented meat and milk production is based on arable crops, such as cereals, soybeans and other pulses and oil crops. Feed concentrates, composed of soybean, cottonseed and other protein-rich crops, are fed to both ruminants and non-ruminants in order to fulfil the calculated needs for specific types of production, for example to dairy cows, piglets, laying hens and in large-scale chicken production. Arable land is also used for grass, alfalfa and other plants for silage or hay. These plants can be biologically advantageous in view of crop rotation but are still competing for arable land.

Various kinds of forage

A large number of different kinds of feedstuff are used in world animal farming. Some of these are more commonly used in market than subsistence oriented farming and vice versa, and some are naturally more familiar in some parts of the world than in others. In addition, many types of fodder are primarily accessible to ruminants that are able to digest a wide range of feed that is difficult for monogastrics to manage. In Box 16.1 you can read more about different categories of animal feed.

Planning for the best possible feeding regime

Assessments of how to feed a particular herd often take the form of feeding plans, electronically or manually calculated. Irrespective of how the plan is made, the existence of a plan is most valuable and soon pays back the time and effort involved. In output driven livestock production (Chapter 15) the point of departure is the output, and what is needed to reach this as optimally as possible, through purchases and/or home produced forage. When animal production is input driven, the starting point is instead the available feeds, and the challenge is to make best possible use of this by distributing it as well as possible over the season and between the animals.

Box 16.1 Animal feed, some examples

1   Nutrient-rich roughage, primarily fed to ruminants:
    ○   Grass and other herbaceous plants in the form of grazing
    ○   Fresh grass fed directly to the animals
    ○   Silage, conserved grass, clover, maize, green early harvested grains, etc.
    ○   Hay, primarily dried grass and clover

2   Relatively nutrient-poor feedstuffs that are widely used as surrogates for more nutritious feed:
    ○   Straw, from grain etc.
    ○   Leaves and woody vegetation
    ○   Haulm and other kinds of crop residues
    ○   Household waste

3   Nutrient-rich feed from arable farming, fed to animals as the main product or as a by-product:
    ○   Grains, such as barley and wheat
    ○   Maize
    ○   Beans, such as soybean and many other kinds
    ○   Oilseed, such as rapeseed, sunflower and cottonseed
    ○   Sugar crops, by-products of processing
    ○   Roots and tubers

Feed plans on the basis of home produced feed require thorough estimates of the available quantities of fodder, plus analyses of their energy and nutrient content. It is also important to keep abreast of the feed market to learn about prices and nutrient content of eventual purchases. By planning, the feed can be more optimally distributed between the animals. Moreover, the plan can reduce the risk of there being a lack of feed during the often critical time just before the next harvest. It should be added that some farmers may have innate skills in assessing the best feeding for their animals which achieve results almost as close to the optimum as a theoretic plan.

Feeding plans can be looked at as equations where the sum of standards for the animals' different kinds of needs is balanced against the energy and nutrient value of the different feedstuffs to be used. The optimal feeding plan combines the feed so that each animal or group of animals is provided with what they need through a balanced combination of various feeds at the lowest possible cost. Standards for energy and nutrient needs are specific to the type of animal, live weight and aim of production. For example, the farmer can find out how his/her Charolais bulls should be fed to gain one kilo live weight per day.

Feeding plans may seem most relevant in large-scale market oriented farming, but they are also valuable in small-scale animal husbandry, where it is necessary to get the best value from each kind of resource. It can, however, be difficult to know what animals are consuming when they are fed combinations of grazing and probably unanalysed by-products, residues and home produced feed. As regards large-scale grazing, it is possible to make plans for the organization and use of grasslands, for which weighing or measuring of the animals can serve as beneficial supplementary tools, provided that these are practically possible.

Water in livestock production

Livestock farming is also deeply dependent on water. Substantial amounts are required for the animals to drink and some kinds of production consume large quantities of service water. Water is used for cleaning stables, pens and grounds; showering the animals, cooling stables and animals in intensive market oriented production in the tropics; washing milk utensils and sometimes for cooling milk.

The animals' needs for water are due to species, body weight, temperature and level of production, which, as stated previously, includes growth, pregnancy, lactation and/or activity. In Table 16.1 you can study some estimates of needs for drinking water at 15°C and 35°C, respectively, in relation to certain types of farm animals, body weight and to milk production when relevant.

Although approximate, the figures in Table 16.1 give an idea of the quantities of water that are needed for drinking. For example, a farm with 1,200 high yielding dairy cows will require more than 120,000 litres of water per day, plus substantial amounts of service water. It is relevant to assume that the higher needs for drinking water in hot climates are accompanied by higher needs for service water too, in order to manage good hygiene and animal welfare.

The accompanying body weights and milk yields in Table 16.1 should also be seen as examples. Two litres of milk per cow per day is relevant for small, poorly

Table 16.1 Approximate needs for drinking water for certain animal species, body weights and eventual milk production

Type of animal	Live weight, kg (example)	Milk production, litres per day (example)	Approximate needs for drinking water, litres per head per day	
			15°C	35°C
Cattle	200	2	22	29
Cattle	680	35	103	127
Sheep	36	0.4	9	20
Camel	350	4.5	32	52
Swine, sow, lactating	175		17	47
Fully grown broiler			0.2	0.6

Source: Adapted from Steinfeld *et al.* 2006b: 129.

fed local breeds, whereas the high producing example, 35 litres, can be found in market oriented dairy herds in, for example, Europe, although the level can be the double in highly intensively fed and managed herds. Likewise the live weights are relevant, but may differ in both directions.

Big commercial herds are generally supplied with water through automatic systems that offer free access to water day and night. Alternatively the animals can be taken to a water source in the surrounding area once or a few times a day (see Figure 16.2). A third alternative is to carry water, which is heavy work and can be very time consuming.

Poor water hygiene is a widespread problem that, among other things, causes problems with infected milk and bad animal health. Bad water in animal production can thus be a problem for both human and animal health. The problems among animals can be diffuse and hard to identify as caused by the water; for instance hampered growth, bad appetite, fertility problems and weak offspring. The preventive measures may include a chain of improved arrangements, such as use of sound and sheltered watercourses, hygienic piping systems and water troughs, plus periodic bacterial analyses of the water. Besides, water analyses are often required by dairy suppliers, because even small quantities of bad milk due to unhygienic water risk large quantities of milk at the dairy. The aforementioned measures can, however, be difficult to achieve, depending on available water

Figure 16.2 Smallholder farming in Cambodia, 2010, with a few cattle and a water pond down to the left.

Photo: Anna Martiin.

sources, regional water conditions, climate, farm economy and in the case of unsafe land tenure conditions.

Outdoors and indoors

Whether animal husbandry is operated outdoors, indoors or as a combination of the two has a great influence on feeding strategies, water supply, labour, handling of manure, fences and a number of other practical arrangements. The outdoor alternatives differ greatly, such as almost endless pastures, intensively fertilized and irrigated arable fields with intensive grazing, grazing of marginal pieces of land such as roadsides, pens with a concrete surface or animals tied up in the backyard. As an intermediate form the animals may be kept outdoors but with access to simple shelters against sun, wind and rain.

Indoor systems are dominated by various forms of tied-up systems, pens and loose housing systems. These major types can differ greatly in terms of animal welfare. You can find dark, damp and confined indoor environments, but also alternatives where the animals are kept in light and airy environments that actually may be superior to what is available for many people.

Seasonal changes in climate, grazing or other circumstances can lead to the need for more than one system, for instance indoor systems when temperatures are low, and outdoor systems during warmer periods. Thus the farmer may have to arrange for double systems as regards feeding, water, energy, land use organization, milking, labour and daily routines.

Animal health

Animal husbandry is more complex than just feeding, watering, housing and milking or collecting eggs. As with successful crop production, livestock farming calls for (1) thorough observation of the animals and their environment, (2) concrete preventive measures to avoid health problems, such as improved water, ventilation and a hygienic surface for the animals, and (3) rapid and sound action in order to handle emerging problems.

Appropriate physical arrangements are no guarantee of successful animal farming, which also requires ambition and a good eye for animals. In smallholder farming, conducted in poor conditions, you may find admirable individual efforts to compensate for material shortages, not least among women and children, who may work intensively for the best possible feeding and tending of animals.

Threats to animal health mean suffering for the animals but also problems for the farmer in the form of lowered production, loss of animals, animal fertility problems, personal worries, time-consuming care of sick animals, and costs for veterinary treatment and medicines. The consequences differ according to the severity of the disease or other health problem as such, but also according to the vulnerability of the individual business and household, and the economic and societal context, as is highlighted in the following quotation:

> One of the significant asymmetries between farmers and pastoralists is that the capital of the latter is tied up in living animals which are subject to catastrophic declines through disease. An epizootic can eliminate an entire herd well before the veterinary services reach the area.
>
> (FAO 2001)

Concerns about animal health include matters of zoonosis and epizootics, such as avian influenza (bird flu) and foot and mouth disease, which we will get back to in Chapter 21, which deals with food safety. An overview of major causes of animal health problems at farm level is given in Box 16.2, where the factors are structured thematically.

Box 16.2 Major causes of animal health problems

Animal environment
- Bad outdoor and indoor environments, such as: extreme temperatures, persistent rains, damp bedding, darkness, confined stables, pens and corrals, high levels of moisture and dust, high levels of ammonium and other gases, dirt, noise

Bad feeding, water problems
- Undernutrition, bad feed hygiene (dust, mould, bacteria), toxic wild plants
- Insufficient amounts of drinking water, bad water hygiene

Insects and pests of various kinds
- Harmful insects and parasites, such as the tsetse fly
- Snakes, predators and similar problems

Contagious bacteria and viruses
- Bacteria and viruses, causing infectious diseases of acute or chronic character, for example in udders and lungs

Fertility and offspring
- Fertility related diseases
- Complications after difficult births
- Weak offspring

Physical injures and other problems
○   Wounds
○   Problems with legs and hooves, at first causing pain and limping, but also causing reduced growth and other kinds of production problems
○   Overwork (draught animals)
○   Stress, due to overcrowded pens, stressful transportation and other factors, of which many are mentioned above

Farm animal reproduction

Reproduction is a vital and necessary part of animal husbandry, and in many cases the focal point around which production is based, not least in milk production. Without functioning and regular cycles of reproduction there are no offspring and no lactation; and without calves, lambs, goat kids, piglets and chicks there is no continued meat production. The dairy farmer thus has to pay attention to all parts of the reproduction cycle: heat detection; mating, including through artificial insemination (AI); pregnancy testing; gestation period; birth; lactation; weaning of calves; new period of heat detection; and so on. Table 16.2 shows the length of the gestation period for common farm animal species. The figures are approximate due to normal variations and to deviations between varieties, for example between different kinds of buffaloes.

Of the animals in Table 16.2, pigs are the only ones which often have more than one litter per year; often around 2 in highly market oriented production. In spite of relatively short periods of gestation, ewes and goats usually give birth once a year, which is also the case for cattle and in some cases for horses. Buffaloes and camels have longer intervals, which may include relatively long dry periods.

Artificial insemination has been used in some countries for more than half a century, and has gradually come to be practised for several farm animal species.

Table 16.2 Approximate gestation periods, expressed in months and days. Longer and shorter periods occur, due to individual variation and differences between varieties of the same species

Animal species	Approximate gestation period
Cattle	9 months, 10 days
Buffalo	10–10½ months
Camels	13–15 months
Horses	12 months
Sheep	5 months
Goats	5 months
Pigs	3 months, 3 weeks, 3 days

Through artificial insemination one male animal may produce thousands or tens of thousands of offspring, with variations between species. This makes it possible to distribute hereditary characters from outstanding individual animals, sometimes on an international scale. At the same time the technology requires thorough testing, so that negative traits will not be spread to thousands of offspring. In recent years more advanced technologies, such as transplantation of eggs, have been developed and spread, not least in high-tech dairy farming. In large-scale egg and chicken production the chicks are supplied by specialized hatcheries, from which they are rapidly delivered to specialized egg or chicken producing plants.

Despite the various technologies, large proportions of the world's animal husbandry are based on natural reproduction, for instance with a ram in the herd, sometimes borrowed from a neighbouring farm to avoid inbreeding. In the following we will touch on breeding and breeds, primarily with reference to market oriented livestock production.

Animal breeding

Farm animal breeding has long since been conducted in the form of so-called selective breeding, which, simplified, means that animals with desirable traits have been selected for breeding. Body size, health, fertility, temperament, exterior, milk yield, length of lactation period, fleece quality, egg yield and shell quality are some major features that have been subject to breeding through millennia and centuries.

Selective animal and plant breeding are similar as regards the basic idea of selecting and breeding on individuals with the most desirable traits in the hope of improving the next generation. Professional animal breeding at research institutes and the like is often, but not always, more complicated to work with, compared with plant breeding. First, animal breeding involves high costs for feeding, housing and labour, often higher than the revenues from parallel production. Second, it is economically and practically difficult to keep herds of a desirable size. Third, animal life cycles are generally longer than growing seasons and thus require many years of research before the results can be put into practice. Fourth, it can be difficult to distinguish between genetic and environmental factors and thus to choose the right animals that should become parents and, fifth, to obtain a desirable genetic change without negative side-effects on other traits. High milk yield capacity may, for example, bring about low protein content in the milk or high still birth frequency. Furthermore, some traits are highly hereditary but others are not, which can make it difficult to maintain the achieved results from generation to generation.

In spite of these challenges animal breeding has made great progress, which is reflected in the animals' exteriors and levels of production (see Figure 16.3). Today, the breeding sector works with advanced technologies, with DNA data and ova transplantation, among other things. Thus far, breeding has been more intensive in species of high commercial interest, in cattle, pigs and chickens.

Figure 16.3 Totally unconcerned about breeding and production.
Photo: Jakob Martiin.

For example, camels and buffaloes have been paid less attention, which, for example, is mirrored in long calving intervals among many buffalo varieties.

Breeds with specific characteristics

Generally speaking, an animal breed is distinguished from another by specific and often visible characteristics, such as colour, size and exterior, which are maintained from generation to generation. Breeds may also differ with regard to production, temperament and movement patterns, although it may not be relevant to claim these as breed specific. In many cases breed characteristics are decided on and specified by associations that work for and highlight a certain breed, for example the Arabian horse and the merino sheep, both with long histories of systematic breeding.

Farm animal breeds are also combined, through systematic cross breeding programmes or more randomly. Cross breeding is widely practised in animal farming and is also subject to scientific breeding, not least as regards pigs and poultry. Among the principal ideas of cross breeding is the aim of benefiting from the strengths of both breeds, at the same time as reducing weaknesses. Successful cross breeding requires, however, careful selection and combination.

The more or less synonymous terms local breed, traditional breed and indigenous breed are primarily identified with reference to a certain region, for example an island, to whose environmental conditions the local breed typically is utterly well adapted. Indigenous breeds are important for biodiversity, for the same reasons as were discussed in Chapter 14. Like indigenous plants, local animal breeds are carriers of a great variety of genes which are even more valuable in the current situation of ongoing internationalization and commercialization of farm animal breeding.

The pros and cons of indigenous animals versus imported pure breeds or cross breeds have been under discussion for centuries. Numerous historic and present examples tell of the spread of contagious diseases due to imported animals, and about problems with the foreign animal breeds thriving in and adapting to new natural environments. Despite this there is no doubt that many breeds have been successfully spread to different parts of the world, not least to regions with similar climatic conditions. The spread of the originally Dutch Holstein cattle illustrates the wide distribution as such, for example to North America and New Zealand, but also shows that it can be problematic to move animals to new, demanding climates and living conditions, like in Sub-Saharan Africa.

Apart from their value for production, animal breeds may have additional value for the individual farmer, for whom a specific breed can be something of a hobby that serves as a source of inspiration in the daily work. Glamorous and prestigious livestock shows with award-winning Angus or Charolais bulls or heifers are part of this world that also may generate extra revenues from the sale of individuals from reputable herds.

We will now leave matters of breeding and breeds, and start summing up matters of animal husbandry. Box 16.3 summarizes the life cycle of the dairy cow, which in part applies to other animals as well. Thereafter you will find a list of major factors of importance for farm animal production.

Box 16.3 The dairy cow in market oriented production, an example

The typical dairy cow in market oriented production gives birth to her first calf at about two years of age, or slightly later. After just over nine months of pregnancy the young heifer is now a cow with a yearly cycle that is characterized by calving and lactation (including heat and pregnancy), plus a few months dry period before the next calf is born. If our cow belongs to a herd that is kept outdoors for grazing during the warmer part of the year and indoors when it is colder, the cow will experience a dramatic shift in daily routines, feed and environment twice a year.

Calving can take place at any time of the year, at least when artificial insemination is used. This makes it possible to plan calving and lactation in line with the dairy market, feeding, labour and other aspects of production on the farm in question. A few days on heat can be expected about every third week, and in the case of artificial insemination it is necessary for the farmer to detect the heat and decide the best possible day, or even hour for insemination. As a rough estimate the cow may be maintained in the herd between three and eight lactations, with large variations depending on the individual's milk production, fertility and health, but also on the farmer's strategy for his/her herd. The threats to health include complications after calving, fertility problems, infectious mastitis, leg and hoof problems, intestinal parasites, and metabolic problems due to an eventual imbalance between feed intake and milk production.

In market oriented production the calf consumes a minor share of the daily milk yield, about 4–6 litres per day, whereas the majority is sold. The daily milk yield is heavily dependent on feeding intensity, health and breed, but 30–35 litres per day is common, with higher levels during the first months of the lactation period, and lower during the last months. Record yields are notably higher than that.

Each cow (and other lactating mammal) has an individual lactation curve, which shows the daily milk yield day by day during the lactating period. As you can see from the two lactation curves in this box, similar yearly production can be achieved in different ways. The cow with the steep graph has a higher peak, which requires high feed intake and highly concentrated feed as long as the peak lasts. Thereafter, production is drastically reduced, because of difficulties keeping the balance between milk and feed, or due to some health problem. The flatter graph is less demanding as regards nutrient concentration, and may include fewer metabolic health problems. If you compare the area below each graph you will find that the flatter alternative in this example gives at least as much milk as the steeper one, but requires less concentrated feed and thus may include more home produced roughage and fewer expensive purchases of feed concentrates.

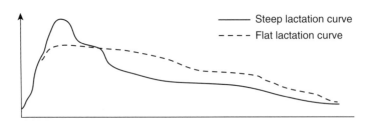

——— Steep lactation curve

– – – – Flat lactation curve

Major factors of importance for animal production

As a parallel to the crop yield influencing factors in Chapter 14, the following list shows the main factors of importance for levels of production in animal farming:

- Feed quantity
- Nutrient content of the feed
- Hygiene quality of the feed
- Farmers' ability to buy supplementary feed
- Water quantity and hygiene quality
- Outdoor and indoor environment
- Climate and weather
- Pressure from insects, parasites and infectious diseases
- Animal fertility
- Animal health
- Animal breed and genetic potential for production
- Access to veterinary service, artificial insemination and advisory service
- The farmers' ambition and eye for animals

Summary

Animal feed is highly decisive for what it is possible to produce. The feeding is also of the greatest importance for the farm economy and animal health. Shortages of energy, protein, minerals and vitamins are directly reflected in production. The individual animal's requirements are generally understood as the sum of its needs for body maintenance and production in terms of growth, pregnancy, lactation and activity. The energy and nutrient needs for maintenance have to be provided for irrespective of production, and can thus represent a major share of the total feeding costs when yields are low.

Whether an animal is a ruminant or not is largely decisive for how the animal should be fed. While ruminants are able to digest and survive on grass and other herbaceous plants, pigs and poultry have to be fed on more easily digestible matter, such as cereals. A feeding plan serves as a beneficial tool for the planning of feed purchases, and the distribution of available feeds between the animals and over the season. Water is another decisive factor in production, primarily as drinking water but also as service water. In addition to concerns about volumes, it is important to maintain water hygiene, which is a source of risks to animal health and indirectly to human health too.

Among the outdoor forms of animal farming there are a wide range of alternatives, ranging from vast pasture lands and intensive grazing of arable land to grazing of marginal pieces of land, confined pens and creatures that are tied up in backyards. You will also find intermediate forms where the animals are kept outdoors but have access to simple shelters against the sun, wind and rain. Indoors farm animals are principally tied up, kept in pens or in loose housing systems adapted to species, age of the animals and other categories.

Animal health problems mean suffering for the animals and problems for the farmer, for instance due to reduced production and animal fertility, lost animals, personal worries and time-consuming tending of sick animals, and costs for veterinary services and medicines.

Regular reproductive cycles are necessary for all kinds of animal farming, without which there will be no dairy products, no eggs and no meat. In addition to the reproduction as such, the breeding of cattle, sheep, pigs, chicken and other farm animals is, like plant breeding, of great importance for yields and other kinds of characteristics. The chapter ends with a summarizing list of the main factors that influence the yields in farm animal production.

Next

We will now leave the concrete work with crops and animals and move on to the fifth and final part of the book. In Chapter 17 you will come across some major aspects of the management of a farm. We will discuss the farm as a system, objective setting and decision making, and discuss farm inputs from more theoretical perspectives.

To discuss

○ Look for figures on yields in different kinds of livestock production, such as buffalo milk, sheep milk, eggs, beef, pork, mutton, chicken and wool.

○ Look for differences in yields of one kind of product, such as cow's milk, in different parts of the world and which you would suggest might be due to different production conditions. Reflect on the dissimilarities you have found, as we did regarding maize yields in Table 14.1 in Chapter 14.

○ Select a category of farm animals that you are interested in and look for examples of how it is recommended they are fed, for instance in the country where you live. Consider types of feed and approximate recommended quantities in relation to production per animal per day.

○ Consider water recommendations for the same animal category.

○ Is the category of farm animals you have selected kept in indoor and/ or outdoor systems where you live?

○ Continue with the same category of animals and the country where you live, and try to find out if the species seems to be threatened by particular kinds of health problems (Box 16.2).

○ What breeds of the selected species are common in the country where you live?

Part V

Managing the farm and the market

17 Managing the farm

In addition to the day-to-day running of the farm, and the challenge of staying on good terms with the weather and the season, it is necessary to have a management perspective on the undertakings. A farm is more than acreage, animals, buildings and technologies; it is a system where production, economy, human resources and external forces interact, and this system has to be planned, organized, directed and controlled.

You will read in more detail about the setting of long- and short-term aims for the farm, and about decisions on what to produce, how to do it, and what quantities and qualities. We will also pay attention to the process of decision making, which can be a matter of small-scale daily decisions as well as questions with decisive long-term consequences. Substantial interest is also paid to the categorization of inputs, with specific emphasis on the allocation of resources at farm level in general, and of arable land in particular.

You may consider this chapter more abstract than the previous crop and animal chapters in Part IV. Market oriented farming with safe access to land serves as a point of reference for some of the discussion, but the principal ideas about the running of a farm are valid for other forms of agriculture too.

After this chapter you are expected to:

- Be aware of farm management as a key factor in farming
- Be able to describe the farm as a system, including its parts and interactions
- Be aware of the importance of setting and resetting objectives for the individual farm
- Give an account of the main stages in the process of decision making
- Be familiar with the terms scarce resources and resource allocation

- ○ Be familiar with the way of categorizing inputs as either land, labour, capital or management
- ○ Be able to discuss alternative allocation of land within the farm

Key words

Farm management, planning, organizing, directing, controlling, scarce resources, resource allocation, farm system, aims of production, decision making, land, labour, capital, management.

Why farm management matters

The management of a farm has much in common with the management of any other kind of business, although agriculture's dependence on weather, seasons and biological rhythms adds additional dimensions. In its widest meaning agricultural and other types of management can be distinguished as matters of the following processes:

- Planning
- Organizing
- Directing
- Controlling

At the same time as farm production differs from many other kinds of activities because of its close dependence on nature, many aspects are ruled like others, such as the impact of supply and demand, the cost of labour and energy, and the world economy at large. This is especially true for market oriented farming but spills over into subsistence farming as well. The influence of both nature and the economy gives agriculture a complex character that speaks for thorough management and preparedness for unpredictable events in crop and animal farming as well as in prices, demand and other economic factors.

The importance of thorough management is in fact so strong that differences in the outcomes from otherwise similar farms may be explained by differences in the farmers' approach to and management of issues. To illustrate what concrete management can be about at farm level, Box 17.1 presents some examples of planning and decision making that often take place in the farmer's mind, in parallel with the practical work in the farmyard, on the tractor or among the animals.

Good farm management typically finds the farmer a step ahead, active and observant, and able to solve practical problems in parallel with continued managerial tasks. The opposite, insufficient farm management and lack of planning, organization,

---

Box 17.1 Farm management issues, some examples

1   How can we use this morning as efficiently as possible?
2   Is there anything we could do to manage another day of drought?
3   Do we dare borrow money to buy more fertilizer?
4   How much should the different categories of cattle be fed to make the best possible use of this year's limited amount of silage?
5   Is this the right day to have the buffalo mated, or is tomorrow better?
6   What is most economical in the long run, repairing the old tyres or buying new ones for the tractor?
7   Do we have to invest time and money in improved drainage before the next season, despite the unusually high interest rates at the moment?
8   If I accept the extra job I've been offered, would it benefit or threaten the farm economy? In the short run? In the long run?

---

direction and control, typically means that the farm will be run *ad hoc*, with the farmer a step behind, frantically busy solving urgent problems.

The *ad hoc* model may be due to the individual but can be also be related to uncertain farming and living conditions because of unsafe access to land, health problems and lack of economic safety nets. It is difficult and hardly inspiring to make plans that will not be realized because the land is lost; or because farming ambitions are overshadowed by illness and medical costs. Still, insufficient management of the farm might result in even more difficult situations, where the farm will rule both the people and the farm economy, instead of the opposite.

The farm, seen as a system

As you know from the previous chapters, global agriculture is based on large numbers of farms that exhibit uncountable alternative combinations of elements, nature, interactions, resource flows and societal impact. Consequently each farm system can be understood as unique; we can not find two exactly identical holdings. We can, however, categorize farms and farm system (see Box 10.2), on a basis of varying criteria such as land tenure, access to irrigation or not, arable and/or animal farming, types of crop production, degree of mechanization, organization of labour, etc. For example farm systems based on coffee production have many similarities and differ greatly from farm systems based on pig production, but there are individual differences between each coffee producing farm as well. Moreover, each individual farm system can be studied in terms of subsystems, such as the crop system and the livestock system at a holding with mixed farming. These systems can be further divided, for instance into the calf rearing

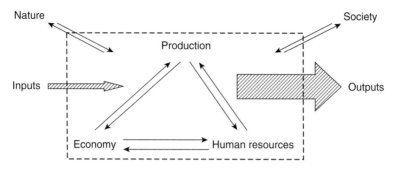

Figure 17.1 The farm, outlined as a system that is open to resource flows into and out of the system, and where farm production, economy and human resources interact under the influence of the forces of nature and local, national and international societies.

system, the milk production system and the silage producing system that are managed within the same farming unit.

You can study an outline of the farm system in Figure 17.1, which shows a farm system with: a) elements such as areas, crops, livestock, labour and technology level; b) influences of nature; c) interaction between production, economy, nature and human resources; d) flows of resources into, within and out from the farm, including purchases, internal use and sale; e) impact of land tenure aspects; f) social and cultural conditions; and g) other kinds of external societal factors, such as agricultural politics and foreign trade.

Setting aims, for the day and the way forward

Each kind of farming, big and small, and with various degrees of market orientation, is dependent on clear objectives to guide the farming activities on the way forward. The objectives can be large or small scale, clearly thought out or diffuse. The setting of aims for a particular farming unit is first and foremost important for the running of the farm, but is also beneficial for communicating with advisers, bankers, and various kinds of sellers and buyers. Objective setting is commonly an issue for the individual farmer, but can in some cases be directly controlled, for example by state interests in the production of certain amounts of food and other kinds of agricultural products.

Almost all farmers have some kind of objective for their business, even if the aims are implicit rather than explicit (see Figure 17.2). A simple but still important aim can, for instance, be to grow at least as much as last year.

We can talk of large-scale and small-scale objectives, and long-term and short-term aims. Long-term objectives cover several years or even decades, and should chiefly be seen as directional aims that may be revised over the years. The long-term aims should be reasonable and inspiring, and serve as the focal point to

Figure 17.2 The objectives at a certain farm may be to maintain animal health, improve the fertility of the cows or to enlarge the herd.

Photo: Jakob Martiin.

which the short-term aims should refer. While long-term objectives in part may be something of a vision, short-term objectives are more concrete. The short-term aim is often limited in time, and specified in terms of quantities or other measurable results. While short-term goals should be related to long-term objectives, it is important that the former are valuable as such, irrespective of whether the envisaged long-term aims will be achieved.

Table 17.1 illustrates long- and short-term objectives at two different farms: one highly market oriented and one primarily subsistence oriented farm. The long-term goal in the first example highlights the maintainance of profitability and the capacity to meet external pressures, which calls for continuous considerations of efficiency, investments, maintenance, competence, and analyses of the market and other parts of society. The second example emphasizes the aim of producing a surplus to sell, in addition to the subsistence aims, which requires improved production and/or expansion as well as continuous attention to demand, prices and ways of selling the produce. The two farmers in Table 17.1 primarily have to pay attention to the short-term aims, to the small steps, which requires active planning, organization, direction and control to make sure that the business is on the right path towards the long-term aims.

Objective setting is a dynamic process that occasionally needs to be reconsidered and modified, due to internal or external circumstances. Farm one in Table 17.1 may, for instance, have to reduce the number of year-round employees from two to one, because of lowered prices of pork, which in turn will require rethinking efficiency and technologies, and changes to the previous objectives.

Table 17.1 Examples of long- and short-term objectives at one highly market oriented and one primarily subsistence oriented farm

	Highly market oriented	*Highly subsistence oriented*
Long-term objective	Maintain the farm as an enterprise that provides for the farmer and two year-round employees, at the same time as the farm is well kept and up-to-date	Increase the production for sale, at the same time as the household is sufficiently supplied with various products for use in kind
Short-term objective 1	Increase the number of delivered hogs by 5 per cent within a year	Improve crop farming with the help of better sowing seed
Short-term objective 2	Reduce the consumption of fuel by 5 per cent per hectare within a year	More frequent weeding, and better timing of the weeding
Short-term objective 3	Introduce an additional crop in the crop rotation system in order to reduce exposure to price volatilities	Explore the possibility of joining a local cooperative, which would facilitate selling the increased production

Detailed aims of production

Short-term objectives are often matters of concrete aims of production, which generally can be expressed in the form of questions about:

o   What to produce
o   How to produce
o   How much to produce, and of what quality

What to produce is highly determined by consumer demand and expected price levels, at the same time as nature related and practical factors limit the alternatives at a particular farm. If the products are aimed at use in kind, crop or animal production is heavily influenced by needs and preferences at the farming unit. The question 'how' can theoretically be answered in terms of resource allocation (see Box 17.3), but more concretely as a matter of methods of production, such as fertilizer, seed, chemicals, machinery, energy and labour, and how the production is organized. It may, for example, be relevant for the farmer to discuss how a certain crop should be harvested, with owned or leased machinery. The third question, how much to produce, is limited by access to land and by the upper limits for what it is possible to obtain per acreage and farm animal. As you know from Part IV, the quality of the sowing seed, amounts of fertilizers and other factors of production determine what can be achieved, although neither volumes nor qualities can be decided with 100 per cent accuracy.

In addition to the aims of production, several other incentives may accompany farmers' motives for being farmers, such as social and cultural aspects, and personal interest in farming as a profession. This kind of perspective might contribute to more nuanced action than in businesses where profitability is the only driving force.

Making decisions

Farm management is largely about making decisions: decisions about planning, organizing, directing and controlling. We make hundreds of small and big daily decisions, and farming is no exception. Many of the decisions refer to detailed matters, such as how much to feed a certain animal or in what order things should be done. Ideally the farmer relates all decisions to the framework that is set by the long- and short-term objectives for the farm. If, for example, improved animal health is an objective, it is natural to make decisions that consequently promote animal health. Where an effort is not in line with the objectives set, it is of the greatest importance to avoid decisions and activities that counteract the objectives set.

Decision making is a gradual process that is described slightly differently by various authors, but can be outlined as the following steps:

- Continuous observations of all parts of the farm system, and of external factors that might influence the farm
- Detection of problems, either (1) upcoming acute problems or (2) suboptimal existing conditions with potential for improvement
- Identification of the problem
- Analysis of the problem
- Search for alternative ways to solve or handle the problem, in line with the overall objectives for the farm
- Choice of the most promising of the alternatives
- Implementation of the selected alternative
- Following the outcome of the decision
- Evaluation of the outcome and taking responsibility

The first stage of the decision process is a matter of observation in order to detect potential problems early. When a problem has been identified, the process of decision moves forward to analysis and the search for alternative solutions to choose between. Depending on the type of problem and the individual farmer, the stage of analysis may be a short or drawn-out process; the latter, for example, may be the case with decisions about big investments. Sooner or later, however, the process has to be moved forward to some kind of decision and implementation. It is easy to underestimate needs for run-in periods for new methods and technologies, which may require time, patience and additional costs before the improvement works as planned. The final step is to take responsibility: to modify things, deal with calculated and unexpected costs, and to adjust to the outcome.

Table 17.2 shows the stages in the decision making process with reference to ordinary kinds of decisions at two different farms. The first example is a French farmer's problems with wheat, while the second describes decision making associated with a sick animal on an Indian smallholding.

As you have already seen, decisions at farm level include very different kinds of problems: dealing with land, labour, fertilizer, seed, animal feed and other kinds of input resources. In the following section we will give particular attention to inputs and how these can be categorized and dealt with from more theoretical points of view.

Table 17.2 Examples of step-wise decision making at farm level

Stages in the decision making process	Example 1 Large-scale wheat production in France	Example 2 Small-scale dairy production in India
Observe	A French farmer drives around between the fields and observes the plant growth.	An Indian dairy farmer milks the cows in the early evening and checks the udder health, as always.
Detect	He finds some kind of disease on several wheat plants in one of the fields.	She finds lumps in the milk from one of the three dairy cows.
Identify	He suspects some kind of rust.	The udder is swollen and the cow seems to have a fever. The farmer identifies the problem as mastitis.
Analyse	The problem can become severe. Something has to be done.	The problem is found to be acute.
Alternative solutions	Alternative solutions according to the farmer's previous experience: • Chemical treatment. Costs versus losses? • Wait and see.	Alternative solutions, according to the farmer's previous experience: • Antibiotics from the veterinary station, 5 km away. But how will she be able to pay? • Frequent milking and other more traditional efforts that are free of charge.
Choose an alternative	Consultation with a plant pathologist. Due to a tricky economic situation at the farm after last year's drought, the farmer is not prepared to take the economic losses of large-scale infestation. He thus decides to apply pesticides as soon as possible.	Consultation with an experienced neighbour. The farmer decides to ask the vet for antibiotics, because of the risk of losing the cow if she does not recover quickly. A prerequisite is, however, that the bill can be paid later.
Implement	Immediate call to a local entrepreneur, who undertakes the assignment and treats the field the same evening.	The farmer walks to the vet. The cow is treated the same evening and during the following days.
Await the outcome	The farmer observes the infested field and his other fields.	The farmer milks frequently, making extra observations and taking extra care for a couple of weeks to make sure that the cow recovers. The milk is again delivered to the local dairy.
Evaluate and take responsibility	The operation seems to have been successful. In addition the farmer observes and reflects in order to learn for the future. He pays the bill from the entrepreneur.	The benefits of the treatment are considered. The medicine is paid for by part of the payment from the dairy.

Categorization of input resources

The classic way of considering input resources is to categorize them as land, labour or capital. The perspective derives from economic thinking in the late eighteenth and early nineteenth centuries and is still in use, albeit in modified versions and often including the management category, which was added later. Today's farming, especially in highly market oriented forms, is more complex than two centuries ago, before the establishment of the fossil fuel regime and before the beginning of large-scale industrialization and urbanization. By that time all kinds of farming were carried out manually or with animal traction, whereas the possibility of replacing manual labour with machinery was not yet in view. This confuses the traditional categorization and can be handled in various ways. You will find suggested explanations of the categories in Box 17.2.

You may already have observed that all kinds of farm production require elements from each category: you cannot farm without land; you cannot farm without labour; you cannot farm without several of the inputs that are included in the category capital; and you cannot farm without managing the processes. In the

---

Box 17.2 Classic categorization of the means of production

Land
The category land includes all nature-given factors that influence farm production, such as: land, soils, topography, temperature, length of day and season, precipitation and humidity.

Labour
The classic definition of labour stands for practical work done by the farmer, paid and unpaid family members and friends, or permanent and casual employees. This understanding of the term labour is narrower than the present one, which often considers labour and labour saving technologies as more or less exchangeable, although the latter may be categorized as capital.

Capital
The category capital includes a wide range of different kinds of assets, including long-term investments as well as stocks of crops and live animals. According to Federico (2005: 40), agricultural capital can be categorized in five groups: (1) improvements that are made to land, such as fences and terraces; (2) farm buildings; (3) farm machinery and other equipment and tools; (4) farm animals; (5) working capital, such as standing crops and stocks. We may also consider capital in terms of durable and non-durable assets, such as buildings and tractors, on the one hand, and seed and livestock, on the other.

Management
In line with the previous discussion in this chapter, farm management means planning, organizing, directing and controlling, through frequent and good decision making.

continued discussion about inputs we will build freely on the classic categorization; for more specific studies, such as theoretical work in terms of formulas and graphs, you are referred to specific courses and literature.

The different kinds of resources that are used in farm production are often considered to be scarce, which calls for continuous efforts to allocate and reallocate the resources in order to be as efficient as possible. Box 17.3 explains more about the approach to thinking about resources in terms of scarcity and allocation, which is closely related to neoclassical economic thought.

Box 17.3 Management of scarce resources

Farm management is often considered as a matter of scarce resources, such as land, labour, irrigation water, crop nutrients, sowing seed and animal feed, and how these should be allocated as efficiently as possible. The term scarce resources is widely used in neoclassical economics, which highlights economics as a matter of scarce resources and efficient resource allocation in line with set objectives. In their *Agricultural Economics and Agribusiness* the agricultural economists Cramer, Jensen and Southgate write:

> In the overall, economics is concerned with overcoming the effects of scarcity by improving the efficiency with which scarce resources are allocated among their many competing uses, so as to best satisfy human wants.
> (Cramer *et al.* 2001: 5)

Striving for the efficient allocation of scarce resources at farm level means that the farmer frequently has to question current resource use and look for potential improvements. The flows of resources and money that are involved in market oriented farming offer a great variety of resource use and resource allocation, for example to exchange time for money. For example, a farmer with little spare time can decide to pay a plumber to mend the water system in the pig stable, and use his/her saved working hours on planning for the coming growing season. Such possibilities are less available in subsistence farming, with its minimum cash flow, and altered resource use thus primarily has to take the form of mutual exchanges within the local society.

Replace one resource by another

Changes in the cost of different kinds of farming resources, or other considerations, can motivate changes in the proportions between land, labour, capital and management. This will first be discussed with the help of an example from agricultural history, before and during the European Industrial Revolution. According to the Dutch economic historian J.L. van Zanden, the late nineteenth and early twentieth centuries experienced increased population, rising prices for grains and reduced costs of labour which made it possible to increase agricultural production through intensified labour. As wages rose after 1870, driven by expanding urban labour markets, continuing productivity increases had to be managed through other inputs than labour, which by this time were made available by the increased supply of inorganic fertilizer and feed concentrates from overseas trade.

Moving on to contemporary agriculture, increased wage levels accompanied by the comparatively low cost of machinery and fossil fuel contribute to the replacement of labour by farm machinery (see Figure 17.3). Substitutions like these are not always possible; it is not a given that increases in some parts of the economy are accompanied by decreases in others. We have, for instance, experienced parallel increases in the cost of land and fertilizers which might prevent otherwise logical action in the form of increased fertilizing to compensate for the increased cost of land, or vice versa.

Figure 17.3 Mechanization can in part be explained by the higher cost of farm labour than of farm machinery and fuel. Thailand, 2010.

Photo: Anna Martiin.

The replacement of one input resource by another may be a more or less perfect matter of substitution, which means that one input resource can be replaced by another with output maintained. Input B is a substitute for input A when B can replace A without any changes in output, all other factors held constant. Maize and wheat, for example, may serve as more or less perfect substitutes for each other, in baking and cookery or as animal feed. This makes the national and global yields of these two crops especially interesting in terms of food supply, food prices, animal production and world food trade.

In *The Economics of Agricultural Development* (2006) the agricultural economists G.W. Norton, J. Alwang and W.A. Masters use the terms 'input-using innovations' and 'input-saving innovations', which can be applied to our thinking in terms of land, labour and capital. In the first case, the purchase of a tractor means increased use of fuel (capital). Input-saving innovations instead reduce the use of some resource, for example labour. The tractor example can thus be seen as both input-using and input-saving. Time-saving working routines and improved animal health are often resource saving without any kind of accompanying resource increase. In the following concluding section of this chapter we will concentrate on allocation of land resources, which is one of the key tasks in farm management. Labour is another, and that is a major focus in Chapter 18, which also deals with the management of the farm.

Allocation of land at farm level

Everyone with access to a piece of land, big or small, has to decide how to use the area. Arable land especially offers many alternative choices, in comparison with pasture and forest land. As you know from previous chapters, arable land can be used for a variety of foods, animal feed, fibres, bio-energy and other non-foods. Once a decision is taken and implemented, other kinds of cultivation will be excluded until it is time for new crops (provided that no additional land is available and that other factors are held constant). Figure 17.4 shows four alternative ways to use a specific area, and illustrates how one kind of tillage excludes another.

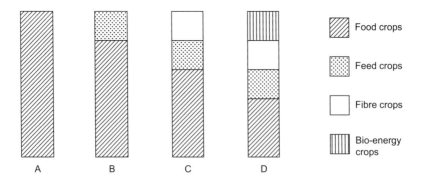

Figure 17.4 Examples of alternative ways to make use of a specific area. The columns represent the total arable area at the farms A–D. Decisions to cultivate one kind of crops (or a mixture of crops) mean that others are reduced or excluded.

The first alternative, A, in Figure 17.4 illustrates a farm where the entire acreage is used for food crops. In B food and feed production are combined, and in C food and feed are accompanied by fibres, such as cotton, although at the expense of the food and feed area. In D food crops cover less than half the area in A, while a major part of the acreage is used for other kinds of crops.

In highly market oriented arable farming the combination of crops may be based on active decisions about the most profitable alternative, within what is practicably possible, whereas household needs are highly decisive for what to grow in subsistence oriented agriculture. Thus we can expect a more multifaceted combination of crops in the latter.

Figure 17.4 can also be studied from national and global perspectives, as demonstrating how the allocation of land for different purposes has consequences for other kinds of production, provided that other factors, such as technology levels, are held constant. A recent example is when arable land is reallocated from food to bio-energy production.

Summary

Good farm management typically finds the farmer a step ahead, active and observant, and able to solve practical problems in parallel with continued managerial tasks. More theoretically expressed, management includes planning, organizing, directing and controlling the business. Insufficient management efforts may be due to the individual case but can also be explained by unsafe farming and living conditions which reduce the possibilities of making plans and seeing them come to fruition.

The management of a farm benefits from a holistic view and a systems perspective. Typically the farm system is characterized by the flows of resources into and out of the system, by processes of production, farm economy, human resources, and by the impact of nature and external societal factors.

Each kind of farming, big and small, and with various degrees of market orientation, benefits from clear objectives to guide the farming activities on the way forward. While long-term goals may serve as a vision for the future, the short-term aims should be more specific. Aims also have to be set for the various kinds of production at the farm, as regards what to produce, how to do it and about the quantity and quality to be produced. In this chapter you have also read about the stepwise decision making process, including two examples.

Farm inputs can be categorized in terms of land, labour, capital and management, which all are necessary for the ability to farm, although in various forms and proportions. In addition, it may be possible to substitute one input for another, because of altered costs and for other reasons. As a final point this chapter includes a discussion about the allocation of arable land at farm level, highlighting alternatives but also the constraints that follow with the character of land as a fixed resource.

Next

Chapter 18 continues the management theme by highlighting various angles on farm work, bottlenecks and the importance of timing. You will also read about alternative ways to structure and organize farming, and about intensive versus extensive and specialized versus diversified production. Attention is also paid to administration, risks and some aspects of advisory services.

To discuss

○ Reflect on the differences in the management of a fully owned farm holding and of a holding with unsafe access to land (Chapter 9).
○ Examine Figure 17.1 and try to concretize the different parts, by applying them to the production of a particular crop and animal production, respectively.
○ Imagine an individual farm, with production and location of your own choice, and suggest a long-term objective plus a number of short-term objectives that support the long-term objective but also seem to be beneficial as such.
○ Suggest a fictional decision making process for a highly market oriented pig producing farmer who observes a tendency towards falling pork prices.
○ Look for examples where one kind of resource use may be replaced by another, for example artificial insemination by natural mating.
○ Which of the bars A–D in Figure 17.4 do you find most relevant for the area where you live?

18 Working with agriculture

The central focus of attention in this chapter is farm work that is dealt with from very different angles, such as: workforce, labour categories, working conditions, responsibilities and skills. We will also discuss structuring of time, and the importance of organizing the work so that it moves on without bottlenecks and similar problems. Furthermore, you will read about different ways of organizing labour and production, through various joint arrangements, occasional collaboration between neighbours and hiring in of machinery or labour.

Whether the production is intensive or extensive, whether inputs and output per hectare or animal are high or low, this influences the use of resources and the farm economy but naturally also the work. The same applies to specialization on a few products, or, on the contrary, to work with many different kinds of production. Moreover, we will touch on administrative tasks, which are not the favourite activity of all farmers, but are both necessary and quite beneficial for the management of the farm. Agricultural insurance and other forms of safety nets are also paid some attention, including reflections on risk averseness in farming. The remaining part of the chapter is devoted to advisory services and other kinds of communication. Many highly market oriented farmers are faced with almost constant flows of commercial and non-commercial information, while others are not. We will consider frequently communicated topics and information channels, and the variety of actors that are involved in the world of agricultural information, which, by the way, might be a part of your current or future job.

After this chapter you are expected to:

- ○ Be able to discuss various factors that influence the need for labour at a particular farm, plus factors that may hamper the possibility of engaging sufficient labour
- ○ Be familiar with some typical characteristics of farm work in various kinds of farming
- ○ Have a fair idea of the importance of timing in crop and animal production and other farming issues

   o   Be aware of the problem of bottlenecks in farm machinery chains, as well as in chains based on manual farm work

   o   Be able to compare and discuss typical intensive, extensive, specialized and diversified agriculture

   o   Be able to give examples of various kinds of administrative task at farm level

   o   Be aware of the existence of advisory services and various marketing activities directed at different kinds of farming, and of frequently communicated topics

Key words

Working conditions and requirements, part time, family farming, timing, machinery chains, bottlenecks, intensive, extensive, specialization, diversification, administration, farm insurance, safety nets, risk, advisory service, information.

The number of people engaged at the farm

There are no linear relationships between the number of people engaged and the acreage or herd size at the farm in question. The labour force is instead decided by combinations of many influencing factors that on the one hand refer to concrete needs and on the other hand to the possibilities of engaging people for the work. You will find a number of suggested factors that belong to the first category in Box 18.1 and to the second in Box 18.2.

    The labour intensity differs enormously and is generally low in highly mechanized large-scale farming but high in smallholder farming. Enormous acreages

---

Box 18.1 Factors that influence the need for labour at a particular farm

- Degree of mechanization
- Crops: kinds of crops and degree of intensity in the production
- Livestock: kinds of farm animals and degree of intensity in the production
- Seasonal peaks
- Access to buffering family labour (Box 18.5)
- Distances to fields (Chapter 10), water, roads, etc.
- Degree and types of post-harvest work
- Hiring in of external services, such as machinery repair
- Time-consuming engagement in farmers' associations, sales cooperatives, etc.
- Other undertakings, such as transportation, road building, etc.

Box 18.2 Factors that influence the possibility of engaging sufficient labour

- Economic possibilities to have people engaged at a particular farm
- The local labour market in general – unemployment or the reverse?
- Competing other jobs
- Access to farm labour with respect to temporary or permanent work
- Access to farm labour with respect to qualifications
- Practical arrangements, such as housing, arrangements for family members, working conditions, etc.

---

and numbers of livestock may be managed by just a few people who produce necessities for thousands or tens of thousands consumers. In contrast, about the same number of people may work intensively on a few hectares, carry water and firewood, and carry out the post-harvest handling and other stages all along to cooking, which at best supplies the household. There are pros and cons with both these polar opposites, but there is no doubt that labour efficiency is higher in the first alternative. Besides, it can be interesting to note that the world's biggest farms employ tens or hundreds of people, whereas the giant companies at the end of the food chain can have tens or hundreds of thousands of people working for them.

Various kinds of farm work

Farm work can differ greatly due to various types of crops and livestock; technologies; social and cultural contexts; over the year; and due to the climate and current weather. In the following, five different kinds of characteristics of farm work around the globe will be discussed. First, farming requires a wide range of skills and responsibilities, ranging from highly qualified to monotonous tasks. Farmers often have to be skilled, flexible all-rounders, able to solve problems that otherwise are dealt with by a specific profession, as illustrated in Box 18.3.

Box 18.3 Similarities between farming and other professions

- Driving a gigantic high-tech combine in a maize field has much in common with other qualified technical jobs
- Assisting a complicated calving has similarities with veterinarian duties
- Manual digging of a ditch could be almost the same as manual road building
- Picking fruit has similarities with work on assembly lines
- Farm management has much in common with the running of any kind of business

The extent to which the farmer has to be a jack of all trades depends, however, on the kind of farming and on the competences among the others on the holding, which leads to a second kind of characteristic. You can find the most varied forms of engagement in world farming, such as: self-employed farmers who work alone; farming carried out by almost all members of extended families; year-round employees; seasonal employees; casual farmhands; and occasionally engaged neighbours and friends who get involved when a helping hand is needed. In addition you can meet hired-in specialists on short visits, such as electricians, veterinarians or consultants in animal nutrition or farm management, although this happens first and foremost on big market oriented farms that are able to pay for these kinds of support.

Third, the working time is not always regular, but rather varies from day to day and between seasons. Peak periods, for example in horticulture, may be followed by less intensive working periods, which may be the same as periodical unemployment for seasonal farmhands. In contrast, dairy farming has to be carried out 365 days a year. Trade unions may regulate working conditions, but it is fair to say that many of the categories working at farm level work comparatively long hours and that, generally speaking, holidays are rare, although they certainly do occur. Besides, the working time can be assumed to be reduced by traditionally work-free days and other cultural events.

Where farm work is combined with off-farm work, even a relatively small holding may occupy the keeper during all the remaining time. You can read about part-time farming in Box 18.4.

Fourth, salaries and other kinds of compensation can take a variety of forms. Skilled and ambitious people may be in high demand and relatively well paid in some countries, where the employees' living standards may be almost equal to those of the household that runs the farm. Many farm workers around the world are, however, badly paid and payment may in part consist of food and accommodation. Bearing in mind this and the fact that much family labour is unpaid (Box 18.5), it is safe to say that world food production in fact is largely supported by underpaid or unpaid labour in both market and subsistence oriented farming.

A fifth kind of characteristic, which farm work shares with many other kinds of undertaking, is that some kinds of work are more visible than others. Ploughing is, for example, more visible to the outer world than administrative tasks and daily routines in animal husbandry, which thus risk being undervalued and overlooked by people who are not directly involved. In many cultures much of the undervalued work is conducted by women, children and elderly people, which is illustrated in Figure 18.1.

Neither access to abundant labour nor investment in an impressive array of machinery guarantees successful farming. It is also necessary to time things well and to organize operations as optimally as possible. This is discussed under the two next headings, which deal with the importance of timing and functioning chains.

Box 18.4 Part-time farming

All over the world it is commonplace to combine farming with other sources of income, in the form of off-farm jobs or complementary activities on the farm. The term part-time may refer to situations where some (as in the Romanian example in Chapter 3 and the Danish example in Chapter 10) or all adult members of the farm household work both on and off the farm. We can assume that most of the many smallholdings around the globe are more or less dependent on additional income. Part-time farming is, however, also common among farmers who run relatively big farms, for whom the off-farm income is necessary to be able to continue farming. In such cases the term part-time farmer may be misleading, because the reason is bad economy rather than lack of work at the holding. A precondition for seeing this as a long-term solution is, however, that it is possible to combine the duties without mismanaging either the farm, the off-farm job or one's health. Among many alternative kinds of farming where part-time farming is involved are:

- Poor subsistence oriented holdings that regularly fail to feed the household
- Small-scale farming that traditionally is run in combination with other sources of income
- Formerly full-time farms that can no longer provide an adequate income
- Farms that serve more or less as a hobby in combination with other sources of income

---

Box 18.5 Family farming

The term family farming is frequently used and is often seen as farming with more or less unlimited access to free labour that is on hand whenever it is needed. In some forms of farming, primarily at market oriented farms, adult sons and daughters are fully paid and live in separate households. In others, adult family members are fully or partly engaged at the farm and live and eat together with other generations, with or without some cash payment. Many family members find it natural to do their best for the family and the holding, thrive on the work and have no other plans than to continue. From the individual perspective cheap family labour may thus be a good and the only solution, without which one would have to give up. In a broader view, however, the system includes elements of exploitation.

The farm household's private economy is often highly integrated with the farm economy, which in part can be positive and more or less natural. There are, however, also risks with this kind of interconnection;

for example, in cases of high indebtedness for farm production, the private economy may be threatened as well.

Farming on the basis of helpful family members may on the one hand be highly sustainable, but can, on the other hand, be vulnerable. Families do not always look the same, which, among other things, means that family labour differs over time. The numbers of family members at home may change, and so do their ages and their health. Small children have to be cared for during some periods, and at the same time or during other periods pregnancy and health problems may occur. Moreover, elderly family members who used to assist with farming may instead be in need of help. Changes within the family will thus influence not only the family as such but also the ability to manage the farm.

Figure 18.1 A woman and a child in the South African countryside, 2011. Walking and carrying are important parts of the work in smallholder farming.

Photo: Viktoria Olausson.

The importance of timing

The importance of timing cannot be overemphasized. Doing the right thing at the right time can be crucial to managing farming and may explain why some farmers are more successful than others. Due to the connection to biological and seasonal rhythms, few or no daily routines can be postponed until the next day, and delayed seeding or weeding will usually have negative consequences throughout the growing season. Similarly, passing the optimal time for mating will probably reduce production, and lack of preparatory maintenance of machinery and tools increases the risk of failure later on. The importance of timing was clear already in ancient Rome, more than 2,000 years ago, when Marcus Porcius Cato (234–149 BC) wrote:

> See that you carry out all farm operations betimes, for this is the way with farming: if you are late in doing one thing you will be late in doing everything.
>
> (Cato and Varro 2006: 17)

Functioning chains and bottlenecks in farm work

Regardless of technology level, it is important to organize the work as efficiently as possible, within the limits set by the available technology in each particular case. Each specific task, such as harvesting, can be looked at as a chain where the links are interconnected and where each link is dependent on the others. For example, efficient utilization of a combine requires wagons or containers where the tank can rapidly be emptied so that the threshing can go on. If the combine has to wait, this creates a bottleneck that is a weak link that hampers the efficiency of the entire harvest chain. Just imagine the divergence between theory and practice when a new combine, bought for a fortune and calculated to have a capacity of five tons of grain per hour, is hampered by insufficient transportation and thus has its capacity reduced to three tons per hour. Bottlenecks naturally appear in manually operated farming too, in small-scale agriculture and horticulture. One stage along the chain can suffer from a lack of people, tools may break or differ in effectiveness, or one person may work more intensively than another. Figure 18.2 illustrates the first case, where the combine's grain tank is emptied into a waiting wagon.

Problems with bottlenecks can be caused by a combination of links in the chain with different capacities, as illustrated above, or by missing labour, machines or draught animals because of machinery breakdown or illness. Moreover, new, often bigger machines may not fit into the previous machinery chain, which can result in the need to upgrade other parts of the machinery chain as well. The first idea of replacing one old farm machine may thus generate accompanying investments well beyond the initial calculation. A common way to deal with problems like these is to work together with other farms and to create more efficient chains, or even to create small separate joint companies for parts of production. You will read more about this in what follows.

Figure 18.2 Combine emptying its tank into a waiting wagon for further transportation to the farm or for direct delivery to a purchaser, 2011.

Photo: Carin Martiin.

Various forms of collaboration between farmers

The physical and legal farm unit is not always the same as the organizational unit. On the contrary, the general farm system, as shown in Figure 17.1 in Chapter 17, may be organized in alternative ways, such as in joint companies or through more temporary kinds of collaboration. The motives can be to get access to sufficient labour for a particular task or peak, or to organize an efficient machinery chain without having to make new investments. Collaboration at farm level can, for example, take the following forms, which often are combined; they are also outlined in Box 18.6.

- A joint company with a small group of farmers whose purpose is to manage a certain kind of production or other kind of undertaking. Examples: large-scale cultivation, storing and marketing of potatoes; irrigation arrangements; maintenance of local roads.
- Hiring in of services from other farmers or from separate machinery stations or the like. Examples: sowing of special crops; spread of pesticides; spread of manure.
- Collaboration between individual farmers. Examples: collaboration on labour; combination of machinery to create a complete and efficient chain for silage harvest.
- Individual farming with temporary hiring in of services. Example: complicated machinery repair.

Box 18.6 Collaborating with neighbouring farms in north-western Europe

The figure at the end of this box outlines how two neighbouring market oriented farms in north-western Europe collaborate on parts of production while other parts are managed independently. The two farmers collaborate fully on arable farming, of sugar beets, wheat and barley, including joint ownership of the machinery. However, animal production, pig farming, is operated individually, except for the manure, which is utilized in the joint arable farming.

After some years of temporary collaboration the joint organization was formalized a decade ago, with the help of an experienced economic adviser, and a few years later the collaboration was extended through a joint investment in a small windmill that forms a completely separate business. From the formal point of view the two farms are run separately, which requires thorough administration of working time and other resources that are put into and taken out of the joint business.

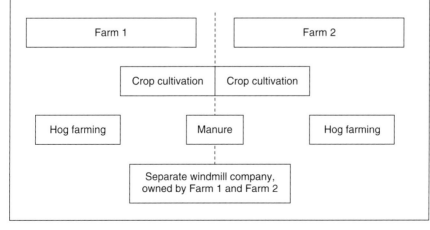

So far this chapter has highlighted the organization and structuring of farms with regard to workforce, working conditions, management of time, bottlenecks and various kinds of collaboration at farm level. Next attention turns to alternative ways of framing production in terms of intensiveness versus extensiveness, and specialization as opposed to diversification. This perspective gives much emphasis to the use of labour, investments and other input resources such as fertilizer and feed, and is thus closely related to input versus output driven production, discussed in earlier chapters.

In the following, the four terms are discussed with a contrasting approach, although it should be remembered that real-world farming includes a great variety of intermediate forms and methods of production where various degrees of intensiveness/extensiveness and specialization/diversification are applied.

Degrees of intensiveness and specialization

Intensive arable farming is characterized by high inputs and high output per hectare of land or per farm animal. The inputs, such as labour, fertilizer, animal feed, agrochemicals, technologies and energy, can be applied in varying proportions, for example intensive manual work but low use of fossil fuel, or vice versa. Accordingly, both manual horticulture and highly mechanized crop farming can be intensive. The 'Green Revolution' described in Chapter 14 was largely a matter of intensification, as it was based on a package of high yielding seeds, inorganic fertilizers, irrigation and high use of agro-chemicals. In large-scale market oriented livestock farming intensive systems are typically found in dairy, pig, egg and chicken production.

Extensive agriculture is often associated with pastoral farming on vast, low-producing areas. You read about this in Chapter 15, where the production of meat and wool on vast grasslands in the US, Latin America and Australia was used as an example of stationary, often large-scale extensive and input driven livestock production. Nomadic forms were illustrated by pastoral animal farming in Africa and Central Asia. Quite different forms of extensive production are found in part-time or even hobby farming, for example in Western Europe, where extensive cattle, sheep or horse farming can be part of landscaping and wealthy versions of country life. It is generally easier to carry on extensive animal than arable production, which is due to the fact that crop farming generally requires more human involvement in the form of tillage, seeding and compensation for lost plant nutrients, compared with continuously green pastures.

Neither intensive nor extensive forms of production are bound to certain species of crops or animals. With some exceptions, it is possible to apply intensive, extensive or intermediate methods of production to almost any kind of crop or farm animal species. Meat and milk production, for example, is found in highly intensive as well as more or less extensive farming. However, the varieties often differ; for example, Holstein dairy cattle are kept in intensive production, while hardier breeds are used in extensive cattle farming. You will find more about intensive and extensive production in Table 18.1, which also deals with specialized and diversified production.

Table 18.1 Examples of intensive or extensive farming in combination with specialized or diversified agricultural production

	Intensive	*Extensive*
Specialized	Dairy farming on large family farms. Chicken production in factory-like production	Large herds of cattle or sheep kept on vast pasture lands in stationary or nomadic pastoral farming
Diversified	Smallholder farming with a few cattle, pigs and poultry, plus cereals, vegetables and fruits	Cattle, sheep and horses on vast pasture lands in combination with tourism

In specialized farming production is concentrated on one or a few products, for example on pork, milk or eggs, which is common in large-scale market oriented farming. It is easier to finance one than several kinds of feeding systems and less demanding to keep up to date with the latest findings in one kind of production. Besides, far-reaching specialization may contribute to a strong professional identity; for example, as a cotton producer, rapeseed producer or merino wool producer, rather than being a farmer in general. On the other hand, the dependence on one or a few products implies higher exposure to risks such as falling prices for the particular product, or to outbreaks of specific plant or animal diseases. Moreover, high degrees of specialization can bring about heavy workload peaks, in the lambing season for example.

Typical diverse farming is found on subsistence oriented smallholdings with a variety of crops and animals, or on relatively small, family operated market oriented farms with a large number of products for sale. Both cases were illustrated in Chapter 3. Many kinds of crops and animals means spreading the risk of pests and diseases, volatile prices and eventual natural disasters may hit different crops and animals differently. What is more, bad results in one kind of production may be balanced by better results in another. Among the drawbacks of diversity, the difficulties of investing and the challenge of keeping up to date have already been mentioned; one should add the difficulties of handling many events at the same time. Several crops may be ready to harvest at the same time, and just at the same moment health problems may suddenly occur among the animals. Diverse production may also be a matter of combining agriculture with other on-farm activities, for instance the refining and direct sale of wool, fruits or cheese, or bed and breakfast arrangements. Diversification has recently been pointed to as an alternative to structural rationalization of small and medium-sized farms in the EU, but is found on all continents. In Table 18.1 you will find the terms intensive, extensive, specialization and diversification, combined and illustrated by different kinds of animal farming.

As mentioned, real farming in various corners of the world includes a huge variety of intermediate forms between the polar opposites in Table 18.1. What is more, the different forms can be combined on a single farming unit; for instance, intensive dairy production plus extensively grazing steers, or intensive horticulture, extensive sheep farming and tourism.

Administrative farm work

Administration undoubtedly belongs to the category of less visible tasks in farming. The extent and character of administrative farm work differs according to regulatory requirements, degree of market orientation, the size and complexity of the business and individual interest in administrative tasks. Regardless of external requirements on accounting and the like, many parts of the administrative work serve as useful managerial tools. This is true even for small businesses and even when the degree of market orientation is low. The forms naturally differ with the situation, but the principles are much the same for all kinds of businesses, and differ in number of zeros in the columns rather than in the task as such. For example, thorough comparisons between all costs and revenues from one or 100 hectares, or from five or 5,000 pigs, provide the respective farmers with a variety of feedback information that can be utilized for future improvements. The following are among the many kinds of administrative tasks you may come into contact with: budgets, follow-up budgets, liquidity plans, investment plans, tax payment plans, crop rotation plans, fertilizer plans, feeding plans, lists of animal birth dates, vaccinations and illnesses.

Despite the many benefits of administration it is fair to say that far from all farmers are fond of these matters. On the contrary, administration may be seen as a workload for which it is difficult to find time in addition to the running of all practical duties. The administrative workload seems to be especially high in countries with complex subsidy systems and regulations, like those in the European Union, where full-time farmers may spend one or two hours a day on administration. Among the variety of topics to deal with at the farm office desk, farm insurance matters certainly appear now and then.

Agricultural insurance and other safety nets

Insurance arrangements for farm buildings, machinery, livestock and crops have long been available through non-profit or commercial companies, for example in the early industrialized European and North American countries. Other countries have less thoroughly developed systems but may still have some kind of insurance systems, through private companies and/or arrangements with the authorities involved, for example in India. In some countries with many poor smallholders so-called micro-insurance is being developed, albeit on a smaller scale than the corresponding and better known micro-finance institutes.

Threats as such cannot be reduced by insurance, but the risk of devastating economic losses can be reduced. However, in particular many smallholders around the world lack any kind of insurance coverage, in part due to the aforementioned lack of insurance systems in the region, in part because of difficulties coping with the fees. This leaves the farmer to rely solely on support from relatives and other informal safety nets. These kinds of safety nets are, however, insufficient and problematic in many respects. Mutual responsibilities between relatives means that many people will be drawn into the troubles, and may have to sell what has just been built up, for example the livestock herd. Such situations may thus pose threats to smallholder farmers, who, like the title of a book by Anirudh Krishna (2011), can be said to live 'One illness away' instead of being able to escape hunger and poverty permanently. Against this background it is natural to state that many farmers are, and have to be, risk averse, which is further commented on in Box 18.7.

As a final part of this chapter we will now turn to the field of agricultural information, which is part of the ordinary running of many market oriented farms, but is also directed at smallholder farming around the world.

Farmers and experts

Experts from many agricultural fields are heavily involved in information and advisory services through direct or indirect contact with the world's farmers.

Box 18.7 Risk averse farmers

Many farmers are comparably cautious and risk averse, which is natural because of the vulnerability that follows with the exposure to both nature and the economy, and the fact that private life and economy are often intertwined with the farming business. Troubles in production will therefore affect the household, and may change the family's entire life.

From the individual farmer's viewpoint it is important to find a balance between caution and the guidance that is provided by previous experience, and openness to new findings in methods of production and other suggested improvements. Big market oriented farms are to an increasing extent being converted into formal companies, from which the private economy is separated and thereby the personal risks as well. This kind of strategy is, however, hardly attainable for all categories of farmers around the world. The following list summarizes some of the threats, grouped by major cause, to which the individual farmer can be exposed:

1   Caused by nature: drought, flood, storms, frost, earthquakes, tsunamis, volcanic eruptions, thunder and lightning, pest insects, plant diseases, animal diseases, human illnesses.
2   Caused by a combination of nature and human activities: soil erosion due to deforestation or overgrazing, salination due to irrigation, absent rains, extended monsoon rains, frequent hurricanes.
3   Caused by societal, economic and other circumstances: rocketing costs, volatile relations between costs and revenues, volatile interest rates, lack of fuel and electricity, altered customer demand, unreliable business partners, volatile political situations, armed conflicts, import and export troubles, troubling trade policies.

Advisory services have been available for centuries or even longer, although with varying purposes and approaches. The history of farmers and experts is not only a success story, but there is no doubt that both farmers' experiences and various experts' teaching, advisory services, field experiments and the like have contributed to improvements in agricultural productivity and to the possibility of feeding the world. The activities have sometimes had too much of a top-down approach, but have also taken the form of mutual exchanges between farmers and experts, with both parties gaining from various findings and lessons learned. Box 18.8 gives examples of topics that are often currently the subject of various forms of agricultural information, with various senders and interests behind them, such as non-profit organizations, public authorities, farmers' organizations and commercial companies.

As shown in Box 18.1, the communicated topics can be rather specific, such as methods of dealing with a certain kind of weed, or more general, such as ideas about rural development. The information is often free of charge and spread more than willingly, particularly by commercial companies but also by non-profit organizations and authorities. In other cases, however, the farmer chooses to pays a certain consultant in order to find solutions to particular problems, for example animal fertility problems, or to get access to an

---

Box 18.8 Topics that are frequently the subject of various information efforts

- Advice for reducing soil erosion
- Improved irrigation technologies
- New findings about crop fertilizing
- Plant varieties
- Pesticides
- New findings about animal feeding
- Farm animal vaccines
- Advice for improved water hygiene
- Information about stricter environmental rules for the handling of manure
- Farm machinery and equipment – new models and functions
- Local adaptation of technologies
- Energy saving technologies
- Information about changes in tax rules
- Information about funding opportunities
- Information about new sales opportunities in order to improve rural livelihoods
- Suggested measures to promote biodiversity in the farmed landscape
- Suggested measures to diversify farming through combination with other farm based activities

inspiring and professional sounding board with whom he/she can air different matters.

The motives behind advice are not always obvious, and it might be difficult for the farmer to identify the sender of a certain kind of information. A field excursion can, for example, be jointly arranged by scientific plant breeders from a public research institute and agronomists employed at a fertilizer company. So-called cross-selling denotes combined service and product sale, which may include several years of frequent contacts and advice on production, plus extensive purchases of the company's products. Arrangements like these may be advantageous for both parties, but also bring about dependency that can involve high costs and indebtedness, which may particularly cause trouble for vulnerable smallholders.

So-called extension services are a specific kind of advisory service that, to simplify, aims to spread knowledge and technologies through successive diffusion from advisers to farmers and then further to neighbouring farmers and others. Box 18.9 gives you an idea of the many channels for information that are used to reach farmers around the world.

Advisers and consultants who represent different organizations may have similar or even shared backgrounds as regards education and experience. Former fellow students can work professionally in the same scientific field, such as in irrigation, crop nutrients or plant diseases, but for the most diverse kinds of employers, ranging from non-profit environmental organizations to national boards and commercial giants. Box 18.10 gives examples of some of the roles performed by experts.

In the end, irrespective of the many experts, it is the farmer who has to value each piece of advice and to adopt or reject it. The farmer can thus be likened to a spider in a web, the one who knows all parts of his/her holding, and the one who has to take responsibility for what is done and what is not done in the long run.

Box 18.9 Common channels for agricultural information

- Field demonstrations
- Visits to farms that are highlighted as good examples
- Adviser visits to individual farms
- Study tours for farmers
- Articles in journals
- Television and radio
- Advertising
- Brochures
- Web information
- Agricultural schools and higher education in agriculture

Box 18.10 Expert roles, some examples

- Communicator of research results to advisers, the media or directly to farmers
- Teacher at various levels of institution, from field schools to universities
- Representative of an agribusiness company, promoting products in various ways
- Representative of a national board or another authority, giving information about rules and regulations
- Representative of a bank, working with funding of farm machinery investments
- Consultant at a small company that specializes in economics and management at farm level
- Expert in hydrology, giving advice on reducing the risks of salination
- Expert in plant diseases, giving advice on reducing the use of pesticides
- Expert in poultry health, giving advice on the indoor environment in large-scale egg production
- Representative of an NGO, teaching smallholder farmers about the organization of cooperatives
- Analyst at a global institute, communicating expected changes in the global food trade
- Analyst, communicating expected changes in agricultural politics at the national level

Summary

The size and character of the labour force at a particular farm is influenced by several factors, such as degree of mechanization, intensiveness of farming and specialization, and by seasonal peaks. Farm work differs widely as regards responsibilities and required skills, and includes labour categories such as self-employed farmers, family labour, year-round employees, seasonal employees, casual farmhands and friends who work more or less for free.

Other variations in farm work refer to working time, working environment, forms of salary and the pay as such. World food production in fact is largely supported by under- or unpaid labour in both market and subsistence oriented farming. The effectiveness of the work is greatly influenced by how the work is organized in terms of good timing and the ability to avoid bottlenecks during crucial operations, such as harvest.

The farm systems can be organized and operated in a number of alternative ways, such as joint companies or different kinds of collaboration between independent farms. Moreover, production as such can be operated intensively, with high inputs and output per hectare or animal, and combined with more or less specialized or diverse production.

In addition to the variety of practical issues, several administrative tasks may have to be carried out, which can be time consuming but provide beneficial tools for the management of the business. Due to the complicated nature of agriculture and close connections between farming and private life, many farmers are typically risk averse. Risk may be reduced with the help of insurance of crops, animals, machinery, etc., although this possibility is not within reach for everybody. Informal safety nets may offer some shelter, although this is far from unproblematic.

Experts from many agricultural fields are involved in information and advisory services. Even though the activities sometimes have had a top-down approach and have not always been successful, there is no doubt that the spreading of research results, field demonstrations, etc. has benefited global agricultural productivity and contributed to increased food production. Among the interests involved in this form of communication are non-profit organizations, public authorities, farmers' organizations and commercial companies.

Next

Chapter 19 deals with farmers' sales and purchases. It covers what and when to sell, and to whom, as well as storage strategies, horizontal and vertical integration, adding value and certification of fam products. You will also read about the current trend of increasingly powerful actors in between farmers and consumers.

To discuss

- If possible, interview a person at a farm about his/her daily working routines and variations over the year.
- What forms of collaboration between farmers seem to exist in the country where you live?
- Select a country and suggest some kinds of production that could be expected at a farm where production is intensive, extensive, specialized, diversified.
- Which kinds of farming, in terms of intensive etc., are applied in the country where you live?
- Look for information about farm insurance, and study what kind of events and damages seem to be covered, for example drought.

- ○ What kinds of safety net seem to be most common among various kinds of farmers in the country where you live?
- ○ What farm related topics are currently highlighted by NGOs, the FAO, authorities, farmers' associations, fertilizer companies, irrigation equipment companies, seed companies, agro-chemical companies, farm machinery companies, animal feed companies? Can you distinguish any common messages from some of these?

19 Beyond the farm gate

Finally, after all the work that has been put into soils, crops and livestock, the farmer has to make sure that the yields are utilized as beneficially as possible – converted either into money or into animal feed, food and other utilities for use in kind. This chapter is about farmers' selling, with a focus on food, but the reasoning is valid for the sale of fibres and bio-energy products as well. We will consider the general characteristics of agricultural markets and discuss farmers' roles as market actors. Furthermore we will touch on the unpredictable nature of agricultural markets as a consequence of nature's impact on the business; on some aspects in view of economic theory; and on problems due to information gaps and poor infrastructure.

You will also study the decision process, which, among other things, includes questions about what crops and animal products to sell, when and to whom. Moreover, you will read about producer cooperatives, and about the principal differences between horizontal and vertical integration of various actors within the agricultural sector. As regards prices and payment, we will pay attention to the fact that the price for farm products is not decided only by demand and supply but also by factors such as agricultural and food politics, trade politics, information gaps and speculation. The chapter ends with a discussion of the increasingly powerful giant retailers that in fact are able to influence the entire food chain, from farm to fork.

After this chapter you are expected to:

- ○ Be able to give an account of some important characteristics of agricultural markets and farmers as market actors
- ○ Be aware of various aspects for farmers to consider about what to sell and when to sell
- ○ Know the major categories of potential purchasers of farm products
- ○ Be familiar with the basic ideas of producer cooperatives
- ○ Understand the principal differences between horizontal and vertical business integration in food production chains

o   Be aware of the adding of value that takes place along various kinds of agricultural product chain
o   Be familiar with the current centralization of power and influence among retailers and other intermediaries along the food chain

Key words

Agricultural markets, market actor, unpredictable events, perfect competition, product differentiation, information, infrastructure, sale, liquidity, quantities, quality, storability, selling time, season, purchaser, producer cooperative, horizontal integration, vertical integration, price, payment arrangements, adding value, intermediaries, retailers.

Towards the final aims of production

Together with the management of production the farmer has to manage the final sale and try to get the best possible value out of the products as they are delivered beyond the farm gate, symbolized by the gate to the right in Figure 19.1. Alternatively he/she has to decide on the best possible internal use. Figure 19.2 illustrates the flows of resources into and out of the typical market oriented farm, with the vertical lines symbolizing the farm gate.

Among the major considerations are seemingly simple decisions about what to sell and/or keep for internal use, when to sell, to whom, at what price, and under what terms of delivery and payment. There are also practical arrangements to deal with, such as storage before delivery. In order to manage this it is important for the farmer to be familiar with the agricultural market in general, with the local market in particular, and with his/her opportunities and constraints as a buyer or seller. It is, however, fair to say that farmers are not always the strongest negotiators, and that poor smallholders in particular may be trapped in situations where crops or animals just have to be sold, and where almost any price is considered as better than nothing.

Agricultural markets and farmers as market actors

Agricultural markets have much in common with other kinds of product markets, but are also impacted by the special circumstances that characterize farming (Chapter 2). In brief, farm product markets are influenced by: the strong bonds to nature; the fact that we all need food; the large number of farms and their comparably small scale; the comparably homogeneous products; problems due to information gaps between farmers and the market actors upstream and downstream from the farm; and obstacles due to poor infrastructure in many rural areas.

Figure 19.1 The farm gate, symbolizing the stage when the farmer's efforts of production are to be converted into money or other benefits. Cambodia, 2010.

Photo: Anna Martiin.

The impact of nature

The impact of and dependence on nature contributes to making agricultural markets more unpredictable than many other sectors. As you know, the yields from crop and animal production fluctuate according to the weather, pests and other nature related problems. The market supply can thus vary substantially, at local, national and regional levels as well as globally, and if poor harvests occur simultaneously in many areas around the globe the world market price will be drastically decreased or increased.

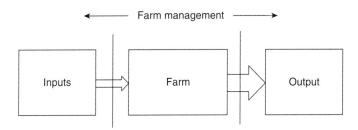

Figure 19.2 The management of a farm stretches beyond the farm gate, both upstream and downstream from the farm. The vertical lines before and after the farm symbolize gates into and out of the farm.

In addition, agricultural markets are characterized by natural seasonal patterns, for instance by the more or less simultaneous harvest of grain in Europe and the US. The season has an especially strong influence on markets for perishable products, such as fresh vegetables and berries, which will rot within hours if they cannot be sold. In situations like these the farmer is exposed to other market actors' arbitrary decisions and, generally speaking, willing to accept almost any price. The seasonal dependency is lower for storable crops, such as grain, but the season is still an influencing factor on the market. Similarly, the production of meat is influenced by seasonal patterns that in turn are decided by grazing seasons and other animal related aspects, as well as by seasonal consumer patterns.

The biological character of farm production can mean a delayed response to altered market conditions. It is easier to press the pause button in factories than in farming, where growing seasons and animals' life cycles rule production and where the invested inputs in crops and animals can be completely lost if the production cycle is not fulfilled. This means that there may be long lags between the first market signals and concrete changes in supply, which complicate the price and farmers' economy. The time lag can, for example, be substantial in production based on permanent crops, such as coffee and cacao.

Another kind of delayed market response should be added: the fact that reduced profits and even severe economic troubles may not be reflected in reduced farming but rather in increased production at individual farms in order to compensate for low prices. Because of strong emotional bonds to farming and rural life, and difficulties in finding another source of income nearby, many farmers may keep farming as long as possible, longer than in many other sectors.

Some business characteristics in light of economic theory

Typically, farm products are comparatively undifferentiated, or homogeneous, and the lack of uniqueness makes it difficult for the individual farmer to benefit from certain qualities of his/her produce. Bread wheat produced by farmer A is commonly more or less similar to the bread wheat that is produced by farmer B, although differences in quality certainly may exist. At a global scale most traders are willing to replace wheat from the US with wheat from Russia, India or France, as long as the quality is acceptable. Hence farmers in regions with unusually low yields will not be able to compensate for this through higher prices as long as the customers can turn somewhere else for similar products. In Box 19.1 you can read about attempts to differentiate farm products, as a way of reducing the drawbacks of homogeneity, and at the same time benefit from the added value that otherwise goes into the pockets of intermediaries.

Furthermore, standard economics textbooks describe the demand for food as relatively inelastic; the demand for food per person is not very sensitive to changing food prices. Alternatively formulated, we have to eat even when food prices increase and we cannot consume unlimited amounts of food if prices go down.

Box 19.1 Product differentiation through certification or other branding

Certification serves as a way to differentiate farm products, for example certification of products as 'organic', as produced in a certain region or as produced under fair working conditions. Other ways are to market the products as special with the help of attractive design or historical references, and to sell the products in a specific environment, for example at the farm or in an attractive shop. This kind of product differentiation is aimed at relatively few and wealthy customers. In addition to adding value to the primary product the various kinds of certifications can have several other values and benefits, such as reduced use of inputs, promoting rural regions, and raising concerns about human working conditions and animal ethics.

In market oriented consumer economies, local and national scarcities may be compensated for by import instead of increased willingness to pay for local production. You may have reflected on the supermarkets' ability to offer abundant amounts and varieties of food irrespective of reality in the surrounding arable fields.

Another statement in textbooks says that markets for farm products have much in common with the definition of 'perfect competition', in that their structure is typically characterized by many small producing units, where the action of one single farmer will not change market conditions generally. Not even if one of the biggest farms in the US doubled cereal production would the national wheat market be directly influenced, though the example might serve as a source of inspiration for others to follow. The structure of the agricultural market can be modified through producer cooperatives (later in this chapter) or by other means, but there is no doubt that many farmers' position in the market can be vulnerable and exposed to pressure from more powerful actors upstream and downstream from the farm. The exposure is, among other things, also connected with lack of information and infrastructure problems.

Information gaps and infrastructure problems

The world's farmers face very different possibilities of getting access to information as such, and of analysing and making use of it. Generally speaking, many highly market oriented farmers make frequent use of electronic sources, in the combine and in the animal stables, and may be well informed about issues such as world market prices, harvest forecasts, supply and demand of various farm products, debates about agricultural politics and about society in general. These well-informed farmers may be on a par with professional advisers, with whom challenging discussions can be rather fruitful for both parties. In contrast, poverty, poor reading and writing skills, and lack of telecommunications pose obstacles to many other farmers' access to this kind of information. We can thus speak of information gaps not only between farmers and other actors along the food, fibre and bio-energy chains, but also between different kinds of farmers around the globe.

Physical infrastructure is another crucial factor in farmers' positions as market actors. It is scarcely possible to sell products if it is not possible to transport them. Production from comparably centrally located fields and stables may be more attractive for purchasers, especially if the products are considered to be equal, while the remote farm risks being disfavoured. The physical distance can also be complicated by lack of passable roads and transportation for the commodities in question. Obstacles like these are common and are considered to be one of the reasons for poverty in smallholder farming in many parts of the world, not least on the African continent:

> In many parts of Africa, poor road conditions prevent farmers from getting to markets where they could sell their excess crops profitably. Poor road conditions include the lack of paved roads, the difficulty of finding transportation into market centers, and the high cost of having to pay unofficial road fees to either customs officials or other agents on the roads.
>
> (Juma 2011: 167)

What to sell, and when?

Once sale has been determined, the farmer has to make a number of more detailed decisions. The decision process that you read about in Chapter 17 referred to planned production by asking what one should produce, how and how much. In the same way farmers' decisions about sale of the products can be formulated as a number of questions, of which you will find several examples in Box 19.2.

If the products are storable, and if sufficient safe storage capacity is available, it may be more profitable to sell all or parts of the yield later when prices may be higher. It is also worth considering if the quality can be improved in a profitable way, for example by lowering the water content in grain, or sorting fruits or potatoes in attractive categories. However, many farmers have no other choice than to sell crops or animal products as soon as possible, often because of difficulties with debts and lack of cash, as discussed in Box 19.3.

Sell to whom?

The potential purchaser may be an old contact to whom the farmer has delivered for a long time, for example all cereals, or the only alternative, for example in remote areas where there is only one dairy plant within a reasonable distance. There are also situations where the farmers' sales opportunities are constrained by

---

Box 19.2 Decisions included in the sale process

- What to sell
- How much to sell
- When to sell
- Whom to sell to
- Whether products should be stored at the farm and delivered in stages
- The form the products should be sold in
- Place of delivery
- Transportation
- What price is acceptable and what the best possible price is
- Payment conditions

---

various kinds of informal dependencies. Most purchasers of farm products are either private actors or cooperatives. The first category includes various kinds of buyers, from one-person firms that are based on personal visits to smallholdings and local markets, to gigantic global players, and all possible alternatives in between. Farmers may also sell directly to consumers, at the farm or at local markets. Producer cooperatives can be strong market actors in some countries; you can read about them in Box 19.4.

Box 19.3 Selling time and liquidity

The liquidity situation, in brief the availability of cash, can be decisive for the sale, as regards time and accompanying aspects. This means that economically pressed farmers may have to sell on less favourable terms than better-off colleagues, who may be able to benefit from higher prices later on. Because of indebtedness or bad storage capacity, poor smallholder farmers, and others, may be forced to sell their produce as soon as possible; and eventually also to sell too much in order to manage urgent liquidity problems. This typically means that the harvest is sold by the end of the harvest season when prices are at their lowest, and that supplementary food must be purchased later on, when prices are at their highest. Sale of fresh milk and eggs is favourable in view of liquidity, due to more or less daily deliveries and frequent payments, which contributes to another kind of economy compared with, for example, beef production, which can require more than a year of feeding costs before any revenues are available. The latter situation may, however, be modified through credits and other arrangements that even out the farm economy over the year.

Box 19.4 Farmers' producer cooperatives

Through collaboration in producer cooperatives farmers are able to act more powerfully as purchasers and sellers than would be possible as individuals. Cooperative activities differ, and can include any of the following: handling and marketing of member farmers' products; supply inputs such as fertilizer, sowing seed, agro-chemicals, fuel, farm machinery and live animals; transportation, services and further processing in mills or dairies, plus marketing of the produce. There are, for instance, marketing cooperatives and supply cooperatives, as well as cooperatives that combine these and other tasks.

The primary aim of farmers' cooperatives is to benefit their members. All members have shares in the cooperative and surpluses are in part funded, in part distributed back to the members. Mutual solidarity between the members and the cooperative is a fundamental principle, and this includes rights and obligations for all parties.

Many countries saw local producer cooperatives develop during the late nineteenth and early twentieth centuries. In Denmark, for example, the cooperative movement grew rapidly and contributed to much of the general societal development, agricultural progress and successful food exporting. Many cooperatives around the world gradually became big national organizations but have also experienced diminished interest among farmers. In contrast, many smallholder cooperatives have been and still are being developed in other parts of the world, for example Latin American smallholder cooperatives for the handling and sale of coffee.

In addition to private enterprises and cooperatives, governments and organizations can act as purchasers of farmers' products. Centrally planned economies are typical examples, but temporary or regular purchases can be made in other countries too, for example to support the farming sector and/or consumer economy. Moreover, food aid can motivate governments and organizations to engage in agricultural markets.

Horizontal or vertical integration

As you already know, farmers are actors at the same level of the agricultural production chain, the farm level. If farmers collaborate, in the form of business relationships or in other ways, we can talk about horizontal integration, which consequently takes place between actors at the same production stage. The two collaborating north-western European farmers in Chapter 18 illustrate this, and so do the member farmers in a producer cooperative.

In the same way, vertical integration refers to integration between at least two successive stages of the agricultural chain. The vertical structure is typical of subsistence oriented agriculture, where all functions along the chain are taken care of within the producing–consuming unit. Vertical structures are, however, also found in large-scale market oriented agriculture, such as in the rearing of hogs or chickens in large-scale mixed farming or factory-like production. Vertical integration in agriculture can take the form of contract production, where the farmer produces in line with an agreement that specifies what to produce and how, and often at a specified price and date of delivery. If the production is integrated with the previous stage, inputs may be supplied as part of the agreement. The farmer may thus guaranteed safe disposal of inputs. On the other hand, his/her decision-making ability can be drastically reduced by the stipulated use of inputs and other rules about methods of production.

In Figure 19.3 you can see the principal differences between horizontal and vertical integration. The food chain has here been turned around in order to show the horizontal chain horizontally and the vertical chain vertically. The horizontal structure is illustrated by the farm level, but could as easily have been shown as horizontal integration between fertilizer producers or dairy plants. The farmers collaborate, for example, on an irrigation system. The vertical structure illustrated shows the farm as an integrated part of a production chain that includes: input supply – farming – slaughterhouse – meat processing – fast-food restaurants.

Figure 19.3 The horizontal structure shows collaborating actors at the same level, in this case farmers, whereas the vertical structure includes different stages of production, here illustrated by input supply, farming, slaughterhouse, meat processing and fast-food restaurants.

Prices at agricultural markets

Prices and price formation in the agricultural sector are complicated matters that we will only touch upon. You may study this as a specific topic during your future studies, but are probably already familiar with the field in the form of discussions about the farm economy or about consumer food prices. High prices in food stores will not automatically mean that the money gets back to the primary producers; there are many processes and actors involved in between. Other questions deal with world market prices and their influence on domestic price levels, or the impact of foreign food aid on domestic prices and the agricultural sector at large.

Recently much attention has been paid to food price spikes regarding expectations for the future and the reasons behind the rises, such as harvest failures, energy and fertilizer prices, speculation and bad weather. As shown in Figure 20.2 in Chapter 20, the world experienced a peak around 2008, and as I write, in July 2012, there are worries about reduced yields in the US due to severe drought, and accompanying concerns about increased world market prices for cereals, bioenergy and other farm products. At the same time as farmers see plants wither, global traders are eagerly following weather and yield forecasts for different parts of the world on their screens, trying to grasp the situation in terms of price levels and dollars.

Volatile prices in agriculture are not only a matter of payment for production but about the cost of inputs too. Fertilizer and energy costs in particular can be crucial in this context. Farmers may pay high prices for inputs at the beginning of the growing season but achieve low price levels for their yield by the end of the season, and the opposite the next year. This causes liquidity problems and makes it difficult to plan.

Price formation in agriculture is complicated and includes a plethora of aspects, many of which you are already familiar with. In brief, and simplified, prices for farmers are influenced by the following factors:

- Supply: total yields of different crops and animal products, globally, regionally, nationally and locally. The production situation in leading export countries is generally given special attention. Supply depends on all the factors that influence production and final yields, as discussed in Parts III and IV.
- Stocks of various products: stocks are very important as regulators from season to season and are of decisive importance for world market prices. Cereals in particular are key players, in the price of both vegetable and animal products (Figure 19.4).
- Demand: total demand, globally, regionally, nationally and locally, with differences due to preferences, consumers' food standards and the ability to pay.
- Food security concerns and purchases for food aid purposes, for immediate use or for storage.

- Seasonal price patterns, which generally mean lower prices at harvest time. Some harvest seasons coincide to a great extent globally, whereas others are more evenly distributed over the year.
- Information is a crucial factor. Knowledge about stocks, sown areas, weather events, forecasted yields, pests and diseases, number of animals reared, consumer demand, bio-energy politics and trade agreements are just a few examples of the many kinds of information that contribute to setting the price of various kinds of farm products.
- Speculation and similar phenomena: speculation can be a cause of price volatility, and can drive prices to problematic levels. The risk of speculation in food can be closely related to forecasts about supply and demand, and other kinds of information.
- Differences between various kinds of farm product markets, such as bulk markets versus markets with differentiated products.
- Costs of production, such as costs for energy, phosphorous and nitrogen.
- Food safety measures (Chapter 21).
- State intervention such as tariffs, taxes, quotas, export subsidies, trade agreements with other countries and various forms of agricultural programmes, as the following quotation comments:

All governments intervene in agricultural markets. Reasons include raising tax revenue, supporting producers' income, reducing consumers' food costs, attaining self-sufficiency…The wide variety of interventions makes measuring their magnitude, impact, and the gains from trade liberalization a formidable task.

(Tweeten 1992: 49)

In addition to the price that is paid to farmers, the products will undergo substantial increases in value, plus modifications through taxes, subsidies and other means that increase or decrease the final consumer price. State intervention may influence the price all along the food chain, from fertilizer and the farm gate price, to processors and retailers. Moreover, the price is influenced by the cost of transportation, packaging, marketing and, not least, by intermediaries' costs and profits. Substantial adding of value thus takes place along the food chain, which is further discussed in Box 19.5.

Payment arrangements

Farm products are paid for in various ways, such as cash on delivery, exchanges in kind, monthly payment for regular deliveries, for example of milk. There are also forms of forward pricing and contracting where the seller and buyer agree on a price for a specific commodity to be delivered later, for example a tractor or a kitchen stove. The arrangements can also be more complicated and include elements of risk management, for example through futures. Future contracts are written standardized contracts where only the price is open to negotiation, whereas

Box 19.5 Adding value along the food chain

Substantial adding of value takes place between the farmer and the consumer, between the farm gate and the food store. The price that is paid to the farmer may in fact be a tiny share of what final consumers are charged. Step by step each involved actor will add to the price: traders, processors, packaging companies, marketers and others that get involved along the food or fibre chain. Generally speaking, the value increases with the degree of differentiation, and the readier the product is for final consumption. A reverse trend, albeit on a small scale, is instead highlighting the farm and direct contact between the farmer and the consumer as a value adding quality.

quantity, quality, place of delivery and date of expiry are decided. The idea is to reduce the risk of price variations, for example during the growing season. Before the date of expiry futures can be frequently traded, without any physical deliveries taking place. The system has been established for a long time, particularly in the US, but is far from ordinary business for most farmers around the world. In these and other more complicated affairs farmers are generally assisted by banks and others. While access to a bank account and telecommunications

Figure 19.4 Silos for storing grain.
Photo: Carin Martiin.

is taken for granted in highly market oriented farming, lack of such access poses obstacles for many smallholders' chances of expanding their economic contacts.

Increasingly powerful actors in between farmers and consumers

From earlier chapters you are well aware of the large numbers of farmers and food consumers around the world: approximately 0.5 billion farm holdings of varying size and even higher numbers of people are involved in the primary stages of the food chain, and about 7 billion food consumers are, or try to be, seated around the tables in the final stage. Generally speaking, fewer people are engaged in between, in the secondary agricultural production that takes place upstream and downstream of the farm. Figure 19.5 indicates approximate proportions between the actors along the food chain when the focus is on the number of people involved. However, highly mechanized farming may generate more jobs in the agricultural sub-sectors than in primary production at the farm, which may be clarified by the plethora of intermediaries that are listed in Box 19.6.

If we switch perspective, from the number of people to the impact and power along the food, fibre and bio-energy chains, almost the opposite picture emerges, a picture where the intermediaries appear as very influential throughout the entire agricultural sector. This tendency has been remarkably strong in recent decades and is illustrated in Figure 19.6.

Strong actors can exercise substantial power along the entire food chain by demanding specific qualities, storability, packaging and time of delivery. The retail sector in particular has become more powerful and has increased the economic pressure on farmers, indirectly and directly. Farmers aiming at delivery contracts with supermarkets often have to manage detailed requirements regarding colour, taste, form and size of vegetables, roots and fruits, as well regarding

---

Box 19.6 The plethora of actors upstream and downstream of the farm

The fertilizer industry; the energy industry (fuel, electricity, equipment for small-scale energy); the transport sector; the seed industry (research, development, sale); the animal breeding industry (research, development, sale); the feed processing industry; the agro-chemical industry (pesticides, hormones, chemicals for cleaning, animal medicines); the farm machinery industries; the farm equipment industry; the building material industry; the advisory service sector; banks and similar organizations; the agricultural trade sector; the food processing industry; the packaging industry; distributors; manufacturers; fast-food markets; restaurants; and institutional food businesses (school, hospitals).

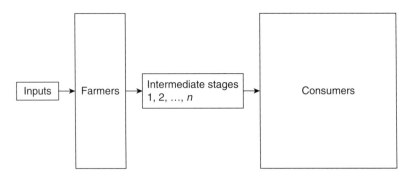

Figure 19.5 Approximate proportions between various actors along the food chain when the focus is on the number of people involved.

storability, quantities, packaging and time of delivery. Despite this, many farmers may compete for contracts and in most cases the supermarket chains prefer to do business with large-scale producers rather than with a large number of smallholders. At the same time, the existence of large stores can make it more difficult for smallholders to sell at local markets as these may lose customers to the supermarkets. Still, farmers often continue to symbolize the product. You may have seen supermarket items showing smiling farmers photographed in idyllic natural surroundings, highlighting the product's closeness to nature, whereas the processing and packaging are toned down. The situation has been formulated critically as:

> retailers' role – they have emerged as the main gateways to consumers, using contracts and specifications to gate-keep between primary producers and consumers.
>
> (Lang 2004: 5)

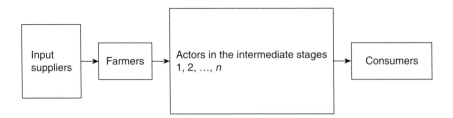

Figure 19.6 The relative impact and power of various actors along the food chain. The approximate relative sizes of the boxes show the imbalances.

Summary

In addition to their practical and managerial work with crops and animals, farmers have to manage the final sale as well as possible. The sale process includes a number of decisions, such as what to sell or keep for internal use, when to sell, to whom, at what price, and under what conditions as regards deliveries and payment. Agricultural markets have much in common with other product markets but are also characterized by their dependence on nature and the fact that we all have to eat. The market is also characterized by a large number of farms, their comparably small scale and by the comparatively homogeneous products, which is close to the definition of perfect competition. Farmers' positions as market actors can be weakened by lack of information, especially in the case of poor smallholders, and farmers in remote areas can be disadvantaged because of poor infrastructure. Private companies of varying size are common as buyers of farmers' products but cooperatives can also be of great importance as purchasers. Vertically integrated production means that farm production is integrated with stages upstream and downstream of the farm, while horizontal integration refers to different forms of collaboration between actors at the same stage of the food chain. Like other commodities, the price of agricultural products is to a great extent decided by supply and demand, but price formation in the agricultural sector is also influenced by several other factors, such as: seasonal variations, stocks, information, speculation, and by government intervention in the form of tariffs, taxes and subsidies. These interventions can impact the price at different stages of the food chain, and can increase or decrease the price to the farmer and/or to the consumer. In recent decades intermediaries along the food chain have gained power and have become rather important players with a great impact on prices and methods of production.

Next

In Chapter 20 the farm gate is left far behind and so is the farmer. Other actors have taken over and arranged for continued handling and sale. Substantial but far from major shares of total farm production are internationally traded, either between countries in the same international region, or across the globe. This trade is the focus of the next chapter.

To discuss

- Who are the dominant purchasers of farmers' products in the country where you live?
- Try to figure out how different categories of farmers in the country where you live sell their products.
- Study the marketing of organic products; or products certified as originating from a certain region; or that are produced under fair working conditions. Next consider how the consumer is informed about each.
- Compare national statistics for the number of farmers, the number of employees in the intermediary sectors and total population.
- Look for food marketing strategies where the farmer is highlighted rather than the middlemen.

20 International agricultural trade

Worldwide agricultural trade is the main theme of this chapter, the penultimate one, before the final discussion of food safety in Chapter 21. The following pages provide an overview where you will read about the international export and import of crops and animal products. We will study this in the form of leading exporting and importing countries, and the most traded products in terms of value and quantities. The major focus is on unprocessed foods, such as wheat and meat, but we will also touch on the trade in animal feed and fibres of vegetable and animal origin. Much of the reasoning is built up around statistics from the World Trade Organization (WTO) and from FAOSTAT, which you are already familiar with. You will be made aware of some peculiarities of trade statistics, for example that a country can export and import the same kind of food, and that this may be consumed in that country or just pass through its borders.

In addition to discussing trading countries and various agricultural products we will also discuss agricultural trade from broader perspectives and touch on economic development, resources and food security. Trade can, it is argued, be a driving force for economic and social development, and a safety valve for food security, but may also cause problems in terms of outcompeted domestic farming and environmentally harmful transportation. With this in mind the final part of the chapter changes focus, from trade as such to import dependency, volatile prices and concerns about production potential in proportion to population needs in some example countries. In addition, you may find several details that recall many of the earlier pages of the book.

After this chapter you are expected to:

- Have a fair idea about international agricultural trade as a share of total production
- Be able to discuss different aspects of the export and import of food from the perspective of farmers and consumers in exporting and importing countries respectively
- Be familiar with the existence of international organizations engaged in international trade

- ○ Be aware of aspects to consider in the analysis of agricultural trade statistics
- ○ Know the leading exporters and importers of agricultural products
- ○ Know the most exported agricultural products and give examples of leading exporters and importers
- ○ Be familiar with the trade in different kinds of meat, dairy products and eggs
- ○ Have a fair idea of the shares traded within and outside the different international regions
- ○ Be aware of the international regions whose export values exceed their import values and vice versa
- ○ Be aware of the extensive trade in feed concentrates
- ○ Have a fair idea about the export and import of vegetable and animal fibres
- ○ Be familiar with the Food Price Index and recent years' volatile food prices
- ○ Be able to discuss arable areas, population and yield levels in terms of export and import, and against the background of the previously learned fundamentals of agriculture

Key words

International trade, trade statistics, export, import, international regions, value, quantity, vegetable products, animal products, fibres, volatile prices, Food Price Index.

International agricultural trade, a multifaceted business

> Agriculture and the food trade have also always been among the most regulated and protected sectors of the economy. This is perfectly understandable considering that a lack of food and excessive spikes in food prices upset economic development and create social unrest.
>
> (Sjauw-Koen-Fa 2010: 18)

The international food trade can serve as a safety valve in situations of scarcities and the risk of hunger, and as a driving force for rural development and economies at large. The trade can, however, also be a complex and disputed field that includes different forms of barriers, inequalities and environmental drawbacks.

The average international agricultural trade in 2007/2010 covered about 16 per cent of the entire volume of agricultural production, according to estimates from

Sjauw-Koen-Fa (2010). There are substantial differences between various products, from typical export products such as coffee, tea, cacao, cotton and rubber, to the opposite. The aforementioned report suggests that about 57 per cent of oilseed is internationally traded, 31 per cent of sugar, but only about 7 per cent of rice production.

Despite the fact that a relatively low average share of total production is internationally traded, the export and import of agricultural products are a highly influential factor for the entire sector on all continents; for farmers, food consumers and the intermediary actors along the food, feed, fibre and bio-energy chains. The impact is direct, through effects on supply and price levels, although to varying degrees depending on agricultural, food and trade politics. Effects are also indirect. Pressure from competing imports can generate restructuring of domestic agriculture and alter methods of production. The types of changes depend on ownership and leasehold patterns, economic and demographic aspects, geography and infrastructure, and have in Europe and North America contributed to increased mechanization and reduced numbers of farmers. Altered consumer demand is another possible effect, which can pose new pressures for farming, for example about the taste, colour and shape of fruits and vegetables.

History includes numerous trade disputes and trade wars but also lots of positive effects such as improved well-being and reduced vulnerability to the sometimes cruel forces of nature. Current debates about agricultural trade can be intense and sometimes provocative meetings between trade promoting international organizations, such as the WTO on the one hand and critical NGOs on the other. Moreover, there are differences between governments that are positive to increased free trade and governments with a more protectionist approach. Box 20.1 illustrates different perspectives on international trade, and mixes positive and negative aspects.

International monitoring of production and trade

International trade in food and other agricultural commodities is intensely monitored by many actors around the world; by governments and financial institutes, and by the WTO and other kinds of organizations with very varied interests. Even more attention is paid by agri-business companies and traders, who follow the trends minute by minute on stock markets in Chicago, Paris and elsewhere.

The monitoring of international agricultural markets has much in common with other kinds of commodity markets, but while most other types of commodities are safely produced indoors, agricultural trade can be abruptly changed by information about heavy rains or long-lasting heatwaves in different parts of the world. Agricultural market forecasts are thus by necessity of a tentative character. Despite this, there is a great interest in information about: sown areas; proportions between crops, such as wheat, maize and soybeans; weather problems; how the crops develop during the growing season; time of harvest; and whether problems in some regions seem to be compensated for by favourable conditions in other parts of the world. These kinds of forecasts are combined with information about

---

Box 20.1 What agricultural trade can do

- Fill gaps in the case of harvest failures and/or imbalances between domestic population size and farm production
- Include various forms of trade barriers and unequal trade relations
- Serve as a driving force for economic and social development
- Generate increases in the income of farming and other parts of the agricultural sector
- Generate business opportunities and commercial benefits along the food chain
- Expose import dependent countries to volatile international prices
- Increase or reduce domestic price levels, for farmers and/or consumers
- Serve as a driving force for positive or negative changes in methods of production, in farming and further along the food chain
- Threaten domestic farm production and/or outperform domestic farmers
- Increase the supply of different kinds of food to consumers, such as fresh fruit all year round
- Conceal agriculture's dependence on nature and seasonal variations through import from other regions
- Increase food transportation, with negative environmental consequences
- Complicate the recycling of nutrients, as products are transported far away from the farm
- Contribute to one-sided agricultural production in the exporting country, at the expense of diverse production for domestic needs
- Cause food safety problems, by risking rapid and large-scale spread of harmful substances and diseases (Chapter 21)

---

changes in food price levels, energy prices, consumer demand, speculation trends and trade agreements; the list goes on. Among the most frequently studied forecasts are the monthly reports from the the United States Department of Agriculture (USDA). You will find a section of the June 2012 report quoted in Box 20.2 and followed up in Boxes 20.3 and 20.4 at the end of the chapter.

Agricultural outlooks are also dealt with by bodies such as the WTO, the International Monetary Fund (IMF) and the Organization for Economic Co-operation and Development (OECD), for whom agricultural trade is one of many tasks, and by banks with a specific focus on agriculture such as the Rabobank. Furthermore, international agricultural trade is monitored by farmers' associations around the world and by associations that promote regional trade, such as the EU, the African Union (AU) and the Mercosur, with some Latin American countries as members. There are also associations for certain kinds of products, for example the International Grains Council (IGC), with the EU, US, India and some more countries represented.

Box 20.2 Forecasting supply and demand for 2012/2013, an example

'Global 2012/13 rice supply and use is little changed from a month ago. Global rice production is projected at a record 466.5 million tons, up less than 100,000 tons from last month. Global 2012/13 exports are raised nearly 1.0 million tons mainly due to an increase for India, now forecast at 7.0 million, up 1.0 million from last month, but down 1.0 million from revised 2011/12. India's 2011/12 exports are raised to a record 8.0 million tons. Import 2012/13 forecasts are raised for Iran and several African countries. Global consumption for 2012/13 is raised 1.0 million tons, primarily due to larger consumption for Iran, Vietnam, and several African countries. Global ending stocks for 2012/13 are projected at 104.2 million tons, down 0.7 million from last month, due primarily to a reduction for India.'

Source: USDA 2012: 3 (World Agricultural Supply and Demand Estimates, USDA).

With food security as its focal point the agricultural market is followed by organizations with food security as a focal point, such as the FAO, the World Food Programme (WFP) and other bodies within the UN sphere. In addition the market is watched by organizations such as Oxfam that have a more critical approach and pay more attention to trade related human and environmental problems than to agri-business. Criticism can, for example, be directed against tariffs and quotas that favour some countries and farmers at the expense of others.

At the same time as there are forces working for more free trade there are other forces working in the opposite direction. The result is mixed, and the present world of agricultural trade involves a plethora of instruments that distort, favour and disfavour: tariffs, quotas, import bans, export bans, export subsidies, transnational commodity agreements, bilateral trade agreements, so-called non-tariff measures and technical barriers to trade, such as restrictions in the case of an outbreak of an animal disease in an export country. Instead, we will move on to trade statistics and some features that have to be taken into consideration during the following account for world agricultural trade.

Points to consider when analysing trade statistics

One of the peculiarities of trade statistics is that a single country may import and export the same kind of commodity, which has similarities with car producing countries that export some of their products and import other brands of cars. Table 20.1 illustrates this phenomenon through the US and German export and import of beef and veal in 2009. According to the table the two countries exported and imported about the same quantities of beef and veal. Uruguay and Japan have been included as contrasting examples that only export or import.

Table 20.1 Export and import of beef and veal in 2009

Country	Export, 1,000 tonnes	Import, 1,000 tonnes
US	514	756
Germany	166	163
Uruguay	254	0.09
Japan	0.6	479

Source: FAOSTAT (accessed 21 October 2012).

Another aspect to consider in analyses of agricultural trade statistics is that a country can be a major exporter without being a leading producer, and vice versa. A country that exports almost all its modest production may hold a more prominent position in international trade statistics than a country with high production but almost no exports. For example, China is the largest producer of pork but exports almost none of this.

Furthermore, it is important to remember that products are exported in various forms; for instance, meat from pigs could take the form of bacon, ham or pork, which means that the total trade can require analysis of more than one statistical category. You will find more examples in the section on the export of animal products.

It may seem unnecessary to say that statistics vary from year to year, but the differences can be substantial. The reasons for this vary too, and can range from altered trade agreements and trade politics to differences in yields. In a good year a normally self-sufficient country can try to sell the entire surplus on the international market but in a bad year the exported figure may be close to zero. Table 20.2 shows big differences, for various reasons, in exports from some more or less randomly selected countries in 2007, 2008 and 2009.

Table 20.2 Differences in exported quantities of some commodities from example countries in 2007, 2008 and 2009

Country	Exported product	Exported quantities, 1,000 tonnes		
		2009	2008	2007
Argentina	Beef and veal	372	214	293
Brazil	Sugar, refined	6,369	5,848	6,916
France	Potatoes	1,964	1,890	1,962
Russia	Wheat	16,821	11,720	14,444
Burkina Faso	Cotton lint	198	141	201
Ukraine	Rapeseed	1,856	2,387	910
US	Maize (corn)	47,813	54,094	57,014
New Zealand	Butter or cow's milk	451	300	364
India	Cashew nuts	117	125	111

Source: FAOSTAT (accessed 21 October 2012).

Figure 20.1 Hong Kong, well known for extensive transfer of various products.
Photo: Anna Martiin.

Yet another aspect to consider is that trade can be a matter of the transfer of products into and out of a country, and that the products may not even be related to the country's farm production. Agricultural trade statistics can thus inform us about trade without mirroring farming. The Belgian banana trade provides an illustrative example. Although no Belgian banana cultivation was reported in FAOSTAT for 2009, the small central European country was a major banana exporter in 2009, behind Ecuador, Colombia, the Philippines, Costa Rica and Guatemala, but ahead of Honduras and other more natural banana exporters. A closer study of the Belgian banana statistics reveals that 1.315 million tonnes of bananas were imported and 1.244 million tonnes exported. Most of the bananas apparently passed both into and out of the country. Figure 20.1 shows a photo of Hong Kong, well known for extensive transfer of various products.

In the following sections we will focus on large-scale international regions, on trade between countries in the same region and with countries in other regions.

Trade within and between regions of the world

Europe provides the largest share of the word's agricultural exports, measured in value. The second largest exporting region is Asia and Oceania, where Australia and New Zealand are important exporters of both crops and animal products. You can follow this in Table 20.3, which also shows how much of the export value is traded between countries in the same international region – how much of European countries' exports go to other European countries, and of African countries' exports to other African countries. The reference to international regions instead of continents is due to the source, WTO trade statistics, in which the term

Table 20.3 Distribution of world agricultural export between international regions, and the shares of the export that are traded between countries within the same international region in 2010

International regions	Share of world agricultural export, %	Share of exports that are traded within the same international region, %
Europe (EU-27 and other European countries)	42	79
Asia and Oceania (primarily Australia and New Zealand)	21	59
North America	16	38
South and Central America	12	17
Africa	4	19
CIS	3	37
Middle East	2	61

Source: WTO 2011: adapted from Table 11.13: 64.

Note: The abbreviation CIS stands for Commonwealth of Independent States, which includes the Russian Federation, Ukraine and other former Soviet Republics.

is applied. As you can see in Table 20.3, the regions are partly the same as the continents.

According to Table 20.3 Europe provided as much as 42 per cent of the total value of the world export of agricultural products in 2010, twice as much as Asia and Oceania. The Americas provided 16 and 12 per cent respectively while small shares of the world agricultural export value are accounted for by Africa, the CIS and the Middle East.

Looking at the column on the far right in Table 20.3 you can see that almost 80 per cent of European exports in 2010 was a matter of intra-regional trade between European countries. The African situation was quite the opposite, with low export values and low intra-African trade. European countries are thus involved in substantial parts of world agricultural trade, which, however, does not exclude other regions from having far-reaching impact – you will see more of this in what follows.

As for the shares of the exports that were traded to countries in other international regions in 2010, only 1 per cent of European agricultural exports were exported to South and Central America, counted in value and with continued reference to WTO statistics.

Of the about 40 per cent of Asian and Oceanian exports that were traded outside this region, about 14 per cent were exported to Europe, 12 per cent to North America, 6 per cent to the Middle East, 5 per cent to Africa and less than 2 per cent to South and Central America. As much as 38 per cent of North American exports went to Asia and Oceania, while 10 per cent went to Europe, 7 per cent to South and Central America, about 3 per cent to Africa and the Middle East respectively, and only 1 per cent to the CIS. Of South and Central American agricultural exports about 26 per cent was exported to Europe and Asia and Oceania respectively. Most of the African export was exported to Europe, 37 per cent of the value, and to Asia and Oceania, 16 per cent. Even the CIS countries exported a great deal to Europe, 24 per cent, followed by Asia and Oceania, 19 per cent. Of the 39 per cent of the total Middle East exports that went outside the region, 12 per cent of the value was exported to Asia and Oceania and 10 per cent to Europe.

Export versus import

International trade in agricultural products can also be considered in terms of export in proportion to import. According to the World Trade Organization's International Trade Statistics 2011 export value exceeded the import value in two regions, Central and South America, and North America. The same year the European export value was slightly lower than the import value, whereas the value of agricultural imports was notably higher than the export value for Africa and the CIS, and even higher for Asia and Oceania, but highest for the Middle East. We will get back to these matters at the end of the chapter, where food importing is discussed from a food security perspective.

Major exporting and importing countries

The European dominance in the value of world agricultural trade remains if we turn from big international regions to a smaller scale. The US, however, is the dominant individual country. The following account refers primarily to countries but considers the EU-27 as a whole, although, as you will see later on, many European countries are important individual traders. In Table 20.4 you will find the fifteen most important exporters and importers as regards values of agricultural products in 2010. According to the table as much as 81 per cent of the total export value was accounted for by the fifteen leading exporters in 2010, while 76 per cent of the import value was accounted for by the fifteen major importers. The share for EU-27 was the same for exports and imports. The share of 39 per cent compared with the previously highlighted 42 per cent in Table 20.3 is due to differences between Europe and EU-27. It should be noted that the WTO definition of agricultural products includes both vegetable and animal food, beverages, tobacco, textile fibres, hides and other raw materials from agricultural production.

Taken together the EU-27 and the US provided half of the value of all agricultural trade in 2010, which it is important to notice in terms of food security and trade relations. You can read more about the kind of exports and imports from many of the countries in Table 20.4. In what follows our attention is turned from summarized values to traded quantities of different commodities. In terms of quantities, world agricultural trade is dominated by crops (Table 20.5). We will therefore also deal separately with traded foods of animal origin.

Table 20.4 The fifteen major exporters and importers and their share of world trade in agricultural products in 2010

Major export countries 2010, value		Major import countries 2010, value	
Country	% of world trade	Country	% of world trade
EU-27	39.1	EU-27	39.1
US	10.5	US	8.2
Brazil	5	China	7.6
Canada	3.8	Japan	5.4
China	3.8	Russia	2.6
Indonesia	2.6	Canada	2.2
Thailand	2.6	North Korea	1.9
Argentina	2.5	Mexico	1.7
Malaysia	2.1	Hong Kong	0.9
Australia	2	India	1.2
India	1.7	Malaysia	1.1
Russia	1.5	Indonesia	1.1
New Zealand	1.4	Saudi Arabia	0.9
Mexico	1.4	Taipei, China	0.9
Chile	1.1	Turkey	0.9
Total share	81		76

Source: WTO 2011: adapted from Table 11.15: 67.

The most frequently traded farm products

As in crop cultivation, wheat and maize are the dominant crops in world agricultural trade. The US dominated the export of both crops in 2009 and provided almost half of the entire world exports of maize. Rice, the third largest cultivated crop, is relatively little traded in proportion to total production. In contrast, a large part of the total soybean production is traded internationally, in the form of soybeans and soybean cakes. The US provided half of soybean exports in 2009 and, taken together, the US and Brazil accounted for 85 per cent of soybean exports in 2009. The same year China was the largest importer of soybeans. Other major crops were sugar and palm oil, whereas chicken meat provided the largest traded quantities of animal product in 2009 (also see Table 20.6).

It is not always clear to what extent agricultural products are utilized as food, feed or for other purposes. Wheat is a major staple food but is also used as feed, for instance in pig production. Barley is to a great extent used as feed but is also utilized to brew beer and for other purposes. Maize, soybeans, palm oil and rapeseed have even wider uses, which is why Table 20.5 includes agricultural products that can be used as food and/or animal feed, food additives, personal care items, bio-energy and many other purposes.

Animal products in the international arena

Many animal products have a high monetary value and are more concentrated in terms of nutrients and other qualities. As illustrated later, there a large number of

Table 20.5 Some major exported agricultural products in 2009 (excluding beverages, unspecified foods and similar items) and major exporting and importing countries

Commodity	1,000s of tonnes	Major exporting countries	Major importing countries
Wheat	146,967	US, Canada, France, Russia, Australia, Ukraine	Italy, Spain, Algeria, Egypt, Iran, Brazil, Netherlands, Indonesia, Japan
Maize	100,657	US	Japan, North Korea, Mexico, Egypt, China, Spain, Iran
Soybeans	81,572	US, Brazil	China, Mexico, Japan, Germany, Netherlands
Soybean cakes	56,839	Argentina, Brazil, US, Netherlands, India	Netherlands, France, Germany, Spain, Italy, Vietnam, Indonesia, Japan, Thailand
Palm oil	35,193	Indonesia, Malaysia	China, India, Netherlands, Pakistan, Germany
Sugar, raw centrifugal	30,581	Brazil	India, US, North Korea, Malaysia, China, UK, Bangladesh, Russia
Rice	29,734	Thailand, Viet Nam, US, Pakistan, India	Philippines, Saudi Arabia, Malaysia
Barley	25,670	Ukraine, France, Russia, Australia, Canada, Germany, Argentina	Saudi Arabia, China, Belgium, Netherlands, Spain, Japan
Bananas	18,322	Ecuador, Colombia, Philippines, Costa Rica, Guatemala, Belgium	US, Germany, Belgium, Japan
Rapeseed	17,107	Canada, Ukraine, France, Australia	Germany, China, Japan, Belgium, Netherlands, Mexico

Source: FAOSTAT (accessed 25 October 2012).

animal product categories and this is worth noticing in the analysis of the statistics. We will begin with the international trade in meat and then continue with dairy products and eggs.

World export of various types of meat

You can find the major categories of different kinds of meat in Table 20.6, which summarizes several sub-categories in FAOSTAT. The figure for poultry meat is dominated by chicken meat but includes duck meat, turkey meat, goose and guinea fowl meat, canned chicken meat, fat liver prep and unspecified bird meat. In addition to the leading exporters, the US, Brazil and the Netherlands, large-scale poultry export is accomplished by many other EU countries, as well as by Thailand and China. The second largest category is termed 'pig meat' in the FAOSTAT

Table 20.6 Exported quantities of different kind of meat in 2009, plus major exporting and importing countries

Kind of product	Exported quantity, 1,000s of tonnes	Major exporting countries, quantity	Major importing countries, quantity
Poultry meat	14,281	US, Brazil, Netherlands	Russia, China, Hong Kong, Japan
Pig meat	12,125	US, Denmark, Germany	Germany, Russia, Mexico
Bovine meat	9,606	Brazil, Australia	US, Russia, Japan
Sheep meat	1,026	New Zealand, Australia, UK	France, UK, China
Goat meat	51	Australia	US, United Arab Emirates

Source: FAOSTAT (accessed 21 October 2012).

statistics, and includes both 'pig meat' as such but also 'bacon and ham', 'pork', 'sausages', etc. 'Bovine meat' is the third largest category, in which buffalo and cattle meat, beef and veal, sausages, dried, salted and smoked and other kinds of bovine meats are included.

A glance back at Figure 7.3 in Chapter 7 points to substantial differences between production and international trade in chicken meat and goat meat. Chicken is widely traded in proportion to production, well in line with the large-scale market oriented chicken production discussed earlier, albeit poultry are of the greatest importance in smallholder farming as well. In contrast, the many goats around the world are primarily found in subsistence oriented small-holder farming, and consequently leave few footprints in the international meat trade.

International trade in dairy products and eggs

The number of alternative categories is at least as large as regards dairy products as meats. FAOSTAT accounts for trade in condensed, evaporated, dry and fresh milk. Moreover, there is skimmed milk and whole milk, plus yoghurt, ghee, whey, cream, butter and cheeses. Table 20.7 has been limited to give a few examples of dairy products, plus liquid eggs. It should be noted that the various kinds of dairy products and eggs differ widely in water content, nutrients and other qualities, which makes it difficult to compare them – 1 kilo of cheese is not the same as 1 kilo of dry milk, which is not the same as 1 kilo of fresh milk.

Global trade in feed concentrates

Feed concentrates are a much debated topic in discussions within the context of agriculture, animal production, the environment and trade. Soybean products in

Table 20.7 Dairy products and eggs, exported quantities in 2009

Commodity	Exported quantity, 1,000s of tonnes	Major exporting countries, quantity	Major importing countries, quantity
Cheese from whole cow's milk	8,891	Germany, France, Netherlands, New Zealand, Denmark	Germany, UK, Italy, France, Belgium, Russia, Netherlands, Japan
Cheese from sheep's milk	42	Italy, France, Bulgaria	US, Germany, UK
Milk, whole, dried	2,275	New Zealand, Netherlands, Argentina, Australia, Belgium, Denmark	Venezuela, China, Algeria, United Arab Emirates
Butter from cow's milk	1,559	New Zealand, Netherlands, Belgium, Ireland	France, Germany, Belgium, UK, Netherlands, Russia, Mexico
Eggs, liquid	266	Netherlands, France, Spain, US, Poland	Germany, UK, France

Source: FAOSTAT (accessed 21 October 2012).

particular have been scrutinized, as regards methods of production and long distance transportation around the world. As you read in Chapter 16, feed concentrates are rich in nutrients and energy and widely used in intensive animal production. Feed concentrates can have different forms, but if we stick with feed cakes FAOSTAT distinguished a large number of different cakes, of which the following are included in the total of 73 million tonnes of feed cakes exported around the world in 2009: cakes of soybean, rapeseed, palm kernel, oilseed, nes (not elsewhere specified), copra, cottonseed, linseed, groundnuts and sesame seed. The 73 million tonnes can be compared with the world's wheat export of 147 million tonnes in the same year. Sizeable global trade in feed concentrates has been going on since the nineteenth century, but the trade has expanded substantially in recent decades. For example, the export quantities of soybean cakes increased from 18 million tonnes in 1980 to 37 million in 2000 and 57 million tonnes in 2009. The threefold increase in three decades is clearly related to increased numbers of animals, intensified feeding, improved yields per animal and enlarged herd sizes.

International trade in fibres

You read about global fibre production in Chapter 8, which highlighted cotton as the dominant vegetable fibre. Cotton lint is also the most traded vegetable fibre, with 6.7 million tonnes exported in 2009, with a value of $9 billion. The second largest fibre is wool (greasy), of which 0.57 million tonnes, with a value of $1.8 billion, was exported in 2009. It could be added that the international wool trade has decreased substantially over recent decades. The exported quantity of valuable silk had an export value of $0.3 billion. Table 20.8 shows the major exporters and importers. As was shown in Chapter 8, China, India and the US were the leading cotton producers in 2009, and, as you can see in Table 20.8, China was also a leading importer.

At the same time as Table 20.8 accounts for export and import it clearly illustrates the location of the textile industry in Asia, from which much of our clothing is delivered. Similarly, you can recognize the jute and wool industries in Table 20.8.

Although fibres are necessary and many countries depend on imports, import dependency on food can be more acute and even more challenging. This is the focus of the text which follows, which widens the previous approach on traded values and quantities to food safety aspects on trade.

Volatile prices on the international food market

It is one thing to choose to import food and another thing to be forced to buy food from abroad. The reasons for importing food are not always obvious, but there is no doubt that some countries are involved in far-reaching international food trade as a business and without a lack of domestic food, whereas others are continuously dependent on food imports. Among the developing countries that often are related to as import dependent are: Egypt, several Sub-Saharan countries, countries in the Middle East, some Central American countries, Bangladesh and North Korea. As regards cereals, basic staple foods, FAOSTAT figures for developing countries in 2009 report the largest net importing of cereals for Egypt. In addition, there are several food-import dependent highly industrialized countries, for example in Europe.

Table 20.8 Fibres of vegetable and animal origin. Export and import (quantities) in 2009

Product	Major exporting countries	Major importing countries
Cotton lint	US, India, Brazil	China, Turkey, Indonesia, Pakistan, Thailand, Mexico, Viet Nam, Bangladesh
Jute	Bangladesh, India, Kenya, Tanzania	Pakistan, China, India, Nepal, Thailand
Silk	China, India	India, China, Italy
Wool, greasy	Australia, New Zealand, South Africa, Germany, UK, Uruguay, Spain, Argentina	China, India, Uruguay

Source: FAOSTAT (accessed 24 October 2012).

Like poor households, import dependent countries can be exposed to volatile food prices, which may bring hardship to the economy and cause social unrest. International food prices are also of great international importance, for economic, political and humanitarian reasons. One of the most frequently referred to sources of information about the global food price situation is the FAO Food Price Index, which is outlined in Figure 20.2.

The FAO Food Price Index is, among other things, seen as indicating food security and the state of food and agriculture generally. The index measures food price changes on the basis of a basket that consists of five commodity group price indices. The FAO presents new figures monthly, which are often commented on in the media and elsewhere, especially if the changes are dramatic. A sudden rise can, for instance, fuel debates about energy and fertilizer prices versus food production, world population increase, climate change and about the risk of speculation in food.

A relatively long period of stable prices at the end of the twentieth century was broken in 2007–2008 when food prices rose dramatically, as is clearly visible in Figure 20.2. The peak at that time is often referred to as the first food price crisis. As there are numerous historical examples of food price crises, this should not be taken literally, but rather as the beginning of a series of international food price crises. A second peak arose soon after, and a third currently seems to be underway, in late July 2012. As an illustration two newspapers are quoted, *The Financial Times* in Box 20.3 and the *Jakarta Post* in Box 20.4.

The concluding part of this chapter puts more focus on food safety than on trade. Remembering the previous discussion of import dependency we will consider food production potential in relation to population, which, at least theoretically, indicates export potential on the one hand but import dependency on the other.

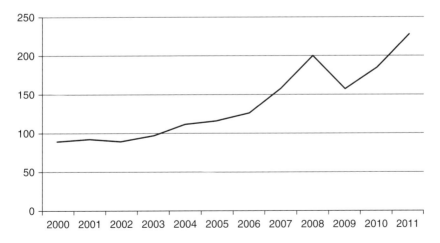

Figure 20.2 FAO Food Price Index, 2000–2011.
Source: FAO Food Price Index 2000–2011 (accessed 17 July 2012).

Box 20.3 Looming crop shortfall despite first-class technologies

'The third food commodities price spike in five years highlights how problems in one corner of the world quickly become a global concern. The US leads the world in agricultural commodity exports, countries and regions as diverse as China, Europe, Egypt and Mexico depend on imports of grain from the boundless fields of states such as Iowa, Illinois, Indiana, Ohio and Missouri. Government officials fret a further surge could induce panic buying by importers or export restrictions in the world's breadbaskets, turning an episode of high prices into a crisis … The impact of a looming crop shortfall in the US, the country with the best seed technology, first-class export infrastructure, the deepest commodity futures markets and plenty of capital available to farmers, also raises unsettling questions about how food supplies will keep pace with a growing population and a warming climate … The US categorises almost half of its corn crop as poor or very poor … More than a third of the soybean crop had the same rating … As recently as mid-June, USDA forecasters estimated farmers who had rushed to sow corn during the extremely warm spring would average 166 bushels on each acre, lifting total US production to a record 14.8 bn bushels … Then, seemingly out of nowhere, prolonged blasts of heat hit emerging stalks and plants … In Missouri, which boasts 57 cattle per square mile, the drought has ruined the grass that calves traditionally graze before they are sold for fattening on feed lots. Farmers are feeding winter hay stockpiles in summertime to keep animals alive …'

Source: Quoted from *The Financial Times*, 30 July 2012, http://www.ft.com/intl/cms/s/0/2866ba4a-da40-11e1-b03b-00144feab49a.html#axzz22JfuMqLd.

Box 20.4 Jakartan soybeans in the shadow of drought in the US

'Record soybean prices in the world's largest soybean exporter, the drought-stricken United States, is pushing up volatile food prices in Indonesia, a major consumer of soybean cakes (tempeh), tofu, cooking oil and soybean milk … Indonesia imports 60 percent of its soybean needs mostly from the US, and the drought has spiked imported soybean prices in the domestic market to Rp 8,000 (84 US cents) per kilogram, from about Rp 5,000 early this year, up almost 50 percent so far in 2012. Across Indonesia, tofu and tempeh producers are reported to have been cutting back on staff due to higher costs. Producers in Bogor and many other cities in Indonesia plan to stop production from July 25 to 27, demanding that the government controls fluctuating soybean prices … Agriculture Minister Suswono said that Indonesia needed an additional 2 million hectares of productive land to make the country self-sufficient in key commodities, of which 500,000 hectares should be allocated for soybean cultivation. "With enough land for our farmers, our dependency on soy and other imports could be drastically reduced," he added. "Our soybean once had its heyday, but with the introduction of imports, our farmers have lost out." Imported soybeans cost less than those locally produced which sell for about Rp 9,000 per kilogram.'

Source: Quoted from the *Jakarta Post*, 30 July 2012, http://www.thejakartapost. com/news/2012/07/25/soybean-prices-unlikely-affect-inflation.html.

Food requirements and the potential to produce

Our discussion about the potential to produce food will be based on a number of example countries. The reasoning is in many ways a continuation and repetition and rehearsal of Chapters 5 and 6 in Part II. The countries included are selected on the basis of criteria such as many mouths to feed, rapidly growing population, access to arable areas, farm production and if the country is an influential player in international agricultural trade. You will find the selected countries in Table 20.9, which also has columns for total arable areas, total population, average arable area per person and a figure for the average yield of cereals per hectare. Cereals were chosen over other crops because cereals are important staples and because they are grown in all the countries. You can also see world figures in the bottom row. What is more, you can compare these data for 1980 and 2009.

Table 20.9 Arable land in relation to the population and average yields in some example countries in 1980 and 2009

Country	Arable land, millions of hectares		People, million		Arable land per person		Average cereal yield, tonnes per hectare	
	1980	2009	1980	2009	1980	2009	1980	2009
China	96.9	110	983	1335	0.099	0.082	2.9	5.4
India	163	157.9	700	1208	0.231	0.131	1.4	2.6
Brazil	45	61.2	122	193	0.369	0.317	1.6	3.5
Mexico	23	25.1	69	112	0.333	0.224	2.2	3.4
US	188.8	162.8	230	308	0.821	0.529	3.8	7.2
Russia	–*	121.8	–*	143	–*	0.852	–*	2.3
Nigeria	27.9	34	76	154	0.367	0.221	1.1	1.5
Tanzania	8	10	19	44	0.421	0.227	1	1.1
Denmark	2.6	2.4	5	6	0.512	0.440	3.9	6.8
UK	6.9	6	56	62	0.123	0.097	4.9	7
World	1,352.3	1,381.2	4,453	6,818	0.304	0.203	2.2	3.6

* Figure missing due to the transformation of the former USSR to the Russian Federation.

Source: FAOSTAT (accessed 28 October 2012) and *World Population Prospects, the 2010 Revision* (accessed 26 September 2012).

Beginning with arable land you can see that especially Brazil but also China, Mexico, Nigeria and Tanzania experienced increases in total arable area from 1980 to 2009, in contrast to the US, the UK and Denmark, where the total arable area was reduced. We might, it is suggested, distinguish an interest for arable land in the example emerging economies, but little interest for maintaining cultivated areas in the second category.

The most dramatic information in the table is the decreased arable area per person, in all the example countries and in the world at large. India and Nigeria faced great reductions, and so did the US. Furthermore, we can see a reducation in arable land per person even in countries where the area per head was low already in 1980, such as China, India and the UK. Today, the largest arable area among the example countries is found in Russia and in the US, and the smallest area in China and India, both with more than a billion people to feed.

The ability to feed the inhabitants with domestically produced food depends on more factors than area per person, thereby on relevant yields. This is indicated by the column to the far right, where you can study average tonnes of cereals per hectare in 1980 and 2009. With the exception of Nigeria and Tanzania, which lag behind, all the studied countries exhibit impressive increases, among them India and Mexico. In many cases average yields have almost doubled in thirty years, in emerging economies as well as in the US, Denmark and the UK. The improved yields have obviously compensated for part of the lost areas and increased populations, although this hardly means that the long-term food supply is secured.

Summary

The international food trade can serve as a safety valve for food security and is an important driving force for the agricultural sector, for rural development and for economies generally. The trade can, however, be complex and include different forms of trade barriers, inequalities between countries and environmental drawbacks. Approximate figures suggest that about 16 per cent of total agricultural production is internationally traded, between countries on the same continent or to the other side of the globe. Typical export products are traded to a higher degree, for example half of oilseed production. International trade in agricultural products is monitored by giant organizations such as the WTO and various UN bodies, but also by governments, agri-business companies and different kinds of interest associations around the world.

Europe stands out as the international region with intensive agricultural trade, of which the major part takes place between the European countries. The African situation is almost the opposite, with low export values and low intra-African trade. Asia and Oceania is the second largest international region in terms of the value of agricultural trade, followed by North America. As regards individual countries, the US is the dominant actor in the export of wheat, maize, soybeans, chicken and more. According to the WTO 81 per cent of the total export value was accounted for by the fifteen leading exporters in 2010, while 76 per cent of the import value was accounted for by the fifteen major importers. In 2010 both the North and South American continents exported higher values than they imported, whereas import values exceeded export values in the rest of the world. As in crop cultivation, wheat and maize are the major exported agricultural products. Rice, the third largest cultivated crop, is relatively little traded in proportion to total production. Soybeans, sugar and palm oil are largely traded.

International trade in meat is dominated by poultry, pig and bovine meat, while the trade in sheep and goat meat is modest or marginal. The dairy trade includes a rich variety of products, for example substantial quantities of cheese. The trade in feed concentrates, especially soybean cakes, is extensive and has increased enormously over recent decades, which also mirrors changes in livestock production generally. Not surprisingly, cotton is the most traded fibre, followed by wool.

Many of the actors on the international food market are engaged for business reasons and may export as much as they import. Some countries are, however, forced to buy food abroad, due to harvest failures and/or insufficient domestic agriculture in proportion to the population. Like poor households, import dependent countries can be vulnerable to increased food prices, which may bring hardship to the economy and cause social unrest. The FAO Food Price Index is a frequently referred to tool for the monitoring of the food price situation, which has been quite unstable since 2007–2008. The concluding part of this chapter puts more focus on food safety than on trade and highlights the ratio of arable land to population, which reveals decreased total areas in some countries and substantially reduced areas per person over recent decades.

Next

The next and final chapter, Chapter 21, deals with food safety, the term used for efforts to ensure that all food is as safe as possible. The subject differs from that of previous chapters by focusing on pathogen microorganisms and toxic substances, rather than on tonnes of inputs and yields. The topic is, however, closely related to all agrarian activities – it is necessary that the food that is produced is safe to eat.

To discuss

○   How would you characterize agricultural trade in the country where you are? As export? Import? Transit trade? Which kind of commodities are most and least traded?

○   Discuss the pros and cons of the international food trade with a colleague, on the basis of Box 20.1.

○   Study the websites of the WTO and IMF and some trade critical organizations at national or international level. What are their missions? What are the similarities and differences between them?

○   Select two countries and compare their imports and exports of food, feed and fibre with the help of the FAOSTAT database.

○   Many of the tables in this chapter include major importers and the like. This does not, however, take account of imports per person. Select a type of food and study imports per person of this commodity with the help of information in the FAOSTAT database. Which countries are major importers from this perspective?

○   Extend Table 20.9 to the year 2030, including expected population increases and other changes that you think may take place; urbanization for example.

○   This chapter contains many details that relate to earlier chapters in this book, such as disappointing plant development at the end of Box 20.3. How many details like these can you find?

21 Making food as safe as possible

In addition to the many efforts to produce enough of various kinds of foods, and all the other concerns that you have read about throughout this book, it is necessary to make sure that the food is safe to eat. Unsafe food is a huge global problem that is considered to be one of the major obstacles to improved living conditions and economic development in many parts of the world. The term food safety differs from the previously often mentioned term food security in that food safety refers to hygiene aspects, whereas food security is broader and includes access to sufficient, safe and nutritious foods.

As food may be contaminated almost anywhere along the food chain, food safety is the responsibility of each actor involved, from input suppliers, farmers and intermediate actors, further on to consumers and recirculation of waste. The fact that food chains often are global matters, with ingredients and actors from almost all over the world, complicates the monitoring and handling of food safety problems, which can require both national and international collaboration between authorities, food chain actors and experts from various fields.

You will also read more specifically about different types of contaminating substances, which in brief can be categorized as pathogenic or toxic microorganisms, chemical or physical contaminants and contamination through environmental emissions. Furthermore, we will again work our way through the various links of the food chain, now in terms of the risk of contamination and other food safety considerations. Some reflections will also be made on food safety concerns as obstacles to trade, and on the practical consequences for agriculture and other actors who are directly or indirectly involved in an outbreak of a food-borne disease.

After this chapter you are expected to:

- ○   Know how the terms food safety and food security are defined
- ○   Know the main categories of potential contaminants in food
- ○   Be able to discuss and give examples of risks of contamination along the food chain

- ○ Be aware of authorities' engagement in food safety matters
- ○ Be familiar with the existence of international collaboration on food safety problems
- ○ Be able to discuss how food-borne diseases can pose obstacles to international trade
- ○ Be able to discuss consequences for agriculture and other actors who are directly or indirectly involved in an outbreak of a food-borne disease

Key words

Food safety, food security, contamination, food-borne diseases, pathogens, toxic, chemicals, environmental emissions, food chain, food safety risks, authorities, international organizations, obstacles to trade.

Food safety: ensuring food is as safe as possible

The expressions food safety and food security are frequently heard in common debate, at international conferences and at universities around the world. Both refer to the importance of food, and to the responsibility of ensuring safe access to food for the entire world population. The term food safety is narrower, however, and deals specifically with hygiene qualities in food, whereas food security refers to access to sufficient amounts of both safe and nutritious food. Box 21.1 shows how food safety and food security are defined by the two UN bodies the World Health Organization (WHO) and the Food and Agriculture Organization (FAO).

Box 21.1 Food safety versus food security

Food safety encompasses actions aimed at ensuring that all food is as safe as possible. Food safety policies and actions need to cover the entire food chain, from production to consumption.

(www.who.int/topics/food_safety/en/ (accessed 3 June 2011))

[Food security] exists when all people at all times have both physical and economic access to sufficient, safe and nutritious food that meets their dietary needs for an active and healthy life.

(http://www.fao.org/hunger/en/ (accessed 2 July 2012))

You have already been reminded of the around 870 million people who are currently estimated to be undernourished. The number of people who suffer from insufficient food safety is not exactly known but the problem has been likened to an iceberg, of which only the tip is visible. According to rough estimates by the WHO Food Safety Programme 2002, unsafe food makes thousands of millions of people ill, among whom many young children die. Moreover, the UN body states that

> The availability of safe food improves the health of people and is a basic human right. Safe food contributes to health and productivity and provides an effective platform for development and poverty alleviation.
>
> (WHO 2002: 7)

Sudden outbreaks and other kinds of problems

Some food-borne diseases are more or less constant acute nuisances in many parts of the world, such as diarrhoea in children. Others take the form of sudden outbreaks. Both these forms of food-borne disease cause immediate threats. There are also more diffuse threats that cause fears for severe health problems later in life, depending on exposure. In contrast to acute danger, increased risk of later health problems is of a relative and sometimes negotiable character in that restrictions and a maximum recommended intake may be altered, for example in the case of food shortages or for economic reasons. You may remember the authorities' decision to recommend a certain maximum recommended intake of radioactively contaminated foods after the nuclear breakdown in Fukushima, Japan, in 2011. Disasters and sudden disease outbreaks generally attract more media attention, such as the examples of well-known outbreaks from the 1980s onwards that you find in Box 21.2.

Box 21.2 Food contaminants and outbreaks of food-borne human
           diseases, some examples

- Bean sprouts contaminated with EHEC bacteria, Germany, 2011
- Vegetables, milk and other foods contaminated with radioactivity, Japan, 2011
- Pork contaminated with dioxin, Ireland, 2008
- Milk contaminated with the chemical compound melamine, China, 2008
- Beef contaminated with BSE agent (mad cow disease, caused by a prion), UK, peak by 1992
- Cooking oil contaminated with dioxin, Spain, 1981

Sources of food contamination

Food safety is threatened by a great variety of different contaminants, of which some primarily cause acute diseases, while others pose future threats to the exposed individual, provided that the exposure is modest. The substances can be categorized as follows:

○   Pathogenic microorganisms
○   Toxic microorganisms
○   Artificial chemical contamination
○   Physical contaminants
○   Environmental emissions

The first category, pathogenic microorganisms, contaminate food, feed or water through harmful bacteria, viruses or other microbes that cause food-borne diseases. Pathogenic bacteria are common and cause far-reaching food safety problems. Examples of food-borne diseases are, as termed by doctors, veterinarians and other professionals in the field: tuberculosis, dysentery, campylobacteriosis, e-coli infections, listeriosis and salmonellosis.

A second source of food contamination is toxins from microbes, such as myco-toxins and moulds. Harmful consequences may appear directly or long after the exposure. This kind of contaminant may, for example, develop in crops during storage, or in later stages of food processing. High humidity and temperatures increase the risk of this kind of threat to foods, for example growth of the kind of moulds that produce aflatoxin. If infected crops, such as cereals, oilseeds and pulses, are used as feed, the contamination may be transmitted further along the food chain, for example to milk.

Third, different kinds of artificial chemical substances may contaminate food, feed or water. Initially the chemicals may have been added consciously, in order to solve a problem or facilitate production in one way or another. Vegetables and fruits can hold residual pesticides, and further along the food chain residual cleaning agents may be found. Among animal products, residual quantities of veterinary drugs may be found. As a fourth kind of contamination, food and feed can be threatened by foreign physical substances, such as small pieces of glass or metal that have found their way into the food somewhere along the food chain.

The fifth category refers to harmful environmental emissions to water, soil and air, for example heavy metals and radioactive particles. Toxic or otherwise unhealthy substances in soil and water can be absorbed by root systems, leaves and other parts of the plants, and are then transmitted to animal feed and human food. Harmful emissions can also be absorbed from the air, or may be left on the surface of leaves and fruits.

Some types of contaminants pose higher threats to food safety in warm and humid climates, which are conducive to the reproduction of many food-borne pathogens and harmful vermin. The same is true of water, which, as mentioned, is another key factor in food safety – without safe water it is not possible to have safe food. Many kinds of food safety problems are thus especially demanding for farmers, food processors and food consumers in warm and humid climates. Paradoxically, this means that food safety issues generally are more demanding in the parts of the world where cooking, water and cooling facilities are poor and the consequences may be the most difficult to handle. In particular, undernourished small children, pregnant women, HIV infected persons and other people with weak immune systems are more susceptible to food- and water-borne diseases. Health care and authorities with food safety ambitions are naturally also of great importance. We will get back to the latter further on in this chapter. Given the severe consequences of unsafe food it is necessary that everybody involved take responsibility for the best possible handling of crops, farm animals, and vegetable and animal foods all the way from farm to fork.

The concern of everybody involved in the food chain

> Food contamination can occur at any stage from farm to table. Everyone on the food delivery chain must employ measures to keep food safe – farmer, processor, vendor and consumer.
>
> (WHO 2009: Fact 8)

The food chain perspective from Chapter 4 is quite useful for helping to recognize and handle food safety matters. Thinking in terms of links along a chain, eventually also in terms of complex webs, helps our understanding of how contaminants find their way into food, how they are spread and how to find potential solutions. You will find the food chain outlined in Figure 21.1, together with several ways through which various kinds of contaminants may enter the food chain.

In view of the mutual interdependencies between the links of the food chain it is obvious that failures anywhere along the chain may cause harm to the later stages. Each actor involved thus has to be aware of the routines that have to be observed in his/her particular work, for example hygienic feed and water; clean hands at milking; cleaning vessels, storage spaces and transport lines; sheltering against sun radiation or moisture, as regards the milk chain at farm level.

Step by step along the food chain

In the following we will discuss each of the main stages of the food chain from the perspective of food safety, and with special attention to crop and animal farming, in line with the general approach of this book.

The input level

Input suppliers and distributors are responsible for the hygiene quality of commodities they sell and handle. Feed concentrate companies, for instance, have to take care of the hygiene of the ingredients and of processing, so that all products

The ways various contaminants enter the food chain:

- Ordinary inputs. Example: non-organic fertilizer with heavy metals; organic fertilizer with harmful microorganisms
- Surrounding environment. Example: air-borne, soil-borne, water-borne contaminants
- Inappropriate storage environment. Example: too hot/cold; too light/dark; air; moisture/dryness
- Additives applied anywhere along the food chain. Example: antibiotics to animals; chemical substances to improve storability or the colour of the food
- Insufficient cleaning. Example: storage; transport; silos; pipes and the like; ventilation systems; packaging; household items
- Infestation by vermin. Example: rats and insects that contaminate the food, and whose damage also opens up the possibility of further damage and contamination by microbial organisms and the like
- Waste that is recycled as inputs despite containing various contaminants

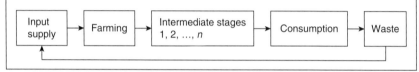

Figure 21.1 The food chain as it was outlined in Chapter 4, here considered in terms of food safety, with an emphasis on the ways through which various kinds of food safety threats may enter the food chain.

are free from pathogens and mycotoxins. Similarly on-farm produced inputs, such as animal manure, have to be properly managed by the farmer.

Crop farming

Crop farming faces the most food safety problems in terms of contaminated irrigation water, manure and agro-chemicals such as pesticides. Moreover, storage calls for special attention. Crops naturally include water after harvest, which makes the fresh crop damp and in need of good ventilation. If this is not maintained, the yield will be threatened by mould and other toxin-producing microbes. The problems and requirements differ greatly with the various kinds of crops, for example between grain and carrots. Depending on the kind of production and delivery strategies, market oriented farmers may invest heavily in optimal storage conditions. Poor smallholders generally lack such facilities, which can be especially problematic in high humidity conditions and long wet periods.

Animal farming

Animal production is, among other things, exposed to contaminants in feed and water, which have to be continuously watched and cared for. While purchased feed mixes and the like are the responsibility of the deliverer, farm produced cereals, pulses, silage and other kinds of roughage have to be watched by the farmer throughout the season so that hygiene does not deteriorate because of mould, vermin and other threats. Moreover, animal foods may be contaminated by manure, which is a vehicle for pathogens that may affect the food directly, or indirectly via infected grasslands or roughage. We can thus speak of feed safety problems too, problems that are discovered either if the livestock get ill, on sampling during the intermediate stages of the food chain or if people get sick after eating certain animal foods.

The often high dependency on purchased inputs in market oriented farming includes pros and cons from the food safety perspective. Processed feeds may be produced under intensive control, but failures can bring about big problems. Like a Trojan horse, a delivery of contaminated feed concentrates may bring pathogenic bacteria onto the farm and into the livestock.

The infection pressure can be high in animal production, with many animals per area, indoors or outdoors, which require frequent cleaning and following of strict hygiene routines. Furthermore, infectious diseases risk being spread through contacts with other herds, and sometimes also through the local wildlife.

Special attention should also be paid to the risk of the spread of infections from herd to herd via purchases of animals from other herds, insufficiently cleaned transportation vehicles, livestock exhibitions and markets, where animals from many different herds come into contact with each other. People can also spread infections, between animal herds or from animals to human beings, which calls for special care when travelling from one farm to another.

In addition, overuse or abuse of veterinary drugs for zootechnical preventive or acute purposes can pose a risk to food safety. The problem appears to be bigger in large-scale animal farming, but antibiotics in particular may also be a problem in poor smallholder farming. Generally speaking, food safety risks at farm level appear to be generally higher in the following:

- animal farming compared with crop farming
- factory-like animal farming compared with extensive animal farming
- warm humid climates in comparison with cold and dry climates

Farming based on internally produced inputs, such as sowing seed, animal feed and animal manure can be seen as more or less closed systems that generally are less exposed to external risks like those described above. At the same time, however, production may be more or less bound to the use internal resources, which means that the farmer can get trapped in a vicious circle where both nutrients and pathogens are recycled.

Continuing further along the food chain

Continuing along the food chain, marketed food commodities in particular are often involved in complex structures with repeated transportation, storage, various kinds of processing, and packaging and repackaging. This includes food risks in terms of bad storage facilities, careless transportation, grinding, mixing, heating, cooling and improper packaging, which all may serve to open the door to microbial growth and other kinds of contamination. Slaughter calls for high levels of hygiene and so does milk processing, which, among other things, requires efficient pasteurization of milk in order to prevent the spread of tuberculosis.

The intermediate stages are generally fewer when crops and animal products are used in kind, which, however, does not exclude the possibility that the products can be moved from one place of storage space to another, and from bigger to smaller sacks, vessels and the like.

Later on along chains for marketed foods we will reach the retailing stage, in the form of street vendors, food stores and supermarkets, where food safety differs greatly with regard to cooling, intermediate storage and individual hygiene (Figures 21.2 and 21.3). Similarly, restaurants and different types of fast-food sale face several food safety challenges, many of which have similarities with those in private households.

The household and waste stages

Food safety problems are often discovered at the household or restaurant level, and this is often where the search for the original source of contamination begins.

Figure 21.2 Animal foods have to be thoroughly cared for.
Photo: Anton Martiin and Ola Carlsson-Fredén.

Figure 21.3 Food being sold in the street. South Asia, 2011.
Photo: Anna Martiin.

The late stages of the food chain include several food safety aspects that have to be considered: high outdoor temperatures, vermin, unclean storage and cooking utensils, and insufficient heating or cooling. Households with no or insufficient water and cooling facilities have to deal with the biggest challenges, but, even so, food losses and food waste are notably high in regions with widespread access to well-equipped kitchens with fridge, freezer, comfortable electric stove and fresh running water. You may have followed this through recent food waste debates that highlight this as a terrible waste of resources that is absurd in view of under-nourishment and world population growth.

Among the problems with food waste the risks to animal health have already been touched on (Chapter 15). Contaminated meat can transmit harmful microbes such as foot and mouth disease (FMD), which poses severe threats to the health of ruminants and swine. FMD is a transboundary disease (TAD), a term used for animal diseases that represent major threats to food security and are of significant importance for food safety, economics and/or trade. The importance of proper handling of animal food waste was demonstrated by an outbreak of FMD in the UK in 2001, which is thought to have been caused by meat contaminated with the foot and mouth virus that had been fed to swine illegally. The outbreak was given much attention in the media and elsewhere and is an illustrative example of how complex these matters can be. In Box 21.3 you will find a list of various complicating

Box 21.3 Food and feed safety problems

- Can occur almost anywhere along the food chain
- Can spread rapidly almost all over the world before the problem is hopefully identified
- Can involve authorities in several countries
- May complicate export and import of agricultural products
- May neither be visible, smell, nor be otherwise detectible with our senses only
- Can exist, without being known, but start to develop under certain conditions, such as moisture
- Include the risk of free-riders who do not bother about hygiene but whose products may be mixed with those of others
- Can involve large numbers of actors, such as:
  a   Deliverers of feed concentrates (including all stages and people involved in the feed concentrate production chain
  b   A certain farm
  c   A specific lorry that proves to have transported contaminated feeds or foods
  d   A complicated pipe system at a feed or food processing plant
  e   Staff at supermarkets or restaurants who forgot to wash their hands
  f   Household members handling the food on cooking or eating
  g   Everyone involved in the handling of waste at each stage

aspects of food safety, several of which you have already read about, and others of which you will read about further on in this chapter.

Authorities' involvement in food safety

The monitoring of food safety, whether it be harmful bacteria, viruses, chemicals or other hazardous substances, is also the responsibility of food safety authorities at the local, national and international levels. With varying ambitions authorities engage in food safety matters through regulation, inspections, guidelines and routine controls. Moreover, outbreaks of food-borne diseases tend to result in far-reaching emergency actions from the authorities due to worries for public health, attempts to restore consumer confidence, protection of the national economy and anxiety about problems in international trade relations.

In contrast with individuals and private actors, representatives of the authorities generally speaking have the competence, right and power to monitor all parts of the food chain; and to intervene when needed. Their work can, however, be constrained by legal restrictions, information problems, and limited rights and opportunities to sample and analyse.

Box 21.4 Food safety, a complex detective story

The search for the original source of contamination can be something of a detective story. Imagine a situation in which a number of people suddenly get ill from a probably food-borne disease. You might have experienced this yourself or in your neighbourhood. In order to find the source of infection the responsible authorities may collaborate with doctors, veterinarians, food scientists, toxicologists, agronomists and microbiologists, who will soon find themselves involved in complicated detective work.

Infected people have to be identified and interviewed about their eating habits during the last two to four weeks. Thousands of samples can be taken, which requires efficient laboratories. A key problem is identifying and finding the original source of contamination. Hopefully the pieces of the puzzle are put together so that the risks can be assessed and appropriate measures put in place before the problems escalate to dramatic levels.

The authorities' food safety work ranges from ordinary controls to emergency actions, such as culling farmers' animals, which presents many difficulties. Substantial efforts may also be made to trace the original source of contamination and to map how it has been spread from there. This can in fact be a complex piece of detective work (Box 21.4). Among others, the European Union pursues far-reaching so-called trace-back marking of farm inputs, living animals, animal products, vegetables and food ingredients. Places of production, vehicles and intermediate stages are registered too, in order to make it possible to trace the origin of harmful contaminants, animal diseases or food-borne diseases. You may remember the earlier reasoning about institutional frameworks, of which food safety issues provide a typical example. Box 21.5 gives more deatil about international agreements and frameworks, and includes some of the complex terms and abbreviations that belong to this part of the world of agricultural economics.

Food safety and international trade

In addition, food safety concerns may cause large disruptions in international trade. The discovery of a food safety problem in one country often leads to rapid reactions in other countries and import bans for periods of time. Thus a certain kind of production may be ruined not only by the contaminant as such, but also by economic trouble and lost future export markets. Some economic compensation may occur, but although this hardly covers farmers' and others' real costs and personal suffering, the authorities' costs can be enormous, considering the cost of administration, expertise, control, compensation and reduced trade.

In particular, countries that rely heavily on food exports can be extremely anxious about losing export markets because of food safety problems. For example,

Box 21.5 Institutional frameworks for food safety

A number of international agreements and systems have been developed in order to safeguard food safety in the world. The already mentioned FAO and WHO coordinate their food safety work through the Codex Alimentarius Commission (CAC). CAC is the official risk assessment body that develops international food standards for the assessment and management of food safety risks, and food safety standards and recommendations for food trade. All CAC guidelines are based on science and risk assessment. CAC is also connected with the WTO and with the SPS agreement (the Agreement on the Application of Sanitary and Phytosanitary Measures) that sets food safety rules for international trade with member states. The SPS agreement means that all countries that comply with the guidelines from CAC and the intergovernmental World Organization for Animal Health (OIE) shall be deemed safe to export on the world market. Any country that wants additional safety requirements must justify these on a scientific basis.

As regards food safety aspects of trade in live animals and animal products, the OIE plays the same role as CAC. The OIE works in collaboration with the FAO, WHO and CAC, and is often described as animals' counterpart to what the WHO is for human health. In the long run the SPS agreement and CAC and OIE standards should facilitate safe trade in food as well as in other kinds of animal products globally, and thereby also food security and economic development.

in 2008 an Irish feed processing plant was contaminated with dioxin. The feed had been distributed to relatively few farms, but the authorities still decided to recall all Irish pork that had been produced that autumn.

What is more, food safety issues can be used, or misused, as a kind of justification for barriers to trade. Import bans may be extended in time, and to include other products as well. Another kind of problem in this context is when poor producer countries have difficulty gaining access to export markets because of difficulty complying with expensive controls and other formal arrangements.

Summary

This chapter highlights agriculture in terms of food safety, and thus the previous emphasis on production has been accompanied by more of a consumer health perspective. Food safety is distinguished from the similar sounding food security in that the first term refers to hygiene qualities in food, whereas food security is wider and deals with access to sufficient amounts of both safe and nutritious food. Many people suffer more or less constantly from problems with acute nuisances in many parts of the world, while sudden and severe outbreaks form another kind of safety problem. There are also more diffuse threats that cause fears for future health problems, rather than acute diseases.

Food-borne diseases and other kinds of contamination can enter the food chain at any stage, and can spread rapidly before the problem is detected and identified. This means that food safety is the responsibility of all actors involved along the food chain, who have to guard against pathogenic or toxic microorganisms, artificial chemical contamination, physical contaminants and environmental emissions. Food and feed contaminants are, however, far from simple to handle, in that the contaminants often are invisible and do not smell, and in that they may originate from almost anywhere in the world. The field is complex, and calls for an interdisciplinary approach and international collaboration between authorities in order to find the source of contamination, assess the risks and handle the many practical problems involved.

To discuss

○   What kinds of food safety concerns seem to be common among food consumers where you live, such as avoidance of some foods or boiling before eating?

○   Study some journals on crop and animal farming and look for articles on food safety related matters. Does there seem to be any ongoing debate?

○   Which are the authorities that are responsible at the local and national level where you live?

Bibliography

Aikins, S.H.M. and Afuakwa, J.J. (2008) 'Growth and dry matter yield responses of cowpea to different sowing depths', *ARPN Journal of Agricultural and Biological Science*, 3 (5 & 6), 50–54.

Alexandratos, N. (ed.) (1995) *World Agriculture: Towards 2010 an FAO study*, Chichester: FAO and John Wiley & Sons.

Allen, D.W. and Lueck, D. (2002) *The Nature of the Farm: Risk and organization in agriculture*, Cambridge, Massachusetts: MIT Press.

Andersen, K.E. (2011) *Communal Tenure and the Governance of Common Property Resources in Asia: Lessons from experiences in Asia*, Land Tenure Working Paper 20, FAO, http://www.fao.org/docrep/014/am658e/am658e00.pdf (accessed 12 August 2012).

AQUASTAT: FAO's information system on water and agriculture, http://www.fao.org/nr/water/aquastat/main/index.stm (accessed 12 August 2012).

Arelovich, R.D., Bravo, R.D. and Martinez, M.F. (2011) 'Development, characteristics, and trends for beef cattle production in Argentina', *Animal Frontiers*, 1 (2), 37–45.

Atwood, D.A. (1990) 'Land registration in Africa: The impact on agricultural production', *World Development*, 18 (5), 659–671.

Badstue, L.B. (2006) *Smallholder Seed Practices: Maize seed management in the Central Valleys of Oaxaca, Mexico*, Wageningen, Netherlands: Wageningen University.

Baker, C.J., Saxton, K.E. and Ritchie, W.R. (1996) *No-Tillage Seeding: Science and practice*, Wallingford: CAB International.

Beierlein, J.G. and Woolverton, M.W. (1991) *Agribusiness Marketing: The management perspective*, Upper Saddle River, New Jersey: Prentice Hall.

Bending, T. (2010) *Monitoring Secure Access to Land: Progress and prospects*, Land Monitoring Handbook, International Land Coalition, http://www.ilc.swerve.it/publications/land-monitoring-handbook (accessed 12 April 2011).

Bernstein, H., Crow, B. and Johnson, H. (1992) *Rural Livelihoods: Crises and response,* Oxford: Oxford University Press.

Binswanger-Mkhize, H.P., Meinzen-Dick, R. and Ringler, C. (2011) 'Policies, rights and institutions for sustainable management of land and water resources', *The State of the World's Land and Water Resources for Food and Agriculture (SOLAW)*, Background Thematic Report TR09, http://www.fao.org/nr/solaw/thematic-reports/en/ (accessed 10 January 2012).

Boserup, E. (1965) *The Condition of Agricultural Growth*, London: Allen & Unwin.

Boyce, J.K., Rosset, P. and Stanton, E.A. (2005) 'Land reform and sustainable development', Working Paper Series No. 98, Political Research Institute, Massachusetts, http://www.peri.umass.edu/fileadmin/pdf/working_papers/.../WP98.pdf (accessed 12 August 2012).

Bradbear, N. (2004) *Beekeeping and Sustainable Livelihoods*, Diversification booklet No. 1, Rome: FAO, http://www.fao.org/docrep/006/y5110e/y5110e00.htm (accessed 21 September 2011).

Brady, N.C. and Weil, R.R. (1999) *The Nature and Properties of Soils*, 12th edn, Upper Saddle River, New Jersey: Pearson Prentice Hall; 14th edn 2008.

Brassley, P. (1997) *Agricultural Economics and the CAP: An introduction*, Oxford: Blackwell Science.

British Society of Plant Breeders (2000) 'Plant breeding: The business and science of crop improvement', http://www.bspb.co.uk/BSPB%20Handbook.pdf (accessed 26 February 2012).

Brittaine, R. and Lutaladio, N. (2010) *Jatropha: A smallholder bioenergy crop: The potential for pro-poor development. Integrated crop management*, 8–2010, Rome: FAO.

Brouwer, F. and van der Straaten, J. (eds) (2002) *Nature and Agriculture in the European Union: New perspectives on policies that shape the European countryside*, Cheltenham: Edward Elgar Publishing.

Brown, J. and Caligari, P. (2008) *An Introduction to Plant Breeding*, Oxford: Blackwell Publishing.

Brown, L.R. (2004) *Outgrowing the Earth: The food security challenge in an age of falling water tables and rising temperatures*, New York: W.W. Norton & Company.

Cakmak, I, Yilmaz, A., Kalayci, M., Ekiz, H., Torun, B., Erenoğlu, B. and Braun, H.J. (1996) 'Zinc deficiency as a critical problem in wheat production in Central Anatolia', *Plant and Soil*, 190, 165–172.

Caldwell, J.C. and Schindlmayr, T. (2002) 'Historical population estimates: Unravelling the consensus', *Population and Development Review*, 28 (2), 183–204.

Cardellino, R. and Mueller, J. (2009) 'Wool and other animal fibres in South America', in FAO and Common Fund for Commodities, *Discover Natural Fibres*, 43–52, http://www.fao.org/docrep/011/i0709e/i0709e00.htm (accessed 21 November 2011).

Caswell, J. and Bach, C. (2007) 'Food safety standards in rich and poor countries', *Ethics, Hunger and Globalization*, 12, 281–304.

Cato, M.P. and Varro, M.T. (2006) *Cato and Varro: On agriculture*, translated by Hooper, W.D. and revised by Ash, H.B., Cambridge, Massachusetts: Harvard University Press.

Chambers, R.G. (2002) 'Information, incentives, and the design of agricultural policies', in Gardner, B.L. and Rausser, G.C. (eds), *Handbook of Agricultural Economics, Volume 2B: Agricultural and food policy*, Amsterdam: Elsevier Science.

Charteris, P.L., Morris, S.T. and Mathews, P.N.P. (n.d.) 'Pasture-based beef production in New Zealand', http://www.pdffinder.net/Pasture-based-beef-production-in-New-Zealand (accessed 3 July 2011).

Chikwendu, D.O. and Arokoyo, J.O. (1995) 'Landownership and access to farm inputs by rural women in Nigeria', FAO Corporate Document Repository, http://www.fao.org/docrep/V9828T/v9828t08.htm (accessed 7 March 2012).

Clay, J. (2004) *World Agriculture and the Environment: A commodity-by-commodity guide to impacts and practices*, Washington, DC: Island Press.

Coldham, S. (2000) 'Land reform and customary rights: The case of Uganda', *Journal of African Law*, 44 (1), 65–77.

Collier, P. (2008) *The Bottom Billion: Why the poorest countries are failing and what can be done about it*, Oxford: Oxford University Press.

Colman, D. (2007) *The Rise and Decline (?) of Agricultural Economics*, paper presented at the IAAE–104th EAAE seminar 'Agricultural Economics and Transition', Budapest, Hungary, 6–8 September 2007, http://www.ageconsearch.umn.edu/bitstream/8526/1/sp07co01.pdf (accessed 10 August 2012).

Coote, B. (1992) *The Trade Trap: Poverty and the global commodity markets*, Oxford: Oxfam Publications.

Cotula, L., Toulmin, C. and Hesse, C. (2004) *Land Tenure and Administration in Africa: Lessons of experience and emerging issues*, London: FAO and IEED, http://www.pubs.iied.org/pdfs/9305IIED.pdf (accessed 8 August 2012).

Cotula, L., Vermeulen, S., Leonard, R. and Keeley, J. (2009) *Land Grab or Development Opportunity? Agricultural investment and international deals in Africa*, FAO, IIED and IFAD, http://www.ifad.org/pub/land/land_grab.pdf (accessed 22 January 2012).

Cousins, B. (2007) 'More than socially embedded: The distinctive character of "Communal Tenure" regimes in south Africa and its implications for land policy', *Journal of Agrarian Change*, 7 (3), 281–315.

Cramer, G.L., Jensen, C.W. and Southgate, D.D. (2001) *Agricultural Economics and Agribusiness*, 8th edn, New York: John Wiley & Sons.

Crossley, P., Chamen, T. and Kienzle, J. (2009) *Rural Transport and Traction Enterprises for Improved Livelihoods*, Diversification booklet No. 10, Rome: FAO, http://www.fao.org/docrep/011/i0525e/i0525e00.htm (accessed 21 September 2011).

Defra (2011) 'The British survey of fertiliser practice: Fertiliser use on farm crops for crop year 2010', York: Defra, http://www.defra.gov.uk/.../defra-stats-foodfarm-environ-fertiliserpractice-... (accessed 12 August 2012).

Defra (2002) 'Origin of the UK foot and mouth disease epidemic in 2001', http://www.archive.defra.gov.uk/foodfarm/farmanimal/.../atoz/.../fmdorigins1.pd... (accessed 10 August 2012).

De Gorter, H. (2002) 'Political economy of agricultural policy', in Gardner, B.L. and Rausser, G.C. (eds), *Handbook of Agricultural Economics, Volume 2B: Agricultural and food policy*, Amsterdam: Elsevier Science.

De Haan, C., Steinfeld, H. and Blackburn, H. (1997) 'Livestock and the environment: Finding a balance', http://www.fao.org/docrep/x5303e/x5303e00.htm (accessed 9 August 2012).

De Janvry, A. and Sadoulet, E. (2001) *Access to Land and Land Policy Reforms*, Policy Brief No. 3, UNU World Institute for Development Economics Research, http://www.staff.ncl.ac.uk/david.harvey/AEF806/AccessToLand.pdf (accessed 9 August 2012).

Delgado, C., Rosegrant, M., Steinfeld, H., Ehui, S. and Curbois, C. (1999) 'Livestock to 2020: The next food revolution', Food, Agriculture, and the Environment Discussion Paper 28, IFPRI/FAO/ILRI, http://www.ifpri.org/2020/dp/dp28.pdf (accessed 13 August 2012).

Dent, D. (2000) *Insect Pest Management*, 2nd edn, London: CAB International.

Dent, J.B. and McGregor, M.J. (eds) (1994) *Rural and Farming Systems Analysis: European perspectives*, Wallingford: CAB International

De Soto, H. (2000) *The Mystery of Capital*, New York: Basic Books.

Diaz-Bonilla, E., Robinson, S., Thomas, M. and Yanoma, Y. (2002) *WTO, Agriculture, and Developing Countries: A survey of issues*, TMD Discussion Paper No. 81, Washington, DC: IFPRI, http://www.netamericas.net/researchpapers/documents/.../Diaz-Bonilla6.pdf (accessed 8 August 2012).

Dicken, P. (2003) *Global Shift: Reshaping the global economic map in the 21st century*, 4th edn, London: Sage Publications.

Dixon, J., Gulliver, A. and Gibbon, D. (2001) *Farming Systems and Poverty: Improving farmers' livelihoods in a changing world*, Rome: FAO.

Dos Santos, L.M.R., Michelon, P., Arenales, M.N. and Santos, R.H.S. (2011) 'Crop rotation scheduling with adjacency constraints', *Annals of Operations Research*, 190 (1), 165–180.

Doye, D. and Brorsen, B.W. (2011) 'Pasture land values: A "Green Acres" effect?', *Choices. The magazine of food, farm and resource issues*, 26 (2), http://www.

choicesmagazine.org/choices-magazine/theme-articles/farmland-values/pasture-land-values-a-green-acres-effect (accessed 10 May 2012).

Duffy, M. (2011) 'The current situation on farmland values and ownership', *Choices. The magazine of food, farm and resource issues*, 26 (2), http://www.choicesmagazine.org/choices-magazine/theme-articles/farmland-values/pasture-land-values-a-green-acres-effect (accessed 28 July 2012).

East Africa Dairy Development Program (2008) *The Dairy Value Chain in Kenya*, http://www.kenyadairy.com/.../1279101361–748142- (accessed 17 July 2012).

Eicher, C.K. (1999) *Institutions and the African Farmer*, Issues in Agriculture 14, CGIAR, http://www.worldbank.org/html/cgiar/publications/issues/issues14.pdf (accessed 28 June 2012).

Eisen, A. and Hagedorn, K. (eds) (1998) *Co-operatives in Central and Eastern Europe: Selfhelp in structural change*, Berlin: Ed. Sigma.

Enserink, H.J. (1995) *Sorghum Agronomy in West Kenya: Investigations from a farming systems perspective*, Amsterdam: Royal Tropical Institute.

Ensminger, M.E. (2002) *Sheep & Goat Science*, Danville, Illinois: Interstate Publishers.

FAO (2011a) *Save and Grow: A policymaker's guide to the sustainable intensification of smallholder crop production*, Rome: FAO.

FAO (2011b) *The State of the World's Land and Water Resources for Food and Agriculture (SOLAW)*, Abingdon: Earthscan, http://www.fao.org/nr/solaw/the-book/en/ (accessed 2 January 2012).

FAO (2011c) *Payment for Ecosystem Services and Food Security*, Rome: FAO, http://www.fao.org/docrep/014/i2100e/i2100e00.htm (accessed 2 January 2012).

FAO (2011d) *The State of Food and Agriculture 2010–11: Women in agriculture: Closing the gender gap for development*, Rome: FAO, http://www.fao.org/docrep/013/i2050e/i2050e.pdf (accessed 27 September 2012).

FAO (2010a) *2000 World Census of Agriculture: Main results and metadata by country (1996–2005)*, FAO Statistical Development Series 12, Rome: FAO, http://www.fao.org/docrep/013/i1595e/i1595e00.htm (accessed 28 October 2011).

FAO (2010b) *Global Food Losses and Food Waste: Extent, causes and prevention*, study conducted for the International Congress Save Food, Düsseldorf, Germany, 2011, Rome: FAO, http://www.fao.org/docrep/014/mb060e/mb060e00.pdf (accessed 15 November 2011).

FAO (2009a) *The State of Food and Agriculture 2009: Livestock in the balance*, Rome: FAO, http://www.fao.org/docrep/012/i0680e/i0680e00.htm (accessed 28 January 2012).

FAO (2009b) *Towards Voluntary Guidelines on Responsible Governance of Tenure of Land and Other Natural Resources*, FAO Land Tenure Working Paper No. 10, Rome: FAO, http://www.fao.org/docrep/fao/011/ak374e/ak374e00.pdf (accessed 9 April 2012).

FAO (2008a) *Compulsory Acquisition of Land and Compensation*, FAO Land Tenure Studies No. 10, Rome: FAO, http://www.fao.org/docrep/011/i0506e/i0506e00.htm (accessed 8 April 2012).

FAO (2008b) *The State of Food and Agriculture 2008: Biofuels: prospects, risks and opportunities*, Rome, FAO, http://www.fao.org/docrep/011/i0100e/i0100e00.htm (accessed 12 December 2011).

FAO (2007) *Good Governance in Land Tenure and Administration*, FAO Land Tenure Studies No. 9, Rome: FAO, http://www.fao.org/docrep/010/a1179e/a1179e00.htm (accessed 8 April 2012).

FAO (2005a) *Fertilizer Use by Crop in India*, Land and Water Development Division, Rome: FAO, http://www.fao.org/agl/agll/docs/fertuseindia.pdf (accessed 26 January 2012).

FAO (2005b) 'Spotlight/2005: Protecting the pollinators', Agriculture and Consumer Department at the FAO, http://www.fao.org/ag/magazine/0512sp1.htm (accessed 12 August 2012).

FAO (2005c) *A System of Integrated Agricultural Censuses and Surveys*, Volume 1. World Programme for Census of Agriculture 2010, Rome: FAO, http://www.fao.org/fileadmin/...and.../FSDS_11_Volume_1_WCA2010.pdf (accessed 28 October 2011).

FAO (2004) *Unified Bioenergy Terminology (UBET)*, Rome: FAO, http://www.fao.org/docrep/fao/007/j4504e/j4504e00.pdf (accessed 25 September 2011).

FAO (2001) *Pastoralism in the New Millennium*, FAO Animal Production and Animal Health Paper 150, http://www.fao.org/docrep/005/Y2647E/Y2647E00.HTM (accessed 20 December 2011).

FAO: Food Price Index 2000–2011, http://www.fao.org/worldfoodsituation/wfs-home/foodpriceindex/en/ (accessed 17 July 2012).

FAO and AGAL: Livestock Information, Sector Analysis and Policy Branch (2005) 'Livestock sector brief, Bangladesh', http://www.fao.org/ag/againfo/resources/en/.../sector_briefs/lsb_BGD.pdf (accessed 10 August 2012).

FAO and Common Fund for Commodities (2009) *Discover Natural Fibres 2009*, proceedings of the symposium on natural fibres, Technical Paper No. 56, Rome, 20 October 2008, http://www.fao.org/docrep/011/i0709e/i0709e00.htm (accessed 30 December 2012).

FAO and IAEA (2008) *Guidelines for Sustainable Manure Management in Asian Livestock Production Systems*, http://www-pub.iaea.org/books/iaeabooks/7882/Guidelines-for-Sustainable-Manure-Management-in-Asian-Livestock-Production-Systems.

FAO/IFAD/WFP (2012) *The State of Food Insecurity in the World 2011: Economic growth is necessary but not sufficient to accelerate reduction of hunger and malnutrition*, Rome: FAO, http://www.fao.org/docrep/016/i3027e/i3027.htm (accessed 30 December 2012).

FAO/IFAD/WFP (2011) *The State of Food Insecurity in the World 2011: How does international price volatility affect domestic economies and food security?*, http://www.fao.org/docrep/014/i2330e/i2330e.pdf (accessed 2 May 2012).

FAOSTAT, the FAO Statistical Database, http://faostat.fao.org/default.aspx?lang=en.

Farrington, J. (1998) 'Organisational roles in Farmer participatory research and extension: Lessons from the last decade', *Natural Resource Perspectives*, No. 14, http://www.odi.org.uk/resources/docs/2915.pdf (accessed 14 March 2012).

Federico, G. (2005) *Feeding the World: An economic history of agriculture 1800–2000*, Princeton: Princeton University Press.

Fellows, P. (2011) *Processing for Prosperity*, Diversification booklet No. 6, Rome: FAO, http://www.fao.org/docrep/015/i2468e/i2468e00.pdf (accessed 8 August 2012).

Finley, E. and Price, R.R. (1994) *International Agriculture*, New York: Delmar Publishers.

Forbes, J.C. and Watson, R.D. (1992) *Plants in Agriculture*, Cambridge: Cambridge University Press.

Forse, B. (1999) *Where There Is No Vet*, London: Macmillan.

Gardner, B.L. and Rausser, G.C. (eds) (2002a) *Handbook of Agricultural Economics, Volume 2A: Agriculture and external linkages*, Amsterdam: Elsevier Science.

Gardner, B.L. and Rausser, G.C. (eds) (2002b) *Handbook of Agricultural Economics, Volume 2B: Agricultural and food policy*, Amsterdam: Elsevier Science.

Gardner, B.L. and Rausser, G.C. (eds) (2001) *Handbook of Agricultural Economics, Volume 1A: Agricultural production*, Amsterdam: Elsevier Science.

Gardner, J. (2011) 'Sharemilking in New Zealand', paper presented at the 18th International Farm Management Congress, New Zealand, http://www.ifmaonline.org/pdf/congress/11_NPR_Gardner_P170-178.pdf (accessed 22 January 2012).

Geers, R. and Madec, F. (eds) (2006) *Livestock Production and Society*, Wageningen, Netherlands: Wageningen Academic Publishers.

Gefu, J.O. (1992) *Pastoralist Perspectives in Nigeria: The Fulbe of Udubo Grazing Reserve*, Uppsala: Scandinavian Institute of African Studies.

Ghatak, M. and Roy, S. (2007) 'Land reform and agricultural productivity in India: A review of the evidence', *Oxford Review of Economic Policy*, 23 (2), 251–269, http://oxrep.oxfordjournals.org/content/23/2/251.abstract (accessed 9 August 2012).

Gloy, B.A., Boehlje, M.D., Craig, L.D., Jurt, C. and Baker, T.G. (2011) 'Are economic fundamentals driving farmland values?', *Choices. The Magazine of Food, Farm and Resource Issues*, 26 (2), http://www.choicesmagazine.org/choices-magazine/theme-articles/farmland-values/are-economic-fundamentals-driving-farmland-values (accessed 8 August 2012).

Giller, K.E. (2001) *Nitrogen Fixation in Tropical Cropping Systems*, 2nd edn, Wallingford: CAB International.

Gooding, M.J. and Davies, W.P. (1997) *Wheat Production and Utilization Systems: Quality and environment*, Wallingford: CAB International.

Gow, H.R. (1998) 'Up- and downstream restructuring, foreign direct investment, and hold-up problems in agricultural transition', *European Review of Agricultural Economics*, 25 (3), 331–350.

Grist, D.H. (1986) *Rice*, 6th edn, London: Longman.

Gupta, A.K. (2004) 'Origin of agriculture and domestication of plants and animals linked to early holocene climate amelioration', *Current Science*, 87 (1), 54–59, http://repository.ias.ac.in/21961/1/333.pdf (accessed 9 August 2012).

Hacket, S.C. (2006) *Environmental and Natural Resources Economics: Theory, policy, and the sustainable society*, 3rd edn, New York: M.E. Sharpe.

Haggblade, S. and Hazell, P.B.R. (eds) (2010) *Successes in African Agriculture*, Baltimore, Maryland: Johns Hopkins University Press.

Hahn, S.K., Reynholds, L. and Egbunike, G.N. (eds) (1992) *Cassava as Livestock Feed in Africa*, Ibadan, Nigeria: IITA.

Hardaker, J.B., Huime, R.B.M., Anderson, J.R. and Lien, G. (2004) *Coping with Risk in Agriculture*, 2nd edn, Wallingford: CAB International.

Hartmann, A. (2012) 'Scaling up agricultural value chains for pro-poor development', in Linn, F.J. *Scaling Up in Agriculture, Rural Development, and Nutrition*, http://www.ifpri.org/sites/default/files/publications/focus19.pdf (accessed 10 August 2012).

Hafez, B. and Hafez, E.S.E. (2000) *Reproduction in Farm Animals*, 7th edn, Philadelphia: Lippincott, Williams & Wilkins.

Hazell, P. (2011) 'Five big questions about five hundred million small farms', Conference on New Directions for Smallholder Agriculture, Rome: IFAD, http://www.ifad.org/events/agriculture/doc/papers/hazell.pdf (accessed 9 August 2012).

Hellin, J. and Higman, S. (2005) 'Crop diversity and livelihood security in the Andes', *Development in Practice*, 15 (2), 165–174, http://www.jstor.org/stable/10.2307/4030077 (accessed 12 August 2012).

Henderson, J. and Gloy, B. (2011) 'Farmland values', *Choices. The magazine of food, farm and resource issues*, 26 (2), http://www.choicesmagazine.org/choices-magazine/theme-articles/farmland-values/theme-overview-farmland-values (accessed 9 August 2012).

Henriksen, J. (2009) *Milk for Health and Wealth*, Diversification booklet No. 6, Rome: FAO, http://www.fao.org/docrep/011/i0521e/i0521e00.htm (accessed 21 September 2011).

Hillocks, R.J., Thresh, J.M. and Belotti, A. (eds) (2001) *Cassava: Biology, production and utilization*, Wallingford: CAB International.

Hodges, R. and Farrel, G. (eds) (2004) *Crop Post-Harvest: Science and technology, Volume 2: Durables*, Oxford: Blackwell Science.

Holzapel, E.A., Lorite, A., de Oliviera, S.A.S. and Farkas, I. (2009) 'Design and management of irrigation systems', *Chilean Agricultural Research*, 69 (Suppl. 1), 17–25, http://www.chileanjar.cl/.../V69_ISpecial%20Edition_2009_ENG_... (accessed 12 August 2012).

Huang, Y. (1998) *Agricultural Reform in China: Getting institutions right*, Cambridge: Cambridge University Press.

ILRI (2000) *Livestock Strategy to 2010: Making the livestock revolution work for the poor*, Nairobi, Kenya: ILRI.

Juma, C. (2011) *The New Harvest: Agricultural innovation in Africa*, Oxford: Oxford University Press.

Just, F. (ed.) (1990) *Co-operatives and Farmers' Unions in Western Europe: Collaboration and tensions*, Esbjerg, Denmark: South Jutland University Press.

Karp, L.S. and Perloff, J.M. (2002) 'A synthesis of agricultural trade economics', in Gardner, B.L. and Rausser, G.C. (eds), *Handbook of Agricultural Economics, Volume 2B: Agricultural and food policy*, Amsterdam: Elsevier Science.

Kellems, R.O. and Church, D.C. (2002) *Livestock Feeds and Feeding*, 5th edn, Upper Saddle River, New Jersey: Prentice Hall.

Krishna, A. (2011) *One Illness Away: Why people become poor and how they escape poverty*, Oxford: Oxford University Press.

Lal, R., Uphoff, N., Steward, B.A. and Hansen, D.O. (eds) (2005) *Climate Change and Global Food Security*, Boca Raton, Florida: Taylor & Francis Group.

Land Administration Law of the People's Republic of China, adopted 1986, amended 1998 and 1999, http://www.chinadaily.com.cn/bizchina/2006-05/08/content_584128_2.htm (accessed 12 August 2012).

Lang, T. (2004) *Food Industrialisation and Food Power: Implications for food governance*, Gatekeeper series No. 114, International Institute for Environment and Development Network Resources Group and Sustainable Rural Livelihoods Programme (accessed 12 August 2012).

Leach, I. and Wilson, R.T. (2009) *Higher Value Addition through Hides and Skins*, Diversification booklet No. 8, Rome: FAO, http://www.fao.org/docrep/fao/011/i0523e/i0523e.pdf (accessed 5 October 2011).

Leeuwis, C. and van Baan, A. (2003) *Communication for Rural Innovation: Rethinking agricultural extension*, 3rd edn, Oxford: Blackwell Science.

Lewan, E., Kreuger, J. and Jarvis, N. (2009) 'Implications for precipitation patterns and antecedent soil water content for leaching of pesticides from arable land', *Agricultural Water Management*, 96 (11), 1633–1640, http://www.sciencedirect.com/science/article/pii/S0378377409001796 (accessed 10 August 2012).

Life Sciences: Biotechnology and food security: 64 pages of insight (2010) http://www.workspace.imperial.ac.uk/.../Public/lifesciences%20mag.pdf (accessed 9 April 2012).

Linn, J.F. (ed.) (2012) 'Scaling up in agriculture, rural development, and nutrition', Focus 19 in the 2020 Vision for Food, Agriculture, and the Environment, Focus 19, IFPRI, http://www.ifpri.org/sites/default/files/publications/focus19.pdf (accessed 10 August 2012).

Lipper, L., Anderson, C.L. and Dalton, T.J. (eds) (2009) *Seed Trade in Rural Markets: Implications for crop diversity and agricultural development*, Rome: FAO and Earthscan.

Lipton, M. (2009) *Land Reform in Developing Countries: Property rights and property wrongs*, London: Routledge.

Livi-Bacci, M. (2001) *A Concise History of World Population*, 3rd edn, Malden, Massachusetts: Blackwell.

Lockie, S. and Pritchard, B. (eds) (2001) *Consuming Foods: Sustaining environments*, Brisbane: Australian Academic Press.

López, R. (2002) 'The economics of agriculture in developing countries: The role of the environment', in Gardner, B.L. and Rausser, G.C. (eds), *Handbook of Agricultural Economics, Volume 2A: Agriculture and external linkages*, Amsterdam: Elsevier Science.

LRF Konsult AB (2010) http://www.lrfkonsult.se/press/Nyheter/Akermarkspriser-2010/ (accessed 8 November 2011).

Lundqvist, J., de Fraiture, C. and Molden, D. (2008) *Saving Water: From field to fork – curbing losses and wastage in the food chain*, SIWI Policy Brief, SIWI, http://www.eldis.org/assets/Docs/39358.html (accessed 10 August 2012).

Lusk, J.L. and Rozan, A. (2006) 'Consumer acceptance in ingenic foods', *Biotechnology Journal*, 1 (12), 1433–1434, http://www.onlinelibrary.wiley.com/doi/10.1002/biot.200600187/pdf (accessed 8 August 2012).

Lutaladio, N., Ortiz, O., Haverkort, A. and Caldiz, D. (2009) *Sustainable Potato Production: Guidelines for developing countries*, FAO, http://www.fao.org/docrep/fao/012/i1127e/i1127e.pdf (accessed 10 August 2012).

McCown, R.L. (2012) 'A cognitive systems framework to inform delivery of analytic support for farmers' intuitive management under seasonal climatic variability', *Agricultural Systems*, 105 (1), 7–20, http://www.sciencedirect.com/science/article/pii/S0308521X11001193 (accessed 8 August 2012).

McDonald, P., Edwards, R.A., Greenhalgh, J.F.D. and Morgan, C.A. (2001) *Animal Nutrition*, 6th edn, Harlow: Pearson Prentice Hall.

Mandala, E.C. (2005) *The End of Chidyerano: A history of food and everyday life in Malawi, 1860–2004*, Portsmouth, New Hampshire: Heinemann.

Mankiw, N.G. (1998) *Principles of Macroeconomics*, Texas: Dryden Press.

Marshall, E. and Chandrasekharan, C. (2009) *Non-Farm Income from Non-Wood Forest Products*, Diversification booklet No. 12, Rome: FAO, http://www.fao.org/docrep/011/i0527e/i0527e00.htm (accessed 21 September 2011).

Martiin, C. (2012) 'Farming, favoured in times of fear: Swedish agricultural politics, 1935–1955', in Brassley, P., Segers, Y. and Van Molle, L. (eds), *War, Agriculture, and Food*, New York: Routledge.

Martiin, C. (2010) 'Swedish milk, a Swedish duty: Dairy marketing in the 1920s and 1930s', *Rural History*, 21 (2), 213–232, http://www.journals.cambridge.org/action/displayAbstract?fromPage=online&aid=7907107 (accessed 12 August 2012).

Merrett, S. (2002) *Water for Agriculture*, London: Spon Press.

Merrington, G., Winder, L., Parkinson, R. and Redman, M. (2002) *Agricultural Pollution: Environmental problems and practical solutions*, London: Spon Press.

Meyer, Gregory (2012) 'US drought: Stuck on dry land', *The Financial Times*, 30 July.

Mkhize, S. (2004) '10 years of subdued land reform', *AFRA News*, No. 57, May, http://www.afra.co.za/upload/files/AN314.pdf (accessed 11 November 2011).

Morgan, K., Marsden, T. and Murdoch, J. (2006) *Worlds of Food, Place, Power and Provenance in the Food Chain*, Oxford: Oxford University Press.

Morris, M., Kelly, V.A., Kopicki, R.J. and Byerlee, D. (2007) *Fertilizer Use in African Agriculture: Lessons learned and good practice guidelines*, Directions in Development, Agricultural and Rural Development, World Bank, https://www.openknowledge.world-bank.org/ (accessed 10 August 2012).

Moschini, G. and Hennessy, D.A. (2001) 'Uncertainty, risk aversion and risk management for agricultural producers', in Gardner, B.L. and Rausser, G.C. (eds), *Handbook of Agricultural Economics, Volume 1A: Agricultural production*, Amsterdam: Elsevier Science.

Moss, C.B. (2010) *Risk, Uncertainty and the Agricultural Firm*, London: World Scientific Publishing.

Mundlak, Y. (2000) *Agriculture and Economic Growth: Theory and measurement*, Cambridge, Massachusetts: Harvard University Press.

Murray, S. (2008) *Moveable Feasts: From ancient Rome to the 21st century, the incredible journeys of the food we eat*, New York: Picador.

Mutsaers, H.J.W., Weber, G.K., Walker, P. and Fischer, N.M. (1997) *A Field Guide for On-farm Experimentation*, Ibadan, Nigeria: IITA/CTA/ISNAR.

Mwantimwa, K. (2008) 'The relationship of indigenous knowledge and technological innovation to poverty alleviation in Tanzania', paper presented at the VI Globelics Conference, 22–24 September 2008, Mexico City, http://www.smartech.gatech.edu (accessed 10 August 2012).

Nachtergaele, F., Bruinsma, J., Valbo-Jorgensen, J. and Bartley, D. (2011) 'Anticipated trends in the use of global land and water resources', SOLAW Background Thematic Report, TR01, FAO, http://www.fao.org/fileadmin/templates/solaw/files/.../TR_01_web.pdf (accessed 2 January 2012).

Nannipieri, P., Ascher, J., Ceccherini, M.T., Landi, L., Pietramellara, G. and Renella, G. (2003) 'Microbial diversity and soil functions', *European Journal of Soil Science*, 54, 655–670, http://www.bashanfoundation.org/paolo/paolodiversity.pdf (accessed 10 August 2012).

Newbold, K.B. (2002) *Six Billion Plus: Population issues in the twenty-first century*, Lanham, Maryland: Rowman & Littlefield.

Nichols, M. and Hilmi, M. (2009) *Growing Vegetables for Home and Market*, Diversification booklet No. 11, Rome: FAO, http://www.fao.org/docrep/011/i0526e/i0526e00.htm (accessed 21 September 2011).

North, D.C. (1994) 'Economic performance through time', *American Economic Review*, 84 (3), 359–368, http://www.classwebs.spea.indiana.edu/kenricha/classes/v640/.../north%201994.p (accessed 10 August 2012).

North, D.C. (1991) 'Institutions', *Journal of Economic Perspectives*, 5 (1), 97–112, http://www.classwebs.spea.indiana.edu/kenricha/classes/v640/.../north%201991.p (accessed 10 August 2012).

Norton, G.W., Alwang, J. and Masters, W.A. (2006) *The Economics of Agricultural Development: World food systems and resource use*, New York: Routledge.

OECD–FAO Agricultural Outlook 2011–2020, http://www.oecd.org/site/oecd-faoagricul-turaloutlook/database-oecd-faoagriculturaloutlook.htm (accessed February 2012).

Olson, K.D. (2004) *Farm Management: Principles and strategies*, Ames, Iowa: Iowa State Press.

Ostrom, E. (2002) 'Common-pool resources and institutions: Towards a revised theory', in Gardner, B.L. and Rausser, G.C. (eds) (2002) *Handbook of Agricultural Economics, Volume 2A: Agriculture and external linkages*, Amsterdam: Elsevier Science.

Ostrom, E. (1990) *Governing the Commons: The evolution of institutions for collective action*, Cambridge: Cambridge University Press.

Oxfam (2011) 'Grow: Food, life, planet', http://www.oxfam.org/sites/www.oxfam.../grow-manifesto-may2011-eng.p... (accessed 9 August 2012).

Pagura, M. (ed.) (2008) *Expanding the Frontier in Rural Finance: Financial linkages and strategic alliances*, Rugby: Practical Action Publishing.

Pant, K.P. (2010) 'Health costs of dung-cake fuel use by the poor in rural Nepal', Report No. 10–14, South Asia Network of Economic Research Institute, http://www.saneinetwork.net/Files/10_14___K_P_Pant.pdf (accessed 11 August 2012).

Parlberg, R.L. (2010) *Food Politics: What everyone needs to know*, New York: Oxford University Press.

Parry, J., Barnes, H., Lindsey, R. and Taylor, R. (2005) 'Farmers, farm workers and work-related stress', Report 362 by Policy Studies Institute for the Health and Safety Executive, http://www.hse.gov.uk/research/rrhtm/rr362.htm (accessed 17 April 2012).

Patil, B.R., Singh, K.K., Pawar, S.E., Maarse, L. and Otte, J. (2009) 'Sericulture: An alternative source of income to enhance the livelihoods of small-scale farmers and tribal communities', Pro-Poor Livestock Policy Initiative 'A Living from Livestock', http://www.fao.org/ag/againfo/programmes/en/.../rep-0903_IndiaSericulture.pdf (accessed 10 August 2012).

Peacock, C. (1996) *Improving Goat Production in the Tropics: A manual for development workers*, Oxford: Oxfam.

Penson, J.B., Capps, O. and Rosson, C.P. (2002) *Introduction to Agricultural Economics*, Upper Saddle River, New Jersey: Prentice Hall.

Perry, T.W., Cullison, A.E. and Lowrey, R.S. (1999), *Feeds and Feeding*, 5th edn, Upper Saddle River, New Jersey: Prentice Hall.

Pimentel, D. and Pimentel, M.H. (2008) *Food, Energy and Society*, Boca Raton, Florida: CRC Press.

Platteau, J.-P. (1992) 'Land reform and structural adjustment in Sub-Saharan Africa: Controversies and guidelines', FAO Economic and Social Development Paper 107, Rome: FAO.

Plieninger, T., Bens, O. and Hüttl, R.F. (2006) 'Perspectives of bioenergy for agriculture and rural areas', *Outlook on Agriculture*, 33 (2), 123–127, http://www.bbaw.de/bbaw/Forschung/Forschungsprojekte/ (accessed 11 August 2012).

Pollot, G. and Wilson, R.T. (2009) *Sheep and Goats for Diverse Products and Profits*, Diversification booklet No. 9, Rome: FAO, http://www.fao.org/docrep/fao/011/i0524e/i0524e.pdf (accessed 15 October 2011).

Potter, R.B., Binns, T., Elliot, J.A. and Smith, D. (2008) *Geographies of Development: An introduction to development studies*, 3rd edn, Harlow: Pearson Prentice Hall.

Pretty, J. (2002) *Agri-Culture: Reconnecting people, land and nature*, London: Earthscan.

Quan, J. (2006) 'Land access in the 21st century: Issues, trends, linkages and policy options', Livestock Support Programme Working Paper 24, FAO, http://www.fao.org/es/esw/lsp/land.html (accessed 11 August 2012).

Reay, D., Hewitt, N. and Smith, K. (eds) (2007) *Greenhouse Gas Sinks*, Wallingford: CAB International.

Reed, M.R. (2001) *International Trade in Agricultural Products*, Upper Saddle River, New Jersey: Pearson Prentice Hall.

Renard, C. (ed.) (1997) *Crop Residues in Sustainable Mixed Crop/Livestock Farming Systems*, Wallingford: CAB International.

Rhodes, V.J. and Dauve, J.L. (1998) *The Agricultural Marketing System*, 5th edn, Scottsdale, Arizona: Holcomb Hathaway.

Richards, J.F. (ed.) (2002) *Land, Property, and the Environment*, Oakland, California: ICS Press.

Rose, S.P. (1997) *Principles of Poultry Science*, Wallingford: CAB International.

Roth, A.V., Tsay, A.A., Pullman, M.E. and Gray, J.V. (2008) 'Unravelling the food supply chain: Strategic insights from China and the 2007 recalls', *Journal of Supply Chain Management*, 44 (1), 22–39, http://www.springerlink.com/content/c2w1k10760336g26/ (accessed 11 August 2012).

Sahoo, A. and Soren, N.M. (2011) 'Nutrition for wool production', *Webmed Central Nutrition* 2 (10): WMC002384, http://www.webmedcentral.com/article_view/2384 (accessed 11 August 2012).

Samboh, E. and Yulisman, L. (2012) 'Soybean prices unlikely to affect inflation', *Jakarta Post*, 30 July.

Sen, A. (2001) *Development as Freedom*, Oxford: Oxford University Press.

Shaw, D.J. (2009) *Global Food and Agricultural Institutions*, London: Routledge.

Sherrat, A. (1983) 'The secondary exploitation of animals in the old world', *World Archaeology*, 13 (1), 80–104, http://www.jstor.org/stable/124640 (accessed 11 August 2012).

Singh, I. (1989) 'Reverse tenancy in Punjab agriculture: Impact of technological change', *Economic and Political Weekly*, 24 (25), A86–A92.

Sjauw-Koen-Fa, A. (2010) *Sustainability and Security of the Global Food Supply Chain*, Rabobank Group, http://www.rabobank.com/content/news/news_archive/073_Wake-up_call_for_food_industry.jsp (accessed 2 May 2012).

Slater, K. (1991) *The Principles of Dairy Farming*, Ipswich: Farming Press.

Smit, J., Nasr, J. and Ratta, A. (1996) *Urban Agriculture: Food, jobs and sustainable cities*, New York: UNDP.

Smith, B.D. (1995) *The Emergence of Agriculture*, New York: Scientific American Library.

Smith, C.W. and Dilday, R.H. (2003) *Rice: Origin, history, technology and production*, Hoboken, New Jersey: John Wiley & Sons.

Smith, H. (2011) 'Greek crisis forces thousands of Athenians into rural migration', *Guardian*, 13 May.

Sobal, J., Khan, L.K. and Bisogni. C. (1998) 'A conceptual model of the food and nutrition system', *Social Science and Medicine*, 47 (7), 853–863.

Soffe, R.J. (ed.) (2003) *Primrose McConnell's The Agricultural Notebook*, 20th edn, Oxford: Blackwell Science.

Southgate, D., Graham, D.H. and Tweeten, L. (2007) *The World Food Economy*, Malden, Massachusetts, Blackwell.

Squires, V. and Tow, P. (eds) (1991) *Dryland Farming: A systems approach. An analysis of dryland agriculture in Australia*, Sidney: Sidney University Press.

Steinfeld, H., Costales, A., Rushton, J., Scherf, B., Bennet, T. and Hall, D. (2006a) *Livestock Report 2006*, Rome: FAO, http://www.fao.org/docrep/009/a0255e/a0255e00.htm (accessed 11 August 2012).

Steinfeld, H., Gerber, P., Wassenaar, T., Castel, V., Rosales, M. and de Haan, C. (2006b) *Livestock's Long Shadow: Environmental issues and options*, LEAD and FAO, http://www.fao.org/docrep/010/a0701e/a0701e00.HTM (accessed 10 August 2012).

Stern, N. (2007) *The Economics of Climate Change: The Stern Review*, Cambridge: Cambridge University Press.

Stoneberg, E.G. (2011) 'Improving Your Farm Lease Contract: A guide to understanding the business of farmland leases', revised by Edwards, W., Iowa State University, http://www. extension.iastate.edu/agdm/wholefarm/html/c2-01.html (accessed 9 August 2012).

Sumner, D.A. and Tangermann, S. (2002) 'International trade policy and negotiations', in Gardner, B.L. and Rausser, G.C. (eds), *Handbook of Agricultural Economics, Volume 2B: Agricultural and food policy*, Amsterdam: Elsevier Science.

Swanson, B.-E., Bentz, R.P. and Sofranko, A.J. (eds) (1997) *Improving Agricultural Extension: A reference manual*, Rome: FAO, http://www.betuco.be/.../Improving%20 agricultural%20extension%20FAO.pdf (accessed 11 August 2012).

Swanson, T. and Vighi, M. (eds) (1999) *Regulating Chemical Accumulation in the Environment: The integration of toxicology and economics in environmental policy-making*, Cambridge: Cambridge University Press.

Swinnen, J.F.M. (1999) 'The political economy of land reform choices in Central and Eastern Europe', *Economics of Transition*, 7 (3), 637–664, http://www.onlinelibrary. wiley.com/doi/10.1111/1468–0351.00029/pdf (accessed 12 August 2012).

Swinnen, J.F.M., Buckwell, A.E. and Mathijs, E. (eds) (1997) *Agricultural Privatisation, Land Reform and Farm Restructuring in Central and Eastern Europe*, Aldershot: Ashgate.

Tamhankar, A.J., Neerkar, S.S., Patwardhan, A.P. and Lundborg, C.S. (2009) 'Rural India perceives that use of antibiotics in farm animals must be influencing antibiotic resistance development in humans: do the regulators think so?', in Lawrence, R., Gulati, A.K. and Abraham, G. (eds), *Antimicrobial Resistance: From threat to reality*, New Delhi: Narosa Publishing House.

Thomas, C.S. (2004) *Milking Management of Dairy Buffaloes*, Acta Universitatis Agriculturae Sueciae, Uppsala: Swedish University of Agricultural Sciences.

Thomas, H. (ed.) (2006) *Trade Reforms of Food Security: Case studies and synthesis*, Rome: FAO.

Thompson, P.B. and Kutach, D.N. (1990) 'Agricultural ethics in rural education', *Peabody Journal of Education*, 67 (4), 131–153.

Thurston, H.D. (1998) *Tropical Plant Diseases*, 2nd edn, St Paul, Minnesota: American Phytopathological Society.

Times Books (2009) *The Times Concise Atlas of the World*, 11th edn, London: HarperCollins.

Tindall, H.D. (1983) *Vegetables in the Tropics*, London: Macmillan.

Tivy, J. (1990) *Agricultural Ecology*, Harlow: Longman Scientific & Technical.

Tracy, M. (1993) *Food and Agriculture in a Market Economy: An introduction to theory, practice and policy*, Genappe, Belgium: Agricultural Policy Studies.

Tripp, R. (ed.) (2009) *Biotechnology and Agricultural Development: Transgenic cotton, rural institutions and resource-poor farmers*, London: Routledge.

Turner, J. and Taylor, M. (1989) *Applied Farm Management*, Oxford: BSP Professional Books.

Tweeten, L. (1992) *Agricultural Trade: Principles and policies*, Boulder, Colorado: Westview Press.

UNICEF and WHO (2009) *Diarrhoea: Why children are still dying and what can be done*, http://www.who.int/maternal_child_adolescent/documents/9789241598415/en/index. html (accessed 18 May 2012).

USDA (2012) 'World agricultural supply and demand estimates WASDE – 507', 12 June 2012, http://www.usda.mannlib.cornell.edu/MannUsda/viewDocumentInfo.do? documentID=1194 (accessed 6 August 2012).

USDA (1999) *Keys to Soil Taxonomy*, 8th edn, Blacksburg, Virginia: Pocahontas Press.

Vanclay, F. (2004) 'Social principles for agricultural extension to assist the promotion of natural resource management', *Austrtalian Journal of Experimental Agriculture*, 44, 213–222.

Van Dam, J.E.G. (2009) 'Environmental benefits of natural fibre production and use', in FAO and Common Fund for Commodities, *Discover Natural Fibres 2009*, 3–17, http://www.fao.org/docrep/fao/011/i0709e/i0709e03.pdf (accessed 21 November 2011).

Van den Ban, A.W. and Hawkins, H.S. (1992) *Agricultural Extension*, Oxford: Blackwell Science.

Van Zanden, J.L. (1991) 'The first green revolution: The growth of production and productivity in European agriculture 1870–1914', *Economic History Review*, 44 (2), 215–239, http://www.jstor.org/stable/2598294 (accessed 12 August 2012).

Von Braun, J. (2011) 'Food security and the futures of farms', *Food Security and the Futures of Farms 2020 and Toward 2050*, Royal Swedish Academy of Agriculture and Forestry's Journal No. 1–2011, 9–16, http://www.ksla.se/.../KSLAT-1-2011-Food-security-and-futures-of-farms.... (accessed 8 August 2012).

Von Braun, J. (2008) 'Rising food prices: What should be done?', IFPRI Policy Brief, http://www.ifpri.org/publication/rising-food-prices (accessed 12 August 2012).

Von Grebmer, K., Torero, M., Olofinbiyi, T., Fritschel, H., Wiesmann, D., Yohannes, Y., Schofield, L. and Von Oppeln, C. (2011) 'Global Hunger Index: The challenge of hunger: Taming price spikes and excessive food price volatility', IFPRI, http://www.ifpri.org/publication/2011-global-hunger-index (accessed 18 November 2011).

Vorley, B. and Fox, T. (2004) 'Global food chains – constraints and opportunities for smallholders', paper for the OECD DAC POVNET Agriculture and Pro-Poor Growth Task Team Helsinki Workshop, 17–18 June 2004, http://www.oecd.org/dataoecd/24/60/36562581.pdf (accessed 12 August 2012).

Weeks, J.R. (2005) *Population: An introduction to concepts and issues*, 9th edn, Belmont, California: Wadsworth Thomson Learning.

Westerndorf, M.L. (ed.) (2000) *Food Waste to Animal Feed*, Ames, Iowa: Iowa State University Press.

 Wheeling, B. (2008) *Introduction to Agricultural Accounting*, New York: Thomson Delmar Learning.

WHO (2009) *10 Facts on Food Safety*, WHO, http://www.who.int/features/factfiles/food_safety/en/index.html (accessed 5 June 2011).

WHO (2002) *Global Strategy for Food Safety: Safer food for better health: Food safety programme 2002*, WHO, http://www.whqlibdoc.who.int/publications/9241545747.pdf (accessed 12 August 2012).

WHO: Food security definition, http://www.who.int/trade/glossary/story028/en/ (accessed 12 August 2012).

Wiebe, K. (ed.) (2003) *Land Quality: Implications for agricultural productivity and food security at farm, regional and global scales*, Cheltenham: Edgar Elgar.

Wiener, G., Jianlin, H. and Ruijan, L. (2003) *The Yak*, Bangkok: FAO.

Wilkinson, J.M. (2003) *Silage*, Lincoln: Chalcombe Publications

World Bank (2007) *World Development Report 2008: Agriculture for development*, Washington, DC: World Bank.

World Bank (1974) *Population Policies and Economic Development*, a World Bank staff report, Washington, DC: World Bank.

World Economic Forum (2010) 'Realizing a new vision for agriculture: A roadmap for stakeholders', http://www.weforum.org/reports/realizing-new-vision-agriculture-roadmap-stakeholders (accessed 11 August 2012).

World Population Prospects, the 2010 Revision (2010) United Nations Department of Economic and Social Affairs, Population Division, Population Estimates and Projections Section, http://www.esa.un.org/unpd/wpp/index.htm.

World Urbanization Prospects, the 2009 revision (2009) United Nations Department of Economic and Social Affairs, Population Division, Population Estimates and Projections Section, http://www.esa.un.org/unpd/wpp/index.htm.

Wrigley, E.A. (1988) *Continuity and Change: The character of the industrial revolution in England*, Cambridge: Cambridge University Press.

WTO (2012) *World Trade Report 2012: Trade and public policies: A closer look at non-tariff measures in the 21st century*, World Trade Organization, http://www.wto.org/english/res_e/booksp.../world_trade_report12_e.pdf (accessed 6 August 2012).

WTO (2011) *International Trade Statistics 2011*, World Trade Organization, http://www.wto.org/english/res_e/statis_e/its2011_e/its11_toc_e.htm (accessed 28 July 2012).

Index

Note: Page numbers in *italic* type represent *figures* and in **bold** represent **tables**.

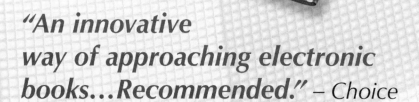